Using Mac OS® X Lion™

ISBN-13: 978-0-7897-4120-2
ISBN-10: 0-7897-4120-2

Library of Congress Cataloging-in-Publication Data

Johnson, Yvonne.
Using Mac OS X Lion / Yvonne Johnson.
p. cm.
ISBN 978-0-7897-4120-2
1. Mac OS. 2. Operating systems (Computers) 3. Macintosh (Computer)—Programming.
I. Title.
QA76.76.O63J6393 2012
005.4'465—dc23
2011035089

Printed in the United States of America
First Printing: October 2011

Trademarks

All terms mentioned in this book that are known to be trademarks or service marks have been appropriately capitalized. Que Publishing cannot attest to the accuracy of this information. Use of a term in this book should not be regarded as affecting the validity of any trademark or service mark.

Warning and Disclaimer

Every effort has been made to make this book as complete and as accurate as possible, but no warranty or fitness is implied. The information provided is on an "as is" basis. The author and the publisher shall have neither liability nor responsibility to any person or entity with respect to any loss or damages arising from the information contained in this book or from the use of the programs accompanying it.

Bulk Sales

Que Publishing offers excellent discounts on this book when ordered in quantity for bulk purchases or special sales. For more information, please contact

U.S. Corporate and Government Sales
1-800-382-3419
corpsales@pearsontechgroup.com

For sales outside of the U.S., please contact

International Sales
international@pearson.com

Associate Publisher
Greg Wiegand

Acquisitions Editor
Laura Norman

Development Editor
Todd Brakke

Managing Editor
Kristy Hart

Project Editor
Andy Beaster

Copy Editor
Paula Lowell

Indexer
Heather McNeill

Proofreader
Williams Woods Publishing

Technical Editor
Jennifer Ackerman-Kettell

Publishing Coordinator
Cindy Teeters

Book Designer
Anne Jones

Cover Designer
Anna Stingley

Compositor
Gloria Schurick

Contents at a Glance

The following appendix can be accessed online at quepublishing.com/using and on the included DVD:

Media Table of Contents

To register this product and gain access to the Free Web Edition and the audio and video files, go to quepublishing.com/using.

The following appendix can be accessed online at quepublishing.com/using and on the included DVD:

Table of Contents

The following appendix can be accessed online at quepublishing.com/using and on the included DVD:

About the Author

Yvonne Johnson has been writing computer books and teaching computer classes since 1982. She has written more than 60 computer books and college texts for well-known publishers on practically every type of software that exists—from operating systems to desktop publishing, from word processing and spreadsheets to databases, from programming to graphic design and web design. Her most recent Mac books include *Using Mac OS X Snow Leopard* (Pearson Education) and *Using Office 2011 for Mac* (Pearson Education).

She started the first proprietary computer-training school in Kentucky and operated it for 12 years, serving local clients such as Brown & Williamson Tobacco and General Electric, and sending out trainers to locations all over the country for the Department of Defense, the IRS, and Fortune 500 companies. During that time, she wrote the curricula for all the software programs taught at the school. After selling the school, she worked as a freelance computer curriculum developer, writing a large percent of the curricula offered by a national computer-training company headquartered in Chicago. She also wrote computer-training material and trained extensively for a computer-training and consulting subsidiary of the *Washington Post*. Ultimately, she took the position of Vice President of Curriculum Development with this company.

Although she has a tremendous depth and breadth of computer knowledge, she has never forgotten how to communicate with beginning learners. She is known for the simplicity of her writing and her ability to explain complex topics in understandable terms. This ability comes from years of delivering classroom training on computer applications to thousands of employees of large and small businesses, military and government personnel, teachers, attorneys, secretaries, and, yes, even Microsoft software support engineers.

Dedication

To my son Todd, who insisted I get a Mac.

Acknowledgments

Writing a book is a team effort, and I appreciate all the people who made this book possible. Thank you Laura Norman, acquisitions editor; Todd Brakke, development editor; and Andy Beaster, project editor—you are a superlative group of editors, and you make writing for Pearson a joy. I'm also grateful to my copy editor, Paula Lowell, and my technical editor, Jennifer Kettell. Many of the people on the team worked "namelessly" behind the scenes to get this book into print, and I want to thank them as well. I do know at least one of these people by name: John Herrin—thanks for all your help with the guidelines for the media elements in the book.

We Want to Hear from You!

As the reader of this book, *you* are our most important critic and commentator. We value your opinion and want to know what we're doing right, what we could do better, what areas you'd like to see us publish in, and any other words of wisdom you're willing to pass our way.

As an associate publisher for Que Publishing, I welcome your comments. You can email or write me directly to let me know what you did or didn't like about this book—as well as what we can do to make our books better.

Please note that I cannot help you with technical problems related to the topic of this book. We do have a User Services group, however, where I will forward specific technical questions related to the book.

When you write, please be sure to include this book's title and author as well as your name, email address, and phone number. I will carefully review your comments and share them with the author and editors who worked on the book.

Email: feedback@quepublishing.com

Mail: Greg Wiegand
Associate Publisher
Que Publishing
800 East 96th Street
Indianapolis, IN 46240 USA

Reader Services

Visit our website and register this book at quepublishing.com/using for convenient access to any updates, downloads, or errata that might be available for this book.

Introduction

The subject of this book is the newest operating system for the Mac, OS X Lion. The book covers system topics, such as installing the software and getting comfortable with Lion's many features, setting up user accounts, installing printers and setting preferences for your hardware, customizing your desktop, managing your applications and files, and using many of the system utilities.

Additionally, the book covers the "work" and "play" applications included in Lion. In the work category, it covers the web browser Safari, iCal, Address Book, Mail, iChat, FaceTime, TextEdit, Widgets, and several applets. In the play category, it covers DVD Player, QuickTime Player, iTunes, Photo Booth, and games.

In the category of keeping your Mac safe, updated, and backed up, it covers security settings in Safari and in the System Preferences, how to update applications, and how to back up and restore files with Time Machine.

The Appendix at the end of the book covers help and support topics including how to use the Help articles in Lion; how to use Apple support, Apple Experts, and the Genius Bar; and how to get free online, video, and hands-on training. The Appendix also discusses the various warranty and business programs that Apple offers.

Although the book is written for beginner-to-intermediate users (people who have purchased a Mac for the first time or people who have upgraded to Lion from an earlier version), the book wastes no space on basic computer skills and knowledge that most people have. For example, instead of teaching you how to surf the Internet, the book focuses on how to use the web browser securely and efficiently.

Using This Book

This book allows you to customize your own learning experience. The step-by-step instructions in the book give you a solid foundation in using Lion, while rich and varied online content, including video tutorials and audio sidebars, provide the following:

- Demonstrations of step-by-step tasks covered in the book
- Additional tips or information on a topic
- Practical advice and suggestions

Here's a quick look at a few structural features designed to help you get the most out of this book.

NOTES
Important tasks are offset to draw attention to them.

LET ME TRY IT tasks are presented in a step-by-step sequence so you can easily follow along.

SHOW ME video walks through tasks you just have to see.

TELL ME MORE audio delivers practical insights straight from the experts.

Special Features

More than just a book, your USING product integrates step-by-step video tutorials and valuable audio sidebars delivered through the **Free Web Edition** that comes with every USING book. For the price of the book, you get online access anywhere with a web connection—no books to carry, content is updated as the technology changes, and the benefit of video and audio learning.

About the USING Web Edition

The Web Edition of every USING book is powered by **Safari Books Online**, allowing you to access the video tutorials and valuable audio sidebars. Plus, you can search the contents of the book, highlight text and attach a note to that text, print your notes and highlights in a custom summary, and cut and paste directly from Safari Books Online.

To register this product and gain access to the Free Web Edition and the audio and video files, go to **quepublishing.com/using**.

About the DVD—for Print Books Only

Print versions of the book also include a DVD with the same step-by-step video tutorials and valuable audio sidebars that are available from the Free Web Edition.

This chapter reviews some of the things you do during the initialization process on a new computer to help allay any doubts you may have about whether you set things up correctly.

1

Initializing a New Computer

I'm assuming that you wouldn't have bought this book about Apple's newest operating system unless you already own a Mac. Either you just bought a new Mac with the Lion operating system, or you already own a Mac and you upgraded to Lion.

If you just bought a new Mac, you've probably already gone through the process of initialization that I'm going to discuss in this chapter, and I'm sure you got through it just fine. However, if you are a true beginner with the Mac, you may have some nagging reservations in your mind. "Did I do everything right?" "Is something going to go wrong later because of a choice I made?" If this describes you, this chapter should help allay your misgivings. If you've already been using a Mac for a while and you are upgrading to the new operating system, flip ahead to Chapter 2, "Upgrading to Lion," which walks you through the upgrade step by step.

Whether you're a new Mac user or an established one, I think you're going to like Lion, the latest version of the operating system, Mac OS X (pronounced oh-ess-ten). Lion has a very cool vibe; its graphics are gorgeous and it's fast and streamlined like a sleek sports car—no waiting at startup, no braking for curves. It shuns even the thought of viruses, worms, and spyware, so you can actually use the Internet without fear of losing your identity or your bank account. The applications just plain work; there are no mystifying quirks, no ifs, ands, or buts. Lion has a very human, even humorous, quality that makes you very comfortable. You also get the feeling that no matter what you do wrong, Lion has some graceful way to rescue you.

Turning On a New Computer the First Time

The thought of getting a new computer and setting it up can be a little intimidating. That's why the Apple Retail Store does a personal setup for you before you leave the store if you purchase your Mac there. If you purchase a Mac online, you still can take it to your local store to be set up or you can do the setup yourself. If you decide to do it yourself, don't worry. Apple really does make things as simple as possible. This section reviews the setup process starting from the point of opening the box. After you have all the hardware out of the box and plugged together (if applicable), you just need to plug into an electrical outlet and press the power button. The rest of the process is completely guided. You just have to follow the prompts to get your Mac software initialized. This initialization process, which sets up the operating system with your user information and preferences, has to be done only once. In general, these are the tasks in the initialization process:

1. Select the language.
2. Select the country or region you are in.
3. Select a keyboard layout.
4. Import data from another Mac.
5. Select your network.
6. Register your Mac with your Apple ID.
7. Answer some questions of interest to Apple.
8. Create your user account by supplying your full name, an account name, and a password, and then taking a picture of yourself or choosing an icon. Lion names your Home folder with your nickname, so to be consistent with the names of other folders on the Mac, I recommend that you capitalize your nickname. (For more information about folders, see Chapter 7, "Using Finder.")
9. Select your time zone.

Now let's see how you fared with some of the initialization processes that you might have questioned during the procedure. If there is anything you need to change or complete, I show you how in the next topics.

Selecting the Language

The Mac OS X operating system comes in several translations. Because you bought this book, I'm assuming that you read English perfectly well, but if you are more comfortable working on your Mac using a different language, you can select the language that you want to use. The Menu bar, menu options, help articles, and so on, appear in the language you select.

SHOW ME **Media 1.1—A Video about Setting the Language Preference**

Access this video file through your registered Web Edition at ***my.safaribooksonline.com/9780132819091/media*** *or on the DVD for print books.*

LET ME TRY IT

Setting the Language Preferences

I'm sure you made the right selection for language, but suppose for one moment that your practical-joking best friend set up your computer for you and selected French or some other language as your default language. Fortunately, icons look the same in any language so you won't have to know the foreign language to correct this problem. Follow these steps to set the language for English:

1. Click the icon that looks like a set of gears in the row of icons at the bottom of the screen. The System Preferences window opens, as shown in Figure 1.1.

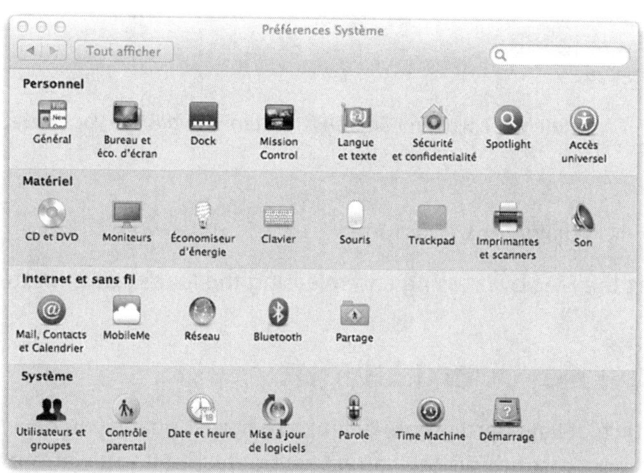

Figure 1.1 *Quel désordre. N'est pas?*

2. Click the blue flag icon in the middle of the top row. A list of languages displays.
3. Drag English to the top of the list (see Figure 1.2) and then click the red button in the upper-left corner to close the window.
4. Click the Apple logo in the upper-left corner of the screen.
5. Click the last option on the menu (or the one above the last option if you see your name in the last option) to shut down the Mac.

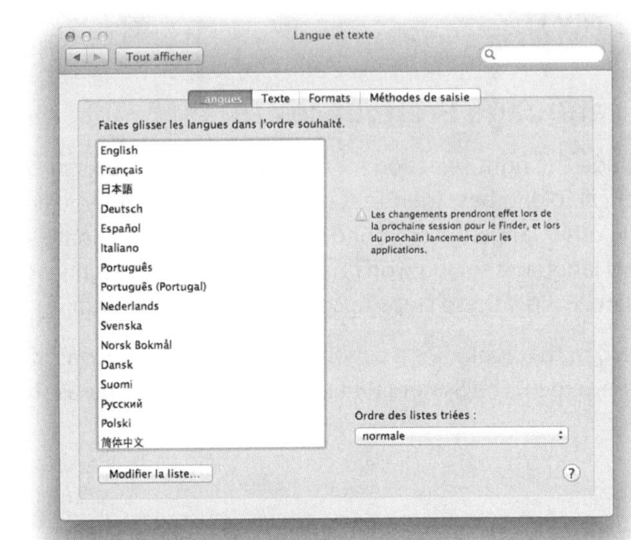

Figure 1.2 *Fortunately, the word for English is written in English so you can readily recognize it.*

6. In the next dialog box that appears, click Shut Down.
7. Restart the Mac by pressing and releasing the Mac's power button.

Selecting a Keyboard Layout

For your choice of keyboard, Apple defaults to the language you have already selected. In most cases this is the correct keyboard, but if you want to use your keyboard for a different language (or additional languages), you have to let Lion know so that it maps the keyboard correctly. For example, if you are trying to use the English keyboard to type in German, there is no key for the German letter ß.

SHOW ME **Media 1.2—A Video about Setting a Language for the Keyboard**

Access this video file through your registered Web Edition at ***my.safaribooksonline.com/9780132819091/media*** *or on the DVD for print books.*

LET ME TRY IT

Selecting a Different Language for the Keyboard

To select a different language for the keyboard, follow these steps:

1. Click the icon that looks like a set of gears in the row of icons at the bottom of the screen. The System Preferences window opens, as shown in Figure 1.3 (this time in English).

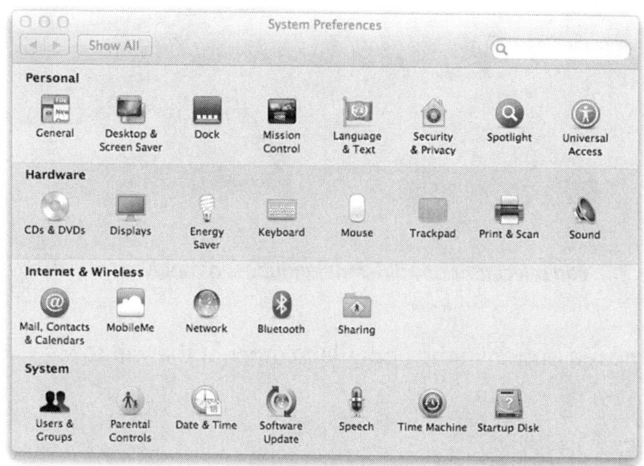

Figure 1.3 *The System Preferences window is the central location for most of the settings that a user is allowed to modify.*

2. Click the Language & Text icon and then click Input Sources.
3. Click the check box for the language that you want to map to the keyboard. Repeat this step for as many different mappings as you want.
4. For your own convenience, I recommend you select Show Input Menu in Menu Bar, as shown in Figure 1.4. If you have multiple keyboards mapped, you can switch back and forth very easily by selecting them from a menu in the menu bar.

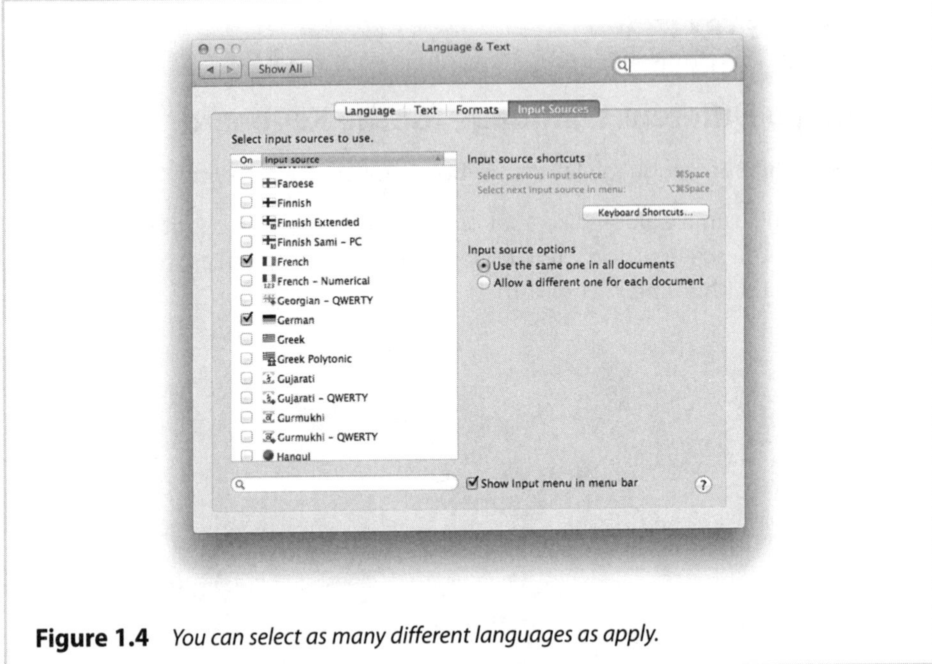

Figure 1.4 *You can select as many different languages as apply.*

5. Click the red button in the upper-left corner of the window.

Importing Data

When you set up a new Mac, if you have an old Mac, you can import its data using the Migration Assistant. Now in Lion, you can do the same with an old PC. You don't have to do this during the initialization process. You can do it afterward by using the Migration Assistant located in the Utilities folder. The Migration Assistant can transfer your user accounts, applications, computer settings, and files, and it's easy to use. Just follow the instructions onscreen after you start the application. If you have lots of applications on your old Mac that you need to reinstall on your new Mac, use the Migration Assistant to transfer them instead of reinstalling them.

Registering the Mac

If you registered your Mac successfully during the initialization you are good to go. If you bypassed this step because you didn't have an Internet connection, you should register as soon as you can.

LET ME TRY IT

Registering Your Mac at a Later Time

Before registering your Mac, you need to have the serial number at hand. Click the Apple logo in the upper-left corner of the screen and click About This Mac. Click More Info. The serial number displays along with other information about your Mac. Then to register, follow these steps:

1. Make sure you are connected to the Internet and then click the second icon in the bottom row of your screen (the rocket ship).
2. Click the tuxedoed Send Registration icon that Lion left for you.
3. When you arrive at the registration web page, follow the prompts to complete the registration.

When you register your Mac, you have to enter your Apple ID, if you have one. If you don't, you have to create one. Your Apple ID contains information about you (your profile) that identifies you to Apple when you want to register another Apple product, make a purchase from the Apple Store or iTunes Store, make an appointment for face-to-face support, and so on.

Editing Your Apple ID

If you want to make changes to your Apple ID, password, or profile information, go to https://www.myinfo.apple.com and click the link to manage your account. Enter your password and click Sign In. When you have made your changes, click Save Changes and then click Sign Out.

If you want to change the Apple ID itself and your original Apple ID is tied to a MobileMe account or an iChat ID, you can't really change it. You have to create a new Apple ID.

Answering Demographic Questions

During initialization, Apple generally likes to collect some demographic information about you such as where you use your Mac (home, business, school, and so on) and the main thing that you do on the Mac (design, music, finance, and so on). Apple always assures you that your privacy will not be invaded with these questions, and I can personally attest to the fact that my privacy has never been invaded with any of the information I have supplied to Apple over the long course of years in which I have purchased numerous new Macs.

Creating Your User Account

Creating your user account is one of the most important steps in the initialization process. You supply three pieces of information to create your account: your full name, a nickname/account name, and a password.

The full name you supply during initialization is your User Account name. You will log in with it when you start your computer and use it to unlock System Preferences and give permission to install application updates. For more information about installing application updates, see Chapter 16, "Keeping Your Mac Safe, Updated, and Backed Up."

The name you supply for your nickname/account name is the name that Lion gives to your Home folder. You cannot change the name of the Home folder, so I hope you created an appropriate name.

The password that you create should be a strong one—that is, one that is difficult to guess. Unlike your Home folder name, your password is not set in stone so if you created a weak password, you can change it at any time.

When you create your user account, Lion automatically makes you an administrator on the computer. As an administrator, you have special privileges and responsibilities: You have the ability to install software and updates, change system preferences, create other user accounts, change passwords, and do anything else that it is possible to do on a Mac.

Purchasing the Extras

When you purchase a new Mac, you have the opportunity to purchase some additional services that can be of great use to you. Some of these services can be purchased after the sale, but some must be purchased at the point of sale.

Purchasing the AppleCare Protection Plan

The AppleCare Protection Plan adds two years to your existing one-year warranty as well as two years to your existing 90-day telephone support. Fortunately, Apple lets you purchase the Protection Plan after the sale, any time within the first year. The effective date of the plan, regardless of when you purchase it or register it, is always the purchase date of the hardware.

Even Consumer Reports, which says, "Just say 'no' to extended warranties," makes an exception for the AppleCare Protection Plan—not because Apples are trouble-prone, but because of the valuable telephone support.

With the Protection Plan, you can literally be worry-free for three years. You can call Apple Support any time you have a question—no matter how small. Because Apple is not only the software manufacturer, but the hardware manufacturer as well, you'll never be caught in the loop where the hardware manufacturer blames a problem on the software and the software manufacturer blames the problem on the hardware. Apple is your one resource for problems or questions.

If any part of your computer or software fails due to defective parts or workmanship, Apple replaces it at no cost. Thanks to my AppleCare Protection Plan, I just received a free, brand-new battery for my almost-out-of-warranty, three-year-old MacBook Pro. You gotta love it! If you spill coffee in the keyboard, however, you're going to have to foot the bill yourself. The plan doesn't cover carelessness.

NOTE

Even after your AppleCare warranty has expired, Apple is good about replacing parts for free if they have known performance issues.

If you purchase AppleCare, you must register it to activate your plan. One crucial piece of information that you need to have before registering is the number assigned to your plan. This number may be referred to as "the registration number," "the enrollment number," "the serial number," or the "AppleCare agreement number." The number is located just above a barcode on an instruction card or booklet that comes inside the AppleCare box.

After you have the number, go to https://www.selfsolve.apple.com/Agreements.do and click Get Started. Then follow the prompts to register the product and activate the plan.

Purchasing One to One

One to One is a program that can only be purchased at the time of the sale. For $99, One to One might be the best money a neophyte Mac user spends on the Mac. As a One to One member you are entitled to the following:

- Setup of your new Mac
- Transfer of your old files to your new Mac
- Installation of all new Apple software
- Exclusive One to One group workshops
- One-hour personal training sessions with an Apple trainer

- Two-hour sessions with an Apple trainer to help you with your own personal projects
- A personalized One to One web page where you can access hundreds of tutorials

Purchasing JointVenture

JointVenture is a program Apple designed for businesses that use multiple computers and other Apple devices. The program includes setting up new Macs, iPhones, and iPads, training employees (up to three two-hour sessions at the Apple Store plus monthly workshops), and ongoing support (anytime updates and loaner computers if yours needs repair). The entry level price for this program is $499.

Keeping Records

Keeping records of your serial numbers, IDs, user names, passwords, and so on can certainly save you some time and headaches in the future. How many times have you fallen for that trick your mind plays on you that says, "I'll remember that"? You have to write these things down, but the minute you do, you have to think of some way to safeguard your information, such as hiding it in the freezer.

I have a sturdy little spiral-bound book that I record all my information in. I don't need to hide it in the freezer because I write any sensitive information in a cryptic way. For example, for a login name or password, if I use a number string that is one of my former street addresses, I don't record the actual number; I record the street name. If I use the letters in my cat's name (I don't really have a cat), I don't write down the cat's actual name, I write "Cat" or "cat," depending on the capitalization. So, for example, if I created a password of "502Fancy" (502 for 502 Orchard Avenue and Fancy for my fictitious cat's name), I would enter the password in my book as "orchardCat." To make the password more secure, I would replace the *a* in Fancy with @. To remember that substitution, I would make it a rule that I use @ for *a* in ALL passwords.

Recording Apple ID Information

The Apple ID information that you need to record is the ID itself and the password. Generally, if you followed Apple's recommendation, you used your email address for the Apple ID.

If you didn't record this information and you have forgotten your Apple ID or your password, go to https://www.iforgot.apple.com. If you have forgotten your password, you can supply your Apple ID, and Apple will email you a link to your account where you can enter a new password. Alternatively, if you can verify the month and day of your birth and answer the security question that you provided when setting up your profile, Apple will allow you to change your password immediately.

If you have forgotten your Apple ID, you can supply your first and last name and up to four email addresses. If any one of the email addresses is the one you originally supplied in your profile, Apple will be able to find your account and will email you a link to your account or allow you to verify the month and date of your birth and answer the security question that you provided when setting up your profile. Whether you follow the link from an email or answer the security question, Apple will display your Apple ID online. At that point, write it down and then click Cancel.

Recording User Account Information

During the initialization process when you created your user account, you supplied Lion with three pieces of information: your full name, a nickname, and a password. Hopefully you wrote these down and put them in a secure place (not on a note stuck to your screen). If you didn't make note of them, then you can at least look up your full name and your nickname, as follows:

- **Full name**—To look up the full name that you supplied, click the icon that looks like a set of gears in the row of icons at the bottom of the screen. Click the Users & Groups icon in the bottom row of icons in the window. Your full name is shown on the left under Current User and on the right in the Full Name field. Click the red button in the upper-left corner of the window to close it.

If you want to change the full name that you originally supplied, simply type a new name in the Full Name field and enter your password when prompted.

- **Nickname/Account Name**—To look up the name that you supplied, click the icon of the blue, two-faced man in the row of icons at the bottom of your screen. It should be the first icon. Click in the box that has a magnifying glass icon. (My mom thinks this is a "Q.") Type **users** and then click File Contains "users." Click This Mac and then double-click the Users folder. Your Home folder name appears under the icon of a House, as shown in Figure 1.5. Click the red button in the upper-left corner of the window to close it.

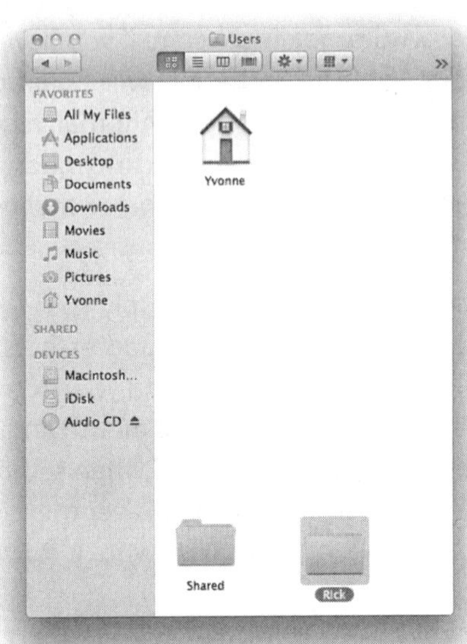

Figure 1.5 *Hopefully your Home folder's name is not something embarrassing like "Sugar Pie."*

- **Password**—Unfortunately, if you didn't write down your password and you have forgotten it, there is no way to find it on the computer. If this happens before you have started creating files, importing pictures, making entries in your address book, and so on, the easiest thing to do is create a new administrative account for yourself. See Chapter 3, "Setting Up User Accounts and Installing Hardware."

Recording AppleCare Protection Plan Information

For the AppleCare Protection Plan you should record the agreement number that is given to you and the expiration date. If you did not record this number, you can look it up by going to https://www.selfsolve.apple.com/Agreements.do and clicking Get Started. Next, sign in with your Apple ID and your password. When you have signed in, you can see all your agreements and their corresponding numbers. Alternatively, you can use a new feature in Lion to check on your warranty and AppleCare Protection plan. Click the Apple menu in the menu bar and click About This Mac. Then click Service in the toolbar and click Check My Service and Support Coverage Status. The first time you do this on your Mac, Lion asks permission to send your computer's serial number to Apple.

In this chapter I take you through the steps to upgrade to Mac OS X Lion and give you a comprehensive overview of what's new.

2

Upgrading to Lion

In this chapter I walk you through the upgrade installation and make some recommendations about what to do next. I also give you an overview of some of the more than 250 new features in Lion.

If you watched the keynote address announcing Lion that was given at the 2011 Apple developer's conference, you could see that the presenters were carried away by the beauty and responsiveness of the new Lion interface. Their enthusiasm and button-busting pride was overpoweringly evident, and you could tell it was real too—not just pumped up for the crowd. While using Lion through the testing period, I came to share their enthusiasm for this new release. After you use it for a while, I think you'll feel the same way.

I know to some hardcore Microsoft users this might sound like the loyal Mac user who has drunk the Apple Kool-Aid, but I've been a hardcore Microsoft user, too, and I feel that Lion is on the cutting edge of the new age of computing that Apple is ushering in with iCloud. The logic behind iCloud is brilliant, and I believe it will shift the whole computing paradigm away from the Mac as the central device to the iCloud. With all my iPhones, iMacs, MacBook Pros, iPads, and MobileMe accounts to keep up with, I see iCloud as an incredible gift Apple is giving me that will make my life so much simpler. For the latest information about iCloud, go to http://www.apple.com.

TELL ME MORE **Media 2.1—A Recording about the iCloud**
Access this audio file through your registered Web Edition at ***my.safaribooksonline.com/9780132819091/media*** *or on the DVD for print books.*

Performing the Upgrade

If you're reading this section, I'm going to assume that you're an "upgrader" who hasn't pulled the trigger yet. If you have already installed the upgrade, you probably have nothing to gain by reading this section unless you just want to relive the experience.

If you've never upgraded a Mac operating system before, you will be pleasantly surprised. When you are finished, you will find that all of your previously set system and application preferences have been retained, your email is still intact, your Safari bookmarks are still there, and all of your data is right where it was before.

This is the first upgrade of Mac OS X that is totally digital. By this I mean that you can only get the upgrade by purchasing and downloading it from the App Store. There is no disc!

Before you purchase the upgrade, make sure your Mac meets all the requirements to run Lion. You must have an Intel Core 2 Duo, Core i3, Core i5, Core i7, or Xeon processor, and you must have the latest update of Snow Leopard installed.

Performing the Install

Just for safety's sake, you should perform a full backup of your computer before upgrading in the unlikely event that something goes wrong. As an experienced user, you probably make backups all the time using Time Machine, so I'm going to trust that you've done that. After backing up your computer, follow these steps to upgrade:

1. Click the App Store icon in the Dock.
2. Type **lion** in the Spotlight search field and press Return.
3. Select the Mac OS X Lion application, click the price and then click Buy App.
4. Enter your Apple ID password and click Sign In. (If you do not have billing information on file, a second dialog box opens asking for your password. Enter your password again and click Billing Info. Complete your billing information and click Done.) The upgrade begins downloading to the Launchpad. You can continue to do other things on your computer during the download. When the download is finished, you see the Lion icon in the Launchpad.
5. To install the upgrade, click the Lion icon in Launchpad and click Continue.
6. Click Agree for the Software Licensing Agreement.
7. Click Agree again to confirm that you really, really do agree.
8. Click Install. Type your password and click OK. The upgrade installs, restarts the computer, and finishes the installation, finally opening to the Setup

Assistant which displays a demonstration of how to scroll and instructions on how to use multi-touch gestures in Lion.

9. Scroll to the bottom of the text as instructed and click Start using Mac OS X Lion.

This is by far the easiest upgrade yet. I'm not sure how they will top this in the next version. I guess Apple will send someone to your location to do the upgrade for you.

Settling In

If you've been through an OS X upgrade before, you know it's fairly painless. The first time you opened some non-Apple applications, you may see a dialog box that said, "You are opening the <name> application for the first time. Are you sure you want to open this application?" You may also have to download a current version of JAVA if you have applications that require it. Other than that, the only settling in you need to do is just familiarizing yourself with the major new features of Lion and taking note of the changes in the look and feel of the new user interface.

If you are a heavy email user, the first thing you might want to do after the installation of the upgrade is launch Mail. The first time you use Mail after the upgrade, you see a message explaining that your existing Mail messages need to be upgraded to take advantage of the new features in Mail. Although the text says it may take a few minutes, I had 282 messages in my Inbox, and it took two seconds to upgrade them!

When Mail opens, take some time to get used to the new user interface. Mail has been so completely redesigned, you'll hardly recognize it, but don't worry; there is a preference that lets you change back to the classic interface if you're not comfortable with the new interface. Initially, the new interface displays two panes. Refer to Chapter 11, "Using Mac Mail," for detailed information and instructions on how to use Mail. Also check out the new look for the conversation view and the new Favorites bar, located just under the toolbar. It has buttons for mail folders that you use most often so you can hide the Mailbox List.

I suggest you look at the Finder next and get familiar with the new All My Files feature. This feature literally lists all your files in one place, categorizing them by type. It's Apple's method of flattening the file structure learning curve. If you use the All My Files feature, you don't have to know the path of any file. All you have to know is what kind of file it is. If you don't know that, you can categorize the files by another criterion, such as Date Last Opened. While you are checking out Finder, looking at the Finder preferences, particularly the Sidebar pane would be worth your while. See Chapter 7, "Using Finder," for more information on using the Finder and setting preferences.

Two new features you will want to learn about right away are Launchpad and Mission Control. Launchpad lists all your installed applications in one easy location that takes its design from the iOS used in the iPad, iPhone, and iPod Touch. Mission Control (think of the control center on the starship *Enterprise*) is the new control center for everything that is running on your user account. See Chapter 8, "Managing Applications," to find out how these two new features can work for you.

As you are getting used to things, you will probably notice that the scroll bars have been redesigned. They don't really display unless you start to use them. This is another new feature design taken from iOS. (Note that some third party apps, such as Office 2011, may still display the older style scroll bars.)

FaceTime and the App Store are also "new" Lion features, but they were actually released months before Lion. If you have Snow Leopard, these two applications were installed for you in an update so you have probably already been using them.

Getting the New Experience

When you upgrade to a new version of the software, you actually miss the new experience—that experience you get when you buy a new Mac. This is because the upgrade keeps all your previous preferences, your desktop background, the icons you have in the Dock, and so on. So, for example, after you install the Lion upgrade, you don't see the stunning new desktop background picture of the Andromeda galaxy. Additionally, you don't really know what the default preferences are for the system and the applications.

To get that "new experience," after an upgrade, I like to create a new user account and use it to explore the new features and defaults. As you may or may not know, each time you create a new user account, Lion sets up the profile as a new, out-of-the-box (or should I say out-of-the-App-Store?) installation. See Chapter 3, "Setting Up User Accounts and Installing Hardware," for instructions on how to set up and delete a new user account.

Exploring Lion's New Features

The Lion release is much more exciting than the Snow Leopard release was, but to be fair, Snow Leopard set the stage for Lion by putting the superstructure in place. It's not just the new features that are exciting, it's also the whole feel of the system. In his part of the keynote address at the 2011 Apple developers conference, Craig Federighi said, "The page feels really alive beneath your fingers," and it truly does. This is due to the responsive scrolling in all directions, the rubber band bounce of the page on the screen, and the multi-touch gestures. A simple swipe makes the pages in a long document fly and a touch stops them on a dime.

The computers that Apple has been building for the last year are built to use the new multi-touch gestures and come with the 2 GB of memory required to run Lion. If you are upgrading an older Mac, I recommend getting the Magic Trackpad so you can get the complete multi-touch experience. And before you upgrade, you will have to increase your memory if you haven't already done so.

The more than 250 new features in Lion are not just changes to the internal workings of the system that you never see. These are changes you can point to in menus, dialog boxes, and toolbars. Some are small, such as new Share options for Vimeo, Flickr, Facebook, and Mail in QuickTime Player, and some are huge, such as Mission Control. I point out almost all the new features in the individual chapters, but in this chapter I highlight the new features that I think will have the most impact on an upgrader like you.

New Features in System Preferences

The System Preferences window is basically the same, but a few of the names have been changed. The Appearance preferences page is now called General, Exposé & Spaces is now called Mission Control, and Accounts is now called Users & Groups.

There are some changes in the settings on many preference pages, but one of the most notable changes is the setting for the restoration of windows when quitting and reopening applications, found on the General page. This setting is part of the new Resume feature in Lion that enables you to start your Mac and pick up where you left off when you quit working the last time.

One other major addition I want to point out is that it's now possible to set up your accounts to use with Address Book, iCal, iChat, and Mail right in the Mail, Contacts & Calendars preferences page shown in Figure 2.1.

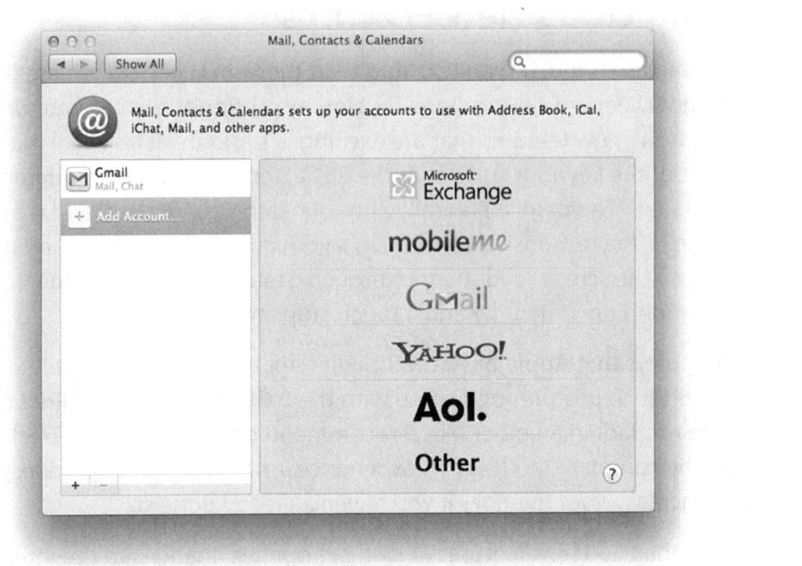

Figure 2.1 *Now you can set up all your accounts all at one time in the Mail, Contacts & Calendars system preferences page.*

New Features on the Desktop

If you like to keep a tidy desktop, you'll appreciate a new command called Clean Up By. It aligns icons with the invisible grid, sorted by name, date modified, date created, last opened, date added, size, kind, or label. After arranging the icons with this command, you can still move the icons freely around the desktop. If you ever used the Sort By command to arrange icons, you know they are immovable after sorting.

If you are exploring the new features of Lion by using a new user account, you will notice that the Dock no longer shows the blue bubble under open applications. You can turn this feature back on by setting an option on the Dock system preferences page. You will also notice that the Application folder has been removed from the Dock and the Launchpad icon, which you will use a lot, has been added. Another new addition to the Dock is the Mission Control icon. See Chapter 8 to learn about Mission Control.

If you're exploring Lion from your previously existing user account, you will have both the Launchpad icon and the Applications folder icon in the Dock.

New Features in the Finder

If you are exploring with a new user account, when you open the Finder, you will not see your Home folder. This is the new default setting, and my guess is that Apple doesn't want to show the Home folder in order to encourage you to use the All My Files feature that I mentioned previously. See Chapter 7 if you don't know how to specify the items that appear in the sidebar.

You can't get a good feel for the All My Files feature and some of the other new features in the Finder using a new account because you don't have any files. Go back to your account to experiment with the Finder. In your account, try the new button in the Finder toolbar that sorts the items in the right pane. Then right-click a file in the finder and notice the option that enables you to send the file as an attachment in email.

With the Spotlight search you can now specify more than one search item in the search box, as shown in Figure 2.2. See Chapter 7 for instructions.

Figure 2.2 *Spotlight uses a new feature called "search tokens."*

New Features in iChat

If you're a frequent "iChatter," you'll really appreciate the way iChat now combines all accounts in one buddy list and combines all accounts for one person under one name. Also new in iChat is the feature that allows you to organize your chats. Each chat has its own tab in the Chat window, and you can rearrange your tabs by dragging them up or down. See Chapter 12, "Using iChat and FaceTime."

New Features in Address Book and iCal

The interfaces of the Address Book and iCal are completely redesigned (see Figure 2.3), but their basic functionality is still very similar to the former versions. iCal does have a new Year view that "heat maps" your schedule so you can see what days are light, average, or heavy, and it has a new feature called Quick Event. You use the Quick Event feature to create an event by supplying four pieces of information in plain English, such as Logan's Birthday on April 28 from 1:00 p.m – 4:00 p.m. See Chapter 10, "Using the Address Book and iCal," to learn more about these features.

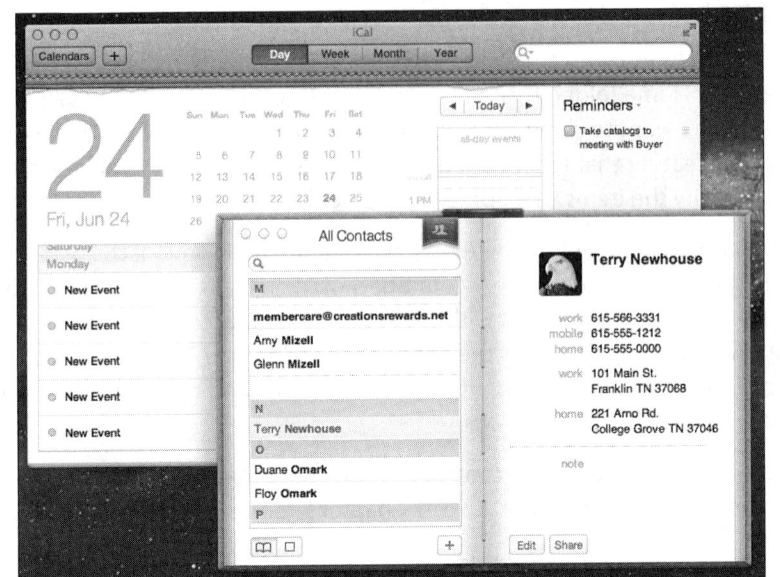

Figure 2.3 *The Address Book and iCal interfaces now look like the "real thing."*

New Features in QuickTime Player

New editing features in QuickTime Player now allow you to trim the beginning or end of a movie and to split a movie into pieces. Additionally, you can rearrange the clips and even drag in new clips from other movies. See Chapter 17, "Having Fun," for instructions on editing your movies.

Other Notable New Features

You can see the new AutoSave and Version feature in applications such as TextEdit, Preview, and Pages. With this new feature, Lion automatically saves your files at intervals while you are working so you don't have to. Each time it saves, it creates a separate version you can access with an interface that is similar to Time Machine. Additionally, you can save a version manually at any time. To learn more about this feature, see Chapter 8.

The Reading List is a great new feature in Safari. It provides you with a location to store pages you want to read at a later time. Click the button with the reading glasses, shown in Figure 2.4, to see this new feature and learn how to use it by referring to Chapter 9, "Browsing the Web."

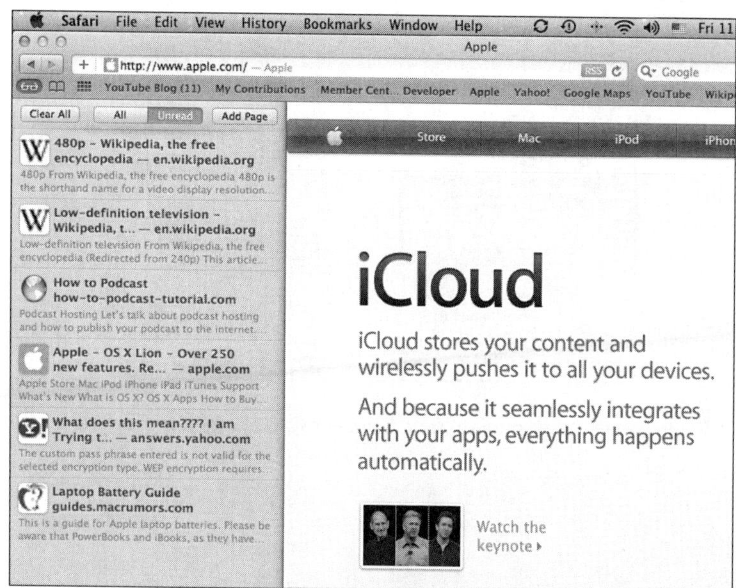

Figure 2.4 *Come back to the Reading List when you have time to read pages you've bookmarked there.*

Take a look at the new System Information utility by clicking the Apple menu, clicking About This Mac, and clicking More Info. This new utility gives you a wealth of valuable information about your system, as the name implies. For example, if you're wondering what's taking up so much room on your hard drive, click Storage and you'll find out! To learn more, see Chapter 15, "Using System Utilities."

Open Photo Booth to see the cool, new, full-screen interface and check out the eight new effects, which, as we all know, is the main reason we use Photo Booth. If you like to make short movies in Photo Booth, you'll be pleased to know that you can now trim off the beginning and the end of your movies to eliminate the parts that show you starting and stopping the recording. Find out how in Chapter 17.

If you need to find a word or phrase in a lengthy PDF document, the new search feature in Preview provides new methods for finding exactly what you're looking for, as shown in Figure 2.5. Learn how to use this feature in Chapter 14, "Using Widgets and Other Applications," and while you're there, check out the new feature that allows you to photograph a signature and insert it in a PDF.

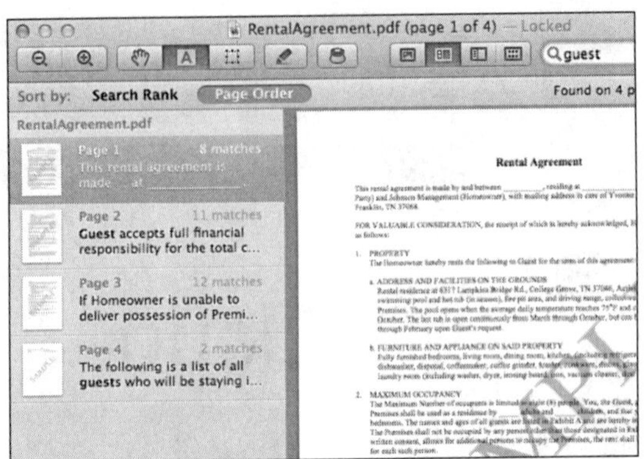

Figure 2.5 *In Preview, the Spotlight search provides a page-by-page summary of what it finds.*

In this chapter you learn to set up user accounts and install hardware such as external drives and printers.

3

Setting Up User Accounts and Installing Hardware

If you just bought a new Mac, then after the initialization process, you probably need to do some things before you can really start using your Mac effectively. In this chapter I cover some of the basics, such as how to change your user password, set up accounts for other users on your Mac, connect and eject external drives, install printers, and set up a simple network.

Customizing Your Own User Account

The first account created on your Mac was your own account. The operating system created it during the initialization process described in Chapter 1, "Initializing a New Computer," and made you an administrator. This means you have all the rights and permissions to do anything you want on the Mac. If you are not the owner of the Mac, but have been given an administrative user account, you also can do anything you want on the Mac. If you do not have an administrative user account, you have to enter the name and password of an administrator on the Mac to make some of the changes to your user account, such as setting Login Options or Parental Controls.

SHOW ME **Media 3.1—A Video about Changing Your User Account Password**

Access this video file through your registered Web Edition at
my.safaribooksonline.com/9780132819091/media
or on the DVD for print books.

Changing Your User Account Password

When you set up your password, if you used a weak password, such as your name, a real word, a date, or simply a string of numbers, then you need to change your password. A strong password has at least eight characters with both characters and numbers, and it never hurts to throw in a capital letter somewhere.

Follow these steps to change your password:

1. At the bottom of the screen, in the Dock, click the System Preferences icon. (It's the one that has a set of gears on it.) The System Preferences window opens.

If you have deleted the System Preferences icon from the Dock, click the Apple in the menu bar and click System Preferences.

2. Click the Users & Groups icon in the fourth row of icons in the window. Your account is selected by default.
3. Click Change Password to open the dialog box shown in Figure 3.1.
4. Type your original password in the Old Password field.
5. In the New Password field, type a new password and this time use a combination of letters, numbers, and for good measure, throw in a punctuation mark as well as a capital letter. Creating a password that is strong yet easy to remember is an art.
6. Type the password again in the Verify field.
7. If you want to (I recommend you do), type a hint to remind yourself of the password and then click Change Password.
8. Click OK for the alert that tells you that your new password is going to replace your current login keychain password.

A *keychain* is a file that stores your passwords for you so you don't have to remember them all. The operating system created your first keychain for you automatically, called the "login" keychain, when it created your user account. By default, your login keychain password is the same as your account password. For more information about keychains, see Chapter 16, "Keeping Your Mac Safe, Updated, and Backed Up."

9. Click the red button in the upper-left corner of the window to close it.

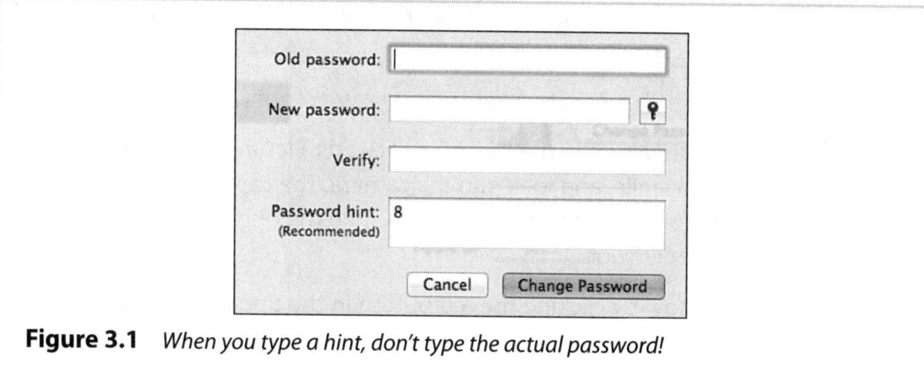

Figure 3.1 *When you type a hint, don't type the actual password!*

TELL ME MORE **Media 3.2—A Discussion about Creating Strong Passwords**

Access this audio recording through your registered Web Edition at
my.safaribooksonline.com/9780132819091/media
or on the DVD for print books.

Changing Your Account Picture

If you chose an icon from the picture library or took a photo of yourself to include as your User Account picture, you may want to change it from time to time. Likewise, you can select a new icon for yourself from the library if you prefer not to use a photo.

To choose a new icon to represent you or take a new picture of yourself, follow these steps:

1. Click the System Preferences icon in the Dock to open the System Preferences window.

2. Click the Users & Groups icon in the fourth row of icons in the window. Your account is selected by default.
3. Click the picture that currently represents your account.
4. Click a different picture in the library or click Edit Picture. Click Take Photo Snapshot, then smile, and look into the camera. The camera counts down from three before it snaps the photo. If you like the photo, click Set; otherwise, take another shot.
5. Close the window by clicking the red button in the upper-left corner.

Launching Applications Automatically at Startup

To make your life easier, you can specify applications that you want to open automatically each time you log in. Just for discussion's sake, suppose you work for the Discs-R-Us company, and as the Vice President of the Rewriteable CDs department, your job is to reformat rewriteable CDs all day long. To make things more convenient for yourself, you can modify your user account so the Disk Utility application launches automatically every time you log in for the day. (What a perk!) Follow these steps to select any application for automatic launch at startup:

1. Click the System Preferences icon in the Dock to open the System Preferences window.
2. Click the Users & Groups icon in the fourth row of icons in the window. Your account is selected by default.
3. Click the Login Items tab in the right pane.
4. Click the Add button (the one with a plus). The Finder opens.
5. Click Applications in the sidebar and select the application that you want to launch automatically.
6. Click Add. The application name displays in the list of items.
7. Repeat steps 4 through 6 for all the applications you want to launch at startup.
8. When finished, close the Preferences window.

If you have an application launching at startup that you no longer want to launch, you can open the Login Items pane in your user account (follow the preceding steps 1 – 3), select the item, and delete it by clicking the Remove button (the one with the minus). Some applications install automatically launching items without your knowing it, so you might want to get rid of these, but be careful. Some applications work best when you allow them to automatically launch as installed.

Sharing Your Computer with Another User

If you want to share your computer with someone else (your sister, for example), you could just let her sit down and start using it, but do you really want your sister reading your email or changing the settings you've made to customize the desktop? If privacy or security is an issue, then a better way to share your computer with her is to create a separate account for her. That way, everything you do on the computer is separated from what she does on the computer, and vice versa. After all, she probably doesn't want you reading her email either. If maintaining separate desktops and email accounts is the issue, rather than privacy or security, setting up separate user accounts is still the way to go.

If you need to share your computer only occasionally with people who just want to get on the Internet or use your printer, you don't need to create a separate account for each person; you can let them use the Guest account. Lion provides a Guest account that is already set up for you to use.

SHOW ME **Media 3.3—A Video about Creating a User Account**
Access this video file through your registered Web Edition at
my.safaribooksonline.com/9780132819091/media
or on the DVD for print books.

LET ME TRY IT

Creating a User Account

As an administrator, you can set up and delete additional user accounts on the computer as the need arises. Even though you have the right to make changes to this part of the system, you will have to unlock the current System Preferences with your account name and password. To set up another user account, follow these steps:

1. Click the System Preferences icon in the Dock and click the Users & Groups icon in the System row. The Users & Groups page opens, as shown in Figure 3.2.

Figure 3.2 *The Guest User account is a default account that is standing by waiting to be enabled.*

2. Click the padlock icon in the lower-left corner of the window.
3. Type your password. If you do not have an Administrative account, you must enter the name and password of an Administrative account. Click Unlock and the padlock opens, allowing you to make changes.
4. Click the Add button (the one with the plus sign just above the padlock icon) to display the form that you must complete to create a new account, as shown in Figure 3.3.
5. Select the type of account you want from the pop-up menu for New Account. Refer to Table 3.1, "Types of User Accounts" to help you make your decision.
6. Type a full name for the account. This will be the login name.
7. Type an account name. This will be the name of the user's Home folder.

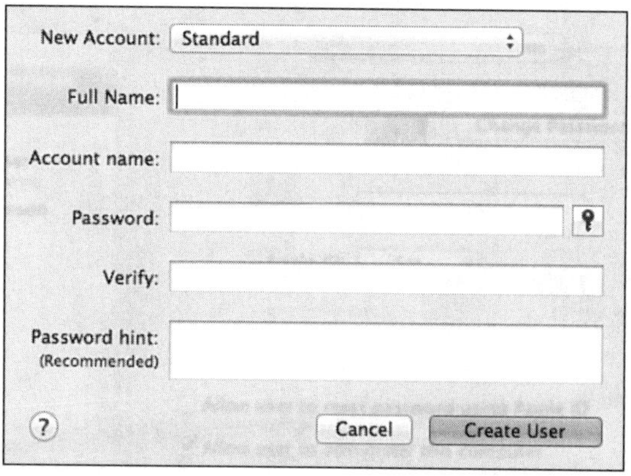

Figure 3.3 *The New Account type defaults to Standard.*

8. Type a password for the account and then type it again in the Verify field.

   Make a note of the full name and password you created to give to the user and keep a copy for yourself. After the account is created, even though you are the administrator, you can't look up the password. If the user forgets the password, you would just have to create a new password for the user.

   If security and privacy are not an issue, you can actually leave the Password and Verify fields blank. If security and privacy *are* the issue, you can click the key icon beside the Password field and let the Password Assistant suggest a strong password for you.

9. Type a hint for the password.

10. Click Create User. The new user account shows up in the sidebar. While it is selected, you can set the Apple ID, if the user has one, and specify additional options for the account, as shown in Figure 3.4.

Figure 3.4 *A new user account displays in the sidebar.*

11. When finished, close the window. Lion closes the padlock automatically when you close the Preferences window.

Table 3.1 Types of User Accounts

Account Type	Privileges
Administrator	Can install software, create, delete, and change user accounts, modify system settings, and change the settings of other users.
Standard	Can install software and change the settings in only his account. (Note that some software may require an administrative password to install even in the user's account.) Cannot create user accounts or change locked system preferences. Cannot create folders outside of his Home folder or the Shared folder.
Managed with Parental Controls	Has at least the Standard privileges, which can then be further limited by the settings made under Parental Controls.
Sharing Only	Can access shared files on a network. Cannot run applications or do anything else.
Group	Includes multiple individual users so that you can make global changes to permissions or sharing privileges for these individuals.

Enabling and Disabling the Guest Account

As mentioned previously, the Guest account is handy for people who just need to use your computer infrequently for something like checking their email on the web or printing a boarding pass. The Guest account is enabled by default in Lion.

Like other user accounts, the Guest account has no access to anything that you or any other user does on the computer with one exception—you can allow the Guest account to access shared folders.

When a guest logs in, he doesn't have to enter a password. When the guest logs out, he has to click Delete Files & Log Out. This is a reminder to the guest that every file he has added to the computer is deleted. Any changes that the user made to the desktop, system preferences, and so on, are reset to the original settings. In other words, Lion cleans house and gets everything ready for the next guest.

If you are logged in as a guest and you don't want to lose your files, you can save your files to a USB drive.

To administer a Guest account, follow these steps:

1. Click the System Preferences icon in the Dock and click the Users & Groups icon in the System row.
2. Click the padlock icon in the lower-left corner of the window.
3. Type your password. If you do not have an Administrative account, you must enter the name and password of an Administrative account. Click Unlock and the padlock opens, allowing you to make changes.
4. Click Guest User in the sidebar.
5. To enable or disable the account, check or uncheck the option Allow Guest to Log in to this Computer.
6. To enable or disable Parental Controls, check or uncheck the Enable Parental Controls option. If you enable them, click the Open Parental Controls button to set the options you want.
7. To enable or disable file sharing, check or uncheck the option Allow Guests to Connect to Shared Folders.
8. Close the window. Lion closes the padlock for you automatically.

Deleting a User Account

When your sister finally buys a Mac of her own, you can delete her user account. One thing to consider before deleting the account is what should happen to the data in her Home folder. Several options are open to you.

LET ME TRY IT

Deleting a User Account

To delete a user account, follow these steps:

1. Click the System Preferences icon in the Dock and click the Users & Groups icon in the System row.
2. Click the padlock icon in the lower-left corner of the window.
3. Type your password. If you do not have an Administrative account, you must enter the name and password of an Administrative account. Click Unlock and the padlock opens, allowing you to make changes.
4. Select the account you want to delete and click the Delete button (the one with the minus on it, located just above the padlock icon). The dialog box shown in Figure 3.5 opens.

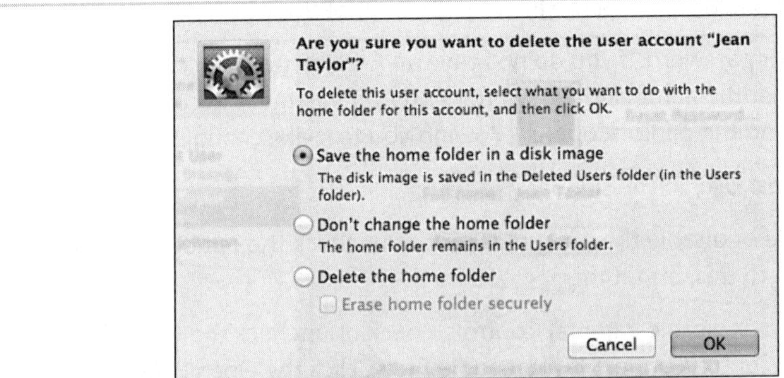

Figure 3.5 *When you delete a user you must decide what to do with the user's Home folder.*

5. If the user has data you want to save, select Save the Home Folder in a Disk Image or Don't Change the Home Folder. Otherwise, select Delete the Home Folder.

6. Click OK. Lion deletes the account and when it is finished, the account name disappears from the sidebar.

7. When finished, close the window. Lion closes the padlock for you automatically.

Logging In and Out

If more than one user account is set up on your Mac, the login process is necessary. To log in when the Mac starts, you click your account name, type the password (if there is one), and press Return or click the arrow in the password field. If you enter an incorrect password, the dialog box appears to shake its head "no" at you. (Sometimes I enter the wrong password a few times just to amuse myself.) If you fail three times to enter the correct password, your password hint is given.

The first time a new user logs in, the desktop and all the System Preferences are set to the factory defaults regardless of what changes you've made to your own desktop and preferences in *your* user account. Remember, user accounts are like Las Vegas—everything that happens in a user's account *stays* in the user's account.

To allow another user (who has a user account) to use the computer, you can log out or simply switch users. To log out, use the keyboard shortcut Shift-Command-Q or click the Apple menu and click the last option on the menu, Log Out *<User Name>* (where *User Name* is the account name). Logging out does not power down the computer; it shuts down all the user's applications and redisplays the log in screen for the next user to log in.

As an alternative to closing all your work and logging off the system completely, you can use the feature called Fast User Switching. The Fast User Switching option is enabled in Lion by default. You'll find the preference for this feature on the Login Options page for each user account in the Users & Groups Preferences window. On this page you can enable or disable the feature and specify what appears in the menu bar if the feature is enabled. You can show the full user account name, the short name, or an icon. I recommend you use the full or short name instead of the icon so you can tell at a glance whose desktop is displaying on the screen.

Switching Users without Logging Out

To quickly switch users, follow these steps:

1. Click the current user name on the right side of the menu bar. The menu shown in Figure 3.6 opens. A check mark appears beside the names of all users who are currently logged in.

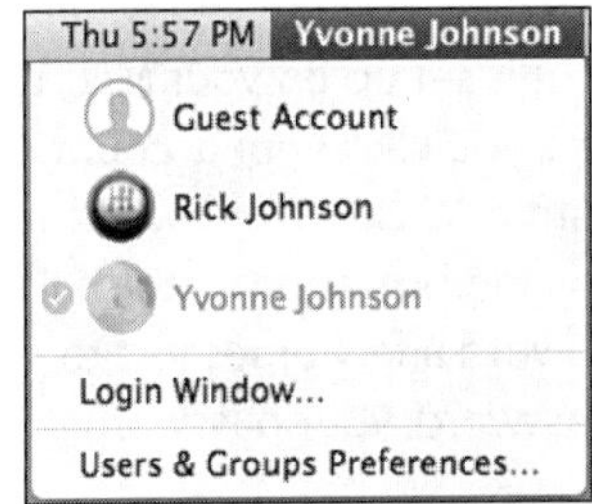

Figure 3.6 *Every user account that is set up on the computer displays in this list.*

2. Click the name of the user account for the user who wants to log in. A log in dialog box opens.

If the user changes his mind about logging in, he can click the Cancel button at the bottom of the screen.

3. Type the password and press Return or click the right arrow in the password field. The desktop for the new user displays, but all the applications and files that the previous user was working with are still open and running (unseen) in the background.

If your system seems to be working very slowly, the possibility exists that a user who is still logged in left a large number of applications open that are using too many system resources.

LET ME TRY IT

Turning On Automatic Login

If you are the only user on your computer, you might like the idea of bypassing the login step altogether. You can do this by turning on automatic login. Without a required login, however, anyone with access to your computer could start it and peruse your data. If that is a low risk for you, by all means, activate automatic login. Follow these steps to turn on automatic login:

1. Open the System Preferences window and click Users & Groups.
2. Click the padlock icon and type your password. If you do not have an Administrative account, you must enter the name and password of an Administrative account. Click Unlock and the padlock opens, allowing you to make changes.
3. Click Login Options.
4. Select your name from the Automatic Login pop-up menu as shown in Figure 3.7.
5. Type your password and click OK.
6. When finished, close the window. Lion closes the padlock for you automatically.

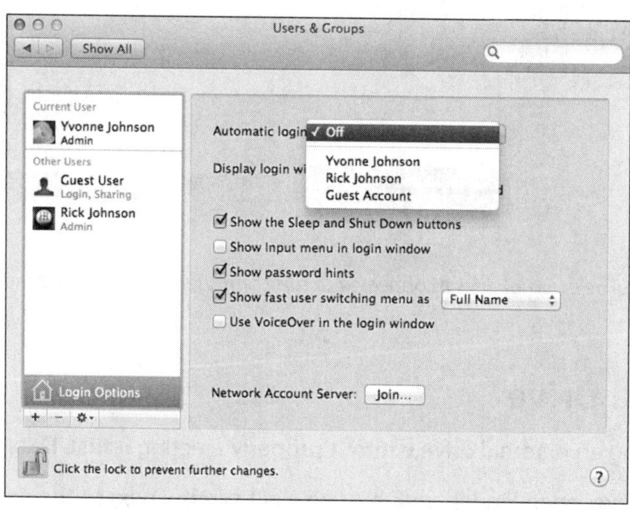

Figure 3.7 *Automatic login allows anyone to use your computer so if your no-good nephew is visiting, you might want to turn this off until he leaves.*

Using External Drives

An external drive is any storage device connected to the Mac via USB or FireWire cable. For example, the drive could be a flash drive, an additional DVD drive, an external hard drive (perhaps one that you use for Time Machine), an iPod, and so on.

For more information about Time Machine, see Chapter 16.

Connecting a Drive

Connecting an external drive is a simple matter of plugging the cable or device into the correct port on the Mac. That's it. The Mac recognizes the drive and lists it under Devices in the sidebar of the Finder, as shown in Figure 3.8.

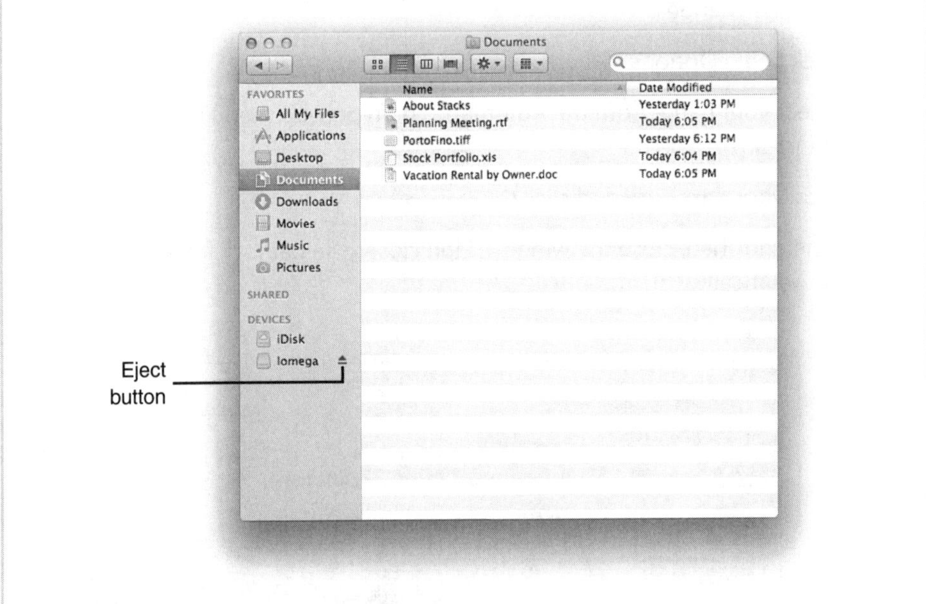

Figure 3.8 *The external device connected to this computer is an external hard drive called Iomega.*

Ejecting a Drive

Never unplug an external drive without properly ejecting it first. Data could be lost.

To eject a drive, open Finder and click the eject symbol next to the drive in the sidebar (refer to Figure 3.8). If you properly eject the drive, its icon no longer shows as a device in the Finder window. Then you can physically disconnect the device from your Mac.

Although not the default, displaying icons for external drives on the Desktop is possible. See Chapter 6, "Customizing the Desktop," to learn how. If you have this preference set, then you can eject a drive by right-clicking its icon and clicking Eject or you can drag the icon to the Trashcan in the Dock. Don't worry; dragging the icon of an external drive to the Trash icon does not delete any data!

Installing and Managing Printers

While perusing a question-and-answer Mac forum one day, I found this post from a PC switcher: "I feel happy and giddy all the time. Also, I have too much free time because I didn't have to figure anything out when I installed my printer and mouse. What should I do?"

This answer was posted: "Enjoy your Mac."

Like everything else, Apple has streamlined printer installation.

Connecting and Using a Printer

Generally, you can connect a new printer to a Mac and use it right away because Lion comes with the most common printer software and selects it automatically when it senses a printer has been connected. Additionally, Mac OS X keeps the software updated automatically via the Internet. The only time you have to do any extra work to install a printer is if you buy an "uncommon" printer.

LET ME TRY IT

Installing a Printer

To verify that Mac OS X recognizes the printer or, if necessary, to install one, follow these steps (in most cases, you probably will have to complete only the first four steps in these instructions):

1. Open any document.

   If you don't have any documents to open, click the Documents stack icon in the Dock and then click the icon for the file named About Stacks.pdf. The document opens in the application called Preview.

2. Click File in the menu bar and then click Print to open the Print dialog box, as shown in Figure 3.9.

3. If your printer is listed in the Printer field, you are good to go. If not, click the Printer pop-up button to display the list of printers installed on your Mac.

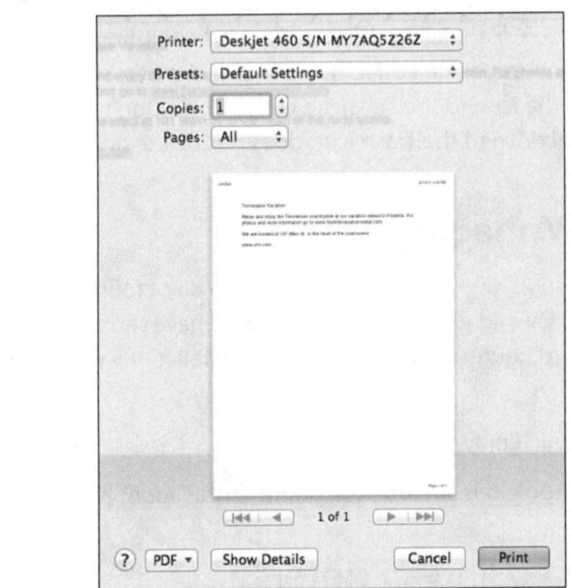

Figure 3.9 *The Print menu contains more options that are currently hidden.*

4. If your printer's name is there, select it and you are ready to click the Print button.
5. If you don't see your printer on the list, click the Add Printer option in the pop-up list, as shown in Figure 3.10.
6. Click the More Printers button. (If you don't see this button, this could mean trouble. You'll have to contact your printer manufacturer for more information.)
7. Choose your printer type from the pop-up menu (for example, Epson USB).
8. After you choose your printer type, it appears in the Printer Name column. Click it and then click the Add button.

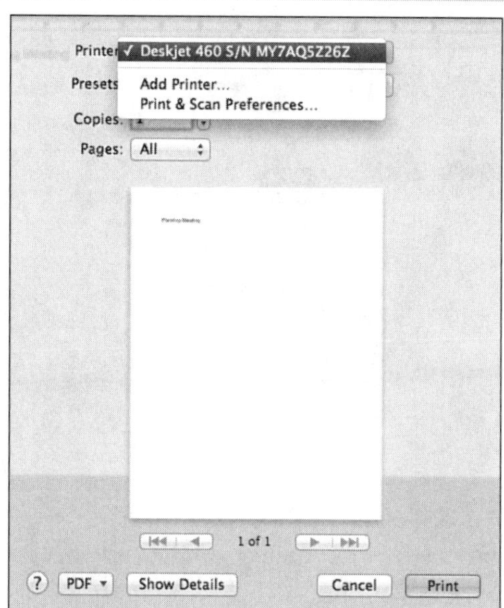

Figure 3.10 *Currently only one printer is installed and it is listed at the top of this pop-up menu.*

In the very unlikely event that your printer doesn't work after installing Lion, unplug it. Then open the Print page of the Print & Scan preferences window and delete the printer. Plug it back in and follow the preceding steps.

Setting a Default Printer

The default printer is the printer that Lion selects automatically every time you send a document to print. The default can be a specific printer, or you can select the option Last Printer Used. Regardless of how you set the default, you can always switch to a different printer before you print if you want to. To set the default printer, follow these steps:

1. Click the System Preferences icon in the Dock.
2. Click Print & Scan. Figure 3.11 shows the Print & Scan window.
3. Select the printer or option that you want for Default Printer.
4. Close the window when you are finished.

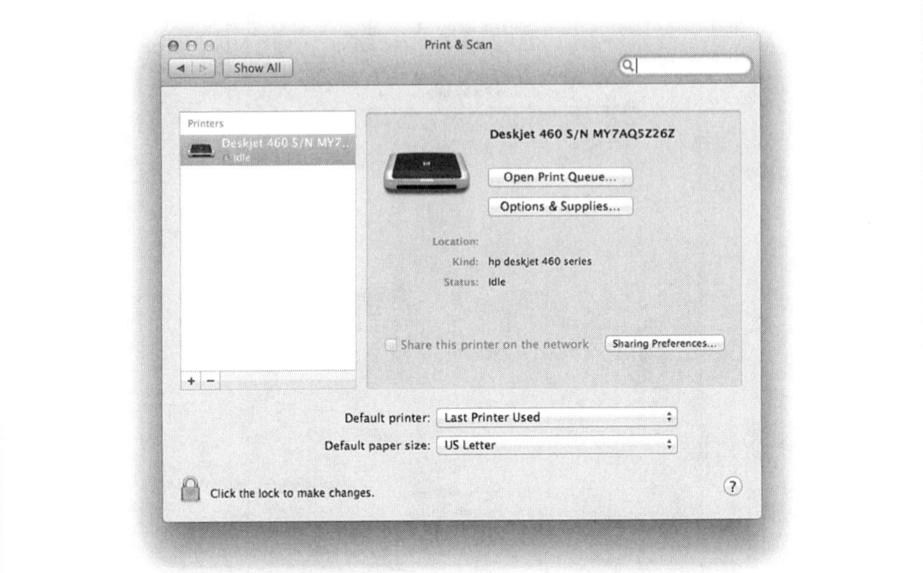

Figure 3.11 *The Last Printer Used option means that you don't really specify a default printer.*

Setting Up a Computer-to-Computer Network

If you have more than one Mac at your location, you might sometimes want the computers to share data or want to print something on a printer that is connected to one of your other Macs. You may quake in your boots at the thought of setting up a network, but setting up a wireless, computer-to-computer network is well within the range of even a beginning Mac user.

The computer-to-computer type of network, also referred to as an "ad hoc" network because it is only temporary, does not require Ethernet, a router, or any special hardware. The only connectivity the ad hoc network uses is Wi-Fi so all computers that you want to include in the network must be Wi-Fi enabled.

If you want to have a "real" network, you can purchase Lion Server from the Mac App Store for $49.99. It has a setup assistant that takes you step by step through the process of setting up your Mac as a server. The Lion Server app includes iCal Server 3, Wiki Server 3, and Mail Server 3.

SHOW ME **Media 3.4—A Video about Creating an Ad Hoc Network**

Access this video file through your registered Web Edition at
my.safaribooksonline.com/9780132819091/media
or on the DVD for print books.

LET ME TRY IT

Creating Your Own Network

One of the following steps could trip you up, and I'm going to warn you about it before you get started so you can be prepared. In step 4, you must specify a channel. The default channel is 11. Using the default channel is not advisable unless you make sure no other device is using that channel. To make sure of this, you must first open System Information and check the Wi-Fi option under Network. If any Wi-Fi device is using channel 11, then you must select a different channel for step 4.

See Chapter 15, "Using System Utilities," for more information about how to open and use the System Information utility.

To create a new network for Wi-Fi-enabled Macs, follow these steps:

1. On the Mac that will be the host, click the Wi-Fi status icon in the menu bar. (If you don't have a Wi-Fi status icon in the menu bar, open System Preferences and click Network. Select the Wi-Fi connection and then click the check box for Show Wi-Fi Status in Menu Bar.)
2. Click Create Network. The dialog box shown in Figure 3.12 opens.

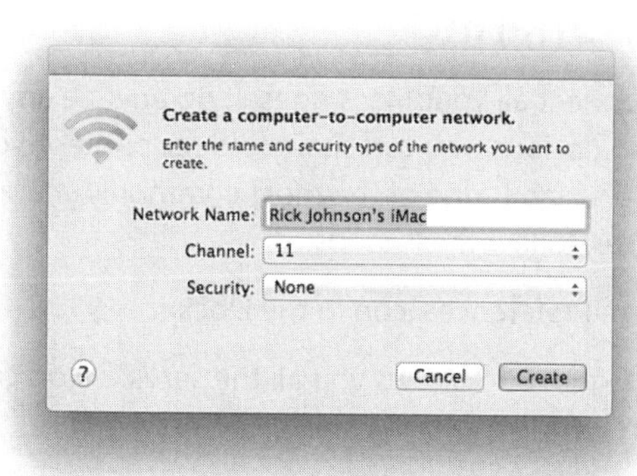

Figure 3.12 *The default channel is 11 but make sure it is available before you use it.*

3. Type the name you want to use for the network if you don't want to use the name provided.
4. Select an unused channel for the network.
5. Select 40-bit WEP or 128-bit WEP for Security. (You also can select None if you don't want to have a password, in which case, you can skip steps 6 and 7.)
6. In the Password field, type an ASCII or a hexadecimal password with the required number of digits (as specified in the dialog box).

   An ASCII password can consist of any keyboard character. Examples of a five-digit ASCII password would include apple, A99le, 123#$, and so on. For a hexadecimal password, you can use any combination of these numbers and characters: 0, 1, 2, 3, 4, 5, 6, 7, 8, 9, A, B, C, D, E, and F, so a 10-digit hexadecimal password might be 12345ABCDE.
7. Type the password again in the Confirm Password field.
8. Click Create. The network is created and your Mac is on the network immediately as you can see from the change in the Wi-Fi status icon.

At this point, your new network should be listed as a network on your Wi-Fi Status menu and on the menus of any other Wi-Fi–enabled Macs within range of your Mac. So now all your Wi-Fi–enabled Macs can connect to each other, but the network evaporates as soon as you change to another network on the host computer or when you restart or shut down.

LET ME TRY IT

Setting Up File Sharing

Just being able to connect all your Macs doesn't do anyone any good unless you turn on some sharing options. You can share folders, printers, your Internet connection, and so on. File Sharing is one of the most commonly shared resources. To turn on file sharing services, follow these steps:

1. Click the System Preferences icon in the Dock.
2. Click Sharing. Figure 3.13 shows you all the services you can turn on for sharing resources.
3. Click the padlock icon and type your password. If you do not have an Administrative account, you must enter the name and password of an Administrative account. Click Unlock and the padlock opens, allowing you to make changes.

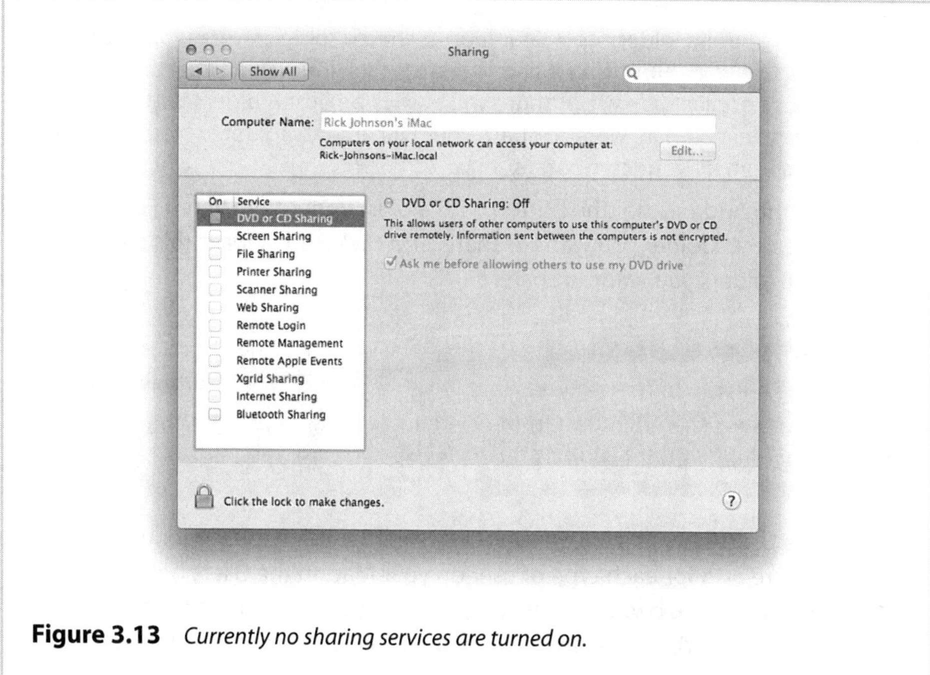

Figure 3.13 *Currently no sharing services are turned on.*

4. Click the File Sharing service to turn it on (see Figure 3.14).

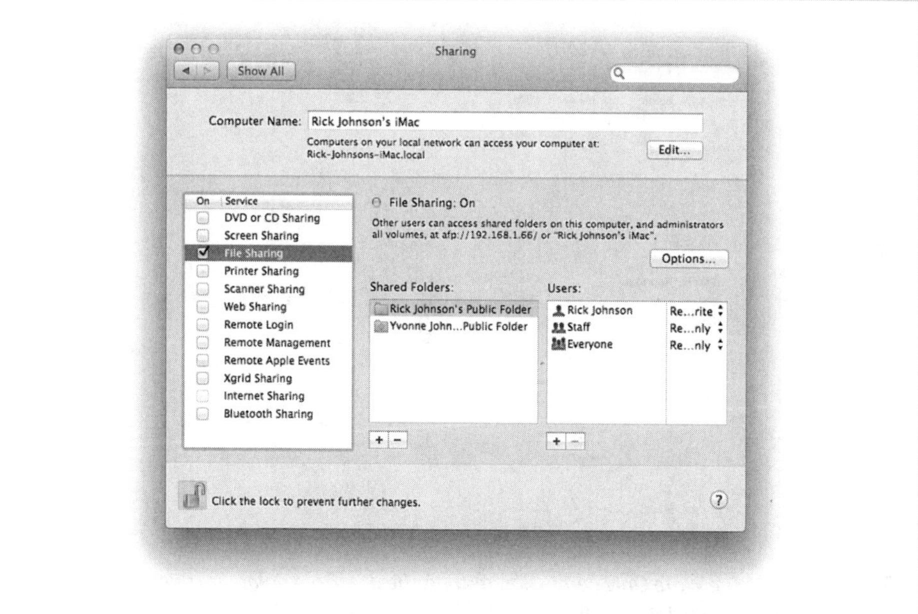

Figure 3.14 *If no folders have been shared, only the Public folders are accessible to other computers.*

The Shared Folders box lists the public folder of every user account set up on the Mac. This is because a public folder is, by definition, a shared folder. Most people don't even know they have a public folder and therefore nothing is in it. You can and should learn how to use public folders, but there will always be other folders you want to share. For example, you may want to share your Documents folder so you can access your main files from all your computers.

5. Click the Add button (the button with a plus) under the Shared Folders box, select a folder you want to share, and click Add. Repeat this step for all the folders you want to share.

To remove a folder from sharing, select it, and click the Remove button (the button with the minus). To remind you what folder you have shared, when you select one of your shared folders in the Finder, the Finder displays a gray bar below the toolbar with the words *Shared Folder*.

6. In the Users box, select a permission level from the pop-up menu shown in Figure 3.15 for each type of user on your Mac. In the Users box, you are listed first as the owner followed by Staff (anyone who has an account on your computer), and Everyone (anyone who can be connected to your computer via any method, such as across a network).

Figure 3.15 *The Write Only permission restricts the user from doing anything except upload to the Drop Box folder in the Public Folder.*

For convenience, you can make the Shared Folder and Users boxes larger or smaller so you can read the content by pointing to the space between the two boxes and dragging left or right.

7. Continue selecting other services, if desired. Each service you select has its own set of options.
8. When finished, close the window. Lion closes the padlock for you automatically.
9. Repeat all these steps for every Mac you want to set up to share resources on the network.

LET ME TRY IT

Accessing Shared Folders on an Ad Hoc Network

To access a shared folder on an ad hoc network and open a file, follow these steps:

1. Click the Wi-Fi status icon in the menu bar and click the name of the ad hoc network. If a password is required, type the password and click OK to join the network.
2. Open the Finder.
3. Under the Shared category in the sidebar, click the name of the computer that has the file you want to use. The shared folders display in the right pane, as shown in Figure 3.16.

   If you are not connected, you may need to click the Connect As button, type your administrative password, and click Connect.
4. Double-click the folder you want to open.

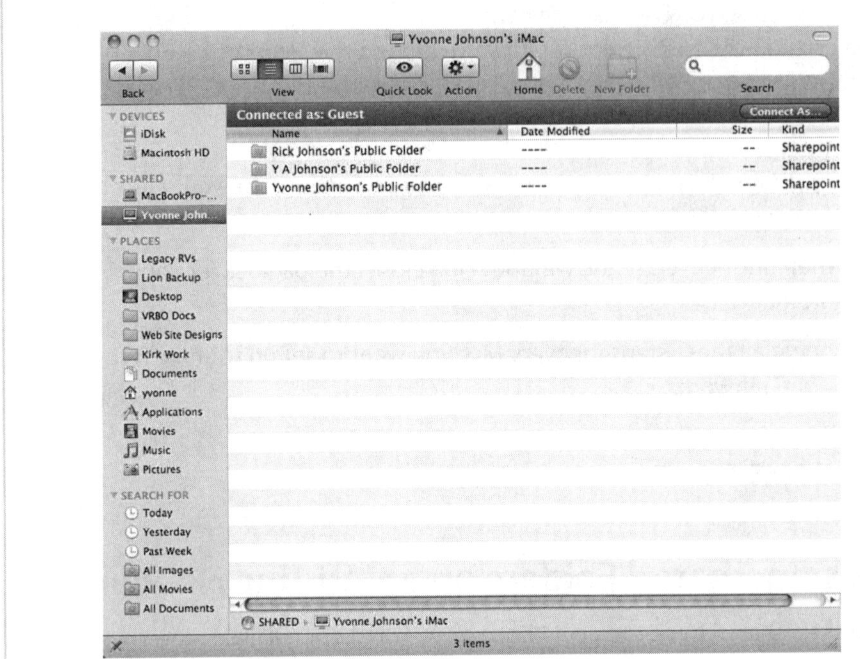

Figure 3.16 *Public folders for all users on the shared Mac display in the list on the right as well as any specific folders that have been shared.*

5. Double-click the file you want to open. Make edits to the file, print it, and so on. Save the file, if necessary, and close it when finished.
6. When you are finished using the network, click the Disconnect button in the upper-right corner of the screen.

This chapter gives you an overview of working with the Lion user interface, including the desktop, menus, important icons on the Dock, and shutting down your Mac.

4

Getting Comfortable with Lion

In this chapter, I help you get familiar with the default appearance and behavior of your Mac—that is, with the original settings that come with a new Mac. I discuss some of the basic features you are presented with when you start your Mac as well as how to use some of the most basic tools and applications, such as the desktop, the menu bar, contextual menus, the Dock, and the Dashboard. Additionally, I show you how to put the Mac to sleep or shut it down.

Exploring the Desktop

The first thing you see after pressing the power button on your Mac is a gray screen with the Apple logo in the middle. After logging in with your user name and password (if logging in is enabled), you see a screen that is referred to as the *desktop*. The new background for the Lion desktop is a picture of the majestic Andromeda galaxy.

If you upgraded from Snow Leopard, your desktop background will be the same desktop you were using before you upgraded, but you can easily change it to the graphic of the Andromeda galaxy. See Chapter 6, "Customizing the Desktop," if you need help with this.

A menu bar at the top extends across the width of the screen. The left side of the menu displays the menu options for the active application. The right side of the menu bar contains Menu Extras (or *menulets*, as many users call them). These are menus represented by icons, and they give you quick access to options for a particular feature, such as the volume level of your sound card. The last icon on the right is the Spotlight. It is an unassuming little icon that looks like a magnifying glass, but, to quote Shakespeare, "Though she be but little, she is fierce." The Spotlight is an unbelievably powerful search tool that is truly amazing. See Chapter 7, "Using Finder," for more details. Between the menulets and the Spotlight is the Fast User

Switching option. By default, this is the full name of the current user. See "Logging In and Out" in Chapter 3, "Setting Up User Accounts and Installing Hardware," for information on how to use this feature.

At the bottom of the screen is a row of icons called the Dock. Figure 4.1 shows the default desktop.

Figure 4.1 *This is the default desktop—straight from the factory with no customizations.*

Using Menus

Now speaking of menus, take a closer look at the menu bar at the top of the screen. Let me begin by saying that there is *always* a menu bar at the top of the screen, but there is never more than one menu bar. Any application you are working in uses this menu bar space to display its menu options.

SHOW ME **Media 4.1—A Video about Using Menus**
Access this video file through your registered Web Edition at
my.safaribooksonline.com/9780132819091/media
or on the DVD for print books.

Notice that the first item on the left is the famous Apple logo. The logo is not just a graphic on the menu bar; it's actually the name of a menu that has options, as shown in Figure 4.2. Next to the Apple logo is the word *Finder*, which appears in bold text. This is the name of the application that currently has the focus (that is, you are working in that application's window), but it is also the name of the second menu on the menu bar. The words to the right of Finder (File, Edit, View, and so on) are also names of menus that work in the application that has focus.

When no other application is active, the menu bar always contains the Finder menu. The Finder is the application that lists and manipulates all the files and folders on the computer. Each time the Mac starts, it opens the Finder application automatically, and this application remains open until you shut down the computer.

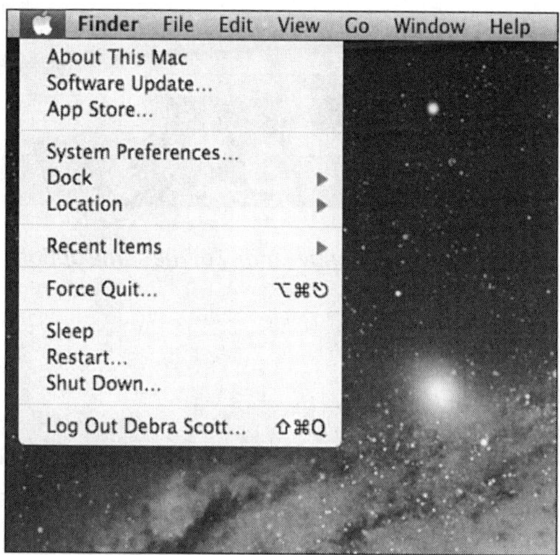

Figure 4.2 *The Apple menu is always the first menu in the menu bar, regardless of what application you are using.*

You can think of the Finder menu bar as a template for all others. Every application you open on a Mac displays a menu bar that has the Apple logo followed by the name of the application, such as Finder, Word, Photoshop, and so on. Figure 4.3 shows you what the menu bar for Microsoft Word for Mac 2011 looks like.

Figure 4.3 *The Word application menu bar has a dozen menu options!*

No matter what application you are using, the Apple menu always has the same commands on it, but the application menus vary by application, as you would expect. For example, the Word menu on the Microsoft Word menu bar has an

Online Registration option that you won't find on the Photoshop menu on the Adobe Photoshop menu bar. By the same token, the Photoshop menu has an About Plug-In command you won't find on the Word menu. Some commands on application menus are generally common to all application menus, however. These include commands such as About, Preferences, Services, Hide, Hide Others, Show All, and Quit.

To the right of the application menu are the additional menus that the application uses. Many applications include some of the same menus as the Finder menu bar, specifically File, Edit, View, Window, and Help, as you can see in Figure 4.4.

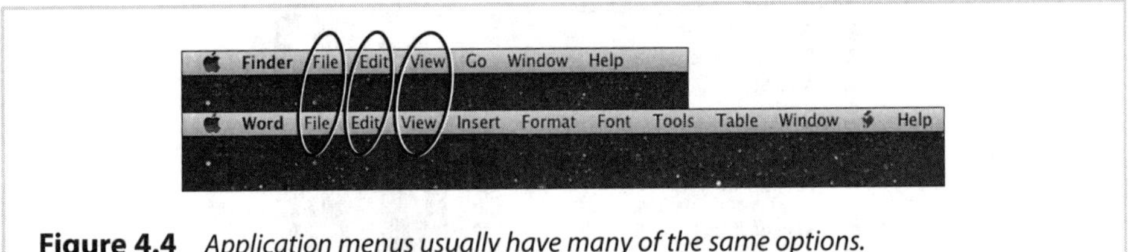

Figure 4.4 *Application menus usually have many of the same options.*

Using the Menu Bar

To use the commands available to you in the menu bar, simply click the name of the menu to display the commands on that menu. Then click the command. Sometimes, commands on the menu have *submenus*. If a menu command has a submenu, it has a right-pointing arrow on the right of the command. To display the submenu, all you have to do is point to the command that has the arrow.

Figure 4.5 shows the submenu for the Sort By command.

Notice in Figure 4.5 that several options on the View menu are "dimmed"—that is, they are light gray instead of black. This means that the commands are not relevant at the moment and, therefore, are not available. Additionally, one menu command shown in the figure (Customize Toolbar) has three dots after it, an ellipsis. Any time you see an ellipsis after a menu command, you know that clicking that command will display a dialog box that contains additional settings or input fields.

One final menu feature you can see in Figure 4.5 is the command's keyboard shortcut—listed just to the right of the command. A keyboard shortcut allows you to perform a command instantly without opening a menu. The shortcuts generally use one or more "modifier" keys (Shift [⇧], Control [Ctrl], Alt/Option [⌘], and Command [cmd]) followed by a regular key (a letter, number, or punctuation mark). To use a keyboard shortcut for a command, first press and hold the modifier keys and then press the regular key.

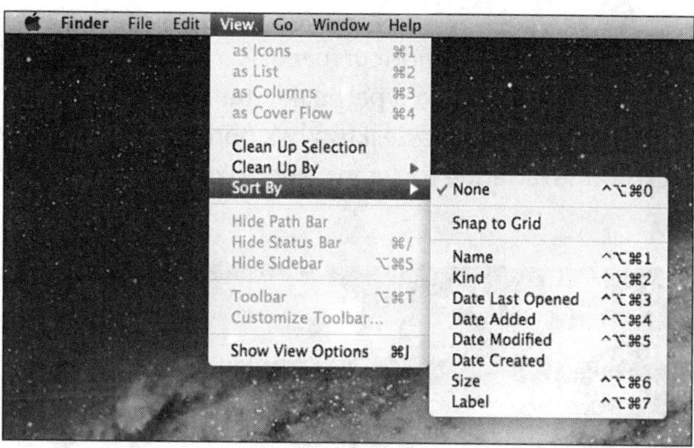

Figure 4.5 *Submenus disappear if you accidentally move the pointer to another option on the first menu while you are trying to click the command that you want on the submenu.*

Most people I know don't use many keyboard shortcuts for two reasons: First, many are difficult to remember, and second, it really seems as fast to use the mouse. But...oops! Your 10,000 shares of stock just took a giant nosedive, and you slammed your mouse down on the desk in frustration, shattering it into pieces! Now what do you do? Unlike my husband, whose mouse and stocks did not revive, you cannot call me into the room to get you out of this mess. All you have is your keyboard to control the computer. Table 4.1 shows the keystrokes to use to access the menu bar and make selections so you can control the computer completely without a mouse.

Table 4.1 Keyboard Shortcuts

Action You Want to Accomplish	Action to Take with the Keyboard
Move to the menu bar.	Press Ctrl-F2. (On some keyboards you may have to use Fn with this shortcut.)
Select a menu on the menu bar.	Use the Right or Left Arrow key to move to the menu you want.
Open a menu on the menu bar.	After the menu is selected, press Return.
Select a command on the open menu.	Use the Down or Up Arrow key to move to the command you want.
Execute a command on the open menu.	After the command is selected, press Return.
Close a menu.	Press Esc. (This also exits the menu bar.)

If you also need to access the Dock, press Ctrl-F3 (or Ctrl-Fn-F3). Then use the Right and Left Arrow keys to move to the icon that you want and press Return to open the application.

Using Contextual Menus

A contextual menu, also called a *shortcut menu*, is a menu that has a limited number of commands that apply just to a particular item in the current situation. For example, the context menu for the desktop has options to create a new folder, change the background, arrange the icons, and so on, as shown in Figure 4.6.

Figure 4.6 *Chapter 6 explains several of the commands on the desktop shortcut menu.*

If you have an Apple Mighty Mouse, Magic Mouse, or a non-Apple two-button mouse, you can display a context menu by pointing to an object and clicking the secondary button. By default, the left side of the mouse is the primary button and the right side of the mouse is the secondary button, but if you are left-handed, you can reverse the buttons by changing the Mouse preferences (see Chapter 5, "Managing Your Hardware"). For ease of writing, I will use the term *right-click* when I refer to clicking the secondary mouse button. If you are a lefty who has switched the buttons, you'll know what I mean. If you have a Magic Trackpad, you "right-click" by clicking with two fingers.

If you don't have a two-button mouse, you can display a context menu by pointing to the particular item and pressing the Ctrl key while you click the item.

Be aware that not every clickable item or space on the screen has a shortcut menu. If no shortcut menu is available when you right-click an item, nothing happens. For example, if you right-click the blank space after the Help menu in the menu bar, no shortcut menu opens.

Using the Dock

The Dock is the flashiest part of the desktop and probably attracts the most attention, so let's look at it in some detail. Notice that it is divided into two sections by a line, which looks like the dotted line in the middle of a highway to me, but technically, it's called the "separator." You can see it in Figure 4.1. It's on the far right, just to the left of the third icon from the right end of the Dock.

Launching Applications

The function of the left side of the Dock is launching applications (*applications* being the official Apple term for "software programs"). Every icon on the left side of the Dock represents an application. Getting familiar with what applications the icons represent might take you a while so until you know them by sight, you can display the name of the application by pointing to the icon. When you point to an icon, the name of the icon shows up in a black label just above the icon.

The Dock does not contain an icon for *every* application that is available on the Mac, but you can add or remove icons so that the Dock contains the applications you use most often. See Chapter 6, "Customizing the Desktop," for details. You can easily access applications that are not represented by an icon on the Dock by using the Launchpad.

To learn more about the Launchpad, see Chapter 8, "Managing Applications."

To launch an application represented by an icon on the Dock, just click the icon. If the application doesn't open instantly, its icon bounces up and down. Either it's excited because it's been selected, or it's impatiently waiting on itself to open. I haven't decided which. When an application has been launched, a glowing blue bubble appears below the icon. You can see it under the first icon in Figure 4.1. This bubble remains in place until you quit the application.

You may also see this bouncing behavior when an application that is running in the background needs your attention. You may need to supply some information or make a selection in a warning or confirmation dialog box.

If you launch an application that doesn't have an icon on the Dock, the application displays its icon on the left side of the Dock with the other application icons until you quit the application. Then the icon disappears. To add the icon to the Dock, while the icon for the application is displayed and before you quit the application, right-click the icon, click Options, and click Keep in Dock.

Notice the first icon in the Dock—the two-faced, blue man (love this metaphor). This is the icon for the Finder application that Lion always launches at startup. Because it is always the current application when the computer starts, its menu is the one displayed in the menu bar, and because Lion never closes Finder, there is always a blue bubble under this icon. I explain more about the Finder in Chapter 7.

Quitting Applications

You literally cannot quit the Finder, but you can quit any other application that you have launched. If you have several programs running, and you want to quit one of them, just right-click its icon in the Dock and click Quit, as shown in Figure 4.7. (Remember, the term *right-click* is relative to the device you are using.)

The shortcut keystroke Command-Q also quits an application, but you actually have to be in the application at the time to use the shortcut.

If you are working in a "pre-Lion" application that does not use the new Autosave feature, you will see an appropriate warning about saving your work before you quit if you haven't done so. If you are using a Lion-compatible application, you can quit the application and everything resumes as it was when you quit and Lion saves your work for you automatically.

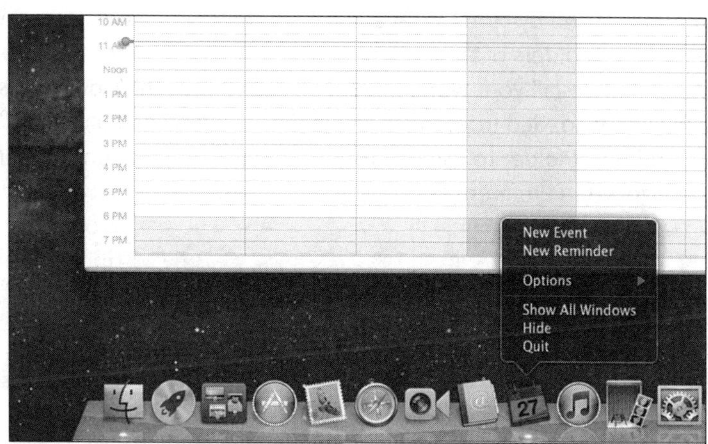

Figure 4.7 *Right-click or Ctrl-click to get this menu.*

Looking at Stacks

Immediately to the right side of the separator in the Dock are two icons that do not launch applications (see Figure 4.8). These icons actually represent folders—the Documents folder and the Downloads folder.

Figure 4.8 *Icons on the right side of the separator represent folders, not applications.*

You can add your own folders to the right side of the Dock and even remove the default folders that Lion puts there for you. I tell you how in Chapter 6, "Customizing the Desktop."

The first icon to the right of the separator line is for the Documents folder, which is the default folder used by Lion for saved documents. If you store all your work in this folder or in subfolders of this folder, the Documents stack icon provides a convenient way to access all your work. The second icon is for the Downloads folder, where all files downloaded from the Internet are stored by default. Note that you can select a different folder to use for storing downloaded files on the General preferences page in Safari Preferences.

As you learn to use the various applications on your Mac, you will see that the right side of the separator also displays other icons temporarily in certain situations. I explain this to you in detail in Chapter 8, "Managing Applications."

SHOW ME **Media 4.2—A Video about Using Stacks**
Access this video file through your registered Web Edition at
my.safaribooksonline.com/9780132819091/media
or on the DVD for print books.

Icons that represent folders have a special name—Apple calls them *stacks*. When you click a stack icon, the individual items in the folder fan out like a deck of cards, as shown in Figure 4.9, or they display in a grid, as shown in Figure 4.10, depending on the number of items in the folder. To open an individual item, just click the item. If the stack displays items in a fan, you must click the icon and not the item name. You actually can choose how you want a stack to display (see Chapter 6), so if you are upgrading from Snow Leopard, and you had selected a display option for a stack, Lion keeps that preference intact for you.

After displaying the items in a stack, if you don't really want to open one of them, you can return the items to the stack by pressing Esc or clicking on a blank area of the desktop. In Chapter 6, I tell you how to customize the appearance of a stack icon in the Dock.

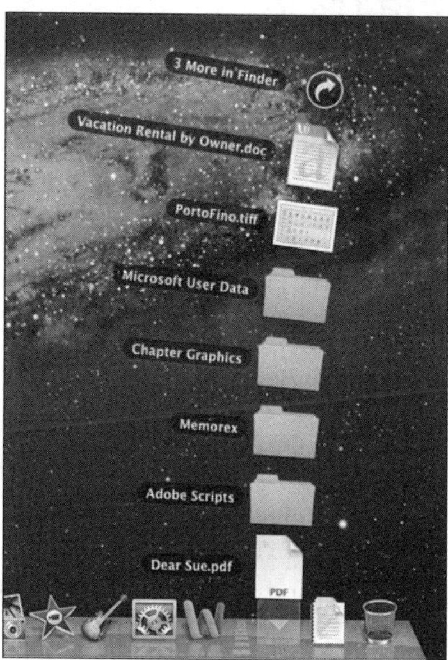

Figure 4.9 *To open an item in the stack, click the icon for the item, not the name.*

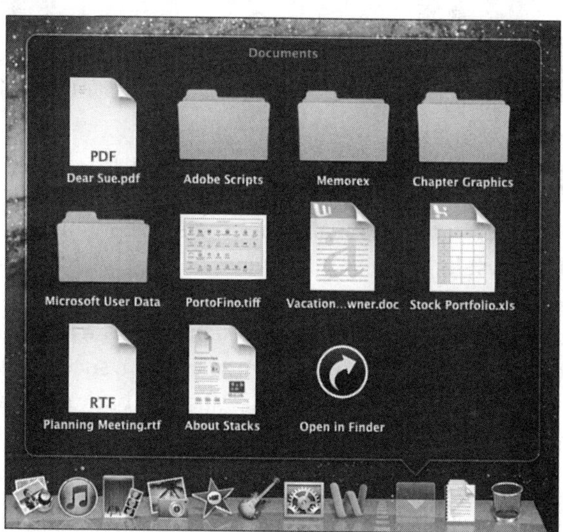

Figure 4.10 *The grid displays the items in the folder in a window that pops up.*

Going through the Trash

The last icon on the right side of the separator is the Trash icon, where deleted files, folders, and applications go until you permanently delete them. On a new computer, the Trash icon is empty, but after you have deleted files, the graphic of the trashcan looks like it has crumpled paper in it.

When you click the Trash icon, a window opens with a list of all the items that are "in the trash." You can go through the trash and take things out again or get rid of them for good. For more information about deleting files and folders, see Chapter 7.

Putting Your Mac to Sleep or Shutting It Down

When you finish working on your Mac for the day, you can put it to sleep or shut it down. It's up to you really, but most Mac users I know leave their Macs running all the time. Sleep mode uses very little power, and it keeps all your applications and work open and in memory. The computer wakes up from the sleep mode within seconds after you press a key or click the mouse so you can get back to work much faster than you can if you have to start the Mac.

The Mac performs many maintenance routines in the middle of the night, or when it recognizes that you're not using it—another reason to use the sleep mode instead of shutting down.

Putting the Mac to Sleep

To put the Mac in sleep mode manually, click the Apple menu and click Sleep. Otherwise, you can just let the Mac go to sleep on its own. After a period of mouse and keyboard inactivity defined in the Energy Saver preferences, the Mac will put both the hard disk and the screen to sleep. Of course, if the Mac is in the middle of a process that doesn't require keyboard or mouse input, such as playing a DVD movie, playing music in iTunes, doing a Time Machine backup, or downloading files from the Internet, it will not suddenly go to sleep in the middle of the process.

If you have a laptop, you have two sets of sleep options—one for the power adapter and one for the battery. Typically, you want to use a shorter time interval for sleep mode when running on battery to conserve the power. For the sake of your laptop battery, you should let the battery run down completely about once a month. This is part of the calibration process. Listen to the audio file I recorded for you that explains what calibration is and how to do it.

TELL ME MORE **Media 4.3—A Discussion about Calibrating a Laptop Battery**

Access this audio recording through your registered Web Edition at ***my.safaribooksonline.com/9780132819091/media*** *or on the DVD for print books.*

LET ME TRY IT

Setting Energy Saver Preferences

To set your computer's energy saver preferences, follow these steps:

1. Click the System Preferences icon in the Dock.
2. Click Energy Saver. The preferences shown in Figure 4.11 are for an iMac.

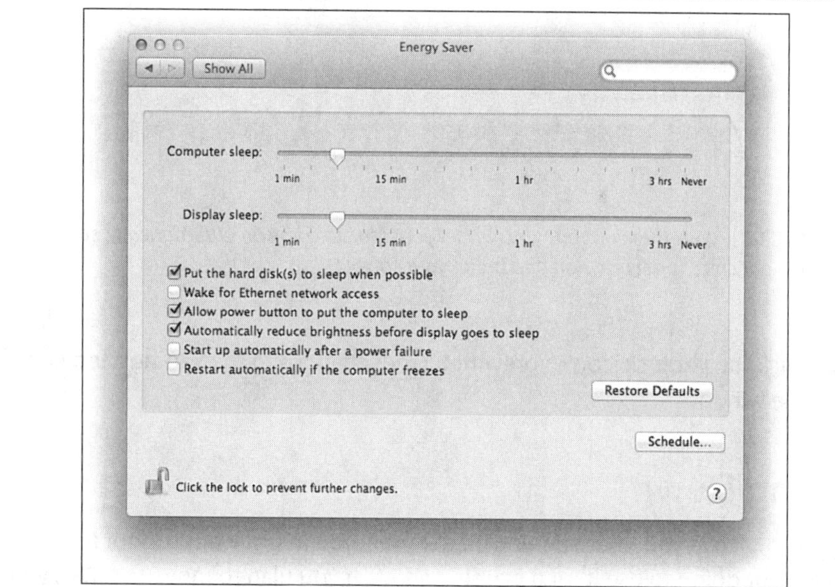

Figure 4.11 *The Energy Saver options are different for a laptop.*

3. If necessary, click the padlock icon and enter the name and password of an Administrative account. Click Unlock and the padlock opens, allowing you to make changes. If your account has administrative privileges, the padlock is open for you when you open the Energy Saver preferences.
4. Set the time on the sliders for Computer Sleep and Display Sleep.

5. Set other options as desired.
6. To set times for automatic startup and sleep, click the Schedule button. Specify the options shown in Figure 4.12 and click OK.

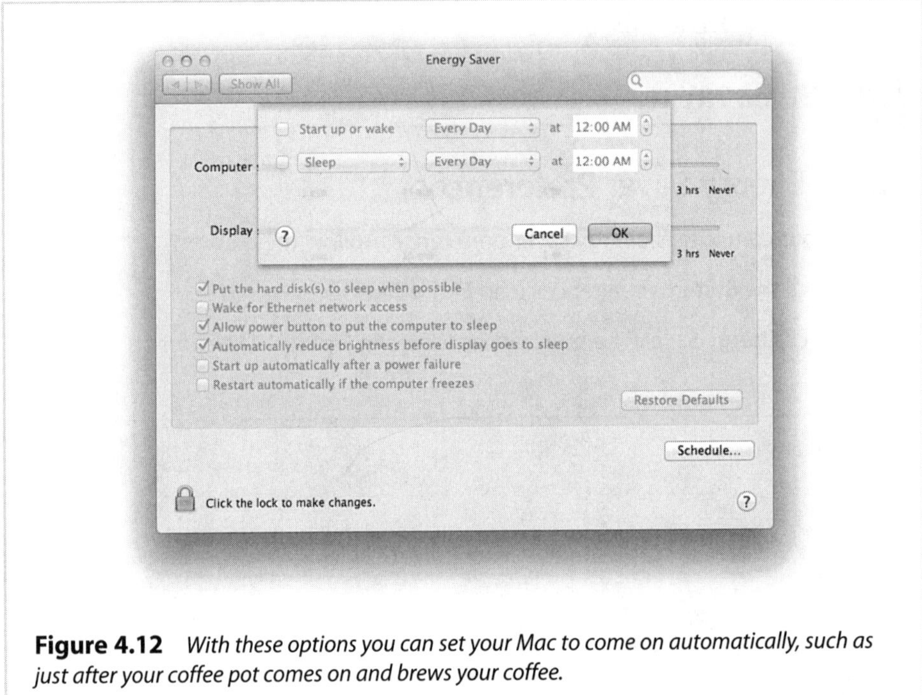

Figure 4.12 *With these options you can set your Mac to come on automatically, such as just after your coffee pot comes on and brews your coffee.*

7. Click the padlock icon to prevent further changes to the settings and close the window.

Shutting Down

Even if you leave your Mac running all the time, you might want to shut it down if you are not going to use it for a couple of days. If you plan to move the Mac, you definitely should shut it down. Moving a desktop computer while the hard disk is spinning could damage the disk. In the case of a laptop, however, if you want to carry the laptop around, all you have to do is close the laptop. It goes into sleep mode automatically when you close the display and the sleep mode stops the hard drive from spinning.

SHOW ME **Media 4.4—A Video about Turning Your Computer Off**
Access this video file through your registered Web Edition at
my.safaribooksonline.com/9780132819091/media
or on the DVD for print books.

LET ME TRY IT

Turning Off Your Computer

Shutting down the computer doesn't mean simply pressing the power button—far from it. No, you must follow the proper shutdown procedure. If you simply turn off the power, you will not have a chance to save your work in a pre-Lion application, should you have failed to do so earlier. If you are the only user logged in, follow these steps to shut down correctly:

1. Click the Apple menu and click Shut Down. A dialog box asks you whether you're sure you want to shut down your computer now. You have 60 seconds to decide. If you do nothing, the Mac shuts down automatically.
2. Before 60 seconds has passed, you can go ahead and click Shut Down.
3. Respond to any prompts that may appear for closing unsaved documents or shutting down applications with unfinished business. When all applications have safely closed, Lion turns off the power for you.

> If more than one user is logged in, then shutting down the computer could cause the other user(s) to lose data. They should be allowed to log off first. When you attempt to shut down the computer, Lion notifies you if there are other users logged on and allows you to switch users (see Figure 4.13). If you don't want to allow other users to log off before you shut down the computer, you can type an administrator name and password and click Shut Down.

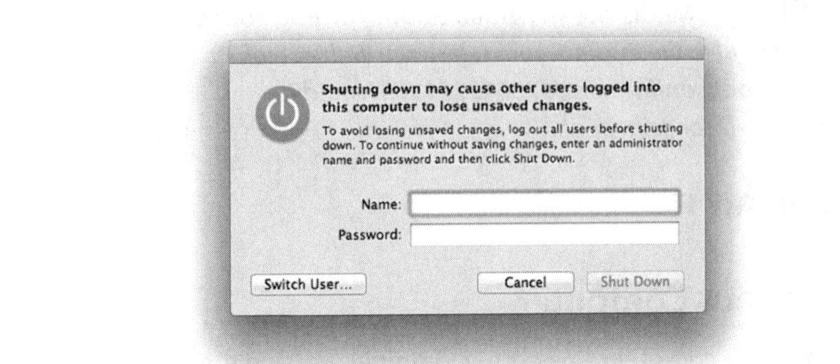

Figure 4.13 *This warning displays if other users are still logged on when you try to shut down the computer.*

This chapter helps you make the optimum hardware settings for the screen, the sound, the keyboard, the mouse or trackpad, and optical drives.

5

Managing Your Hardware

In this chapter, I introduce you to the new System Information application in Lion. Additionally, I show you the settings that control the screen, the speakers, the keyboard, mouse, trackpad, and optical drives (CD and DVD drives).

Learning about Your Mac

Before reading this chapter, you should familiarize yourself with the components of your own system if you need to. Lion provides a new way for you to do that in its new System Information application. This new application gives you general information about your software and hardware, but can also give you detailed information.

SHOW ME **Media 5.1—A Video about Getting System Information**
Access this video file through your registered Web Edition at
my.safaribooksonline.com/9780132819091/media
or on the DVD for print books.

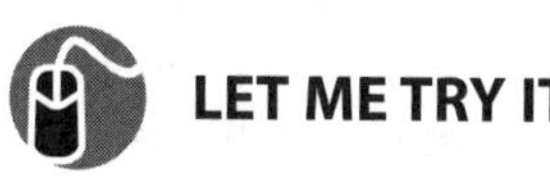

Getting System Information

To get information about your system, follow these steps:

1. Click the Apple menu in the menu bar and click About This Mac.
2. Click More Info. The window shown in Figure 5.1 opens. On the right side of the window you have information about your Mac, including the speed and type of processor, the amount of memory, the name of your graphics card, your Mac's serial number, and the operating system version.

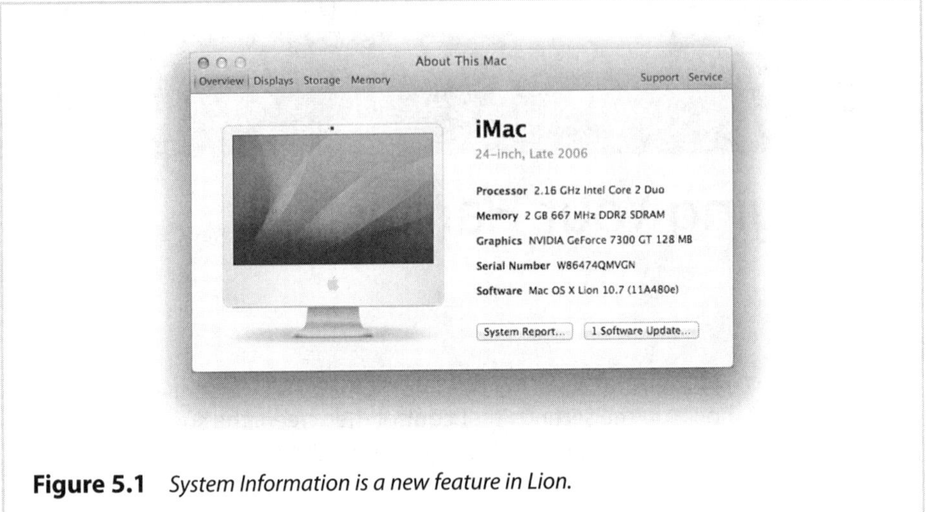

Figure 5.1 *System Information is a new feature in Lion.*

3. Click Service in the toolbar to get information about your warranty, AppleCare Protection Plan, and about your options if your warranty or protection plan has expired.
4. When finished, close the window.

See Chapter 15, "Using System Utilities," for more in-depth information about System Information.

Exploring System Preferences

Before reading much farther, you need to know a little more about what makes Lion tick. Every computer operating system and every computer application is based on a group of settings that control how certain things about the system or application behave in given situations. Often, you'll hear this group of settings referred to as the *defaults*. The defaults are the choices that the programmers who wrote the application made for you. Often, my husband will get frustrated with the way an application does things and say, "Why can't you make the program do such and such?" Sometimes the answer is, "Well, you can if you know where to set the option for that behavior." In these situations, the programmers have given the user the opportunity to change from the default setting to another setting. Sometimes the programmers don't provide an option. Then I have to tell my husband, "That's just the way it works and you can't change it"—not a popular answer.

In Lion, the defaults that you can change are called *preferences*. The system preferences have their own special icon in the Dock, which opens the System Preferences window. If you have deleted this icon in the Dock, you can access the System Preferences from the Apple menu.

The System Preferences window is like a large department store with so many departments and so many items in stock that you need an information counter you can walk up to and say, "Where would I find...?" The Spotlight search box in the top-right corner of the System Preferences window is the information counter you are looking for. If you are having a problem with something or just want to make a change and you suspect there is a system preference that governs it, try typing a relative word or phrase in the Spotlight box. For example, if you want to make the text and graphics larger on your screen, you could type "resolution." If you want your Mac to talk to you, type "speak." As you type the search phrase, Mac OS X lists topics related to the words, and it highlights the appropriate icons in the System Preferences window, as shown in Figure 5.2. You can choose an item from the list, and the appropriate window opens, or you can click a highlighted icon in the window.

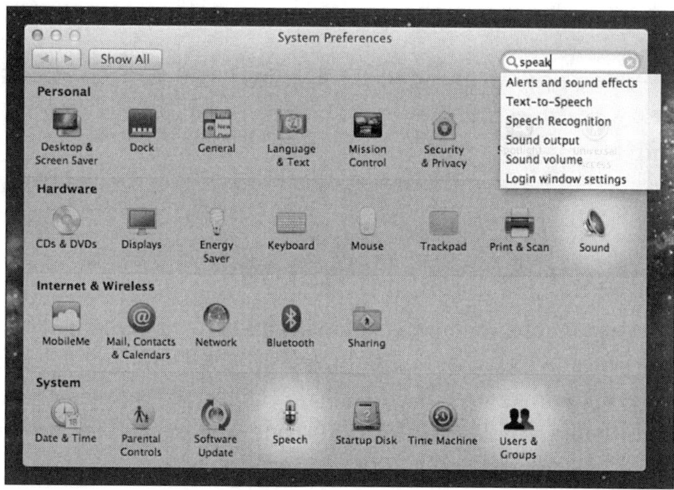

Figure 5.2 *Use the Spotlight to find what you are looking for in the System Preferences window.*

After you open a specific preferences window and make settings, you do not have to close the window if you want to make modifications to other system preferences. You can click the Show All button in the top left (see Figure 5.2) to go back to the System Preferences window.

Because you might be reading this book as a reference instead of sequentially, every set of instructions for setting preferences includes the step to close the window as the last step. Just remember that closing the window is not necessary if you want to set preferences in other categories.

Most preference windows have more than one pane. To access the pane you want, click the appropriate tab at the top of the window. When you close a preference window with multiple panes, Mac OS X remembers the last pane you looked at so when you open the same preferences window again, it displays the last pane that you viewed. Because of this "sticky behavior," I always include a step to click the appropriate tab, but I include the caveat "if necessary."

Instead of slogging through the legion of system preferences in a chapter devoted just to preferences (what a boring chapter that would be), I discuss specific system preferences as they are relevant so you'll find them sprinkled throughout this book.

In addition to system preferences, every application has its own preferences that control the way the specific application behaves. The application Preferences command is always located on the application menu, the first menu to the right of Apple's logo in the menu bar. This menu is always named the same as the actual name of the application. So in the Word application, the Preferences option is located on the Word menu; in the Photoshop application, the Preferences option is located on the Photoshop menu; and so on.

Controlling the Screen Brightness

Two keys on your keyboard control the brightness of your screen: F1 turns the brightness down, and F2 turns the brightness up. Over time, Apple has changed the location of keys on its keyboards, but you can locate the keys by their icons. Look for icons that resemble a sunburst. The one with longer sunrays is the one that makes the screen brighter.

If you have a laptop, your screen's brightness automatically adjusts to ambient light by default although you can still manually control the brightness using the brightness controls. To see where the ambient light option is set, click the System Preferences icon in the Dock, click Displays in the Hardware row, and click Display to open the Display pane if necessary. When you are finished, close the window.

Adjusting the Sound

All Macs have built-in speakers for playing music, listening to videos, and making interface sound effects. Using the speakers, your Mac can even tell you the time or read to you from a file.

Using the Keyboard to Adjust Sound

Three keys on your keyboard control your computer's sound: F10 turns it off, F11 turns it down, and F12 turns it up. Like the brightness adjustment keys, these functions may be located on different keys on older keyboards, but you also can identify them by their icons. One looks like a speaker with many sound waves coming out of it. This one makes the sound louder. The other icons have only one sound wave (for turning the sound down) and no sound waves (for turning the sound off), respectively.

Both F11 and F12 also turn the speakers on after they've been turned off.

Setting Sound Preferences

Setting the volume level in the Sound preferences window is possible, but what's the point? Doing it with the keyboard is so much easier. Other preferences in the Sound preferences window are worth looking at, however. They include setting the default alert sound and its volume, turning interface sound effects on or off, and hiding or displaying the volume control in the menu bar.

SHOW ME **Media 5.2—A Video about Setting Sound Effect Preferences**
Access this video file through your registered Web Edition at
my.safaribooksonline.com/9780132819091/media
or on the DVD for print books.

LET ME TRY IT

Setting Sound Effects Preferences

Sound preferences include settings for effects, output, and input. Unless you are making an audio recording, you probably don't need to make any changes to output or input settings. To set effect preferences, follow these steps:

1. Click the System Preferences icon in the Dock.

2. Click Sound in the Hardware row (second row).

3. Click Sound Effects (if necessary) to display the options shown in Figure 5.3.

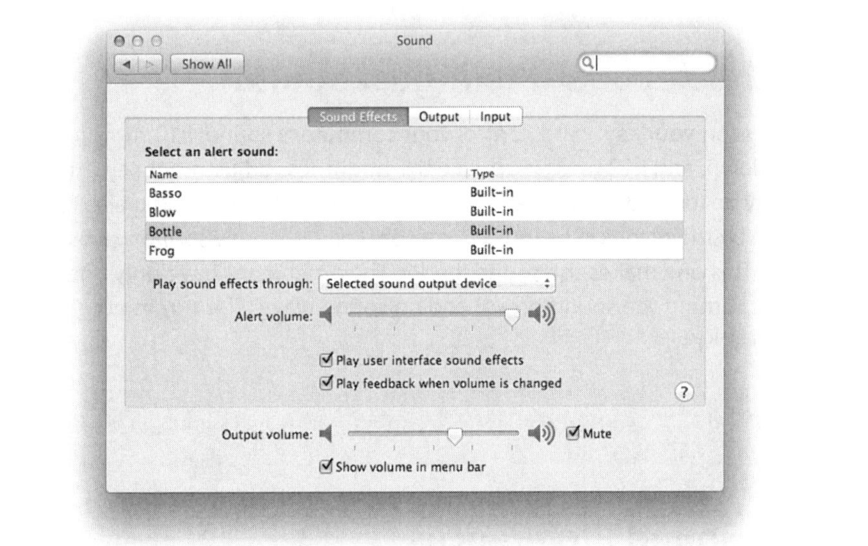

Figure 5.3 *The Sound Preferences window has three tabs: Sound Effects, Output, and Input.*

4. Click an alert sound in the list to hear it play. When you find the one you want, click it to select it. This will be the sound that plays when you try to do something that is not allowed or the computer needs more information from you.

5. Set the volume of the alert by dragging the slider for Alert Volume.

6. Check or uncheck Play User Interface Sound Effects. I recommend you select this one. It causes a sound to play when you perform certain tasks, such as deleting. So if you accidentally delete something, such as an icon on the Dock, the sound alerts you that you've done something that perhaps you didn't even know you did.

7. Check or uncheck Play Feedback When Volume Is Changed. This option plays a sound as you turn the volume up or down with keys on the keyboard.

8. Check or uncheck Show Volume in Menu Bar. (If you select this option, a speaker icon displays in the Menu Extras on the right side of the menu bar,

and you can use that icon to control the speakers instead of using the function keys.)

Showing the volume adjustment in the menu bar gives you one more way to adjust the volume without opening the Sound preferences window.

9. Close the window.

Setting Keyboard Preferences

A keyboard is a keyboard. You type with it. How many preferences could there be? As you can see in Figure 5.4 the preferences for the keyboard are pretty sparse! Some preferences seem almost insignificant. For example, you can change how fast a key will repeat when you hold it down, and you can determine how long you have to hold the key down before it starts repeating. You might use repeating keys in a chat or email, as in "That is so coooool!"

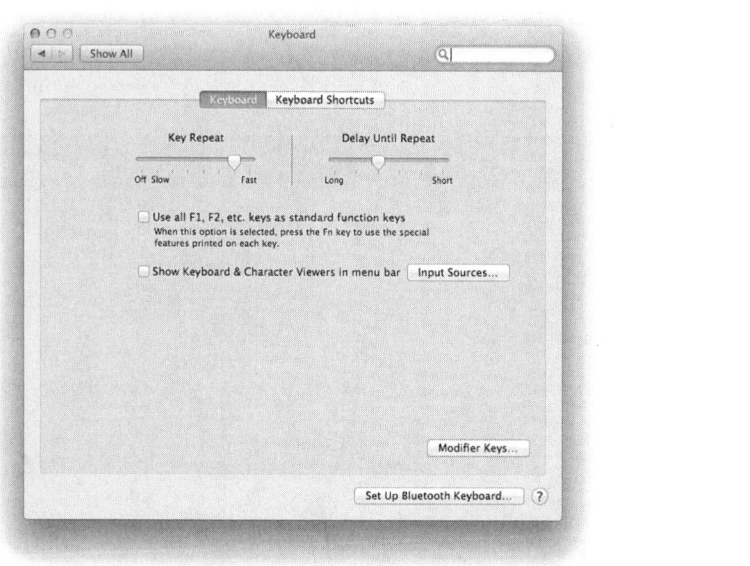

Figure 5.4 *Set the performance of the function keys on this pane of the Keyboard preferences.*

The option to set the function keys may be useful to you. Many function keys can have two functions. For example, you get one function when you press the F11 key and a different function when you press the Fn key in conjunction with the F11 key.

On my keyboard, F11 performs the special function pictured on the key (decreasing the volume), and Fn-F11 performs the standard function (moving everything out of the way to display the desktop). Depending on which function you use most (for all keys in general), you can select this option to use the function keys as standard functions. Then to use the function keys for the special feature printed on the key, you must press Fn with the function key.

One other preference you might want to set is on the Keyboard Shortcuts tab. It is the Full Keyboard Access option, and it enables you to move to each control in a dialog box or window by using the Tab key. By default, the Tab key moves only to lists or text boxes. To change the default setting, click the Keyboard Shortcuts tab and click All Controls at the bottom of the window.

If you have a MacBook Pro model laptop, one very cool keyboard preference is available for you. You can set a preference to illuminate the keyboard in low light conditions; it's perfect for typing in the car at night on a long road trip (when you're not driving, of course). You also can specify what period of inactivity will turn off the illumination. After the illumination goes off, though, just touching the keyboard turns it back on. You'll find these settings on the Keyboard page of Keyboard Preferences as shown in Figure 5.5.

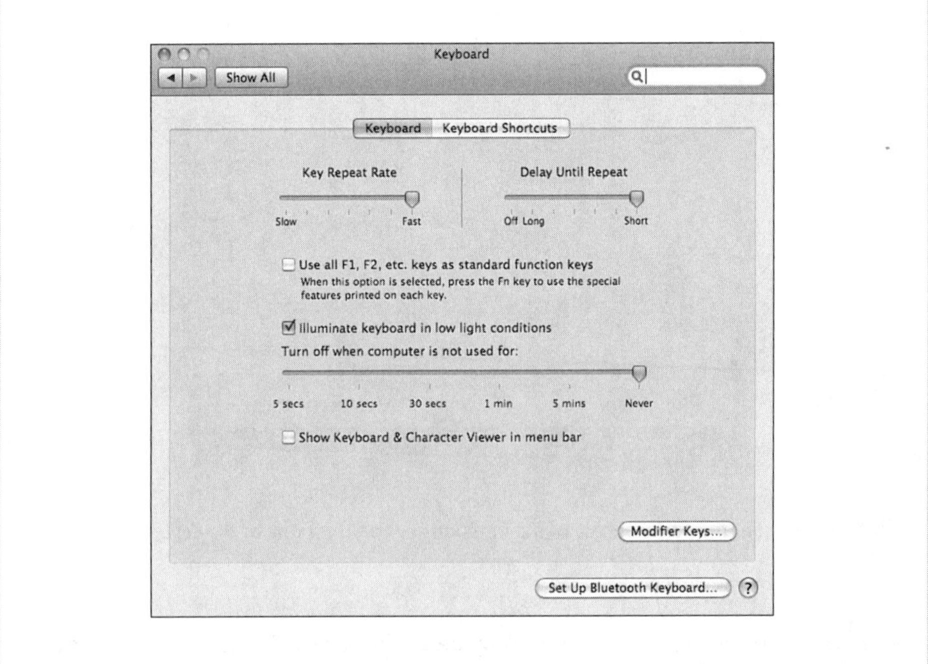

Figure 5.5 *Set illumination options on this page of the Keyboard Preferences window.*

Press F6 to make the keyboard illumination brighter and F5 to dim it. On older MacBook Pro models, press F10 to make the keyboard illumination brighter and F9 to dim it.

Operating the Mouse or Trackpad

All new model Macs come with the Apple Magic Mouse—except, of course, the Mac Mini and the MacBooks. The Mac Mini comes with no mouse, and the MacBooks come with a built-in trackpad.

The Magic Mouse is the successor of the Apple Mighty Mouse, which came out in 2005. Like the popular 1940s cartoon character, the Mighty Mouse had super powers—it was a "buttonless" mouse with not just one hidden button, but two. It was the first multi-button mouse Apple produced, and like the cartoon character's theme song, "Here I come to save the day," it saved the day for all the PC switchers who sorely missed their right-clicking. Going its predecessor one better, the Magic Mouse is the world's first mouse that responds to multi-touch gestures.

Using the Mouse

You might be a new Mac user, but I'm pretty sure you know how to use a mouse. If you need help with pointing, clicking, dragging, and so on, ask any six-year-old. To use multi-touch gestures on the Magic Mouse, use the surface of the mouse just as you would the surface of a Trackpad or your iPhone. For example, to scroll left or right, you just swipe one finger across the mouse to the left or right and to display Mission Control, double-tap the surface. (Note that double-tapping is not the same as double-clicking.) Again, you probably can get help from a six-year-old on this. (My four-year-old granddaughter can do anything on my iPhone and she can't even read!)

Setting Mouse Preferences

Mouse preferences that are available depend on the type of mouse you are using. Generally, you can set preferences for tracking (how fast the mouse moves the pointer on the screen), double-click speed, and scrolling speed. If you have a two-button mouse, you can specify which button is the primary button and which is the secondary button. (Remember, in this book, I use the term *right-click* to refer to clicking the secondary button or two-finger tapping on a Magic Trackpad.)

SHOW ME **Media 5.3—A Video about Setting Magic Mouse Preferences**
Access this video file through your registered Web Edition at ***my.safaribooksonline.com/9780132819091/media*** *or on the DVD for print books.*

LET ME TRY IT

Setting Magic Mouse Preferences

Your Mac recognizes the kind of mouse you are using, so when you perform step 1 and open the preferences for a mouse, you will see preferences that apply specifically to your mouse. To set preferences for a Magic Mouse, follow these steps:

1. Click the System Preferences icon in the Dock and click Mouse (in the second row) to set preferences.
2. Click Point & Click, if necessary. Figure 5.6 shows the Point & Click Preferences pane. This pane has instructional movies to show you how the gestures work. (Leave it to Apple to tuck a video in a dialog box!)

Figure 5.6 *The preferences shown in this figure are for the Magic Mouse.*

3. The first option in the Point & Click pane, Scroll Direction: Natural, is selected by default. This feature is new in Lion, and it is just the opposite

of what you may be used to in previous versions of OS X. If you can't adjust to the new direction, deselect this option.

4. The Secondary Click option is not selected by default, which means you have to press the Ctrl key when you click to get the secondary click function. I always turn this on! After you click the check box, then you can click the popup button to select which side of the mouse should be the secondary click side.
5. The Smart Zoom option is selected by default. It allows you to double-tap (not double-click) with one finger to zoom in on text or graphics in applications such as Safari and Preview.
6. Using the slider, set the speed for Tracking. This setting determines how fast the mouse pointer moves on the screen as you move the mouse.
7. Click the More Gesture tab.
8. Click the popup button for Swipe between Pages and select the option you want (one finger, two fingers, or both). Because two fingers are used for scrolling between full-screen apps (the next option), you may want to leave this option set on one finger.

Using a Trackpad

Apple's laptop, the MacBook, comes with a trackpad built in, but now Apple produces an independent trackpad, the Magic Trackpad, that you can use with any Mac. A trackpad moves the pointer onscreen and performs clicking and dragging actions. It can do everything that a mouse can do, and then some. The Magic Trackpad, like its brother the Magic Mouse, uses multi-touch gestures as does the built-in trackpad on the newer MacBook laptops.

To use a Magic Trackpad, you touch the trackpad with one, two, three, or four fingers in various ways to accomplish various actions. Using one finger you can control the pointer onscreen or tap the trackpad once, twice, or three times like a mouse click, double-click, or triple-click. With two fingers, you can scroll vertically, horizontally, or diagonally. With your thumb and index finger you can rotate an image or use a pinching gesture to open or close. With three fingers you can swipe right or left to page forward or back. With four fingers, you can swipe up or down to open Expose or swipe left or right to switch applications.

For all these gestures, you can set the tracking speed. Additionally, you can set a speed for double-clicking and scrolling.

Setting Trackpad Preferences

Although the Magic Trackpad has many possible gestures, you may not want to use all of them. You can select the gestures you want to use in the Trackpad Preferences window. To set options for the Trackpad, follow these steps:

1. Click the System Preferences icon in the Dock.
2. Click Trackpad in the Hardware row (second row).
3. Set the speed for tracking, double-clicking, and scrolling.
4. Select each gesture you want to use for one, two, three, and four fingers. A video demonstrates the gestures for you when you point to an option.
5. When you are finished, close the window.

Using CD/DVD Drives

All new Macs, with the exception of MacBook Air, come with a built-in optical drive called a SuperDrive. It reads and writes DVDs (even Double Layer) and CDs at super-fast speeds ranging from 8 to 24 times normal speed.

If you have an older Mac, and you are not sure what kind of discs to buy, you can see what type of discs your optical drive can write to by opening the System Information application. For more information about System Information, see Chapter 15.

Inserting and Ejecting Discs

The SuperDrive is a slot-loading device, which means you simply push the disc into a slot and the drive grabs it and seats it properly. After a disc is inserted, the name of the disc appears in the Finder sidebar under the Devices category.

To eject a disc, you can open Finder and click the eject symbol next to the name of the disc in the sidebar (see Figure 5.7) or press the eject key on the keyboard. (Look for a key that has the same symbol on it as you see in Figure 5.7.)

Displaying icons for optical drives on the Desktop is possible. If you have this preference set on the General pane of the Finder Preferences, you can eject a disc by right-clicking its icon and clicking Eject or you can drag the icon to the Trashcan in the Dock.

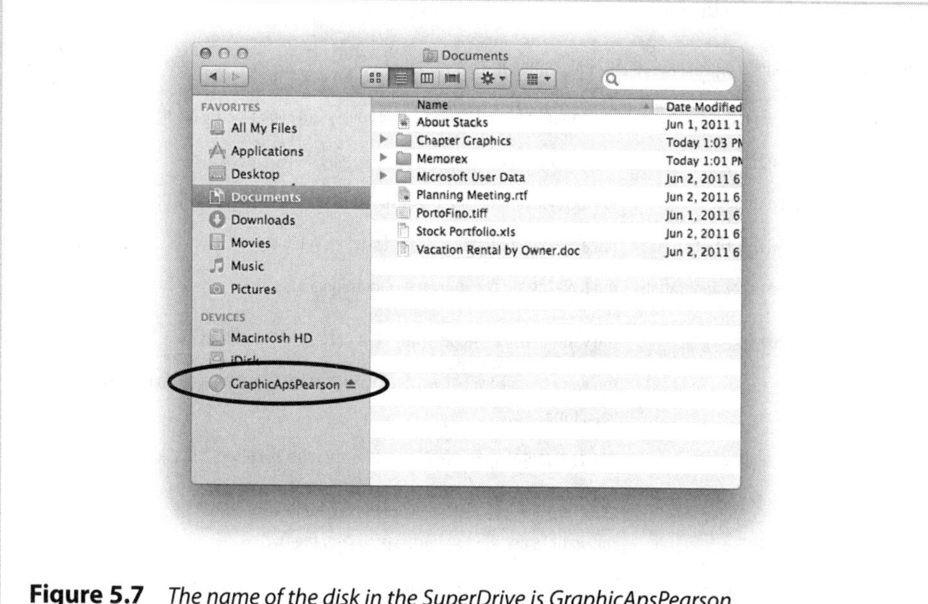

Figure 5.7 *The name of the disk in the SuperDrive is GraphicApsPearson.*

Setting Preferences for CDs & DVDs

The default preferences for CDs & DVDs determine what happens when you insert a particular type of disc in the optical drive. Figure 5.8 shows the default preferences. After you have been using the Mac for a while, you may want to change some of these options, but for now, they are probably just fine. If you are curious about what your options are for each type of disc, refer to Table 5.1.

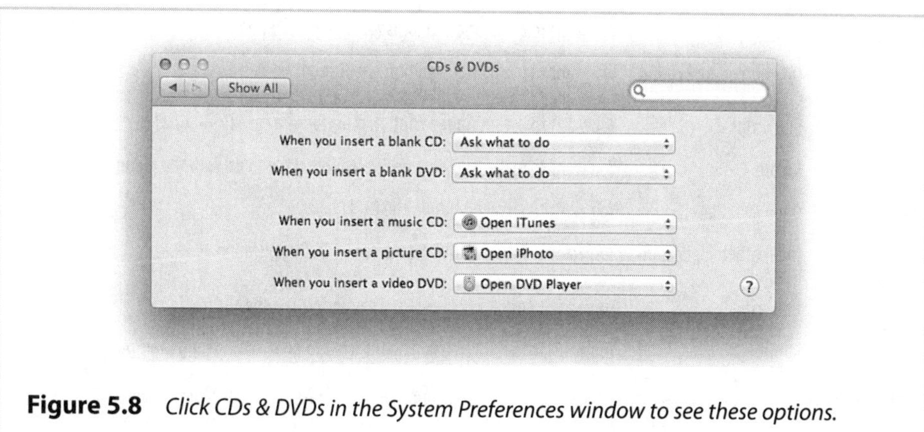

Figure 5.8 *Click CDs & DVDs in the System Preferences window to see these options.*

Table 5.1 Options for CDs and DVDs

Type of Disc	Options	Use This Option If. . .
Blank CD	Ask what to do	You do something different almost every time you insert a blank CD.
	Open Finder	You use Burn Folders. See
	Open iTunes	You always want to create a music CD when you insert a blank disc.
	Open Disc Utility	You always want to burn a data CD when you insert a blank CD.
	Open other application	You have installed your own disc-burning application.
	Run script	You want to use an AppleScript* that performs a specific routine.
	Ignore	You want to make your own decision about what you want to do in your own good time.
Blank DVD	Ask what to do	You do something different almost every time you insert a blank DVD.
	Open Finder	You use Burn Folders.
	Open iDVD	You want to use iDVD to burn a project to the DVD.
	Open iTunes	You always want to create a music DVD when you insert a blank DVD.
	Open Disk Utility	You always want to burn a data DVD when you insert a blank DVD.
	Open other application	You have installed your own disc-burning application.
	Run script	You want to use an AppleScript* that performs a specific routine.
	Ignore	You want to make your own decision about what you want to do with the DVD.
Music CD	Open iTunes	You want to play the CD or otherwise manipulate it in iTunes.
	Open other application	You want to use a different application to play or otherwise manipulate the CD.
	Run script	You want to use an AppleScript* that performs a specific routine.
	Ignore	You want to make a decision about what to do on a case by case basis.
Picture CD	Open iPhoto	You want to archive your photos for viewing in iPhoto.
	Open other application	You want to use a photo-editing application.
	Run script	You want to use an AppleScript* that performs a specific routine.
	Ignore	You want to make your own decision about what to do with the pictures.
Video DVD	Open DVD Player	You want to view the DVD in the DVD Player.
	Open other application	You want to view the DVD in a different DVD application.
	Run script	You want to use an AppleScript* that performs a specific routine.
	Ignore	You want to make a decision about what to do without being prompted.

*AppleScript is a type of programming language that can create routines that use a series of commands to perform tasks.

TELL ME MORE **Media 5.4—A Discussion of AppleScript**
Access this audio recording through your registered Web Edition at ***my.safaribooksonline.com/9780132819091/media*** *or on the DVD for print books.*

From the menu bar to the Dock, this chapter shows you how to customize the desktop.

6

Customizing the Desktop

The default Lion desktop is just fine as it is, but we all have different ideas about exactly how we want our computers to look and behave. Mac OS X throws the door wide open for customizations. In this chapter, we will look at some of the ways you can customize your desktop.

Changing the Background

Although the graphic of the Andromeda galaxy is the default Lion desktop background, Mac OS X provides numerous additional graphic files in several categories for you to choose from if you want to change the desktop background to something different, as shown in Figure 6.1. The graphic files supplied by Lion include full-color photographs of nature, plants, and famous artwork, as well as abstracts, patterns and solid colors. Even black and white photos are available.

Each background graphic is stunning, but you can use one of your own favorite photos instead—that vacation photo in the Swiss alps, your new sports car, your son in his T-ball uniform. Do you have too many favorite photos to select just one? No problem. Display them all in order, or randomly, at an interval that you specify. Your desktop becomes a perpetual slideshow—a virtual digital picture frame.

Using a slideshow-type background uses more system resources, but you won't really notice any sluggishness unless you are running a large number of applications simultaneously.

Figure 6.1 *As a salute to the new version of OS X, you could use the Lion graphic for the background.*

LET ME TRY IT

Changing the Desktop Background

Before you get too carried away with such a rich graphic desktop, you need to know that the desktop can be a very important work area if you want it to be. You probably will have numerous icons on the desktop that you use frequently. If that's the case, you might want to use a solid color or muted pattern for the desktop so that the icons don't get lost in the graphics of the background. Alternatively, you can select a photo that has some neutral space in it and group all your icons in that space. To change the desktop picture, follow these steps:

1. Right-click an empty spot on the desktop to open the shortcut menu and then click Change Desktop Background. The Desktop & Screen Saver preferences window opens to the Desktop pane, as shown in Figure 6.2.

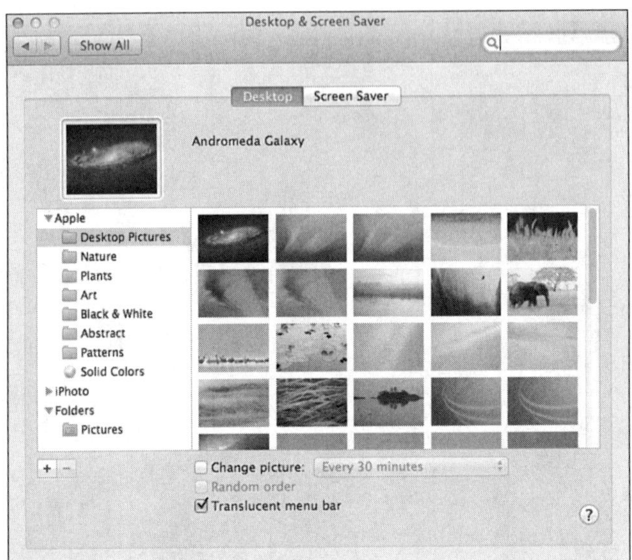

Figure 6.2 *If you don't see iPhoto in your sidebar, it means that you don't have any photos in iPhoto.*

Using the familiar interface of the Finder, the sidebar lists categories of sources of graphics, and the right pane shows the graphics available in the selected source. Click the triangles (to the left of each category) to hide or display the sources under each category.

2. Click a source in the sidebar and then click the graphic you want to use from the right pane or click Solid Colors in the sidebar and select a color. If you don't like any of the default colors, click Custom Color (a new feature in Lion) and select a color from any tab in the Color Inspector.

To use one of your own photographs, click a source under iPhoto or click the Pictures folder. To create a slideshow with all the pictures in a selected source, choose Change Picture and then specify a time interval. Choose Random Order if you want to mix it up a bit.

3. Close the window and see if you like what you selected.

TELL ME MORE **Media 6.1—A Discussion about Creating Neutral Space in a Photo**

Access this audio recording through your registered Web Edition at ***my.safaribooksonline.com/9780132819091/media*** *or on the DVD for print books.*

If you have several user accounts on your Mac, encourage each user to choose a different background. This is a good way to help you quickly identify who is logged in when you look at the screen from a distance.

Using a Screen Saver

The purpose of a screen saver is to keep changing the images on a the old CRT (cathode ray tube) screens to prevent the burning of an image on the screen during periods of inactivity. This is no longer an issue for LCD (liquid crystal display) screens, and it hasn't been for quite a few years; but screen savers live on—they have just become part of the computer culture.

Essentially, screen savers are harmless and entertaining, but they fall under criticism by some because they use more energy than simply putting the computer in sleep mode. This is true, but I have calculated that if all Mac users worldwide stopped using screen savers for a year, we would save only enough electricity for me to go from here to the mall in a Chevy Volt. Unfortunately, we would not save enough energy for me to get back home, so I would have to stay at the mall all day (shopping) while the Volt recharges its battery. In other words, if you want to use a screen saver, go ahead. If you still feel guilty, try saving energy by turning off your printer when you're not using it.

Turning On the Screen Saver

Mac has some cool screen savers. You can preview as many of them as you want before you select one. Follow these steps to select and use a screen saver:

1. Click the System Preferences icon in the Dock and click Desktop & Screen Saver (located in the first row of icons).
2. Click the Screen Saver tab, if necessary, to display the pane shown in Figure 6.3.

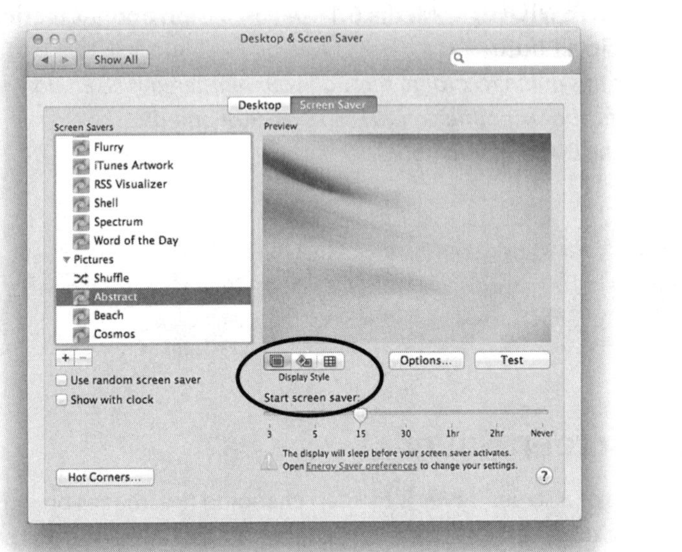

Figure 6.3 *You can view the screen saver in the Preview box or click Test to see it full screen.*

3. Select a screen saver in the Screen Savers list on the left and watch the preview on the right. (Screen savers in the Pictures category have additional options for display styles as pointed out in Figure 6.3.)

4. Click Show with Clock if you want to display the time. (The time doesn't show up in the preview, so click Test to see it on the screen. Press any key or move the mouse to return to the Preferences window.)

5. On the Start Screen Saver slider, select a period of time. This is the amount of time of inactivity that the screen saver will wait before appearing. If you select a time that is greater than the time you have selected for the screen to go to sleep after a period of inactivity, an alert at the bottom of the screen tells you your screen will sleep before the screen saver activates (see Figure 6.3). Below the message is a link to the Energy Saver preferences where you can change the sleep setting if you want. Alternatively, you can change the time for the screen saver instead.

6. Close the window when finished.

If you use a slide show screensaver, Lion has some new controls built in for you that allow you to interact with the photos in the screensaver. When the screensaver starts displaying the photos, press any cursor arrow key to display the controls and then use the controls to browse through the photos.

LET ME TRY IT

Turning On the Mosaic Effect Screen Saver

My favorite screen saver is the mosaic effect with the iPhoto library. It's truly amazing, but I can't use this one because I would never get any work done. To use this screensaver, you must have at least 100 photographs. The more photos you have, the better this feature works. Follow these steps to set it up:

1. Click the System Preferences icon in the Dock and click Desktop & Screen Saver (in the first row).
2. Click the Screen Saver tab, if necessary.
3. Select iPhoto under Pictures in the left pane.
4. Click the Mosaic button in the Display Style bank of buttons (located under the bottom-left corner of the Preview box).
5. Watch and enjoy!

Working with Icons on the Desktop

The desktop has three roles on the Mac:

- It functions as the background on your screen.
- It is a folder in your Home folder.
- It performs some of the functions of the Finder.

In its role as background on your screen, it can use a graphic background, as you've seen in the previous topic. In its role as the Desktop folder, it displays icons for any files or folders you store in your Desktop folder. In its role as the Finder's helper, it can display icons for devices including your hard drive, external drives, optical drives, iPods, and servers. The desktop's Finder functions are turned off by default so none of these device icons display on the desktop. If you choose to display the icons for drives or other devices, which I'm about to show you how to do, just remember that the devices are not really located in the Desktop folder. The desktop is just acting like the Finder and making the drives or devices accessible to you.

Working with Device Icons

Even though Mac OS X hides all device icons by default, I still recommend showing external disks and CDs, DVDs, and iPods on the desktop. This allows you to easily eject them by dragging their icons to the Trash.

LET ME TRY IT

Showing or Hiding Device Icons

You can display device icons on the desktop by following these steps:

1. Click Finder in the menu bar and then click Preferences.
2. Click the General icon at the top of the window if necessary. If you haven't changed any of the default settings for the preferences, then your screen should match Figure 6.4.

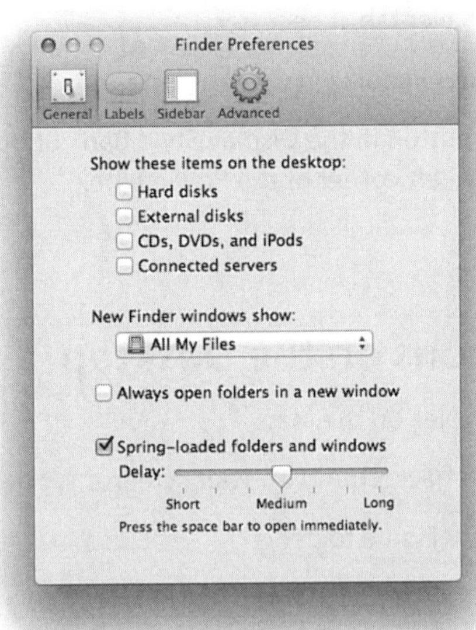

Figure 6.4 *The Finder Preferences window has three more tabs with additional preferences.*

3. Select each type of device that you want to display as an icon on the desktop. I don't recommend that you select the hard drive. You really have no business with it, so why put it in harm's way? You may want to display external disks, CDs, DVDs, and iPods, and connected servers to give yourself easy access to these devices.

4. Close the window when finished.

Be aware that no icon will display for a CD or DVD drive just because it is connected. The icon only displays if a disc is inserted. Unlike the Windows operating system, Mac OS X does not show a CD drive or DVD drive if it is empty.

Adding and Deleting Icons on the Desktop

I've already told you that the desktop displays icons for any files or folders you store in your Desktop folder, so you've probably already figured out that adding or deleting a file or folder to the Desktop folder in Finder adds or deletes an icon for the file or folder on the desktop. It also works the other way—any file or folder you drag to the desktop shows up in your Desktop folder in Finder. Chapter 7, "Using Finder," covers the mechanics of adding and deleting files and folders.

SHOW ME **Media 6.2—A Video about Adding an Alias to the Desktop**
Access this video file through your registered Web Edition at
my.safaribooksonline.com/9780132819091/media
or on the DVD for print books.

LET ME TRY IT

Adding an Alias to the Desktop

Another type of icon that can display on the desktop, in addition to device icons and files/folder icons, is an icon for an alias. An alias is not a file or a folder, but merely a pointer to the actual file or folder. To create an alias on the desktop, follow these steps:

1. Open the Finder and select the file or folder in the right pane for which you want to create an alias.

2. Click File in the menu bar and then click Make Alias. The alias displays in the right pane and it is selected, as shown in Figure 6.5.

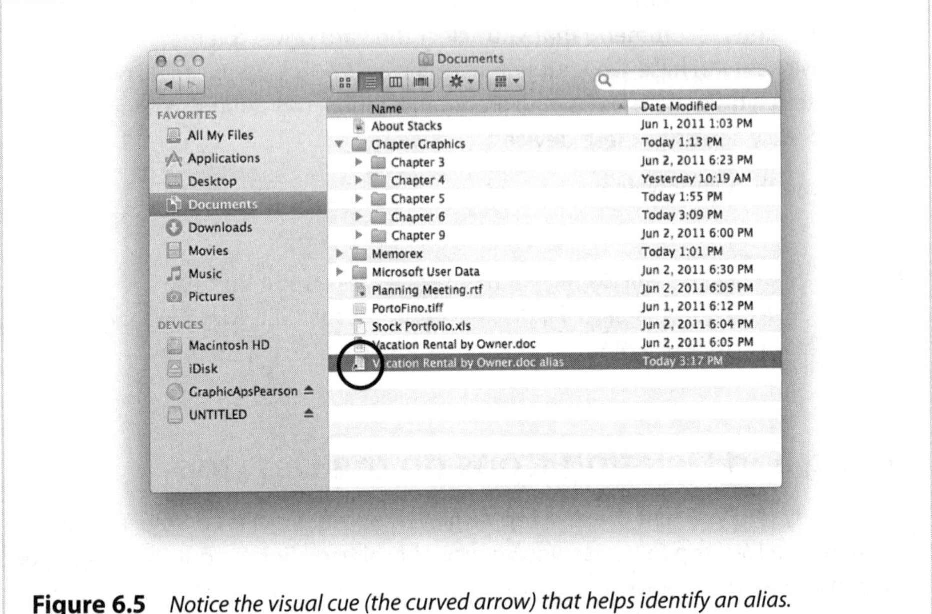

Figure 6.5 *Notice the visual cue (the curved arrow) that helps identify an alias.*

3. Drag the alias icon out of the Finder window and drop it on an empty spot on the desktop.

To delete an icon on the desktop, drag it to the Trash icon on the Dock. Release the icon when you see the word *Trash* above the Trash icon. If you have interface sound effects turned on in the sound preferences and you have your volume turned up, you should hear the sound of the trash hitting the can.

Alternatively, you can right-click the alias and click Move to Trash.

Deleting an icon for a file or folder actually deletes the item, but deleting an icon for an alias does not delete the original file or folder associated with the alias—a good reason to use aliases on the desktop instead of actual files.

If you are a brand-new user, and you don't have any icons on your desktop, you won't be able to perform some of the tasks in the next activities. I suggest you create four or five aliases of the About Stacks.pdf or About Downloads.pdf files and drag them to the desktop so you can try the steps in the next two topics.

Arranging Icons on the Desktop

You can arrange the icons on your desktop by dragging them to any location. After you have positioned the icons where you want them, you can line them up with each other vertically and horizontally by using the Clean Up command on the desktop's shortcut menu (see Figure 6.6). This command aligns the icons with an invisible grid.

If you don't want to arrange and align the icons manually, you can let Mac OS X do it for you with the new Clean Up By command, available on the desktop's shortcut menu shown in Figure 6.6. The Clean Up By command aligns icons with an invisible grid and sorts the icons at the same time. After arranging the icons with this command, you can still move the icons freely around the desktop.

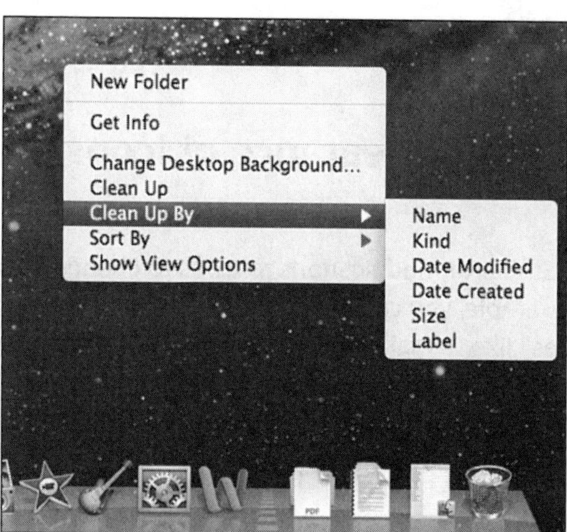

Figure 6.6 *You have six options to choose from for sorting the icons using the Clean Up By command.*

To change the spacing of the invisible grid, close any Finder windows that are open and right-click the desktop to open the shortcut menu. Click Show View Options. Move the Grid Spacing slider, shown in Figure 6.7, to the left to make the grid tighter or to the right to make the grid larger.

If you have a Finder window open when you select Show View Options, the view options refer to the Finder and not the desktop.

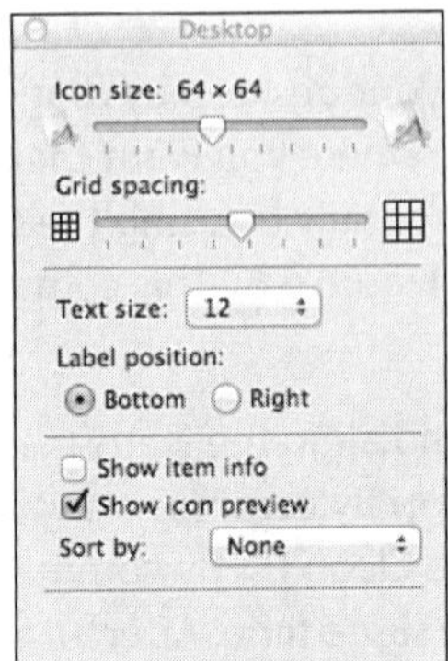

Figure 6.7 *Use this window to control the appearance and spacing of icons on the desktop.*

Customizing the Appearance of Icons on the Desktop

You can make a number of modifications to icons to change their appearance on the desktop. For example, you can change the size and the location of the label. One of the changes I like to make to icons is showing the item information. When the Show Item Info option is selected, you can see additional information about a desktop item that can be very helpful. For example, if the item is a folder, you can see the number of items in the folder. If the item is a graphic file, you can see the pixel size of the image.

SHOW ME **Media 6.3—A Video about Customizing Desktop Icons**
Access this video file through your registered Web Edition at
my.safaribooksonline.com/9780132819091/media
or on the DVD for print books.

LET ME TRY IT

Customizing Desktop Icons

All options for customizing icons on the desktop are located in the View Options window. As you make changes to the icon options, you can see the results on the desktop even before you close the View Options window. To change the appearance of icons, follow these steps:

1. Right-click the desktop to open the shortcut menu and click Show View Options. Figure 6.8 shows the Desktop options. (If you don't see the word *Desktop* at the top of the window on your screen, you have a Finder window open. Close the Finder window and you will then see the Desktop options shown in Figure 6.8.)

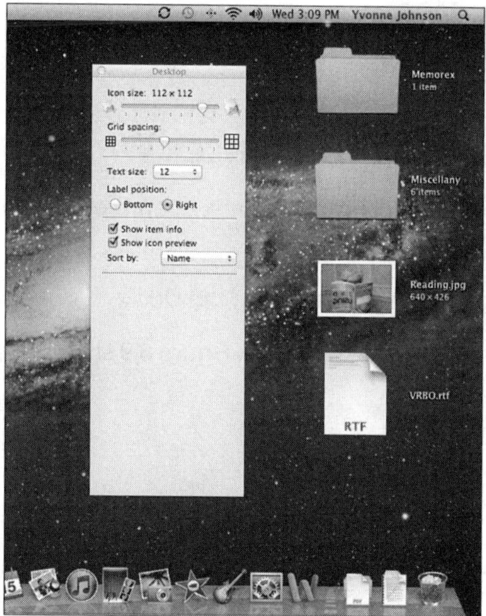

Figure 6.8 *As you make changes in this window, you can see the results on the screen.*

2. Make any changes in the window that you want for the size, grid spacing, label position, and so on.
3. Close the window when finished.

The label for an icon is the name of the file or folder. You can change the text of the label to whatever you want—something shorter perhaps—but realize you are actually changing the name of the item. To change the label, click the icon and press Return. Type the new text and press Return again.

Customizing the Appearance of the Dock

Because the Dock is a key component in the operation of your Mac, customizing it to your needs and preferences is important because you're going to be using it a lot to launch applications and access files. Like the new car on the showroom floor, it looks and runs just fine the way it is, but to get exactly what *you* want, you need to order a model with some additional options—maybe drop an option or two that the floor model has, select the wheels you like, or add the stealth-mode feature (Batmobile models only).

LET ME TRY IT

Opening the Dock Preferences Window

To make any changes to the Dock, you must open the Dock preferences window. Follow these steps to open the window:

1. Click the System Preferences icon in the Dock.
2. Click Dock (located in the first row). Figure 6.9 shows the default settings for the Dock.

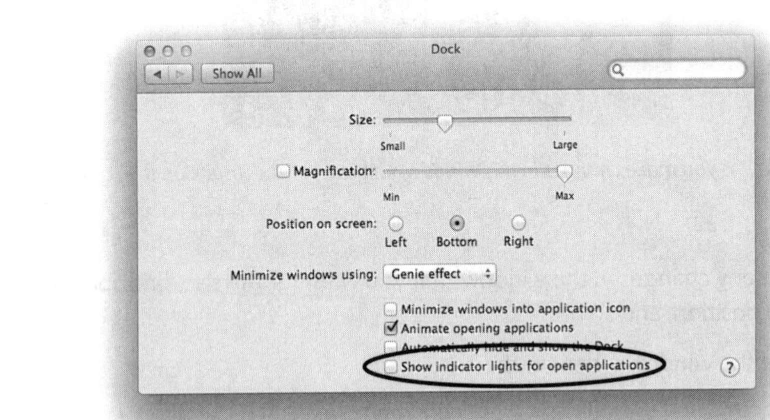

Figure 6.9 *The Show Indicator Lights for Open Applications option is new in the Dock preferences.*

Positioning and Sizing the Dock

As you know, the Dock's default position is at the bottom of the screen, but in the Dock preferences window, you can change the position to the left or right side of the screen. Because the screen is wider than it is tall, leaving the Dock at the bottom of the screen gives you more space to use if you intend to load the Dock up with many icons. On the other hand, an application window could make better use of the space at the bottom of the screen if the Dock occupied a position on the side. For example, you could make a document window taller so you can see more of the document on the screen if the Dock were not in the way at the bottom.

Another approach to reclaiming space on the screen is hiding the Dock when it's not needed. (This is what I call the "Batmobile stealth-mode."). To hide the Dock when not in use, select the option Automatically Hide and Show the Dock in the preferences window. The Dock hides when not in use and reappears when you point to its location with the pointer. This is not one of my favorite features. I don't like it because the Dock pops up too much accidentally when I get the pointer too close to its location.

To change the size of the Dock, use the Size slider in the Dock preferences window. You can make the icons in the Dock smaller or larger, thus making the total size of the Dock smaller or larger, but, ultimately, the number of icons you have in the Dock determines how large or small the icons are, especially if you add a large number of icons.

Try this shortcut for sizing the Dock: Point to the separator. The pointer changes to a two-headed arrow. Drag the separator left or right or simply drag up or down.

If you have so many icons in the Dock that the icons are not very large or if you have purposely set the size of the icons to a small size due to the size of your screen, you can compensate for this with magnification. As you run the pointer over the icons in the Dock, the icons closest to the pointer are magnified.

To set the magnification, click Magnification in the Dock preferences window and then use the slider to set the size of the magnification. You can test the feature while the Dock preferences window is still open.

Animating the Dock

Notice the option in Figure 6.9 for Animate Opening Applications. When this option is selected, application icons bounce up and down while the application is opening. Serious-minded users might think this option is just plain silly, but it does have a utilitarian side. If an application that is running in the background, possibly hidden under other windows, has a problem or needs input from you, its icon bounces up and down to get your attention.

Working with Icons in the Dock

I'm sure the selection of icons in the Dock has been scientifically determined by extensive research on the icons that are the most popular with Mac users, but I like to think of the default configuration of the Dock like my husband thinks of the speed limit—it's just a suggestion.

Fortunately, Mac OS X sees it my way. Within certain limits, you can modify the icons that appear on the Dock and arrange them in any order to suit your needs.

Deleting Icons in the Dock

Deleting icons that you don't think you'll use is the first change you should make to the Dock. Then you'll know how much space you have for the icons you want to add.

To delete an icon in the Dock, drag the icon off the Dock. It's that simple. You'll see a little puff of smoke and hear a "poof" as the icon goes to meet its maker.

Deleting an icon from the Dock is so easy that sooner or later you're going to delete one by accident. You might not even notice which icon you deleted, but you'll hear that little "poof" and see the puff of smoke, and you'll know what you've done. Oh, no! Is there an undo? No. Have you deleted something that is going to cause untold pain and misery? No. Can you find out which one you deleted? No. Eventually, though, you'll figure it out. You'll start to click the iCal icon, and it won't be there. Then all you have to do is add it back to the Dock, as detailed in the next section.

Deleting the Finder icon or the Trash icon is not possible. Although deleting the Launchpad icon is possible, it's only a temporary deletion. The next time you log in, the icon will be back on the Dock.

Adding Application Icons

As you know, all icons on the left side of the Dock represent applications. The key word in that last sentence is *represent*. The icons in the Dock are not the applications themselves; they are just links to them. That's why you do no great harm if you accidentally delete one.

To add an application icon to the Dock (like the one you accidentally deleted), find the application file and drag its icon to the Dock. So how do you find an application file? Use one of these methods:

- Open Launchpad and scroll to the page that contains the application's icon.
- In the Finder menu bar, click Go, Applications.
- Click the Finder icon in the Dock to open the Finder window and then click the Applications folder in the sidebar.

When you drag an icon to the Dock, be careful to drag it between two icons and don't let go until the icons that are in the way move aside. If the icon you are trying to drag to the Dock just won't go in it, you might be trying to put the wrong kind of icon on the wrong side of the separator. Adding any type of icon except an application icon to the left side of the Dock is impossible. Adding an application icon to the right side of the Dock is also impossible. Remember that the right side is for file or folder icons only.

Customizing Icons in the Dock

In Lion, only three icons appear on the right side of the Dock separator. The first two are special icons for folders and they are called *stacks*. In Snow Leopard, the icon for the Applications folder also appeared with these two icons. If you upgraded to Lion from Snow Leopard, your Applications icon will still appear on the right side of the Dock (unless, of course, you had previously removed it).

These special stack icons can have two different appearances. They can look like a stack of icons, as shown on the left side of Figure 6.10, or they can look like a folder, as shown on the right side of Figure 6.10. When the icon looks like a stack, it displays a preview icon for each item in the folder, but the icons are stacked on top of each other like a deck of cards, so only the top icon shows completely, but parts of other icons might show behind the top icon. If the items in the folder change, a new icon may come to the top of the stack and the icon for the stack would change to the preview of the new item.

Figure 6.10 *Compare the two different looks that the special stack icons can have.*

I personally prefer all the stack icons to look like folders. It distinguishes them from other icons that can appear on the right side of the separator. To select the icon appearance you want to use, right-click the icon to display the menu shown in Figure 6.11. Then click either Folder or Stack, as you prefer.

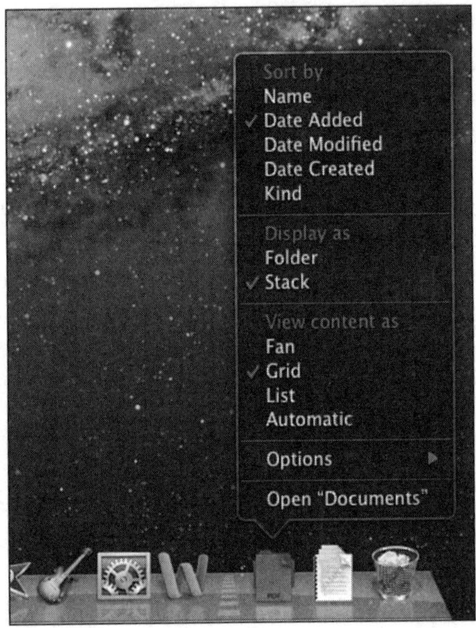

Figure 6.11 *Notice the sorting and viewing options that appear on this menu.*

Notice the four options under View Content As. If you select Fan, the content spreads out in an arc. If the folder contains too many items to display in the arc, the item at the top of the arc is a link that opens the folder in the Finder window. If you select Grid, all the items in the folder display in a pop-up window. The last icon in the pop-up window is a link that opens the folder in the Finder window. If you select List, the items display as a list. And finally, if you select Automatic, which is the default option, Mac OS X decides whether to show a fan or a grid, based on the number of items in the folder.

Adding Folder and File Icons to the Dock

You can add a folder to the right side of the Dock separator by dragging the folder to the desired location. The best way to find the folder you want to add may be to open the Finder, although you could have a folder on the desktop that you just drag to the Dock. Remember that dragging a folder to the Dock creates a stack.

After dragging the folder to the Dock, you may want to customize the icon as described in the previous topic in this chapter.

In addition to folders, you can drag icons for your frequently used files to the right side of the Dock. Clicking the icon for a file opens the file.

Rearranging Icons on the Dock

After you get all the icons you want on the Dock, you can move them around by dragging them so that they are in some sequence that is logical to you. Note that you cannot move the Finder icon or the Trash icon, and, of course, you cannot drag icons across the separator.

Setting Date and Time Preferences

By default, Lion shows the day of the week and the time on the right side of the menu bar. Mac OS X determines what defaults to set for your date and time preferences based on information you supply when you initialize your computer, described in Chapter 1, "Initializing a New Computer." If your location changes, and you need to reset the date, time, and/or time zone, you can make the changes in the Date & Time preferences window.

Having the correct date, time, and time zone set on your computer is important because the computer uses this information to timestamp files and email. By default, if you live in the U.S., your computer keeps the correct time, even the switch to and from daylight savings time, by continually communicating with time.apple.com.

Setting the Date, Time, and Time Zone Preferences

There may be times when you travel that you may want to keep your computer set to your home time zone as a point of reference, especially if you need to refer to iCal to confirm the time of events that will occur when you return home. When Lion changes the time and time zone for you automatically, you can change it back manually by following these steps:

1. Click the System Preferences icon in the Dock and then click Date & Time (located on the fourth line).

2. If necessary, click the Date & Time tab.
3. If you do not have administrative rights in your user account, click the padlock and enter the name and password of an Administrative account. Click Unlock and the padlock opens, as shown in Figure 6.12. If you are an administrator on the Mac, the padlock is open when you open the Date & Time preferences window.

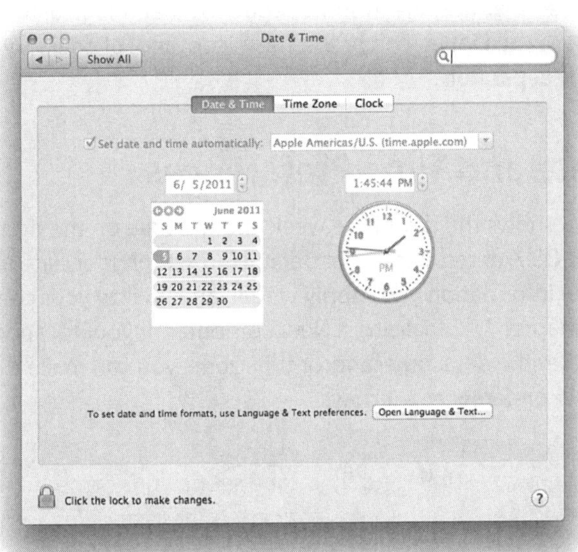

Figure 6.12 *Notice that the Date & Time pane has a link to the Language & Text preferences, where you can set date and time formats in the Format pane.*

4. Deselect Set Date and Time Automatically.
5. Type the correct date or click the correct date in the calendar.
6. Type the correct time or drag the hands of the clock to the correct time.
7. Click Save.
8. Click the Time Zone tab to display the pane shown in Figure 6.13.
9. Click Set Time Zone Automatically Using Current Location, or click the map where your city is located. A red dot in the time zone marks the closest city to you, and (new in Lion) the entire time zone region is outlined on the map. Select your city or the closest city to your location from the Closest City pop-up menu.

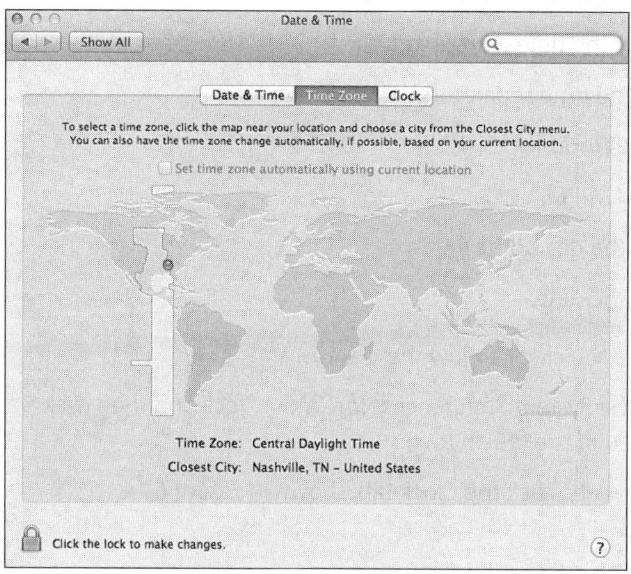

Figure 6.13 *If you travel to a different time zone, Lion can automatically change to the correct time zone if you have an Internet connection.*

10. Close the Date & Time window. Lion closes the padlock automatically.

Have you ever wondered what time zone a particular city uses—especially one that you know is probably very close to the border of another time zone? Click the area on the map that is the approximate location of the city and then check the Closest City pop-up menu to see whether the city is listed. If the city is listed (and only major cities are, so don't expect to see Monkey's Eyebrow, KY) and you select it, the time zone region on the map displays the correct time zone for that city.

Customizing the Clock

If you like an uncluttered menu bar, or you just don't like watching the clock, you can hide the day and the time that displays there by default. If, however, you like seeing the time in the menu bar, you can customize it to the *n*th degree. You can do any of the following:

- Display the clock as digital or analog.
- Display the time with seconds.
- Flash the time separators. (That's annoying!)
- Use a 24-hour clock.
- Show AM/PM.
- Show the day of the week.
- Show the date.

To customize the clock, follow these steps:

1. Click the System Preferences icon in the Dock and then click Date & Time (located in the fourth row).
2. If necessary, click the Clock tab, shown in Figure 6.14.

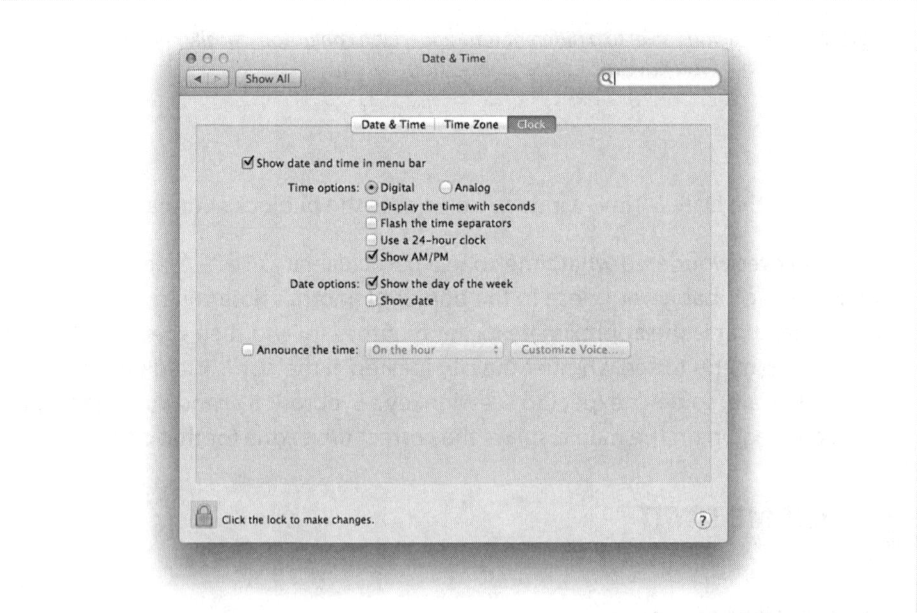

Figure 6.14 *You can make changes to the clock without unlocking the padlock.*

3. Uncheck Show Date and Time in Menu Bar if you don't want to see this information in the menu bar.
4. If you do want to see the date and time in the menu bar, select the Time Options you want and then select the Date Options you want.
5. Close the window.

SHOW ME **Media 6.4—A Video about Announcing the Time**
Access this video file through your registered Web Edition at
my.safaribooksonline.com/9780132819091/media
or on the DVD for print books.

LET ME TRY IT

Announcing the Time

If you are the type who lets the time get away from you, even if it is displayed on the screen, you might try letting the computer nag you by announcing the time every half hour or so. Here's how to set that up:

1. Click the System Preferences icon in the Dock and then click Date & Time (located on the fourth row).
2. If necessary, click the Clock tab.
3. Click Announce the Time.
4. Select a frequency from the pop-up menu.
5. Click Customize Voice to display the options shown in Figure 6.15.
6. Select a voice from the pop-up menu and then click Play to see whether you like it. You can adjust the rate and volume while the voice is playing.

This may take a while because you'll have to try all the male voices and then all the female voices. Then you'll have to click Show More Voices and try all the novelty voices, such as Deranged and Hysterical. To save you some time, I'll tell you that my favorites are Alex and Victoria.

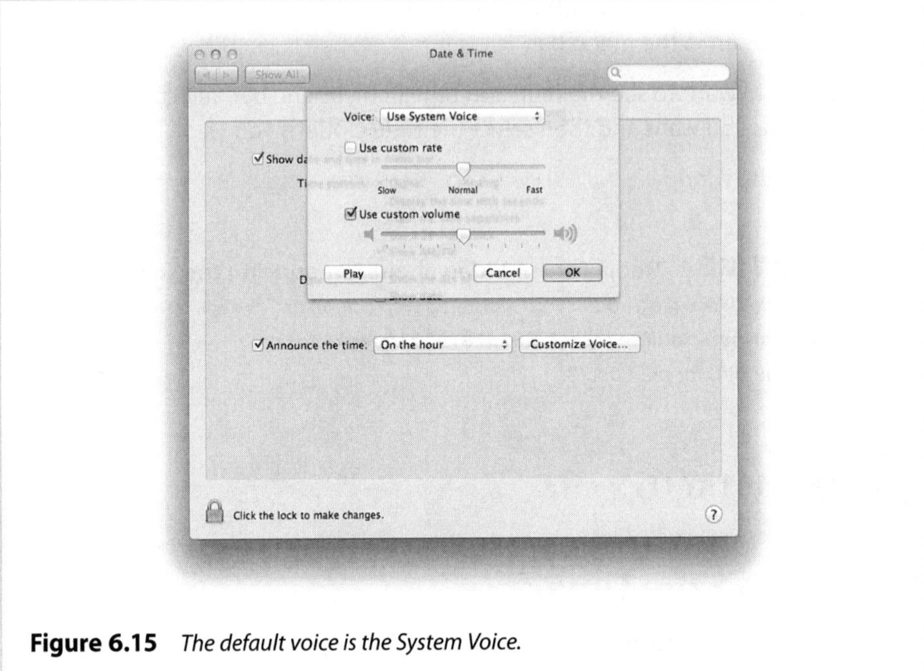

Figure 6.15 *The default voice is the System Voice.*

7. When you are finished, click OK.
8. Close the window.

If you want to use a different format for the date and time, you can. For more information on setting the format preferences, see Chapter 7.

This chapter explains how to work in the Finder to find, copy, move, and delete files and folders.

7

Using Finder

The Finder application lists and manipulates all the files and folders on the computer. It takes its name from the fact that you can find anything on the Mac with the Finder. Primarily, you use Finder to find and open files, but its other functions also include creating new folders, and copying, moving, renaming, and deleting files and folders. This chapter covers all those tasks as well as how to customize many aspects of the Finder.

Identifying Components of the Finder Window

Click the Finder icon in the Dock to open the Finder window, as shown in Figure 7.1 Notice the components of the Finder window pointed out in this figure.

The Finder window has a title bar and toolbar, and it can display two panes. The pane on the left is called the sidebar; the pane on the right doesn't have a name, so call it anything you want. If you don't see the sidebar, turn it on by selecting View, Sidebar.

The title bar, at the top of the window, displays the name of the source that is selected in the sidebar. In Figure 7.1 you can see that All My Files is selected in the sidebar and that name displays in the title bar. Additionally, the title bar has three buttons on the left. You probably already know that the red button in the title bar is the one that closes the window and the yellow button minimizes the window in a disappearing-genie-like swoop to an icon on the right side of the Dock separator. The green button (the Zoom button) makes the window larger or smaller.

Exploring the Sidebar

The sidebar has a list of sources categorized as Favorites, Shared, and Devices. The Devices category can list hard disks, any external disks, flash drives, or iPods that are attached to the computer, and any optical drives that have CDs or DVDs in them. Additionally, if you have purchased MobileMe, iDisk can be listed under Devices.

Within about a year, MobileMe will be discontinued and replaced by iCloud services that will be free. At that time you will probably see something different under Devices in the sidebar.

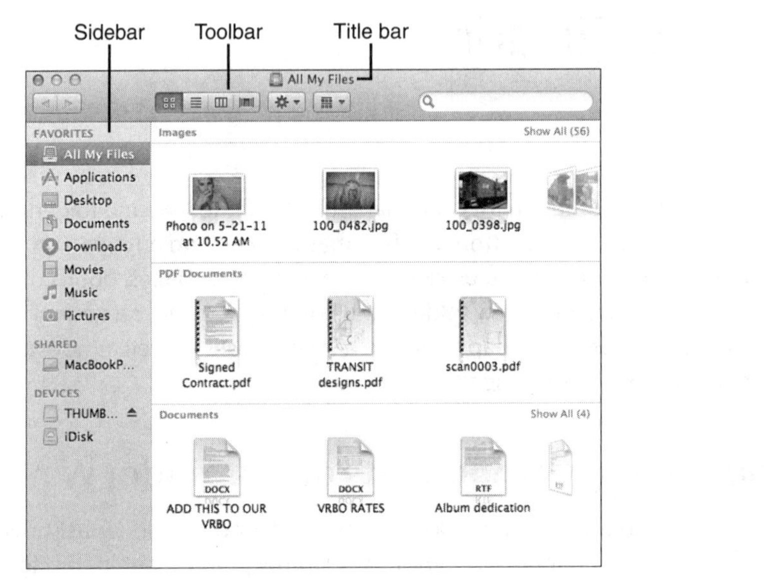

Figure 7.1 *The first time you use the Finder, the view is set to the Icon view.*

The Shared category can list Back to My Mac, connected servers, such as a network server at work, and Bonjour servers. Back to My Mac is a screen-sharing capability that is included in a MobileMe account, and Bonjour servers are servers that are set up on a local network that allow network users to chat (using iChat, for example).

The Favorites category can list the following default sources: All My Files, Applications, Desktop, Documents, Downloads, Movies, Music, Pictures, and your home folder (which generally is your name, depending on what you specified during setup of the computer). The list of sources in the Favorites category is not a hierarchical list. The Favorites category simply lists folders that you tend to use the most. If you have other Wi-Fi–enabled Lion computers within range, you also will see a listing for AirDrop in the sidebar. AirDrop is a new feature in Lion that enables you to send files to other computers via Wi-Fi. Later in this chapter, you learn how to remove folders and add your own folders to Favorites.

I find it curious that Lion lists all the possible folders under Favorites except your home folder. Of course, you can add this in the Finder preferences window.

Notice that when you point to the name of a category, such as Favorites, the word Hide appears on the right. If you click Hide, the items under the category name disappear. Point to the category name again, and the word Show appears, as shown in Figure 7.2. Click Show to display the items in the category again. This new feature in Lion replaces the "disclosure triangle" that used to appear before each of the category names in the sidebar.

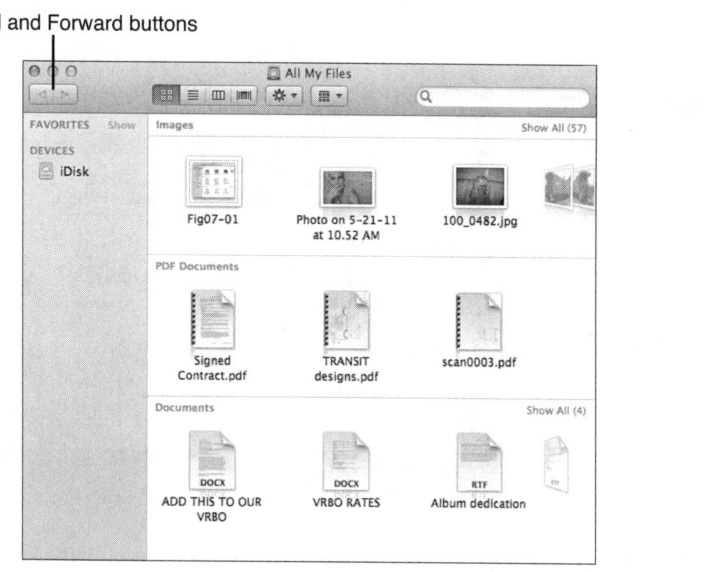

Figure 7.2 *When you click Hide, the list of folders under Favorites disappears and the Hide button changes to Show.*

When you click a source in any category in the sidebar, the items in that source display in the pane on the right. For example, clicking the external drive called Thumb. . . in the Devices category shows the files and folders that are on that drive in the pane on the right, as illustrated in Figure 7.3. Notice that the title bar of the finder shows the complete name of the drive (Thumb Drive). Clicking Documents under the Favorites category displays all the files and folders in the Documents folder, replacing what was in the right pane with the content of the new source; it doesn't open a new window. To quickly go back to the external drive again, click the button in the toolbar that has the left-pointing arrow. Then, to go back to Documents, click the button that has the right-pointing arrow. These buttons work like the Back and Forward buttons in a web browser (see Figure 7.3).

Another new feature in Lion allows you to change the size of the items in the Finder's sidebar. You find this option on the General page of System Preferences.

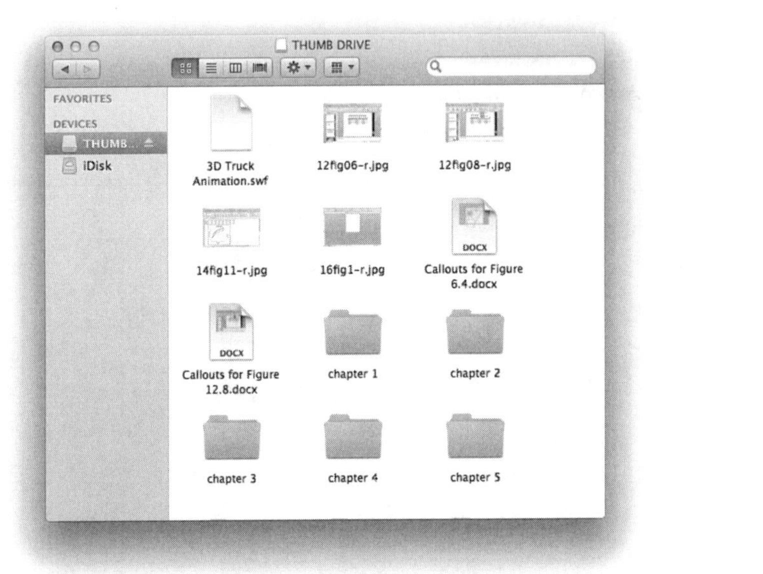

Figure 7.3 *The right pane displays the content of the source selected in the sidebar.*

Using Finder Views

The Icon view, shown in Figure 7.4, is the default view for the Finder, but Finder provides three additional views: List, Column, and Cover Flow. In each view, the pane on the right is different. To switch to a different view, click the button in the toolbar for the view you want (see Figure 7.4).

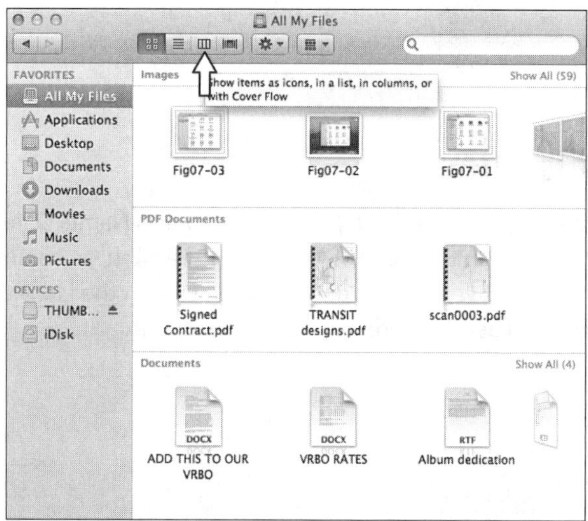

Figure 7.4 *When you point to the view buttons the description of the buttons displays.*

Using the Icon View

The Icon view uses icons in the right pane to represent the content of the source selected in the sidebar. You can arrange the icons in this view by dragging the icons to different locations as you want. For example, you might want to drag all the files that you are currently working on to the top of the window. When you drag icons to new locations, existing icons do not move aside for you. To realign the icons in a tidy grid again, select the icons that are out of alignment, right-click the desktop, and click Clean Up Selection. This command can have surprising results. You might have to work with the Clean Up feature a little bit to fully understand it. Hint: The size of the Finder window can have a bearing on how this feature cleans up!

If you are viewing All My Files in the Icon view in the Finder, you cannot drag the icons at all.

In the Icon view, if you have an icon for a .doc file or a PDF file, when you point to the icon for the file, a set of back and forward arrows appear, and you can use these to scroll through the pages. If you have an icon for certain types of movies (QuickTime formats), when you point to the movie icon, a play button appears, and you can play or pause the movie. Because the pages of the document or the movie display in the icon itself, you might want to increase the size of the icon so you can actually see something. Finally, if you point to a music file, a play button displays. Clicking it plays the music in the file.

The Cover Flow view also provides the same viewing capability for PDF and movie file icons.

Using the List View

Figure 7.5 shows the List view. By default, this view lists Name, Date Modified, Size, Kind, and Date Added (in that order). If you can't see all these columns, make the Finder window wider. If you are looking at All My Files in the List view, the columns are Name, Kind, and Last Opened.

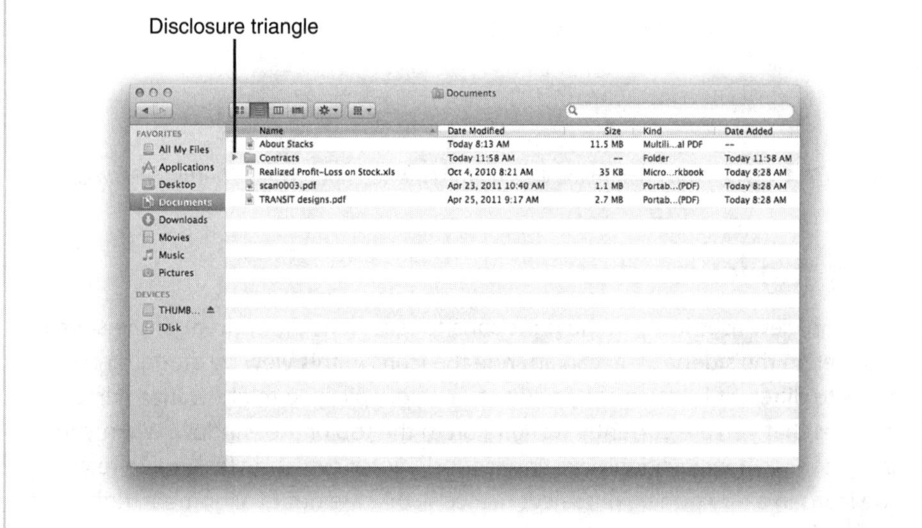

Figure 7.5 *When you cannot see all the columns in the List view, make the window wider.*

The List view uses the disclosure triangles to hide or display sub-items. If you click the triangle when it is pointing to the right, it reveals the sub-items. Click the triangle when it is pointing down and it hides them. Click a column heading and you sort all the items in the view by that column. Click the column heading again to sort in the opposite direction.

In Figure 7.6, the screen on the left shows items sorted in ascending order by Date Modified. The screen on the right shows the same items sorted in descending order.

You can move any of the columns in the List view to rearrange them, except for the Name column. It must remain in place as the first column. To move a column, drag the column title to the left or right. To change the width of a column, point to the right side of the column title until you see a double-headed arrow, and then drag to the left or right.

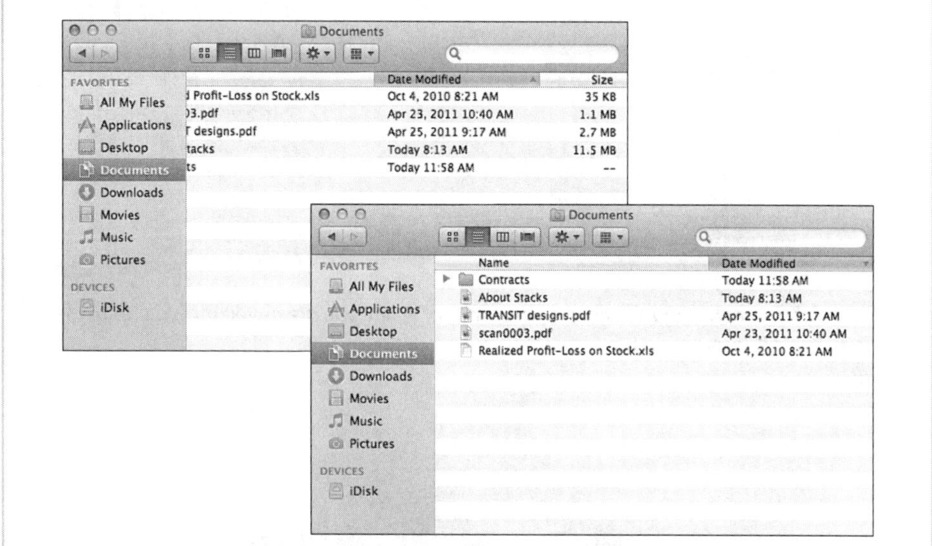

Figure 7.6 *Notice the triangle in the Date Modified heading indicates ascending or descending sort.*

Using the Column View

Figure 7.7 shows the Column view. This view can drill down through nested folders, column by column, until you select a file, and then it shows a preview of the file in the last column. In Figure 7.7, for example, the first column shows the content of the source selected in the sidebar. The content of the folder selected in the first column is shown in the second column. The third column shows a preview of the file selected in the second column.

If you want to see all the columns as you are drilling down, make the Finder window as wide as possible before you start.

Using the Cover Flow View

The Cover Flow view, shown in Figure 7.8, uses the List view in the bottom pane and a graphic 3D view in the top pane. The items contained in the source that you select show as previews in the top pane. If you are an iTunes user, you are already familiar with the Cover Flow view.

Figure 7.7 *Use the Column view to keep track of where you are as you move up and down in hierarchical folders.*

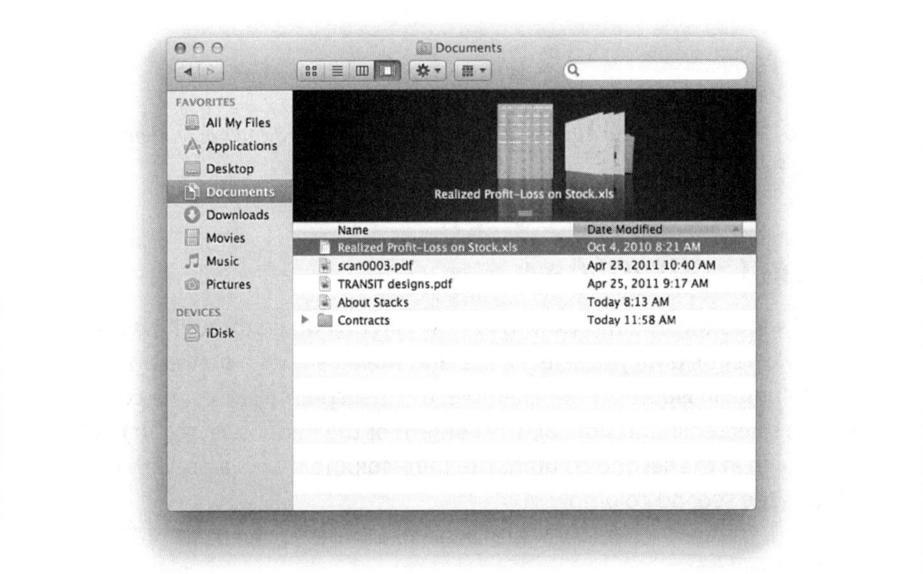

Figure 7.8 *Use a swiping motion on a Magic Mouse or Magic Trackpad to scroll left and right in Cover Flow view.*

You can scroll through the items in the graphic pane by swiping one finger left or right across your Magic Mouse or Trackpad. In the Cover Flow view, scrolling through content is synchronized in both panes. In other words, the item previewed in the top pane is the item selected in the bottom pane, and vice versa.

To get the most out of Cover Flow view, make the graphic area larger. Point to the bottom of the graphic pane and drag it down when the cursor arrow changes to a hand.

Changing the Item Arrangement in a View

Lion gives you a new button in the toolbar that allows you to quickly sort the items that display in the right pane of the Finder. This button is available in the toolbar in all views. By default, when you open the Finder, All My Files, displayed in Icon view, is sorted by Kind. Finder uses a heading for the name of each kind of file.

Figure 7.9 shows the button and the options available on its menu for regular files and folders. If you select the Applications folder in the sidebar, the menu has only the options shown in Figure 7.10. So if you want to see the files that you recently modified displayed at the top of the Finder pane, you would choose Date Last Modified.

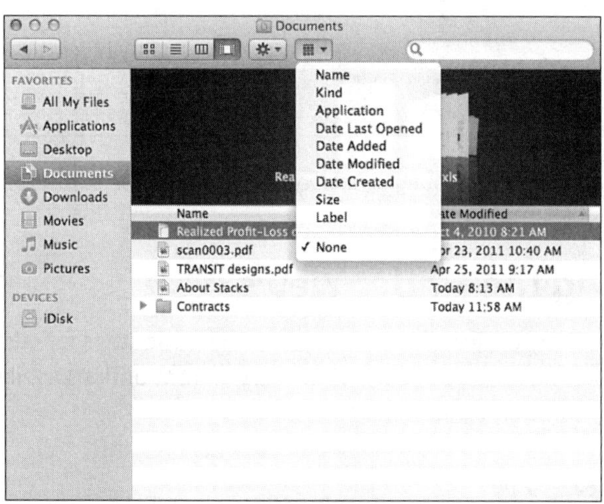

Figure 7.9 *This menu is the same in every view.*

You cannot collapse a category in All My Files in any view, but the Icon view has a Show All and a Show Less feature that is accessible in each category. If you click Show All, the Finder displays all the files in the particular category or as many as it can within the window. If you click Show Less, you can see one row of files in a particular category and then you have to scroll to see more files. To scroll the files horizontally, point to a category and swipe one finger to the left or right if you have a Magic Mouse orTrackpad. To scroll with the keyboard, use the right or left cursor arrow key. To move to a different category with the keyboard, use the up and down cursor arrow keys.

By default, All My Files shows fewer files in each category.

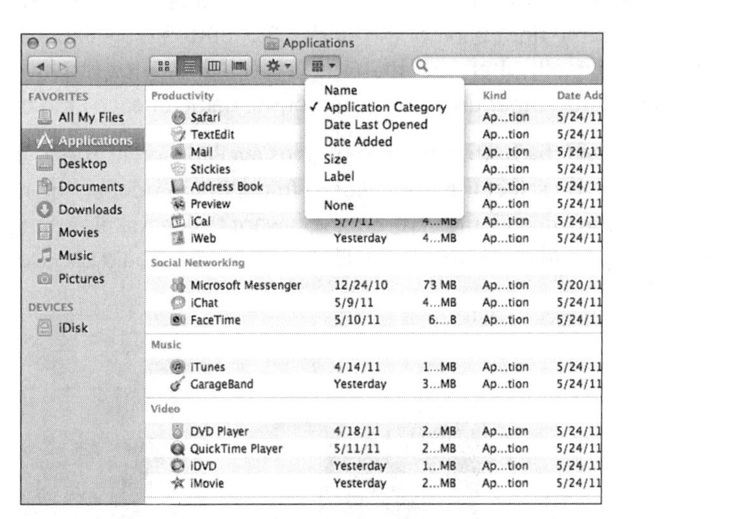

Figure 7.10 *This menu for arranging applications is the same in every view.*

Customizing the Finder Views

Each view has many options for customizing. The basic steps for customizing each type of view are the same, but each view has different options available, as shown in Figures 7.11 through 7.14.

LET ME TRY IT

Setting Options for Each Finder View

To set options for any one of the Finder views, follow these steps:

1. Click the Finder icon in the Dock.
2. Click the view button in the toolbar for the view you want to customize.
3. Click View in the menu bar and click Show View Options.
4. Select the options that you want. Refer to Figures 7.11 through 7.14 to see the options available for each view.

5. Close the window.

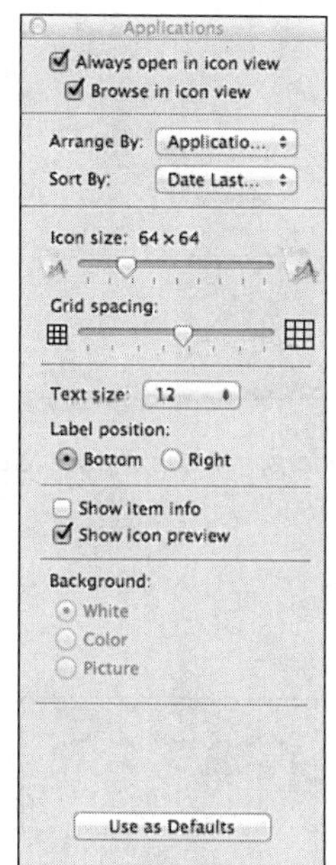

Figure 7.11 *In the Icon options, you can customize the size of icons and their label text.*

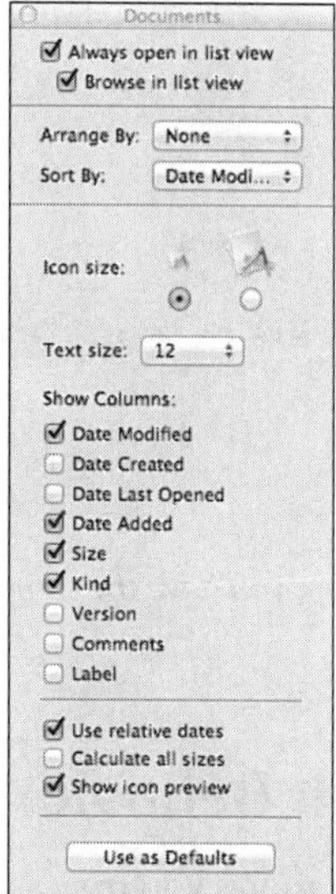

Figure 7.12 *In the List options, you can select the columns you want to see.*

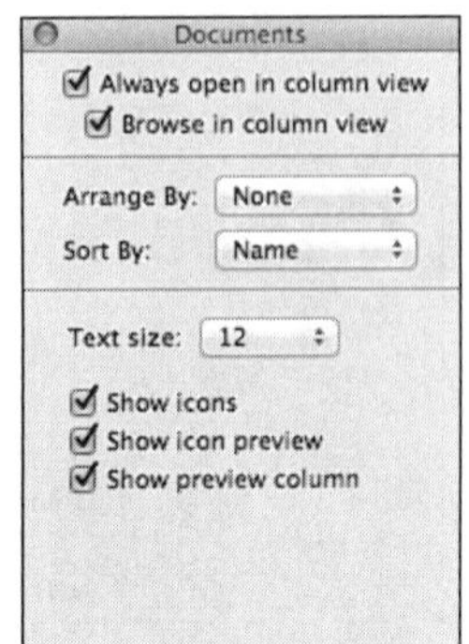

Figure 7.13 *In the Columns options, you can choose to display or hide the last column, the preview column.*

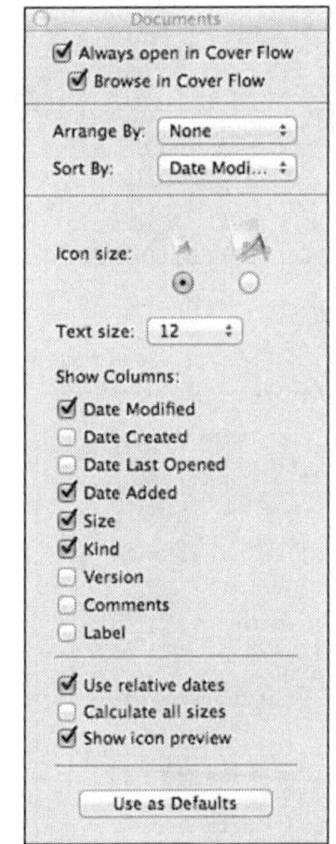

Figure 7.14 *In the Cover Flow view, you have the same options as you do for the List view.*

Observing the Default Behavior of the Finder

As you use the Finder more and more, you may start to notice that the Finder has a memory. For example, it remembers where you last positioned it on the screen when you closed it, and it goes right back to that location the next time you open it.

The Finder window has a default size. If you make the window smaller than the default size, the Finder remembers the size, and the next time you open it, it opens to that size. The opposite of this is not true, however. If you make the Finder window larger than the default size, the next time you open the Finder, it opens in the default size.

Unlike its predecessor, Snow Leopard, Lion does not continue to use the same view persistently. Instead, the Finder remembers the views you use for viewing particular folders. If you use the Icon view to look at the Desktop folder, the next time you look at the Desktop folder, the Finder displays it in Icon view. For example, if you look at the Desktop folder in the Icon view and then you look at the Documents folder in the List view, when you switch to the Desktop folder again it displays in the Icon view. Then when you switch to the Documents folder, it displays in the List view.

The Finder even remembers if you leave its window open when you log out, and it opens the window the next time you log in. It does this even if you do not select the log out option Reopen Windows When Logging Back In.

The default behaviors of the Finder described in this section cannot be changed.

Customizing the Finder

Although you cannot change the default behaviors described in the previous section, you can change many other Finder behaviors. These include the default source to view, the number of windows to use, the default view that Finder uses when it opens, and even the default view for a particular folder. In addition to these behaviors, you can customize the Finder's toolbar, sidebar, and menu bar and hide or display the status bar and path bar.

Exploring the Default Source to View in the Finder

By default, every view opens the same source—a new feature in Lion called All My Files. This feature lists all your user files in categories. The categories are dynamic, and by that I mean that the Finder analyzes your files and creates categories for them on the fly. For example, you might start out with the categories of Images, PDF Documents, and Documents, but if you create a spreadsheet, a new category called Spreadsheets appears for All My Files.

I suspect that this feature may be an attempt to wean the user away from knowing or caring where files are stored. It's also a step toward the new iCloud service that will be available in the fall of 2011. To learn more about iCloud, see Chapter 16, "Keeping Your Mac Safe, Updated, and Backed Up."

LET ME TRY IT

Setting the Default Source to View

If you want to see a particular folder instead of all your files when the Finder opens, you can specify a folder other than All My Files as the default folder that Finder always opens. Follow these steps:

1. Click Finder in the menu bar and click Preferences.
2. Click the General tab, if necessary.
3. Click the pop-up button for New Finder Windows Show and select the folder you want.
4. Close the Preferences window.

LET ME TRY IT

Setting Multiple Window Use

If you want to open a new window every time you open a folder in Finder, you can set an option to do that. This might be a good practice if you copy or move files between folders frequently; however, opening a new Finder window manually if you want one is also possible. To set the multiple window behavior as a default, follow these steps:

1. Click Finder in the menu bar and click Preferences.
2. Click the General tab, if necessary.
3. Select the box for Always Open Folders in a New Window, as shown in Figure 7.15.
4. Close the Preferences window.

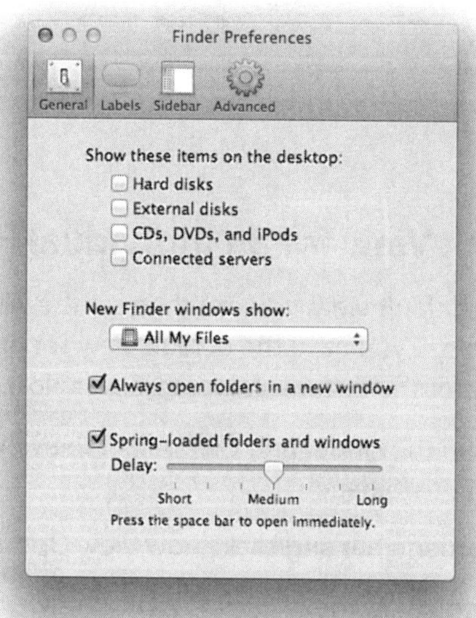

Figure 7.15 *If you start getting too many Finder windows, you always can go back and deselect the option to open new windows.*

LET ME TRY IT

Setting the View in Which Finder Always Opens

You may want to open the Finder in the same view every time if you use the Finder for the same thing most of the time. For example, if you typically use the Finder to locate files in subfolders, you might want the Finder to open in the Columns view. Follow these steps to set the default view of the Finder:

1. Click the Finder icon in the Dock.
2. Click the view button in the toolbar for the view you want to make the default.
3. Click View in the menu bar and click Show View Options. Regardless of the view you select, the first option in the window is the same. Refer to Figures 7.11 – 7.14.
4. Click Always Open in <*Name of View*> View.

At this point, you have set the view for only the selected folder.

5. Click Use as Defaults to make the view the default view for all folders.

6. Close the window.

LET ME TRY IT

Setting the Default View for an Individual Folder

After you have set the default view, you can then set the view of individual folders if you want. For example, if you have the default view set on List, you might want to set the default view for the Pictures folder to Cover Flow.

1. Select the folder in the Finder and then select the view that you always want to use with the folder.

2. Click View in the menu bar and click Show View Options.

3. Click Always Open in *<Name of Current View>* View.

4. Close the window.

Customizing the Finder Toolbar

By default, the Finder toolbar has eight buttons plus the Spotlight field. You can add, delete, and rearrange the buttons in the toolbar to suit yourself.

LET ME TRY IT

Modifying the Toolbar

To me the most valuable modification you can make to the toolbar is to add three more buttons—specifically the Delete button, the New Folder button, and the Burn button. Although you can also remove buttons from the toolbar, I think you'll find you need all the buttons that are there by default. Follow these steps to modify the toolbar:

1. Click the Finder icon in the Dock to open the Finder window.

2. Click View in the menu bar and click Customize Toolbar. The dialog box shown in Figure 7.16 opens.

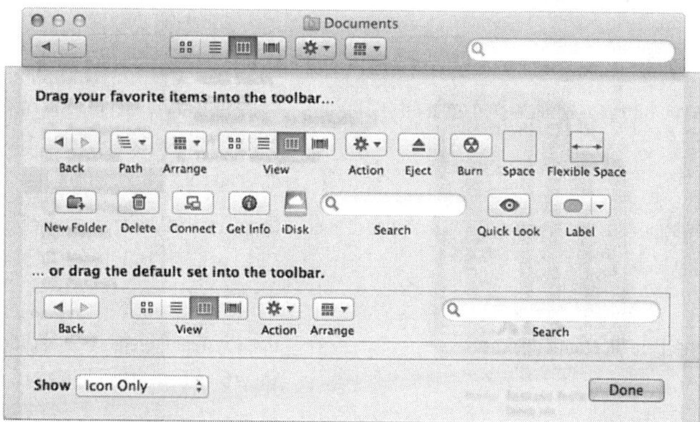

Figure 7.16 *This dialog box lists all the buttons you can place on the Finder's toolbar.*

3. I recommend you drag the spacers (the blank boxes) off the toolbar first. Then drag any new items you want to add into the toolbar.
4. Drag a Space or Flexible Space into the toolbar anywhere you want to separate buttons.
5. In the Show pop-up menu, I recommend you select Icon and Text.
6. If you need to start over at any time, drag the default set into the toolbar.
7. When you are finished, click Done.

Customizing the Menu Bar

If you feel the need to tweak every last item that can be customized, you can make yet another modification for purely aesthetic reasons. You can change the appearance of the menu bar. The default setting for the menu bar makes it translucent. To remove the translucent setting and make the menu bar solid, open the System Preferences window and open the Desktop pane of the Desktop & Screen Saver preferences. Deselect Translucent Menu Bar and close the window.

A more substantive type of modification to the menu bar is the addition or deletion of Menu Extras (also called menulets) on the right side of the menu bar. Table 7.1 describes some of the useful menulets you can add to the menu bar and tells you how to add them.

Many applications you install on your computer also add their own icons to the menu bar.

Table 7.1 How to Add Useful Menulets

Menulet	Description	How to Add
AirPort	Lets you turn your wireless card on or off	Open System Preferences and click Network. Select AirPort in the left pane. Select Show AirPort Status in Menu Bar.
Battery (laptops only)	Shows you how much power is still available in your laptop battery	Open System Preferences and click Energy Saver. Click the Battery tab. Select Show Battery Status in the Menu Bar.
Bluetooth	Connects to Bluetooth devices	Open System Preferences and click Bluetooth. Select Show Bluetooth Status in Menu Bar.
Clock	Displays the time (and date, if specified)	Open System Preferences and click Date & Time. Click the Clock tab. Select Show Date and Time in Menu Bar.
iChat	Displays a menu with options for Status (Offline, Available, Surfing the Web, and so on), Current iTunes, and Show Buddy List	Open iChat. Click iChat in the Menu Bar and select Preferences. Click the General tab if necessary. Select Show Status in Menu Bar.
TimeMachine	Displays the status of a backup in progress	Open System Preferences and click TimeMachine. Select Show Time Machine Status in the Menu Bar.
Volume	Allows you to turn the volume up or down using a slider	Open System Preferences and click Sound. Click the Sound Effects tab. Select Show Volume in Menu Bar.

SHOW ME **Media 7.1—A Video about Adding the Eject Button to Menu Extras**

Access this video file through your registered Web Edition at ***my.safaribooksonline.com/9780132819091/media*** *or on the DVD for print books.*

LET ME TRY IT

Adding the Eject Button to the Menu Bar

One other very useful menulet you can add to the Menu Extras is the Eject button. The steps to add this menulet to the menu bar are different from all the other menulets, and they are a little more complicated. Follow these steps to add the Eject button to the menu bar:

1. Open the Finder and click the icon for the Mac's hard drive under the Devices category.

If you do not see an icon for the hard drive, click Finder in the menu bar, click Preferences, click the Sidebar tab, select Hard Disks (under Devices), and close the window.

2. Navigate the following path: System->Library->CoreServices->Menu Extras.
3. In the Menu Extras folder, find the file named Eject.menu and double-click it. The Eject button appears immediately in the menu bar.

To remove most menulets from the menu bar, you can repeat your steps to open the appropriate Preferences pane and uncheck the option to show the menulet. A quicker way is to press the Command key while you drag the icon off the menu bar. This second method is the one you must use to remove the Eject button.

Customizing the Sidebar

The items you see in the Finder's sidebar are only a starting point—you have a great deal of control over what appears there. You can select from a list of default items for each category to determine whether you want them to be included in the sidebar or not.

LET ME TRY IT

Selecting the Default Sources in the Finder Sidebar

I highly recommend that you make some changes to what you see listed in the Favorites category in the sidebar. I suggest you add your home folder to the sidebar and delete any other items you don't think you'll need. To select the items you want to display in the sidebar, follow these steps:

1. Click Finder in the menu bar and then click Preferences.
2. Click the Sidebar tab, if necessary. The sidebar pane is shown in Figure 7.17.
3. Check items you want to display and uncheck items you want to hide.
4. Close the window.

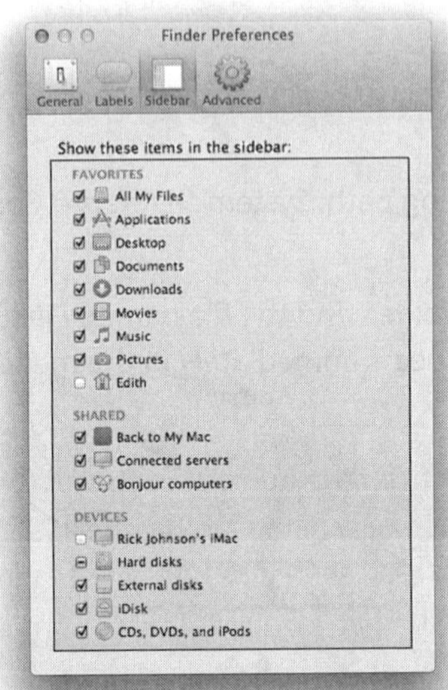

Figure 7.17 *Select the default Favorites, Shared, and Devices you want to display in the Finder sidebar in this pane.*

Each item listed in the sidebar is not the *real* item, but an alias for the item. Normally aliases have a curved arrow added to their icons, but those in the sidebar do not.

LET ME TRY IT

Adding Files or Folders to the Sidebar

In addition to showing or hiding the default items in the sidebar, you can add your own files or folders at will. To add a file or folder to the sidebar, follow these steps:

1. Click the Finder icon in the Dock.
2. Navigate to the file or folder you want to add so it is visible in the right pane.
3. Drag the file or folder in the right pane to the Favorites category in the sidebar, dropping it where you want it.

I recommend that you do *not* clutter the sidebar with individual files. For quick access, a better place to put a file (or an alias to a file) is on the desktop or on the right side of the Dock.

You also can change the order of items within the categories in the sidebar by simply dragging the items to new locations. To delete an item from the sidebar, simply press the Command key as you drag it off the bar or right-click the item and click Remove from Sidebar. If you delete an item by mistake (say, your home folder), don't panic. You haven't lost all your files. Remember the items in the sidebar are only aliases. If you delete a default item by mistake, just open the Sidebar tab of the Finder preferences window and put a check in the box for the item you deleted. If you delete an item that you placed on the sidebar yourself, simply find it in the Finder and drag it back again.

Viewing the Status Bar and Path Bar

When both the status bar and the path bar are visible, the status bar is located at the very bottom of the Finder window and the path bar is right above it. The status bar contains valuable information about the number and size of files or folders you have selected. If you do not see the status bar, turn it on by selecting View in the menu bar and then clicking Show Status Bar. The path bar displays the path of the selected item. For example, if I select the Desktop in the sidebar, the path is Macintosh HD -> Users ->Yvonne->Desktop. If you do not see the path bar, turn it on by selecting View in the menu bar and then clicking Show Path Bar. After you select either of the show commands on the View menu, both the Show Status Bar command and the Show Path Bar command change to a Hide command so you can turn off the display when you want to.

When you use the Icon view in the Finder, if you have the status bar visible, it contains a slider control that you can use to make the icons larger or smaller.

Exploring the File Structure

The remaining topics in this chapter deal with creating and deleting folders and copying, moving, and deleting files. To really be able to perform these tasks in the Finder efficiently, you must understand the file structure of your hard disk. For example, knowing the file structure reveals that what you see in the right pane of the Finder is a hierarchical listing, whereas what you see in the Finder sidebar is *not* a hierarchical listing at all. It is, rather, a list of items provided for your convenience. This can be confusing for new users, especially those coming from the Windows environment in which the Explorer looks and functions similarly to the Finder but has a hierarchical listing in both the sidebar and the right pane.

So start your exploration of the file structure at the root of the hard drive. If you are not familiar with the term *root* as it applies to a drive, think of it as the primary level. A folder also has a root. Again, it is the primary level of the folder. By default, the root of the hard drive has only four folders: Applications, Library, System, and Users. Figure 7.18 shows the folders in the root of the hard drive as well as the folder in the root of the System folder and the folders in the root of the Users folder.

The Users folder contains the home folders of all users who have user accounts set up on the Mac.

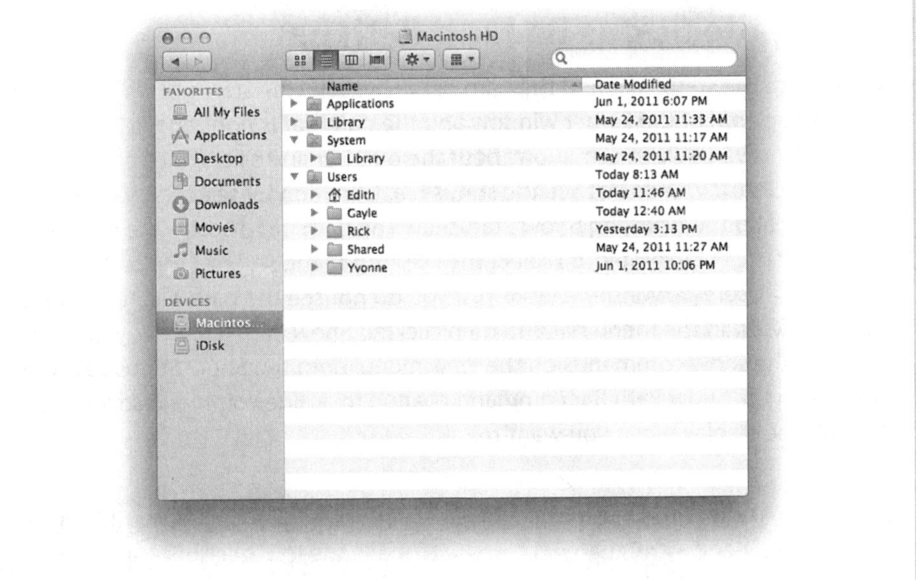

Figure 7.18 *Clicking the triangle beside the folder name reveals the folders in the root.*

As a user, you won't really be tromping around in the folders in the root of the hard drive. In fact, if you are a beginner, you should definitely not trespass in these folders unless you are guided by an Apple expert.

Two exceptions to the "no trespassing" rule exist, and Mac OS X gives you access to the two exceptions via Favorites in the sidebar. One exception is your home folder, which is in the root of the Users folder, and the other exception is the Applications folder. If you customize the sidebar and put your home folder on it, you can then access the folder without opening the Users folder on the hard drive where you could do some damage. The other exception is the Applications folder, also located in the root of the hard drive. It contains all the default software on the Mac. You can open this folder and double-click anything in it to launch the application, again without having to open the hard drive.

The folder that holds all your user files is the home folder. It's not called "Home" folder; it's called whatever you specified for the "short name" during the initial setup of your computer. For example, my home folder is called Yvonne. The home folder contains the following folders by default:

- **Desktop**—This folder holds all the files and folders found on your Desktop, the background of the screen.
- **Documents**—Apple designed this folder to be the default folder for storing most of your files. Therefore, when you issue the command to save a file you are creating (as in the TextEdit application), the default location suggested for the file is the Documents folder.
- **Downloads**—This folder is set as the default location for any files you download from the Internet. The default is set on the General pane in the Safari preferences window.
- **Movies, Music, Pictures**—These folders are the default folders for iMovie, iTunes, and iPhoto, respectively. This means that when you save a file in the iMovie application, the application suggests the Movies folder as the location where the new file should be stored. You don't have to take the suggestion, of course, but in the long run, you may find that it has its benefits. For example, if you store photos in folders all over the place instead of in the Pictures folder, those pictures won't be readily available for use as a desktop background.
- **Public**—This folder can contain any files you want to share with people on your network or with other user accounts on your Mac. Anything you put in this folder can be accessed without a password, can be viewed or copied, but cannot be changed or deleted.

If you upgraded from Snow Leopard to Lion, you also will have a Sites folder.

Every user on your Mac has the same set of folders in his home folder. This is how Mac OS X keeps each user's work and preferences separate. Because the Applications folder is in the root of the hard disk, all users have access to it and can, therefore, run all applications unless restricted by Parental Controls or unless a user installs a program somewhere in his own home folder.

Creating Different Types of Folders

With the Finder, you can create three different types of folders: a regular folder (one that holds files as well as other folders), a Smart Folder (one that gathers files that meet specific search criteria and continually updates itself), and a Burn Folder (a folder that holds files you want to burn to a CD or DVD).

Determining What Folders You Need

Creating a folder is relatively simple. Figuring out which folders to create is more difficult. Before you begin creating all the folders you need, think about how you want to organize your work.

In the Documents folder, storing files such as word processing documents, spreadsheets, presentations, and PDFs makes sense. Rather than creating folders for the different *types* of files you will be creating, creating folders that reflect the purpose or subject matter of the files you will be creating is usually better. For example, instead of creating one folder named Spreadsheets, you might create three folders named Budgets, Client Billing, and Bids.

If you ever do need to see all your spreadsheets at one time, remember that you can click All My Files in the Finder sidebar. Alternatively, you can arrange the items in a particular source by Application using the new button in the toolbar. (See "Changing the Item Arrangement in a View" discussed previously in this chapter.)

TELL ME MORE **Media 7.2—A Recording about the Folders You Might Need on Your Hard Drive**

Access this audio file through your registered Web Edition at ***my.safaribooksonline.com/9780132819091/media*** *or on the DVD for print books.*

Creating New Folders

After you have figured out a logical structure to contain all your files, you can start creating the folders you need. Creating these folders and storing your files in them before your files proliferate is a good idea.

In Lion you now have more than one way to create a folder. A new command in Lion, New Folder with Selection, allows you to select the items that should go in a folder and create the folder "around them," so to speak.

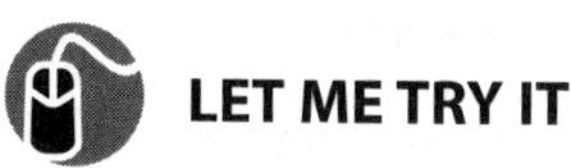

Creating a Folder the Traditional Way

To create a new folder using the traditional method, follow these steps:

1. Open the Finder and change the view to Columns.

You can create a new folder in any view, but the Columns view is the most efficient because it displays the hierarchy so well.

2. Click the folder that should hold the new folder.
3. Click File in the menu bar and then click New Folder, or if you took my advice to add the New Folder button to the toolbar, click it. (You can also use the keyboard shortcut, Command-Shift-N.) A new folder appears in the column to the right with the name **untitled folder**. The complete text of the name is selected and waiting for you to type a new name.
4. Type the name you want to give the folder and press Return. If several files or folders are in the same location as the new folder, the folder moves to a new place in the list based on how the list is sorted.

By default, folders and files are listed in the Finder in alphabetical order by name, but they could be sorted by other criteria, such as Modified Date.

After you've created a folder, you can drag it from the Finder to the right side of the Dock where it functions as a stack. See Chapter 6, "Customizing the Desktop," for more information about stacks. When you click a stack, you see the items in the folder as a fan, a grid, or a list. You can scroll to see all the items in the folder if you are in the grid or list view. If you are in the fan view, you can click Open in Finder to see all the items.

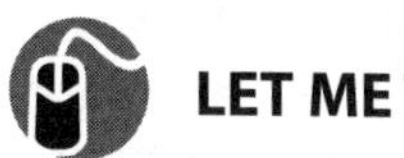

Selecting Files and Folders for a New Folder

To create a folder with the Lion New Folder with Selection command, follow these steps:

1. Select the files and/or folders that should go into the new folder.
2. Right-click the selection and click New Folder with Selection. The new folder is created containing the selected items. The default name of the folder (New Folder with Items) is selected, waiting for you to type your own name.
3. Type a name for the folder and press Return.

Working with Smart Folders

A Smart Folder is a virtual folder that has search criteria attached to it, such as "all JPG files on the hard disk with a creation date after May 2011." Each time you open the Smart Folder, the Finder looks for all the files on the hard disk that currently meet the two search criteria and lists them as if they were located in the same folder. A Smart Folder can contain items from many different locations.

SHOW ME **Media 7.3—A Video about Creating a Smart Folder**
Access this video file through your registered Web Edition at
my.safaribooksonline.com/9780132819091/media
or on the DVD for print books.

Creating a Smart Folder

If you constantly search for the same criteria, the time has come to save the criteria as a Smart Folder. For your convenience, you can even add the Smart Folder to the sidebar when you create it. To create a Smart Folder, follow these steps:

1. Click the Finder icon in the Dock.
2. If you want the search to look only in a specific folder, open it by double-clicking it in the Finder.
3. Click in the Spotlight search box and type a criterion such as **jpg** or **May**. (The Spotlight search box has an icon of a magnifying glass.) An appropriate pop-up menu opens with options for you to choose from, such as Filename Contains "jpg" or "May 2011." Files anywhere on the Mac that meet both the text and the date criteria appear immediately in the right pane.
4. If you select Filename Contains, then you will see a search token called Name in the Spotlight search field. The search token has a pop-up menu

with the options Filename or Everything. If you select a date, a search token called Date appears in the Spotlight search field, but there is no popup. The files that appear in the list can meet the date criterion in any of the date fields, including Date Created, Date Modified, Date Added, or Last Opened.

5. To narrow the search to the folder you selected in step 2, click the name of the folder in the Search bar (just to the right of "This Mac").
6. Click the button with the plus (under the Spotlight search box) to add another search criterion line (see Figure 7.19).

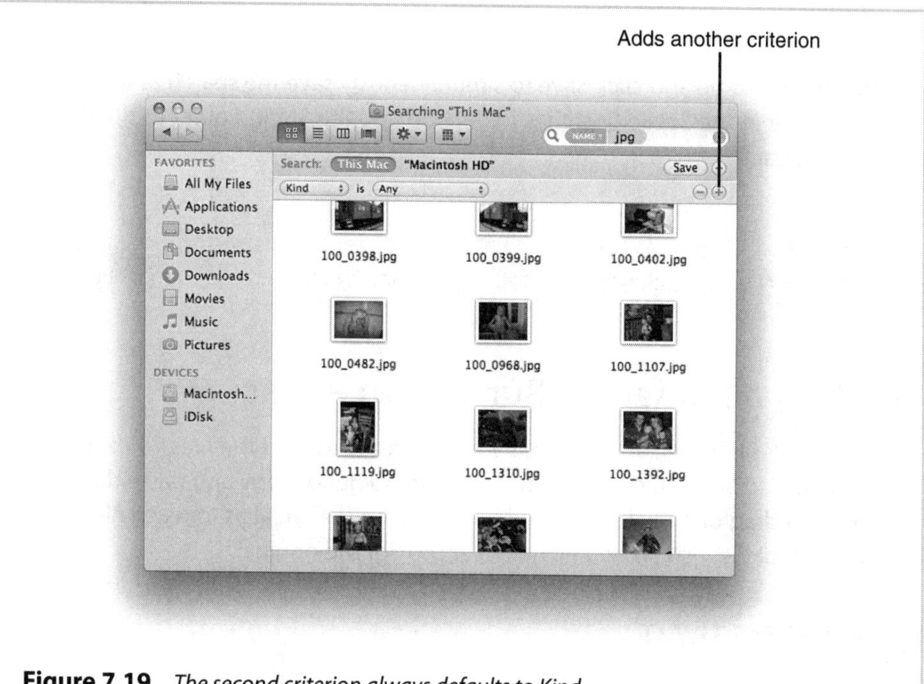

Figure 7.19 *The second criterion always defaults to Kind.*

7. Select an option from the Kind pop-up menu and complete the new criterion using the appropriate additional search token pop-up menus or text boxes. Alternatively, select Other from the pop-up list, select an option from the long list of possible options, click OK, and complete the new criterion.
8. Repeat steps 6 and 7 for additional criteria.
9. Click Save. The dialog box shown in Figure 7.20 opens.

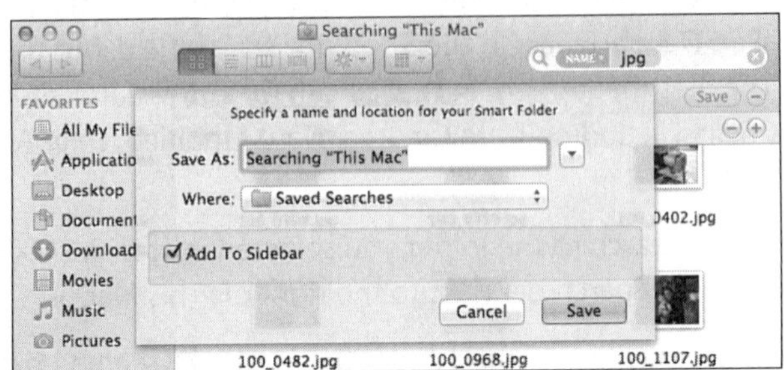

Figure 7.20 *Adding Smart Folders to the sidebar makes them easily accessible.*

10. Type a name and click Save to simultaneously save the search as a Smart Folder in the Saved Searches folder and add the Smart Folder to the Finder sidebar.

You can start the process of creating a Smart Folder by pressing Option-Command-N or by clicking File in the menu bar and clicking New Smart Folder.

Creating a Folder for Burning to a Disc

A burn folder is a special folder that you can create to hold the files you want to burn to a disc. You can drag files into the burn folder or copy and paste them. When you drag or copy files to the folder, Lion creates an alias for each file—a link to the actual file instead of making a real copy of the original.

LET ME TRY IT

Creating a Burn Folder

If you need to send Mom a CD with photos of the kids or you just want to back up some files, you can follow these steps to create the special folder called the burn folder:

1. Open the Finder and open the location where you want to create the burn folder.
2. Click File in the Finder menu bar and then click New Burn Folder. A new folder called Burn Folder appears in the right pane, as shown in Figure 7.21.

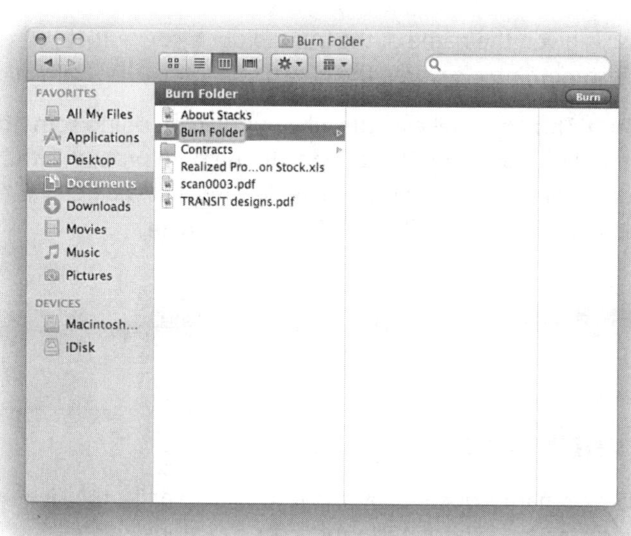

Figure 7.21 *The new Burn Folder is selected and waiting for you to enter a new name.*

3. Type a name for the folder and press Return.
4. Copy or move the files and folders that you want to burn on a disc into the new burn folder.

LET ME TRY IT

Burning the Files to a Disc

After you have placed files in a burn folder, you are ready to burn the disc. Follow these steps:

1. Open the Finder and select the burn folder.
2. Click File in the menu bar and click Burn "*<Folder Name>*" to Disc. (The folder name you have selected appears in the menu command in quotation marks.) You are prompted to insert a blank disc. You can insert a blank disc before you even do step 1, but I prefer to do it at this point because the dialog box that prompts you to insert the disc also tells you how much space you will need on the disc and you can make sure your disk has enough capacity for what you are trying to burn on it.

3. Insert the disc and wait for the prompt to close automatically.
4. The disc is given the name of the burn folder by default. If you want to name it something else, type the new name in the Disc Name field.
5. Click Burn. This could take a little while so plan on doing something else while the disc is burning. The last step in the burn process is the verification. If the disc is verified as reliable, you're finished. If it can't be verified, you'll probably need to use a different disc and try again.

Do not work in the files while they are burning to the disc.

Working with Files

To find, preview, rename, open, copy, move, or delete a file, the Finder is your one-stop-shopping location. Finder performs these functions on files and folders alike. In fact, to the computer, a folder is nothing more than a file. So in this section, when I talk about what you can do with a file, this also includes folders.

Finding Files

One way to find a file is to look for it with your own eyes—the "eyeball method." Suppose you know you created a file called Budget.txt, and you remember you saved it in the Documents subfolder named Personal. You can click the Documents folder in the Finder sidebar, click the triangle beside Personal in the right pane (if you are in the List view), and then just look for the file.

If you can't remember the name of the file, but you know you created it last month, you could sort the files in the folder by date and look for it that way. (In the List view, to sort by date, click the Date Modified column title.)

To sort in any view, click the View menu and click Arrange By. Then click the criterion you want to sort by, such as Name or Date Modified.

Using Color Labels

Applying a colored label to a file is a good way to make the file stand out in a crowd when you are using the eyeball method. To apply a color label, select the file, click the Action button in the Finder's toolbar, and click the color you want from the list shown in Figure 7.22.

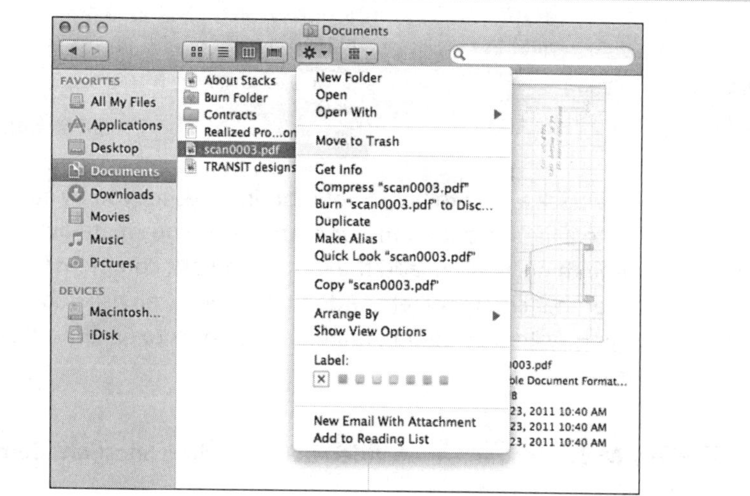

Figure 7.22 *Choose a color from the seven provided to make a file or folder stand out.*

If you apply different color labels to several files, you may benefit from sorting the files by color in the List view, but first, you have to display the Label column in the view. Right-click any column heading and click Label. After you add the column to the view, you can click the column heading to sort on that column.

To make the colored labels even more useful, you can assign a name to each color. Open the Finder preferences and click the Labels tab. Double-click the existing text beside the label ("red," for example), type the name you want to assign, such as "school project," and press Return. Close the preferences window when finished. When you want to apply a color label to a file as described previously, just point to the color to see the name assigned to it.

Using Spotlight in the Finder

The eyeball method is fine to use if you really know where your files are, but what if you have no idea? Then it's time to use the Spotlight to search for the files. To find a file, follow steps 1 through 8 in the "Creating a Smart Folder" instructions earlier in this chapter.

> In Lion you can drag items that Spotlight finds from the results pane into email or into AirDrop. Also new in Lion is the Web Search result. If you select one of these results, Lion opens Safari, searches for the term on the web, and displays the results using your default search engine.

You can stack the deck a little to help Spotlight find files for you by adding Spotlight comments to a file's information. For example, as you create different files that relate to the same thing, you can add the same Spotlight comment to each so that you can search for that comment later. Additionally, you can use Spotlight comments as a tagging system by adding multiple keywords to ensure a file is found by various searches.

SHOW ME **Media 7.4—A Video about Adding Spotlight Comments to Files**
Access this video file through your registered Web Edition at ***my.safaribooksonline.com/9780132819091/media*** *or on the DVD for print books.*

LET ME TRY IT

Adding Spotlight Comments to Files

To add a Spotlight comment to a file, follow these steps:

1. Open the Finder and select the file.
2. Click the Action button in the Finder toolbar.
3. Click Get Information.
4. Type your comments in the Spotlight Comments box at the top (shown in Figure 7.23) and close the window.

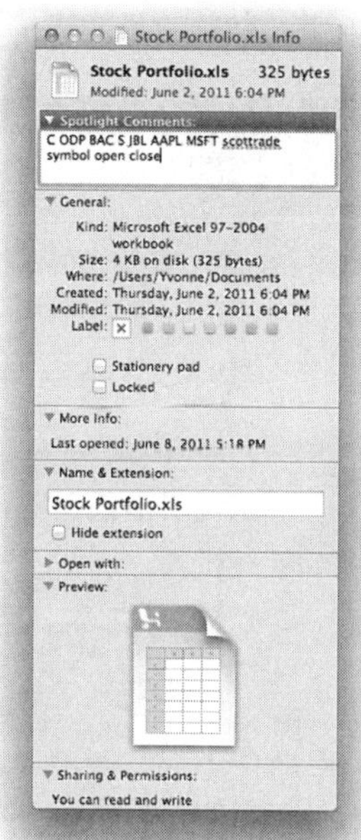

Figure 7.23 *Add Spotlight comments to make files easier to find.*

Using Spotlight in the Menu Bar

The Spotlight button on the far right side of the menu bar is similar to the Spotlight in the Finder, but it is much more powerful. It reaches into the deepest crevices of the computer and finds everything that matches your search criteria. It lists the top 20 results in 14 different categories, including applications, System Preferences, documents, folders, mail messages, contacts, PDF files, web pages in your history, and so on. Figure 7.24 shows the search results for the word *roman*.

You can point to each result and see the item in its own window. To see all the results, click Show All in Finder at the top, and a Finder window opens with all the results displayed. You can sort the items by Name, Kind, or Last Opened by clicking the corresponding column heading.

Using the power of the Spotlight, you can perform many otherwise-lengthy procedures very quickly. Here are a few examples:

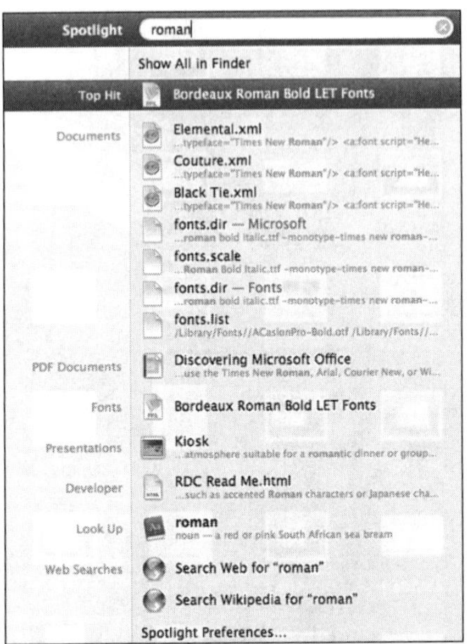

Figure 7.24 *Spotlight lists the result it thinks you are really looking for as the Top Hit.*

- To find the address of a business associate who is listed in your Address Book application, just type the name of the street if you know it, or type the person's name in the Spotlight search box. Spotlight lists the Address Card entry, and you can click the entry to open it.
- To look up a word in the dictionary, type the word in the Spotlight search box and just point to the definition in the list to read it in a pop-up box or click the result to open the Dictionary application where you can look it up in the thesaurus or Wikipedia.
- To do a quick calculation, type the formula in the Spotlight search box, such as .0256 * 5,280 and you will see the answer in the search results.
- To launch an application or utility, type the name of the program and click the link for it. I almost always use this method to open Disk Utility because it is buried in the Utilities folder inside the Applications folder.
- To search for certain types of files, type "**kind:**" followed by the type. For example, you can type "kind: images" or "kind: music." The results show a list of the 20 most recently used files of the type you specify.
- To set the system preferences for a particular feature, type a search phrase such as "screen saver" or "mouse." Click the appropriate link listed under System Preferences.

Using Quick Look

Sometimes you have to see the content of a file to know whether it's the one you want. With the Quick Look feature, you can see the content without actually opening the file. To preview a file with Quick Look, select the file in the folder and press the spacebar or click the Quick Look button in the Finder toolbar (the button that looks like an eye). When the Quick Look window opens, click the Full Screen button in the upper-right corner to see a full screen view. Use an appropriate swiping gesture (depending on your device) to navigate between images or between pages. To exit the Full Screen view, press Esc. When you are finished viewing, press the spacebar again or click the Quick Look button again.

You also can use Quick Look to view several files at one time. Just select all the files you want to view and press the spacebar. The Quick Look preview window shows the first file, and you can use the Next and Previous buttons to navigate through all the files, or you can go into the Full Screen mode and click the Play button to cycle through the files automatically (see Figure 7.25). Using this technique, you can select a group of photographs and create a temporary slideshow with Quick Look. Additionally, while you are in full screen mode, you can use the Camera button to add a photo to iPhoto or use the Index Sheet button to see all the files on a grid.

Figure 7.25 *Each file displays about three seconds in an automatic slideshow.*

If you select a folder instead of a file and click the Quick Look button, you just see a larger image of a folder icon, but you also see information that no other view gives you—the size of the folder. This information is critical, for example, if you need to know whether the content will fit on a CD or DVD. Another way to find out the size of a folder is to select the folder in the right pane of the Finder, click the Actions button in the toolbar, and click Get Info.

Opening and Closing Files

When you are working in an application (such as TextEdit), you can open a file you have created with that application by using the menu command File, Open. A mini version of the Finder opens (see Figure 7.26), and you can navigate to the file and then double-click it to open it.

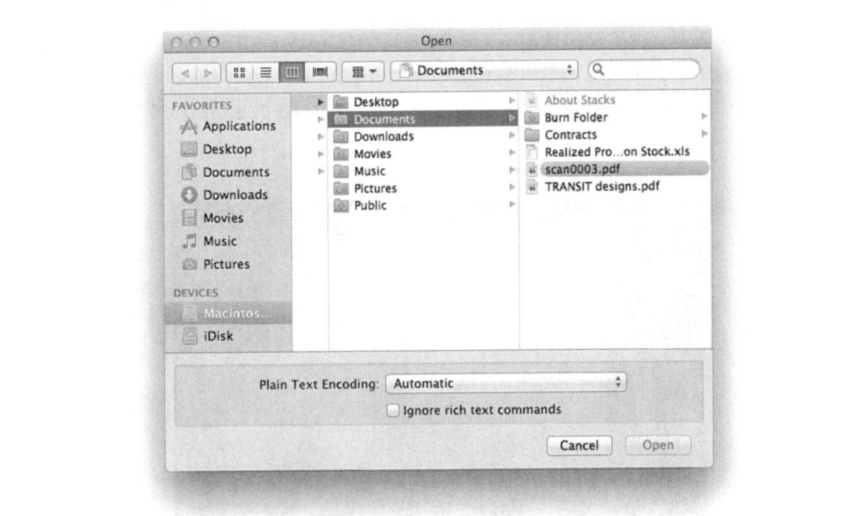

Figure 7.26 *The title bar of the Finder tells you that you're using the Open command.*

If you don't have the application open yet, you can open the Finder, find the file, and double-click it to open it. This obviously opens the application at the same time.

Renaming Files and Folders

On many occasions, you may need to change the name of a file. Maybe you misspelled it, you need a more descriptive name, you need a shorter name, and so on.

To rename a file, select it in the Finder and press Return. Then type the new name and press Return. Remember that a folder is simply a file, so the same steps apply to changing the name of a folder.

Now that you know how to change a folder name, don't get the bright idea that you should change your home folder name from harryhenderson to Harry, for example. Renaming your home folder is a very grave mistake. Recovering from this error is not easy. Data could be and most likely will be lost. Just don't even go there.

In addition to the home folder, you should not rename the following items:

- The system folders found on the hard drive
- Application files
- File extensions (the letters after the period at the end of the filename)

Renaming an application most likely will render it incapable of launching. Renaming it again with the correct name might fix the problem, but it may not. You may have to reinstall the application.

To keep you from accidentally falling into error, Lion does not show the extensions for all files. For example, it hides the .app extensions. If you want to see all file extensions, click Finder, Preferences, Advanced, and select Show All Filename Extensions.

Renaming a file extension may make the file unrecognizable to the application that created it and you may not be able to open the file. In that case, you can simply rename the extension back to its original name and the application will again be able to open the file.

Opening Multiple Finder Windows

By default, the Finder keeps only one window open. This is a good setting because if Finder opened a new window every time you open a different folder, you would soon have your desktop cluttered with Finder windows. There are times, however, when having two Finder windows open at the same time is much more convenient. This facilitates copying from one folder to another or moving a file to a new location.

To open a new Finder window when you need it, click File in the menu bar and then click New Finder Window. Alternatively, you can use the keyboard shortcut Command-N.

Copying Files

You probably know all the reasons you might want to copy a file, so let's get down to basics. No two files can have the same name if they reside in the same folder. If you copy and paste a file in the same folder, Mac OS X automatically appends "copy" to the end of the new filename (just before the extension). If you do it again, Mac OS X appends "copy 2" to the new filename, and so on. If you copy a file from one folder and paste it into a different folder, the copy retains the same name as the original.

LET ME TRY IT

Copying Files Using Shortcut Keys

I like to use a keyboard shortcut to copy and paste files. This method has the added benefit of allowing you to copy the files once, but paste them multiple times. Here's what to do if you want to use shortcut keys to copy files:

1. Open the Finder and select the file (or multiple files) you want to copy.
2. Press Command-C to copy. This one is easy to remember because C stands for copy.
3. In the Finder, select the new location for the file.
4. Press Command-V to paste. I have always remembered this keystroke by thinking of the V as a pointed shovel that is going to plant the file in the new location.
5. Repeat steps 3 and 4 if you want to copy the same files to multiple locations.

If you have trouble remembering the keystrokes, you can always use the menu commands instead. They are Edit, Copy and Edit, Paste. One more way to copy and paste is to use the context menu. Right-click the file you want to copy and click Copy. Then right-click the destination and click Paste Item.

LET ME TRY IT

Copying Files by Dragging

Another way to copy files is by dragging, and here's where opening a new Finder window comes in handy. This is the way I like to proceed if I'm using the dragging method:

1. Open two Finder windows.
2. Set the view in one window to List and the other to Icon. The List view is easier to use to make your selections, and the Icon view gives you a bigger target for dropping the files.
3. In the List view window, select the file (or files) you want to copy.
4. Begin dragging the selection and then press the Option key. A green circle with a plus in it displays to indicate that this is a copying procedure. If you are dragging more than one file, the number of files you are dragging appears in a red circle—just one more new perk in Lion.

Step 4 is a little cumbersome on a trackpad, which is why I prefer the keyboard shortcut.

5. Drop the selection in the right pane of the Icon view window.

Moving Files

If you mistakenly put a file in the wrong folder, then, of course, you will want to move it, but that probably doesn't happen too often. The files I move more than any others are the files I download from the Internet. Remember that these files automatically go into the Downloads folder. For example, each month when I download my American Express bill, it goes into the Downloads folder, and then I move it to my Amex folder located in the Documents folder.

SHOW ME **Media 7.5—A Video about Moving Files by Dragging**
Access this video file through your registered Web Edition at
my.safaribooksonline.com/9780132819091/media
or on the DVD for print books.

Moving Files by Dragging

The steps for moving a file, or a group of files, are almost identical to the steps for copying files by dragging. Follow this procedure to move files:

1. Open two Finder windows.
2. Set the view in one window to List and the other to Icon. As I said before, the List view is easier to use to make your selections, and the Icon view gives you a bigger target for dropping the files.
3. In the List view window, select the file (or files) you want to copy.
4. Begin dragging the selection and then press the Command key. You get no visual cue for the Command key like you do when you press the Option key to copy a file, but If you are dragging more than one file, the number of files you are dragging appears in a red circle as it does when you copy.
5. Drop the selection in the right pane of the Icon view window.

If remembering that the Option key goes with the Copy command and the Command key goes with the Move command is difficult for you, just think of the federal employee who has been *co-opted* (Copy – Option key) by the KGB and is *copying* secret documents. Or think of the fact that you are *commanding* (Command key) the files to *move*!

If you should happen to drag files from one place to another without pressing either the Option key or the Command key, the files may be copied, or they may be moved, depending on the source and destination. If you drag *from* and *to* a location on the *same* disk, Mac OS X moves the files. If you drag *from* one disc *to* another disc, Mac OS X copies the files.

Sending Files by AirDrop

In Lion, you can send files wirelessly to any Lion user around you who also uses AirDrop. (Lion automatically discovers these computers for you. Since AirDrop is a wireless method, the computers must be within range.) To send a file, follow these steps:

1. Open Finder and select the file you want to send.
2. Click the AirDrop icon in the sidebar. All computers that are using AirDrop in the range of your computer appear in the right pane. If the computer owners are in your Address Book, the name, and if available, the photos and Apple IDs for each user appear.

3. Drag the file to the name of the person you want to send the file to and confirm that you want to send it. When the recipient accepts the transfer, Lion transmits the file to the recipient's Download folder. The file is encrypted during transfer and Lion creates a temporary firewall between your computer and the receiving computer during the transfer so no one else can access your computer during the connection.
4. Close the Finder window when finished.

To cancel receiving a file during transfer, click the Downloads icon in the Dock and click the X that appears on the file that is being downloaded.

Moving Files to the Trash (Deleting)

The quickest and easiest way to move a file (or a folder) to the Trash is to select it and press Command-Delete. Another option is to drag the file/folder to the Trash icon in the Dock. If you drag to the Trash icon, be sure you see the word *Trash* before you drop the file or folder. Otherwise, you will have successfully moved the file or folder to the desktop instead of deleting it. One other option is to right-click the item and click Move to Trash on the context menu.

To see what's in the Trash, click the Trash icon. The Finder window opens displaying all the items in the Trash.

With the Finder window open to the Trash folder, you can perform the following tasks:

- Put a previously deleted file back where it originally was by selecting the file and pressing Command-Delete or by clicking File in the menu bar, and then clicking Put Back.
- Empty the trash by clicking the Empty button or by clicking Finder in the menu bar and then clicking Empty Trash. (The command on the menu bar is always available even if the Trash window is not open.) When you empty the trash, the files are permanently deleted. You cannot retrieve them.
- Open a file with Quick Look by selecting the file and pressing the spacebar.

This chapter explains how to work with, install, and update applications.

8

Managing Applications

Applications are the heart and soul of any computer. In this chapter, you learn how to handle application windows on the desktop and how to handle the files that applications create. Think of this as an overview that applies to all the applications discussed individually in subsequent chapters.

Using Launchpad

The Launchpad, one of the new features in OS X Lion that takes its design and functionality from iOS (used in the iPhone, iPad, and iPod), bumped the Applications folder completely off the Dock and established its own icon (a rocket on a silver disc) prominently in the second position on the left—just to the right of the Finder. The Applications folder still exists, but now you use the Launchpad to launch applications from the Dock instead of the Applications folder.

If you upgrade to Lion, the Application folder remains on the Dock if it is there before you upgrade.

When you click the Launchpad icon in the Dock, all your applications (or "apps" in techspeak) display on your Mac in full screen mode, as shown in Figure 8.1. Each app is represented by its icon, and the name of the app appears under the icon. (Some labels under apps are so long they cannot be fully displayed, but you cannot change these labels because they are the actual filenames of the applications.)

Pinch three fingers and your thumb on the Magic Trackpad to open Launchpad.

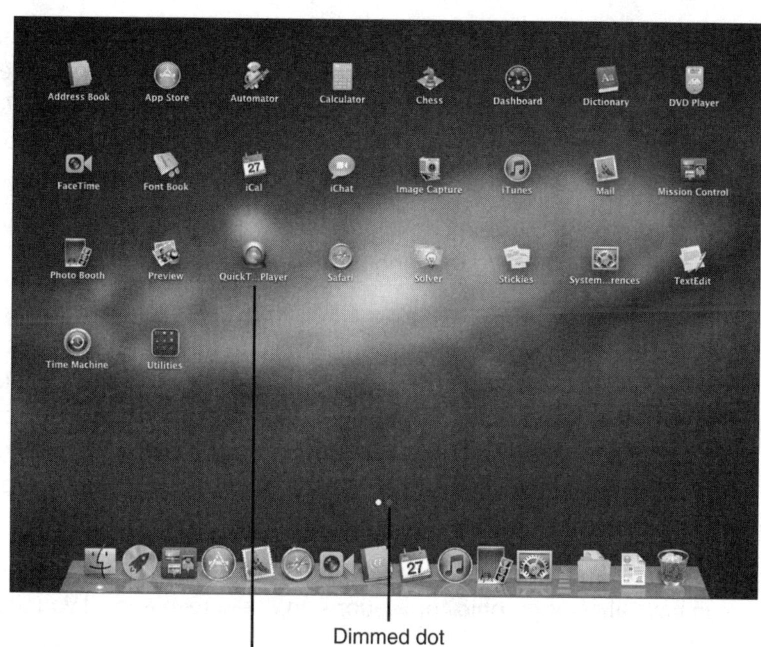

Figure 8.1 *The Launchpad is a full-screen feature.*

Looking at Figure 8.1, you can guess that these are not all the apps on the Mac. Another screen contains more apps. To get to the next screen of apps, you can do one of the following:

- Press the right arrow key.
- Click a dimmed dot (located just above the Dock, as shown in Figure 8.1).
- Do a two-finger swipe from right to left if you have a Magic Mouse or Trackpad. Note that this only works if you have the two-finger swipe preference set to the Navigate option.
- Do a three-finger swipe if you have a Magic Trackpad.

To close the Launchpad, you can click its Dock icon again, press Esc, or click anywhere in the background. The next time you click Launchpad, it redisplays the same page you were on when you closed it. If you had a folder open when you closed Launchpad, it reopens to that folder.

Arranging Apps in the Launchpad

The first thing you will probably want to do is arrange the apps on the screen. You might want the apps you use most to be more accessible—on the first screen and closer to the top perhaps, or maybe you're an alphabetical kind of person. Regardless, you can arrange the app icons in the order you want, on the screens you want, and in the folders you want.

To move app icons, open the Launchpad and simply drag the icons to the new locations. When you are finished rearranging, just click the screen.

Moving an icon from one screen to another is also possible. Just drag the icon to the appropriate edge of the screen (right edge to go to the next screen, left edge to go to the previous screen) and hold it there until the other screen appears. (If you aren't careful when you drag icons to the next or previous screen, you can shoot right past the one you want. If that happens just drag the icon back in the other direction.) When you are on the correct screen, continue dragging the icon to the location where you want to put it on that screen.

Dragging icons to different screens enables you to group applications. For example, you can have all your graphic applications on one screen and all your games on another screen.

> While you are dragging icons around, you might want to drag a few to the left side of the Dock so you can start the application from the Dock instead of the Launchpad.

Adding Apps to the Launchpad

The Launchpad has an icon for every default application installed on your Mac. As you install new applications, from the Mac App Store, for example, more icons are added to the Launchpad. If you install an application from another source and it doesn't place an icon in the Launchpad for you, you can easily add the icons for the applications yourself. Just open the Finder, open the Applications folder, drag the application icon to the Dock, and drop it right on the Launchpad icon.

Working with Folders in the Launchpad

Some software programs break up their code into multiple application files. For example, the software that accompanies one of my Hewlett-Packard printers has the following apps that appear on the second page of my Launchpad: HP Photosmart Stitch, HP Photosmart Share, HP Photosmart Studio, HP Photosmart Create, and so on. To organize the apps that appear in Launchpad and make things a little more compact, I created a folder for all these apps and called it HP. Figure 8.2 shows the open folder in Launchpad.

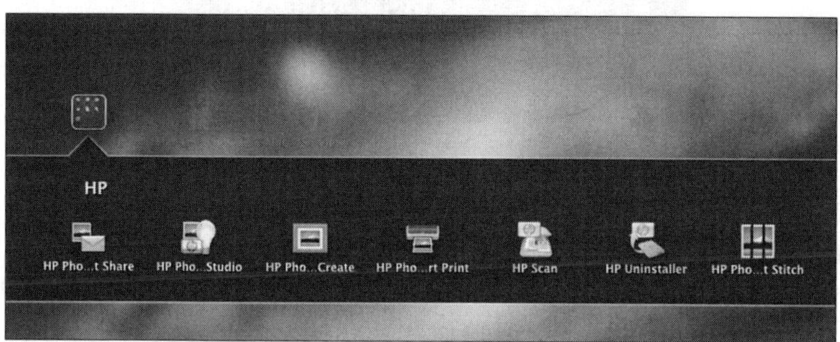

Figure 8.2 *The HP folder holds all the HP applications for the Photosmart printer.*

To access an app in a folder, click the folder to open it and then click the app.

SHOW ME **Media 8.1—A Video about Creating a Folder in Launchpad**
Access this video file through your registered Web Edition at
my.safaribooksonline.com/9780132819091/media
or on the DVD for print books.

LET ME TRY IT

Creating a Folder in Launchpad

To create a folder in Launchpad, follow these steps:

1. Open Launchpad, drag an icon in Launchpad, and drop it on top of another icon in Launchpad that you want to include in the new folder. The two icons appear together in a dark gray band, as shown in Figure 8.3. Lion gives the folder an appropriate name, such as Productivity, Utilities, Board Games, and so on, and it has no qualms about giving a folder the same name as one that already exists.

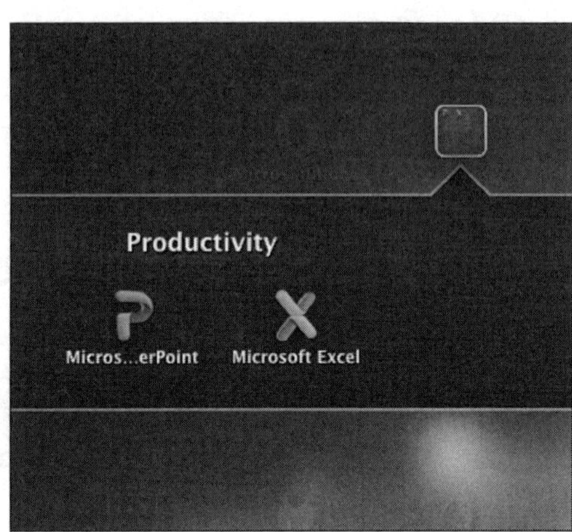

Figure 8.3 *Lion called this folder Productivity.*

2. To rename the folder, click the name, type a new name, and press Return or click the mouse anywhere outside the title box.
3. Click anywhere outside the dark gray band to close the folder.
4. To add additional apps to the folder you just created, drag the app icons individually to the new folder and drop them on the folder icon.

To delete a folder, open it and drag icons out of the folder until the folder disappears.

Deleting Icons in Launchpad

The icons that you see in Launchpad are not aliases or links to the "real" applications; they *are* the applications. So if you delete an icon in Launchpad, you are deleting the actual application. Let me repeat this more strongly. When you delete an icon in the Launchpad, you are permanently and irrevocably deleting the application from your Mac. There is no undo, but, of course, you can always reinstall the application. If you have purchased the app from the App Store, you can reinstall it any time. See "Installing Apps from the Mac App Store" later in this chapter.

LET ME TRY IT

Deleting Applications from Launchpad

Applications that are part of OS X Lion, such as the Address Book, Mail, iTunes, Photo Booth, TextEdit, and so on cannot be deleted within Launchpad, so you are safe there. To delete an application that is not part of the operating system, follow these steps:

1. Open the Launchpad, point to any icon, and click it, holding the mouse button down until all the icons start to wiggle. As shown in Figure 8.4, the icons that you can delete have an X in the upper-left corner.

Figure 8.4 *Launchpad icons that do not have an X cannot be deleted from the Launchpad.*

2. Click the X in the upper-left corner of the application you want to delete. A warning dialog box opens.

As an alternative to steps 1 and 2, you can hold the Option key down while you click the X.

3. Confirm that you want to delete the application by clicking Delete in the dialog box.
4. Delete other icons if desired.
5. Click the screen when finished. The icons stop wiggling.

Opening and Closing Applications

In Lion, when you launch an application, the application icon appears in the Dock (if it doesn't happen to be in the Dock) and a glowing blue bubble displays under the application's icon. By looking at these bubbles, you can always tell whether an application is open or not. Knowing whether an application is running or not is really not that important in Lion any more because when you turn off the computer, you don't have to close all your applications. Three new features that work in conjunction with each other—Autosave, Versions, and Resume—make it unnecessary to save your work and close your applications.

Although the glowing blue bubble still displays in the Dock by default when an app is running, you can turn off this indicator in the preferences window for the Dock. See Chapter 6, "Customizing the Desktop."

Using Autosave

With Autosave, Lion automatically saves your work while you are working so you don't have to. Of course, you have to manually save a new file the first time, but after that, Lion is on the job. Lion automatically saves a version of a document when you open it and at least every hour while you are working on it (or more often if you are making significant changes). Of course, you still can save manually at any time as well.

Before you get too excited about this new feature, a word of caution: Not all third-party applications are on board yet. For example, Microsoft Office for Mac 2011 does not use Lion Autosave or Versions, and if you try to close a Microsoft document, spreadsheet, or presentation without saving it, you're still prompted to save your work. Don't ignore these prompts. If you close without saving, you are going to lose data.

You can witness Autosave in Apple applications, such as TextEdit and Preview. One visual cue you can look for is a pop-up button just to the right of the file's name in the title bar, and if the document has been changed since the last save, the word *Edited* appears to the right of the file name.

Using Versions

When Lion saves a version, it saves it within the document. Using a TimeMachine–like interface (see Figure 8.5), you can browse through the versions and revert to any previous version or copy something from a previous version and paste it into the current version.

In addition to the versions that Lion saves for you automatically, you can save versions yourself. Just click File in the menu bar and click Save a Version.

When you email a file that has versions, only the most current version is sent. None of the other versions are sent.

SHOW ME **Media 8.2—A Video about Browsing Versions**
Access this video file through your registered Web Edition at
my.safaribooksonline.com/9780132819091/media
or on the DVD for print books.

LET ME TRY IT

Browsing Versions

To view all the versions that have been saved in a document type that supports this feature, follow these steps:

1. Click the pop-up button to the right of the document name in the title bar. (If you don't see a pop-up button, just point to the right of the document name, and it will appear.)
2. Click Browse All Versions. Figure 8.5 shows the interface that is so similar to Time Machine.
3. Click the title bar of a version (on the right) to bring it to the front so you can see it. Alternatively, you can click a date on the time line on the right side of the screen.
4. Click Restore to replace the current document with the version selected on the right. You are returned to the application window and the document version you restored is the current version.
5. If you don't want to make any changes, click Done.

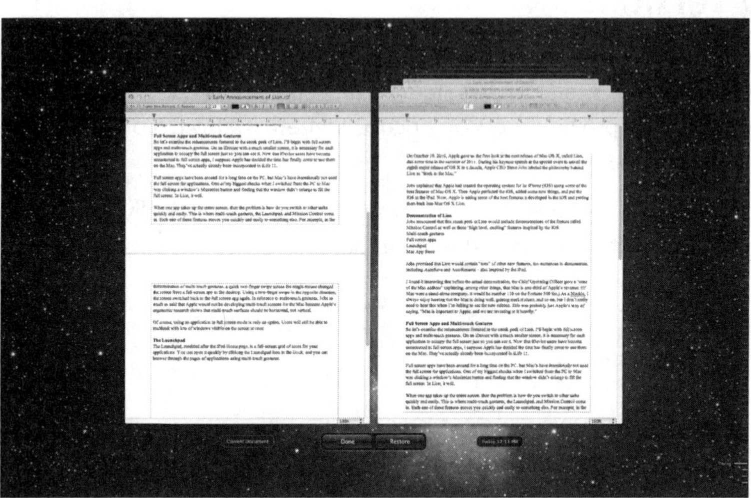

Figure 8.5 *The current document is on the left and the versions are on the right.*

LET ME TRY IT

Deleting a Version

You can weed out some of the versions that you know you don't want by deleting them. To delete a version, follow these steps:

1. Click the pop-up button to the right of the document title in the current document window. (If you don't see a pop-up button, just point to the right of the document name, and it will appear.)

2. Click Browse All Versions.

3. Click the title bar of the version you want to delete. It comes to the top (if it wasn't the version on the top).

4. Point to the right side of the document title and click the pop-up button. Click Delete This Version, as shown in Figure 8.6. A warning dialog box opens.

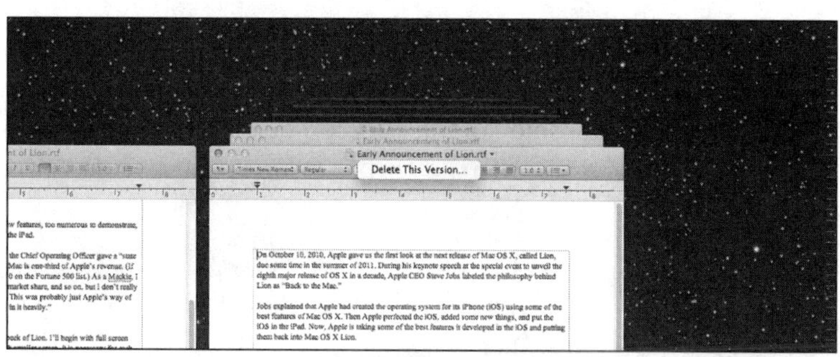

Figure 8.6 *The pop-up button in the version isn't visible until you point at it.*

5. Click Delete in the dialog box.

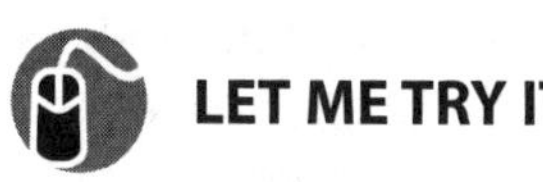

LET ME TRY IT

Saving a Version as a New Document

Undoubtedly you have used the Save As command to save a new file based on the current file. In Apple applications that use versions, that command is gone. It's been replaced with Duplicate, but saving a version as a new document is an even better option because you can do it at any time and with as many different versions as you want. To save a version as a new document, follow these steps:

1. Click the pop-up button to the right of the document name in the title bar of the current document window. (If you don't see a pop-up button, just point to the right of the document name, and it will appear.)
2. Click Browse All Versions.
3. Click the title bar of the version you want to save as a new document.
4. Press the Option key; the Restore button on the screen changes to Restore a Copy. Click this button while you have the Option key depressed. A new document opens in a new window. The name of the new document is the same as the original document with the word *copy* appended to the end (after the extension).
5. Click File in the menu bar and click Save.
6. Give the file an appropriate name, specify the save location in the Where field, and click Save.

Using Resume

The Resume feature, which is enabled by default, allows you to close an application with your documents and inspector windows still open and resume just where you left off (right down to the position of the insertion point) the next time you launch the application.

An inspector window for an application could be a color palette, a font box, a media browser, a list of layers, and so on. It is a window that enables you to change or enhance a file.

If you have unsaved work when you close an application or shut down your Mac, the AutoSave feature also kicks in to save your work. For example, suppose you are in the middle of editing a contact card in your address book. You have made several changes to the card, but you have not clicked Done yet. If you quit the Address Book application and then relaunch it, your Address Book will reopen to the contact card you were working on and the AutoSave feature will have saved the edits you made to the card.

The Resume feature works the same way if you shut down your Mac with all your apps open. The next time you start the Mac, all the applications and their files that you had open previously reopen.

If, for some reason, you want to turn off the Resume feature in applications, open the General system preferences and clear the check mark for the Restore Windows When Quitting and Re-Opening Apps option. The change in the option does not take effect until the next time you log in.

If you want to turn off the Resume feature when restarting the Mac, clear the check mark for the Reopen Windows When Logging Back In option (in the dialog box that opens when you shut down or log out), as shown in Figure 8.7. The next time you log out or shut down your computer, the check mark for this option will be back in the dialog box!

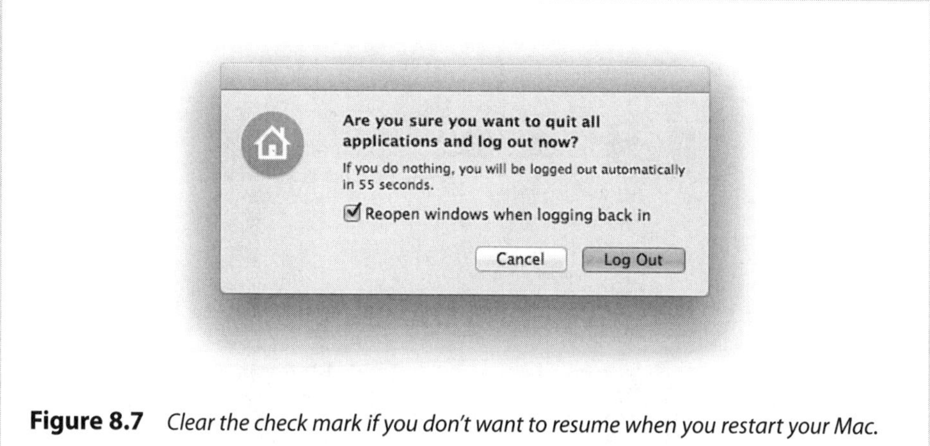

Figure 8.7 *Clear the check mark if you don't want to resume when you restart your Mac.*

Forcing an Application to Quit

It doesn't happen too often, but sometimes an application quits responding—that's computer-speak for *freezes up*. When this happens, the SBBOD (Spinning Beach Ball of Death) appears and keeps spinning indefinitely. It means that you have to force the application to quit.

Historically, Windows PC users were so used to programs freezing up that they hardly thought anything of it. PC users called the reboot keystroke combination (Ctrl-Alt-Del) the "three-fingered salute." For a Mac, the keystroke Command-Option-Esc opens the Force Quit Applications window.

LET ME TRY IT

Force Quitting a Frozen Application

If you have to force an application to quit, you may lose unsaved data! Some applications automatically back up your file while you are working, so you might not lose everything—just what you have done between the automatic save and the time the application freezes. To close an unresponsive application, follow these steps:

1. Press Command-Option-Esc. The Force Quit Applications window opens as shown in Figure 8.8. The window lists all applications that are running.

Figure 8.8 *This window shows that Preview is frozen.*

2. Select the unresponsive application in the window and click Force Quit. A dialog box opens asking, "Do you want to force *<application name>* to quit?"
3. Click Force Quit. A dialog box opens and you can either send a report to Apple or just ignore the incident. If you click Report, a report will be sent to Apple (if you have an Internet connection), but you will never receive any feedback. The report simply serves to help Apple improve its applications.
4. Close the Force Quit window.

Instead of using the shortcut keys (Command-Option-Esc), you can click the Apple menu and click Force Quit. The trick is that you can't click the Apple menu while you are in the frozen program. You have to click into another application (such as Finder) and then click the Apple menu. Memorizing Command-Option-Esc is really much easier. Alternatively, you can right-click the application icon in the Dock and click Force Quit.

Working with Windows

By default, when you launch an application, it opens in a window. A window's shape is defined by a title bar at the top and boundaries on all three other sides. Some windows have a bar at the bottom called a status bar.

Using Full Screen Mode

In previous versions of Mac OS X, an application window never took up the entire screen, not even when you clicked the Maximize button (the green button in the title bar). If you wanted the window to occupy the entire screen, you had to stretch it out manually. In Lion, you have a new Full Screen mode that hides all extraneous elements, such as menu bars and toolbars, and automatically sizes the window to occupy the full screen. The theory is that the full screen mode allows the user to focus his full attention on the window without distractions.

Not all third-party applications support this feature yet.

To enter Full Screen mode, click the control in the upper-right corner of the window. (The control has two arrows pointing in opposite directions.) When in Full Screen mode, point to the bottom of the screen to redisplay the Dock if you need to use it. Point to the top edge of the screen to redisplay the menu bar and toolbar so they are accessible. While the menu bar is displayed, you can click the Full Screen control again to exit Full Screen mode.

If you have several full screen windows open, you can swipe left and right with two fingers to move between them (using a Magic Mouse or a Magic Trackpad). Of course, you must have your preferences set for this gesture.

Using the Normal Screen Mode

When you have multiple windows open at the same time in the normal screen mode, you need to know how to navigate between them, resize them, move them, and so on.

Resizing and Moving Windows

If you need to make a window larger or smaller, point to any corner or any window edge and drag the window to the desired size. Another way to resize a window is to use the green Zoom button on the left side of a window's title bar. The Zoom button alternates between a larger and smaller size window. It works like this: You open a window and it opens to a particular size. You use the sizing handle to make the window larger. You click the Zoom button and the window goes back to the smaller size. You click the Zoom button again and the window goes back to the larger size. The opposite also works. You can make the window smaller than it was when it first opened and use the Zoom button to alternate between those two sizes.

To move a window to another location on the screen, point to the title bar and drag it. This works for all applications. One application, the Address Book, has additional moving capabilities. You can actually click anywhere on the Address Book and drag it to another location.

You can also drag part of the window off the screen at the left or right edge or at the bottom of the screen. This capability can come in handy when you need as much space on the screen as you can get.

Minimizing Windows

When you want to remove an application window from the screen temporarily, you can minimize it by clicking the yellow Minimize button in the upper-left corner of the window. By default, minimizing a window sends a preview of the window down to an icon on the right side of the Dock.

If you have folders on the right side of the Dock that use the stack icon, differentiating a stack from a minimized window is difficult. That's why I like to use folder icons for stacks. To learn how to change a stack to a folder, see Chapter 6.

Another problem with windows that are minimized to the Dock is that you can't always tell what they are. When you are ready to open one back up on the desktop, you might not be able to tell which icon in the Dock to click. You can view all the windows at once to help you determine which one you want. Right-click the application's icon in the Dock and click Show All Windows. Minimized windows for the application display below the line as thumbnails, as shown in Figure 8.9, and open windows display above the line. Click the window you want to make active or press Esc to exit this mode.

An alternative to minimizing the window to the right side of the Dock is minimizing to the application icon on the left side of the Dock. To make this the default, click the System Preferences icon and click Dock. Click Minimize Windows into Application Icon. Both methods have pros and cons, and I discuss them for you in the following audio recording.

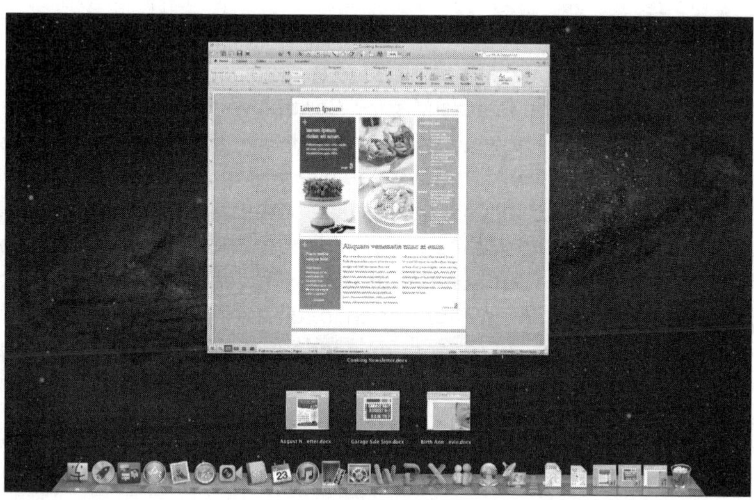

Figure 8.9 *Minimized windows display as thumbnails.*

TELL ME MORE **Media 8.3—A Discussion about Contrasting Two Methods for Minimizing Windows**

Access this audio recording through your registered Web Edition at ***my.safaribooksonline.com/9780132819091/media*** *or on the DVD for print books.*

Closing Windows

Another way to manage open windows is to close the ones you aren't currently using with the red Close button in the title bar. In many cases, closing an application's window does not close the application. It simply hides the window in the application's icon on the Dock. If you click the application's icon, the window opens again.

Switching Between Windows on the Desktop

Instead of minimizing windows, if it is more conducive to what you are doing, then you can leave all your windows open on the desktop and size and arrange them so they are all visible at once. For instance, you might have two windows side by side, with three other windows underneath. Of course, only one window at a time can be active. To make a different window active, click any visible part of the window. If there is no visible part of the window to click, then click the application's icon in the Dock to bring the window forward.

Using Mission Control

Working in smaller windows, as described in the previous topic, can be limiting, but thanks to the new Lion feature Mission Control, you don't have to! You can make all your windows as large as you want and navigate between them using Mission Control. Mission Control shows you everything that is running on your Mac, including Dashboard, all your spaces (see "Working with Spaces" later in this chapter), and all open windows. As shown in Figure 8.10, the row at the top contains a thumbnail for the Dashboard, a thumbnail for each desktop (or space) you have set up, and if you have any apps open in full screen, they also have individual thumbnails across the top. All other open windows are grouped by application below the row of thumbnails. All you have to do to navigate to a different window or space or even the Dashboard is click it in Mission Control.

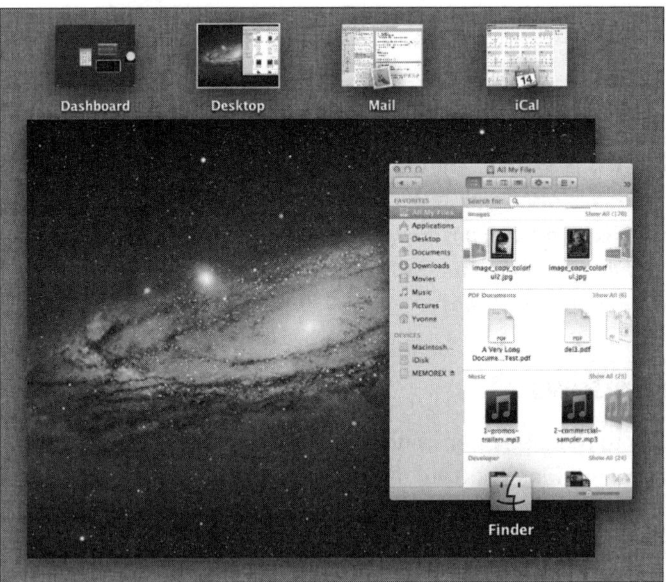

Figure 8.10 *By default Mission Control considers Dashboard a space and displays it at the top of the screen.*

You can open Mission Control in several ways:

- Click the Mission Control icon in the Dock.
- Swipe up on your trackpad using three fingers.
- Press the Mission Control key (F3).

- Press Control-Up-Arrow.
- Click Launchpad in the Dock and click Mission Control.
- Point to a hot corner that has been assigned to Mission Control. (A hot corner is any corner of the screen that performs a function that has been assigned to it.)

To assign Mission Control to a hot corner, click the System Preferences icon in the Dock and click Mission Control. Click Hot Corners. Click the pop-up button for the corner you want to assign, click Mission Control, and click OK. Close the preferences window.

There are also several ways to close Mission Control. You can press the same keys again that you used to open Mission Control, swipe down on your trackpad with three fingers, or (my favorites) press Esc or click on a blank spot on the desktop.

Working with Spaces

The Spaces feature lets you organize windows into groups that you can display on the same desktop. Each space is like having a separate monitor attached to your computer. You can use Spaces to divide your work into different areas. For example, in one space you could trade stocks and use your spreadsheet application to track your trades; in another space you could use iPhoto and PhotoShop. By using different spaces, you also keep your desktop from getting cluttered.

SHOW ME **Media 8.4—A Video about Creating Spaces**

Access this video file through your registered Web Edition at ***my.safaribooksonline.com/9780132819091/media*** *or on the DVD for print books.*

Creating Spaces

In previous versions of OS X you were limited to four spaces, but in Lion you can create as many spaces as you need. To create a space, follow these steps:

1. Open Mission Control.
2. Point to the upper-right corner of the screen until you see a plus, as shown in Figure 8.11.

Figure 8.11 *The plus only shows up when you point to the area.*

3. Click the plus. Mission Control adds a Desktop to the line of thumbnails in the top row.

SHOW ME **Media 8.5—A Video about Adding Applications to a Space**
Access this video file through your registered Web Edition at
my.safaribooksonline.com/9780132819091/media
or on the DVD for print books.

LET ME TRY IT

Adding Applications to a Space

Suppose that you are creating a space to work on your schedule and email. Having three applications assigned to this space would be helpful: Address Book, iCal, and Mail. Follow these steps to assign an application to a space:

1. Open Mission Control.
2. Click the Desktop icon at the top for the space to which you want to assign the application. Mission Control closes itself and opens that space.

3. Right-click the icon in the Dock for the application you want to assign and click Options. If the application doesn't have an icon in the Dock you must open the application so it will.

4. As shown in Figure 8.12, your choices under Assign To are All Desktops, This Desktop, and None. Additionally if the icon is already assigned to a Desktop you will see the Desktop listed with a check mark beside it. Click This Desktop.

Figure 8.12 *The pop-up menu for icons in the Dock allows you to assign an app to a space.*

If you select All Desktops, whenever you launch the application in one desktop, it will open in all of them. If you select None, the application will open in whatever desktop you are working in.

5. Repeat steps 3 and 4 for all applications you want to add to the space.

If all this seems a bit confusing, I recommend that you get used to working with multiple windows on one desktop before you try using Spaces.

After you have spaces set up you can move from one desktop to another using one of these methods:

- Swipe left or right with three fingers to scroll left or right through the spaces.
- Open Mission Control and click the Desktop you want to go to.
- Press the Control key in conjunction with the number key for the number of the desktop you want to go to.
- Press the Control key in conjunction with the left or right arrow key to scroll left or right.

Deleting a Space

When you no longer need a space you have set up, such as Desktop 2, Desktop 3, and so on, you can delete it, but you cannot delete the space called Desktop—the default desktop. Follow these steps to delete a space:

1. Open Mission Control.
2. Point to the Desktop you want to delete until you see a Close button appear in the upper-right corner.
3. Click the Close button.

Installing and Updating Applications

Mac OS X comes with quite a few applications that will take you a long way, but unless you only use your Mac for email and surfing the web, inevitably you will want or need to install some additional applications on your Mac eventually.

Installing Apps from the Mac App Store

Installing applications on a Mac has always been simple, especially compared to installing a program on a PC. With the new Mac App Store, installing a program is completely automated. All you do is find the application you want, click one button, sign in to the App Store with your Apple ID, if you aren't already signed in, and then you can walk away if you like. The App Store downloads the application to Launchpad. While the application is downloading, a progress bar appears under the Launchpad icon in the Dock. When the progress bar is gone, the program is installed and ready to launch.

> Don't worry. If you lose your Internet connection during the download, the Mac App Store will restart the download when the connection is restored. If you had to quit the Mac App Store during the middle of the download for some reason, the Mac App Store will restart the download the next time you launch the App Store.

LET ME TRY IT

Installing Purchased Apps on All Your Macs

After you have purchased an application or downloaded a free application, you can install it on all your Macs free of charge! You can do this several ways, but in my opinion, the following is the easiest and most straightforward method. Follow these steps:

1. Launch the App Store on a Mac that does not have the application installed.

2. Sign in with your Apple ID (click Store, Sign In) and click Purchased in the toolbar. A list, like the one shown in Figure 8.13, displays all the apps you have purchased or downloaded for free. If the application has an Install button beside it, you can install it on the current computer.

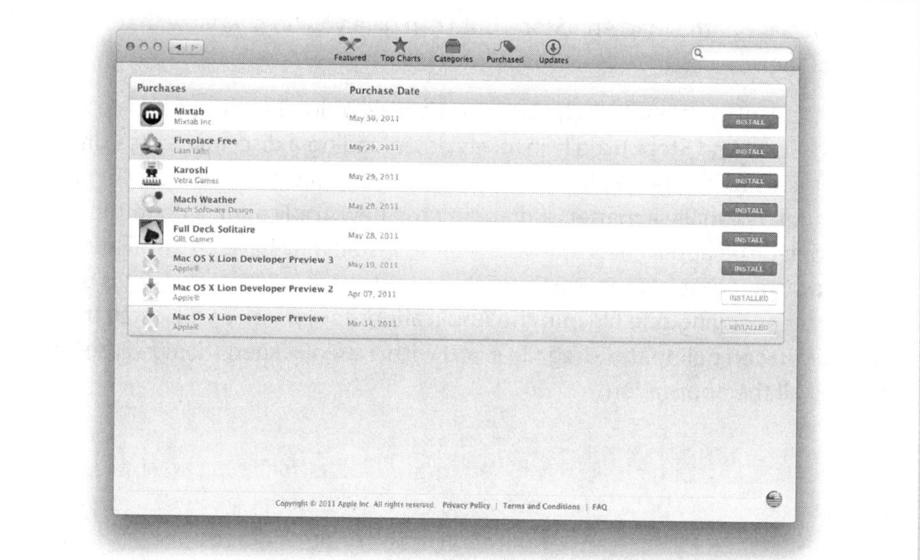

Figure 8.13 *All your purchased and free applications display on this list.*

3. Click the Install button for the application you want to install. Repeat this step for as many of the applications as you want to install to the current computer.

4. Repeat steps 1 through 3 for every Mac that you want to install the applications on.

The steps above also work for reinstalling an application.

Installing Updates from the Mac App Store

If an application that you have purchased from the App Store has an update that needs to be installed, you will see a number on the App Store icon in your Dock. For example, if two updates are available for two of the apps you have purchased, the App Store icon will have the number two on it.

To update your apps, go to the App Store and log in, if necessary. Click Updates in the toolbar and then click the updates you want to install.

Installing Other Mac Applications

Of course, applications are still out there that are not sold through the Mac App Store. To install one of these programs, you have to go back to the old-school methods. Naturally, I can't cover the exact steps for installing every application that exists outside of the Mac App Store, but I can give you an overview that covers most of them.

The process of installing an app that you have downloaded from a source other than the Mac App Store usually involves downloading a disc image file (.dmg), which needs to be opened in order to access the application file. Installing the application is usually a matter of dragging the new application icon to the Applications folder. The application that you want to install may have an installation or setup assistant that guides you through the process, but the end result is usually the same—copying one file into the Applications folder. After you install the application, you can delete the .dmg file if you wish. I usually keep them in case I need to reinstall the application.

The Applications folder is always the suggested folder for installing applications, but you can install applications anywhere in your Home folder, and they will run perfectly well. By installing an application in your Home folder, however, you make it inaccessible to others who log on to your computer. Generally, no good reason exists to install an application anywhere but in the Applications folder, unless you are *trying* to deny other users access to the program.

Getting the Most from the Mac App Store

You can shop for applications in the App Store in a couple of ways. You can browse through apps by clicking the Featured button in the toolbar or the Top Charts button. Featured apps fall into these categories: New and Noteworthy, What's Hot, and Staff Favorites. The Top Charts fall into these categories: Top Paid (in other words the applications with a fee attached that were downloaded the most times), Top Free, and Top Grossing.

Another way to shop is to click Categories in the toolbar and select one to browse. Figure 8.14 shows the Categories page.

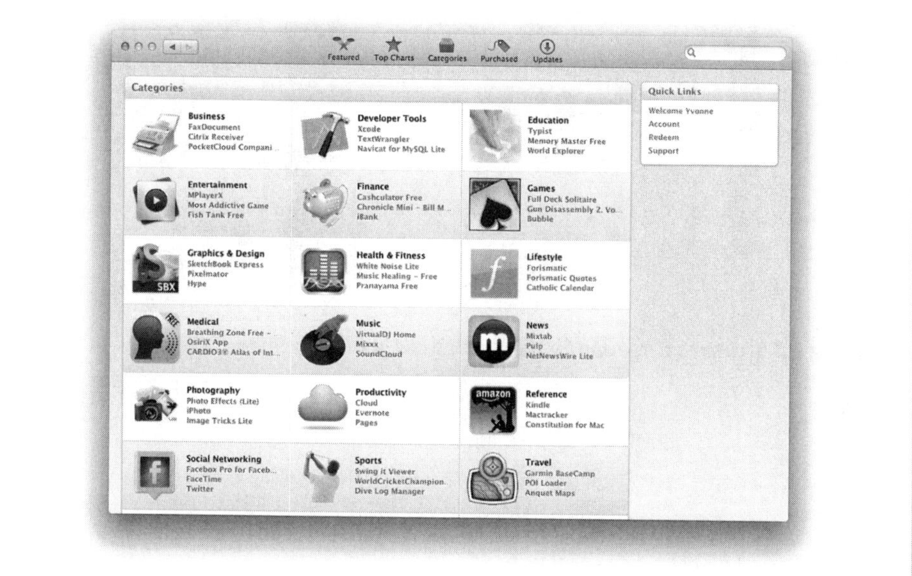

Figure 8.14 *Click a category to select it.*

Finally, you can search for an application using the Spotlight search field. You might search for a keyword that describes the application you are looking for, a manufacturer's name, the application name, and so on,

When one of these three methods yields a result that you might be interested in, you can click the app's name or icon to get more information about it. Figure 8.15 shows the typical information that you can find on an app. At the top of the screen is a description of the application and the cost. Below the description are graphics of the application, and to the right of the graphics is information such as the released date, the version number, the size of the file, the requirements, and so on. To me the Customer Ratings and the Customer Reviews, below the graphics (see

Figure 8.16), are the most helpful information on the page. Notice in Figure 8.16 that you can sort the reviews by Most Helpful, Most Favorable, Most Critical, and Most Recent.

Figure 8.15 *Here's a free app for the classic word game Hangman.*

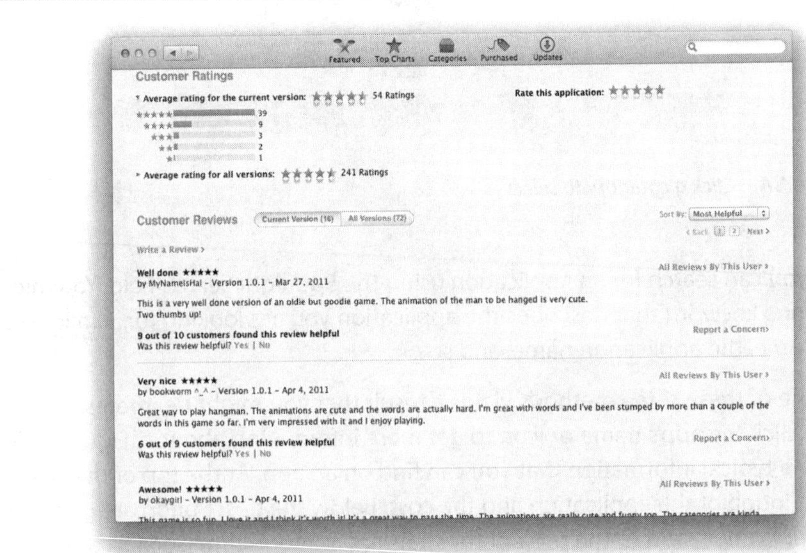

Figure 8.16 *User reviews can help you decide whether the app is for you or not.*

Controlling Access to Applications

Using Parental Controls, you can simplify the version of Finder; deny a user access to all applications, widgets, and utilities except the ones you specify; limit or deny use of App Store Applications; and block the user from modifying the Dock. Additionally, you can view a log of the applications that the user has accessed.

LET ME TRY IT

Setting Parental Controls for Apps

To set parental controls for applications, follow these steps:

1. Click the System Preferences icon in the Dock.
2. Click Users & Groups (in the fourth row).
3. Click the padlock and type your password. If you do not have an Administrative account, you must enter the name and password of an Administrative account. Click Unlock and the padlock opens.
4. Select the user account you want to restrict from the list in the sidebar.
5. Click the Enable Parental Controls check box, if necessary.
6. Click the Open Parental Controls button.
7. Click the Apps tab, if necessary. Figure 8.17 shows the Apps pane.
8. To simplify the Finder, click the check box for Use Simple Finder. When you select this option, the Dock is also simplified and the user is automatically not allowed to modify the Dock.
9. To limit the applications, click Limit Applications and then make selections for Allow App Store Apps and Allowed Apps. Any application you do not allow that usually appears on the Dock will still appear on the Dock, but when the user tries to launch the application, a dialog box opens explaining that the user does not have permission to use the application. An administrator can override the control by clicking Always Allow or Allow Once. Of course, the administrator has to type his name and password.

Figure 8.17 *You can limit the applications a user has access to on this pane.*

Your choices for App Store Apps range from don't allow access to any app purchased through the store to allow access to all apps. In between these two ranges are ratings that are used by the App Store to advise parents of the suitability of an app for a certain age child. The rating "up to 4+" has no objectionable material. The rating "up to 9+" may not be suitable for children under 9 years of age, and so on.

10. If you have not selected Use Simple Finder, you can select Allow User to Modify Dock.
11. Close the window when finished. Lion locks the padlock for you.

To see what applications the user has been accessing, you can return to the Apps screen and click the Logs button. The log lists the number of times an application has been used and the total time it has been used.

This chapter focuses on the unique features of Safari that make web browsing more efficient and enjoyable.

9

Browsing the Web

The Internet has grown to such huge proportions that even its inventors could not come close to imagining its potential at its inception in 1969. All you need to tap into it is an Internet service provider (ISP). Mac supplies everything else you need in the way of hardware (a modem) and software (the web browser called Safari).

This chapter assumes you already know a great deal about browsing the web, so no time is wasted on covering the basics, so it does not cover how to type a web address or what a hyperlink is. Instead, this chapter discusses some of the features in Safari that will turn you into more of a power user on the web, including browsing in tabs or windows, setting parental controls, working with bookmarks and the new Reading List feature, saving web content, customizing the toolbar, and adding extensions to Safari.

Launching Safari for the First Time

To launch Safari, click the Safari icon in the Dock—the one that looks like a blue compass—or click its icon in Launchpad. The first time you launch the application, it welcomes you and displays previews of a dozen popular websites, as shown in Figure 9.1. At the bottom of the screen, it explains that as you browse the web, it will take note of your favorite sites and display them above (instead of the ones it has preselected for you).

At this point, you can do any of the following things:

- Click one of the website previews to go to that site.
- Type a web address in the box at the top left and press Return to go to a specific website.
- Type a search phrase in the Google search box at the top right and press Return to display Google search results.

Apple's own website is the first preview in the first row. If you are a new Mac user, I recommend that you go there first and familiarize yourself with the site. When you are finished browsing, click Safari in the menu bar and click Quit Safari.

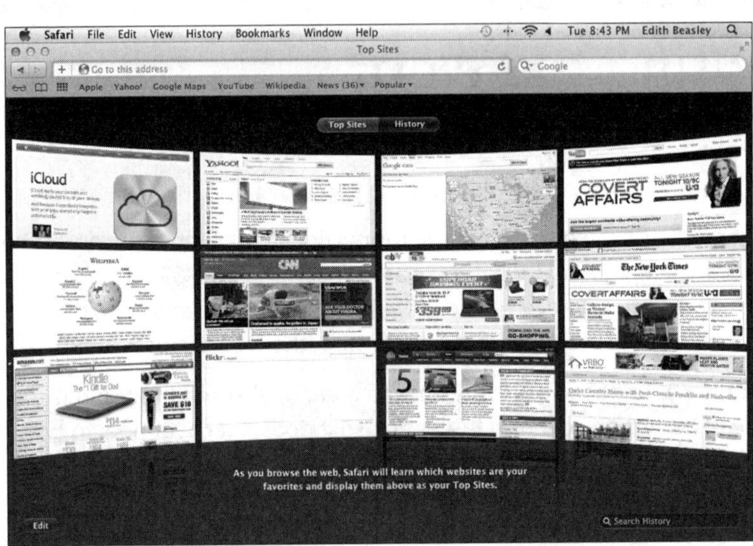

Figure 9.1 *To see a short description and the address of a previewed web page, point to the preview.*

The next time you launch Safari, don't expect to see the 12 previews again. By default, Safari is set up to go straight to "startpage" on the Apple website. Then the next time you launch Safari, the last page you viewed will open. This is because in Lion, applications resume where they left off.

Setting Safari Preferences

To get the most from your Internet experience, knowing how Safari is set up and how you can customize its operation for the way you like to browse is a good idea. As you probably already know, most of the settings for Safari are made in the Preferences window.

To set Safari preferences, click Safari on the menu bar and then click Preferences. On the General pane of Safari's preference window, as shown in Figure 9.2, you can see that the New Window Opens With preference is Homepage. That's why you don't see Top Sites when you launch Safari after the first time. If you want to use Top Sites when you open Safari, change this preference to Top Sites. Top Sites *is* the default for New Tabs Open With, which means that if you use tabs for web browsing instead of windows, each new tab you open will open with Top Sites. If I have to connect to the Internet using my broadband wireless modem, I change this setting to Empty Page because I don't like to wait for the Top Sites to load every single time I open a tab—not that they take that long, mind you. I'm just a nanosecond kind of girl.

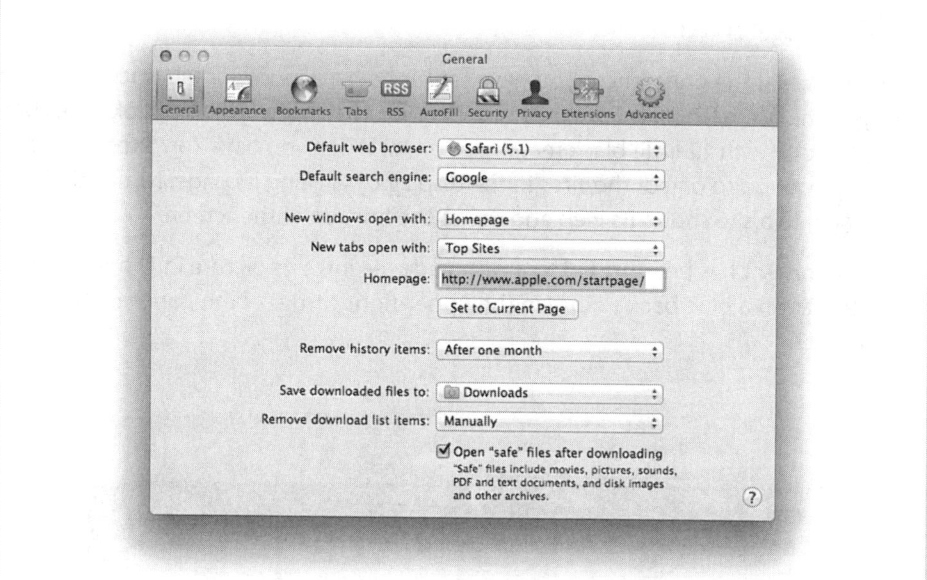

Figure 9.2 *Click Safari, Preferences, General to get to this pane.*

Now notice that the Homepage preference is set for the Apple website. Even if you don't set Safari to open to a home page, you should still change the Homepage preference to the address of a site that you frequent. Later in this chapter, you learn how to add a button to the toolbar that will take you immediately to the home page you specify here. If you know the address you want to use, you can type it in the text box now, or at some point, when you are on the website, you can come back to this window and click the Set to Current Page button.

One other important preference that Mac OS X turns on for you by default is the blocking of pop-up windows. This setting is located on the Safari menu.

I would describe all other preferences in Safari as "fine-tuned." You don't need to worry about them. If you're concerned about security, don't be. You can refer to Chapter 16, "Keeping Your Mac Safe, Updated, and Backed Up," if you are curious.

TELL ME MORE **Media 9.1—A Discussion about Setting Safari Preferences**

Access this audio recording through your registered Web Edition at ***my.safaribooksonline.com/9780132819091/media*** *or on the DVD for print books.*

Using Top Sites

Regardless of the preferences you have set for how a window or tab opens, you can toggle the use of Top Sites anytime with the Top Sites button in the Bookmarks bar. (It's the one with 12 little black rectangles on it.) When you have Top Sites turned on, you can go to one of the sites in the display by clicking its page. Notice that pointing to a site shows its web address at the bottom of the screen.

If new content has been added to a web page recently, its picture in Top Sites has a white star on a blue background in the upper-right corner of the page, as shown in Figure 9.3.

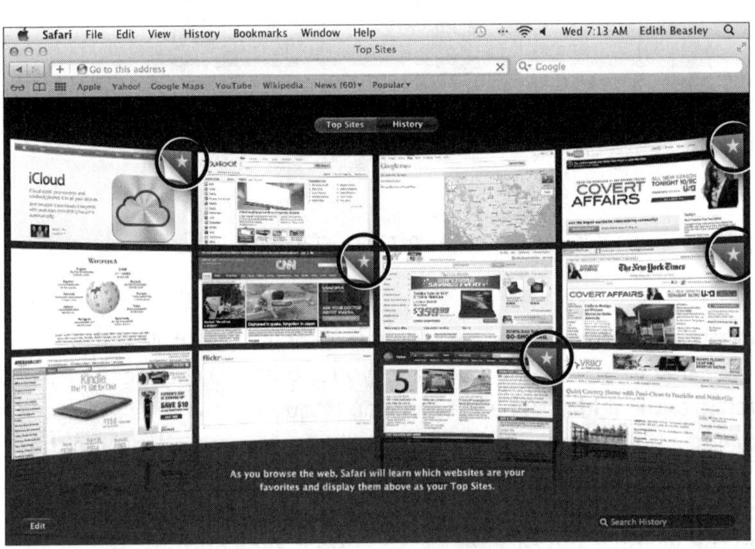

Figure 9.3 *The new content stars help keep you current on your favorite sites.*

SHOW ME **Media 9.2—A Video about Customizing Top Sites**

Access this video file through your registered Web Edition at ***my.safaribooksonline.com/9780132819091/media*** *or on the DVD for print books.*

LET ME TRY IT

Customizing Top Sites

Remember that Lion provides you with default sites when you first start using Top Sites, but you can quickly make Top Sites exactly what you want. To customize Top Sites, follow these steps:

1. If necessary, click the Top Sites button to display Top Sites.
2. Click the Edit button at the bottom left of the screen (refer to Figure 9.3).
3. Choose Small, Medium, or Large for the display.
4. Click the X button to eliminate a site.
5. Click the Pin button to keep a site from being replaced.
6. To add a site, open another window, go to the site, and then drag the icon in front of the website address to the Top Site window and drop the address where you want it in the order.

Some websites, such as Google, for example, have their own icons, but if a site doesn't have a proprietary icon, the generic icon of a globe appears before the address.

7. Rearrange the sites by dragging them to different locations.
8. When you are finished customizing, click the Done button.

You don't have to be customizing Top Sites to add a site. Any time you have a webpage open that you want to add to Top Sites you can add it by clicking Bookmarks in the menu bar. Then click Add Bookmark and select Top Sites from the pop-up menu. You can type a different name for the site if you want and then click Add.

Setting Parental Controls

If you have children of your own or supervise children, you undoubtedly have given them some guidelines you want them to follow concerning computer use. With Mac OS X, you can help enforce the guidelines using Parental Controls.

Using the Parental Controls feature, you can control the following web activities:

- Allow unrestricted access to websites or restrict access to adult websites and list additional websites you want to restrict.
- Restrict access to *all* sites *except* the ones you specify.
- Restrict the amount of time the computer is used.

SHOW ME **Media 9.3—A Video about Setting Parental Controls for Web Use**

Access this video file through your registered Web Edition at ***my.safaribooksonline.com/9780132819091/media*** *or on the DVD for print books.*

LET ME TRY IT

Setting Parental Controls for Web Use

If you have user accounts set up on your Mac for children, you can set parental controls to ensure your guidelines for web usage are being followed—at least on your computer. To set parental controls, follow these steps:

1. Click the System Preferences icon in the Dock and click Users & Groups.
2. Click the padlock icon and type your password. If you do not have an Administrative account, you must enter the name and password of an Administrative account. Click Unlock and the padlock opens, allowing you to make changes.
3. Select the user account you want to restrict, click Enable Parental Controls, and then click Open Parental Controls.
4. Click the Web tab, shown in Figure 9.4, and set the options you want. It's difficult to limit a user to websites that might have adult content even if you try to list all the sites you don't want to allow. I find, for limiting what children can see, it is easier to select Allow Access to Only These Websites. Lion has a good start on sites that are acceptable and of interest to children. You can add to these as more sites come to your attention.
5. Close the window. Lion locks the padlock for you.

Figure 9.4 *Websites you might want to allow access to are listed, but you can add or remove sites from this list.*

Browsing in Tabs or Windows

By default, when you click a link to go to a new page, Safari opens that page in the current window. If you want to work in more than one window, you can click File in the menu bar and click New Window. Browsing in multiple windows allows you to compare websites side by side or open two windows to the same website so that you can follow different links.

If you frequently want to open two windows on the same site to follow different links in each window, change the Safari Preference for New Window Opens (located on the General tab) to Same Page to facilitate this kind of browsing.

If you want to work in one window with tabs for each new site you go to, you can click File in the menu bar and click New Tab each time you want to go to a new site. Working in a tabbed window is neat and efficient. You have only one window open, yet you know exactly what else is open because each tab displays a title identifying the site, as shown in Figure 9.5.

Figure 9.5 *The more tabs you have open, the smaller the tabs get and the titles are more difficult to read.*

> Command-T is an easy shortcut to remember for opening a new tab.

To close a Safari window, click the red Close button in the window. To close a tab, point to the tab to display the Close button (which will appear on the left side of the tab) and then click it.

Navigating the Web

When you boil things down, you have only two ways to get to a website. You can type a web address in the address bar, or you can click a link. If you type the address, you needn't type *http://www* in the web address. Just type the domain name, such as apple.com. If an address you don't want to go to already appears in the Address bar, triple-click to select it (or click the icon to the left of the URL) and type the new address. If you are clicking links to browse the web, the links may be in a list of Google search results, in Top Sites, on the current page, in your Bookmarks, in your History, in a Contact or email message, or even in a document.

Anyone who has spent much time on the Internet at all knows how easy you can start down one path and get off on a tangent that leads to another tangent, and so on. Safari provides a couple of methods to help you get back on course. After you have viewed several pages, the newest way to navigate in Safari is to swipe left and right with one finger on a Magic Mouse or two fingers on a Trackpad.

If you just want to retrace your steps within the current website, you can Command-click the title in the title bar to display a list of the pages you have viewed in the current site, as shown in Figure 9.6. To go back to one, just click it in the list. This works for windows and tabs within a window as well.

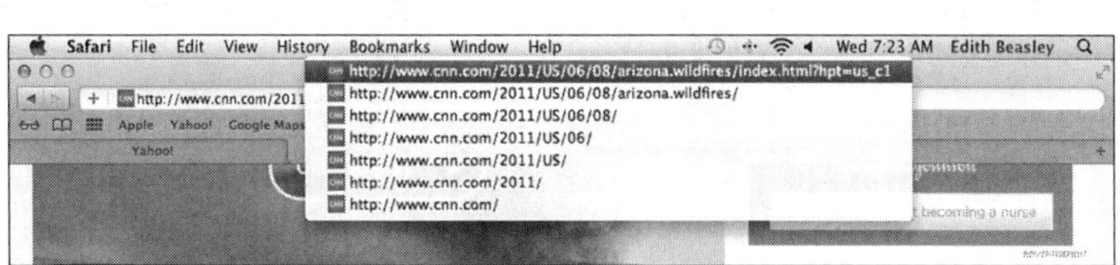

Figure 9.6 *To see this list, you must click the title, not just anywhere in the title bar.*

If you need to retrace your steps to other websites that you have visited in the current window or tab, you can go back one page at a time by clicking the Back button in the toolbar. An alternative method is to point to the Back button, hold down the mouse button to reveal a list of your last pages, and click one of those. The Back button's partner, the Forward button, reverses your direction again if you have been clicking the Back button. It also displays a list if you point to it and hold down the mouse button.

If you need a longer list of your clicking activities—everywhere you've been today, for example—you can open the History menu to access a complete list of links. In addition to the sites you've visited today, links to other dates also appear on the menu, as does the Show All History option.

Safari keeps web pages in your History list from one day up to one year or until you remove them manually. You set this preference in the General pane of Safari's preferences window.

Working with Bookmarks

A bookmark is a link that you save so you can go back to a particular web page. Safari has a Bookmarks bar just below the toolbar that has bookmarks preloaded for you. You can add more bookmarks to this bar and remove any of the preloaded bookmarks you don't want.

Bookmarking a Web Page

When you go to a web page that you want to bookmark, click the Add Bookmark button (the button with the plus mark, to the left of the Address bar). Click the pop-up button and select a location for the bookmark if necessary. (The last selection you made for location is always remembered in this dialog box so if you want to save the bookmark to the same location you last used, you're all set.) Type a different name for the bookmark if desired and click Add.

When you click the pop-up button to select a location for a bookmark, you see that your choices are Reading List, Top Sites, Bookmarks Bar, all the folders on the Bookmarks Bar as well as any folders you have created, and Bookmarks Menu. If you have not created any folders, then only two folders are listed in the location menu—News and Popular.

Using a Bookmark

To go to a web page that you have bookmarked, you can use one of these four methods:

- If the bookmark is on the Bookmarks bar, click the bookmark. If you have too many bookmarks on the bar to display, you might have to click the double arrow at the right end of the Bookmarks bar to reveal the bookmark you want.
- If the bookmark is in a folder on the Bookmarks bar, click the pop-up button for the folder and then click the bookmark in the list.
- If the bookmark is on the Bookmarks menu, click Bookmarks in the menu bar and click the bookmark you want.
- If the bookmark is stored in a folder that you have created (you learn how to create folders in the next section), click the Show All Bookmarks button in the Bookmarks bar to view the bookmarks list, as shown in Figure 9.7. Select the folder in the left pane and then double-click the bookmark in the right pane.

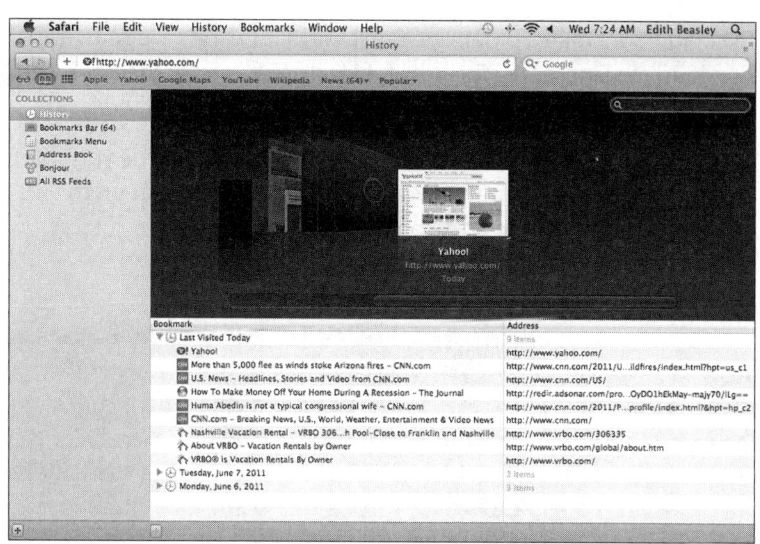

Figure 9.7 *The sidebar lists all sources of links.*

Organizing Bookmarks

One logical way to organize bookmarks is to put them in folders. You might begin by saving your bookmarks in the News or Popular folders because they're the only ones available at first, but after a while, you'll need to create your own folders.

SHOW ME **Media 9.4—A Video about Creating a Bookmark Folder**

Access this video file through your registered Web Edition at
my.safaribooksonline.com/9780132819091/media
or on the DVD for print books.

LET ME TRY IT

Creating a Bookmark Folder

Think about the way you use the Internet and the sites you go to, and it will be very apparent to you what folders you need. For example, I have folders for Shopping, Investing, Novel Writing, Technical Writing, and so on. To create a new folder for bookmarks, follow these steps:

1. Click Bookmarks in the menu bar.
2. Click Add Bookmark Folder. The Bookmarks list window opens, as shown previously in Figure 9.7. The new folder displays under the Bookmarks category in the left pane with its name (*untitled folder*) selected.
3. Type a name for the folder and press Return. The next time you want to add a bookmark, the name of your new folder will appear on the list of places where you can add the bookmark.
4. Close the bookmarks list window when you are finished.

You can move, copy, and delete bookmarks in the list window using the same techniques you use in the Finder to move, copy, and delete files. For example, to move a newly created folder to the Bookmarks bar, select the Bookmarks bar in the sidebar and then drag the folder (listed under Bookmarks in the sidebar) to the right pane. Drop the folder where you want it to appear in the order. You also can create a folder directly in the Bookmarks bar by right-clicking the bar and clicking New Folder.

Customizing the Bookmarks Bar

You can customize the Bookmarks bar in the following ways:

- To rearrange the order of bookmarks, drag the bookmark you want to move to the left or right.
- To move a bookmark currently on the bar to a folder on the bar, drag the bookmark and release it on top of the folder.
- To rename a bookmark, right-click the bookmark and click Edit Name. Type a new name and click OK.
- To create a new folder on the Bookmarks bar, right-click the bar, click New Folder, type the name of the folder, and click OK.
- To delete a bookmark or a folder in the bar, right-click the bookmark or folder and click Delete.

Harnessing the Power of Bookmarks

Here's a power play that will put you right up there with the Mac gurus—opening all the sites that you visit daily with one command. Here's how you set it up: Create a new folder and add it to the Bookmarks bar. Add bookmarks to your favorite sites to the new folder. Then when you want to open all your favorites at once in different tabs, click the pop-up button beside the folder name in the Bookmarks bar and click Open in Tabs. Each of your daily favorites opens in a tab, and you can start reading the first tab while the other sites are opening.

SHOW ME **Media 9.5—A Video about Setting Auto-Click in Safari**
Access this video file through your registered Web Edition at
my.safaribooksonline.com/9780132819091/media
or on the DVD for print books.

LET ME TRY IT

Setting Auto-Click in Safari

The Auto-Click feature is yet another way to automate the process of opening all the sites in a folder on the Bookmarks bar. You can do it with a single click. To set the Auto-Click feature for a folder, follow these steps:

1. Click the Show All Bookmarks button in the Bookmarks bar. (It's the button that looks like an open book.)
2. Click Bookmarks Bar in the sidebar.
3. Select the folder in the bottom pane.
4. Click the check box for Auto-Click, as shown in Figure 9.8. The next time you click the folder in the Bookmarks bar, all the bookmarks in the folder will open.

You cannot set this option for folders that you create that are not on the Bookmarks bar. Of course, you can move a folder to the Bookmarks bar and then set the feature.

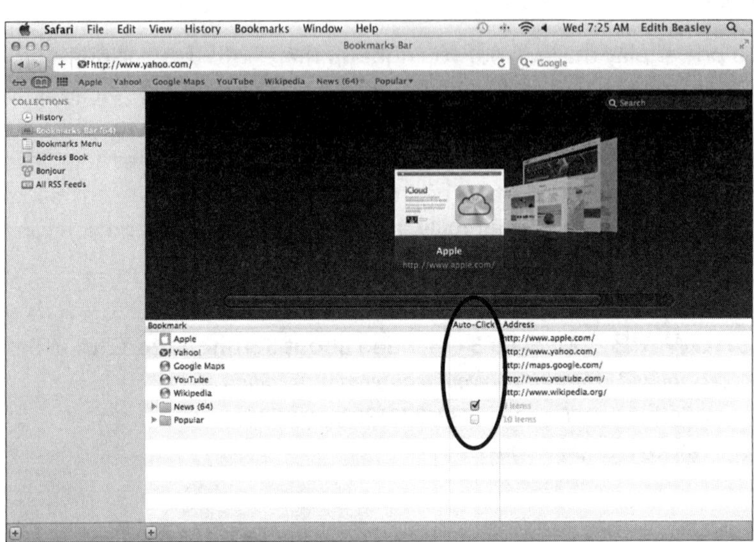

Figure 9.8 *An Auto-Click check box appears only beside folders.*

Downloading and Viewing Files

Many websites have files that you can download, including widgets, applications, music, movies, graphics, and so on. To download a file, simply click the link. The download jumps to the download button and begins downloading. To open the download window and watch the progress of the download, click the download button. (Note that the Download button only appears once you start downloading a file.) It's located in the upper-right corner of the window, just below the full-screen control. When the download is finished, the size of the download displays under the name of the downloaded file, and the file opens if it is a *safe* file (for example, movie, picture, sound, PDF, text file, disk image, and other archives).

While downloading a file, if you change your mind, first pause the download by clicking the **X** to the right of the filename and then click the Clear button. Remember that, by default, Mac OS X saves downloaded files in the Downloads folder.

Most files you can view on the web are PDF files. When you click a PDF file on a web page, it opens onscreen where you can view the file or save it to your hard drive. While viewing the file, you can even copy text from it.

As you are viewing a web page, take advantage of Smart Zoom, one of Lion's new features, to zoom in and out on text and graphics. Depending on your device, you can double-tap or use a pinching motion.

Saving Web Content

One common way to save web content is to select the content on a web page and then copy and paste that content into a document. This method is good to use if you are compiling research and want to pull content from multiple sites into one location.

If you want to save all the information on the web page just as it appears, you can save the page as a web archive. The Web Archive format saves everything on the web page (graphics, movies, and so on). This takes up some space on your hard drive, of course. In some cases, you may want to save a page because it is a receipt for a purchase you have made on the Internet. You'll love the way Safari eliminates the need to print the page by saving the page as a web receipt in its own special folder.

If you just want to go back and read the page at a later time, you can simply add the page to your Reading List. The Reading List is a new feature in Lion that uses bookmarks, but the new feature gives you much more control over the bookmarks.

If photos or graphics are what you're after, you can save them to disc, add them to iPhoto, or even make a web graphic your desktop background.

LET ME TRY IT

Saving a Web Page as a Web Archive

To save a web page as a web archive, follow these steps:

1. Click File in the Safari menu bar and then click Save As. The dialog box shown in Figure 9.9 opens.

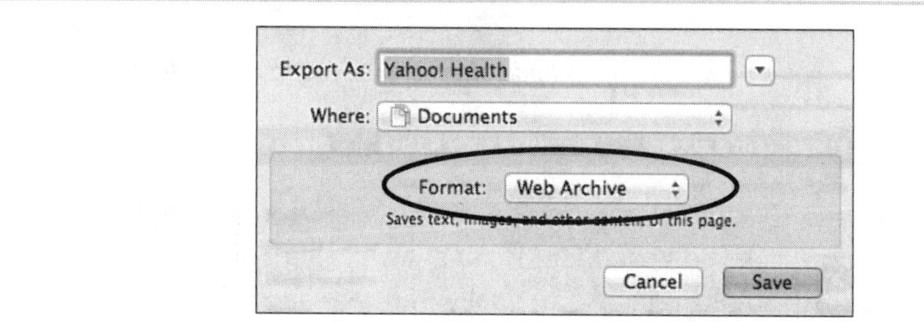

Figure 9.9 *Web Archive is the default format for exporting a file.*

2. Type a different name for Export As, if desired.
3. Select a location where you want to save it and then click Save.

Saving a Web Receipt

To save a web page to the Web Receipts folder, follow these steps:

1. While the web page is displayed onscreen, click File in the Safari menu bar.
2. Click Print to open the Print dialog box.
3. Click the PDF button to display the pop-up menu shown in Figure 9.10.

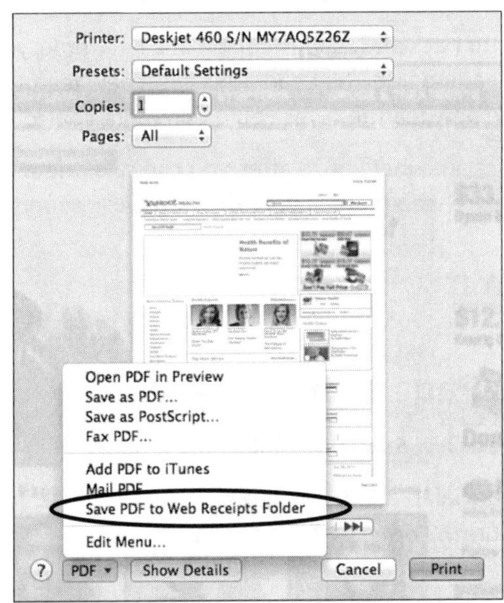

Figure 9.10 *Lion creates the Web Receipts folder the first time you save a file to it.*

If you have applications installed, such as Paperless (which stores receipts) or Scrivener (which can store PDFs used for research), you will see options to save in PDF format to those applications. Additionally, you can save a PDF file to any location, not just to the Web Receipts folder.

4. Click Save PDF to Web Receipts Folder. You do not have an opportunity to name the file and the Print dialog box closes.

Saving a Graphic

If you just want to save a graphic that appears on a web page, one quick way to save it is to drag the graphic to your desktop. Otherwise, you can right-click the graphic and click one of the following:

- Save Image to "Downloads"
- Save Image As
- Add Image to iPhoto Library
- Copy Image

If you select Save Image As, you can select the location where you want to store the saved file. If you select Copy Image, you can then paste it in a file.

LET ME TRY IT

Saving Links

The Reading List, which appears in a sidebar in the Safari window, is a list of links that you save so you can come back to them again when you have more time to read them. This is a new feature in Lion. You can choose to see all the links in the list or just the ones that you have not read yet. Additionally, you can clear all the bookmarks. To add a page to the Reading List, follow these steps:

1. Click the Reading List button in the Bookmarks bar. (It's the one that looks like a pair of reading glasses.) A sidebar opens, as shown in Figure 9.11.
2. Click the Add Page button to add the current page to the list or Shift-click a link to add the link's page to the list. Figure 9.12 shows the Reading List with items in it and the buttons across the top that allow you to clear the list or view all or only unread pages.
3. Click the Reading List button to close the sidebar.

Alternatively, you don't have to open the Reading List to add a page to it. You can right-click any page and click Add Link to Reading List.

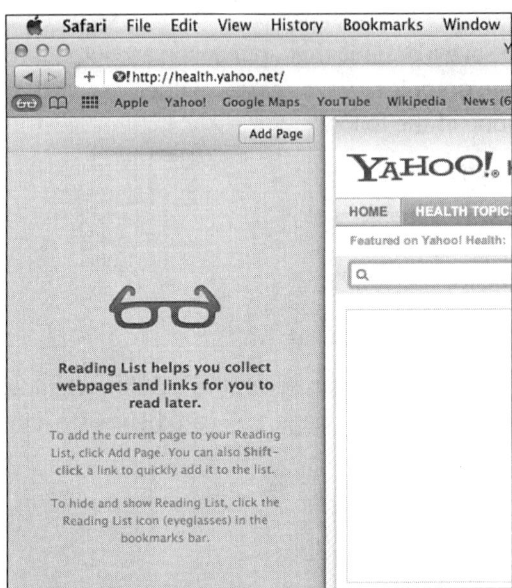

Figure 9.11 *The Reading List looks like this before you add any pages to it.*

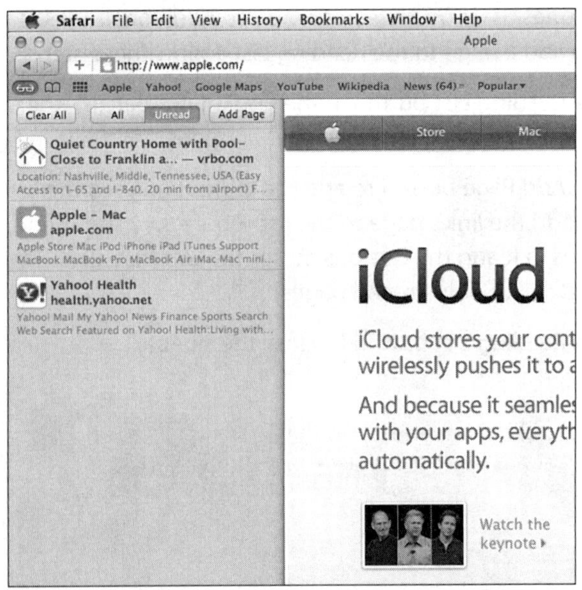

Figure 9.12 *Click Unread to list only the pages you have not read yet.*

Customizing Safari's Toolbar

The Safari toolbar, located just above the Bookmarks bar, has very few buttons in it by default, but Safari has quite a few buttons that you can add. I recommend that you think about adding the following buttons:

- **Home**—This button allows you to go back quickly to the site you have specified as the home page. (The home page preference is located on the General tab of the Safari Preferences.) Going to the home page quickly might be even more important to you now because of the fact that when you start Safari it resumes where it left off when you closed it, opening whatever page you last viewed.
- **New Tab**—Add this button if you like to browse in tabs.
- **Downloads**—This button displays the download window where you can monitor the progress of an item that is downloading to your computer.

To modify the toolbar, click View in Safari's menu bar and then click Customize Toolbar to open the dialog box shown in Figure 9.13. Drag the buttons you want onto the toolbar and click the Done button when finished.

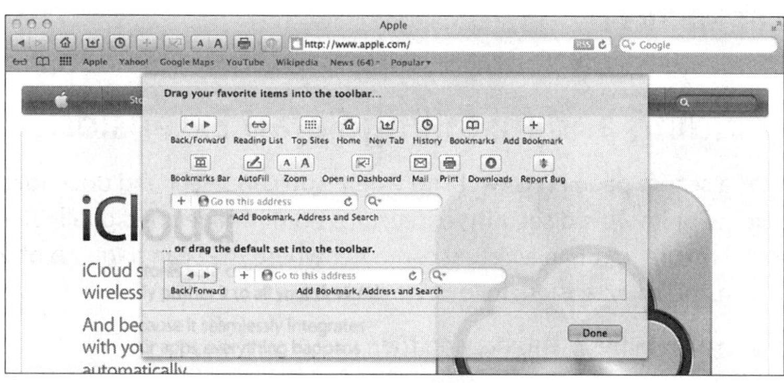

Figure 9.13 *As you add more buttons to the toolbar, the address box gets smaller to accommodate them.*

Adding Extensions to Safari

Extensions are applications created by third-party developers that extend the functionality of Safari by adding a new feature. For example, here are some of the extensions that are available:

- **AdBlock**—Removes all ads on all web pages.
- **Twitter for Safari**—Brings real-time trends and information to every web page and allows you to tweet about the web page you are viewing.
- **Facebook Photo Zoom**—Enlarges photo on Facebook.
- **Print Plus**—Allows you to print just the content that you have selected on a web page.
- **Close All Tabs**—Allows you to close all tabs in the Safari window except for the one you are currently viewing.
- **1-Click Weather**—Adds a button to your Safari toobar that takes you directly to www.weather.com for temperature and weather conditions for your specified Zip code.

LET ME TRY IT

Downloading and Installing Safari Extensions

Apple has a secure page on its website where you can select and download extensions safely. For improved security, extensions on this page are digitally signed and sandboxed (made to run in a virtual container where they can harm no other program). To install an extension, follow these steps:

1. Click Safari in the menu bar and then click Safari Extensions.
2. Select a category from the sidebar on the left, which is shown in Figure 9.14. (You may need to scroll down on your screen to see the categories.)
3. Find an extension that you want and click the Install Now button beside it.
4. After the installation, you may need to open the Extensions preferences page to configure the extension. Click Safari, Preferences, and click the Extensions tab. Figure 9.15 shows the extension for 1-Click Weather.
5. Make any necessary settings and then close the Preferences window.

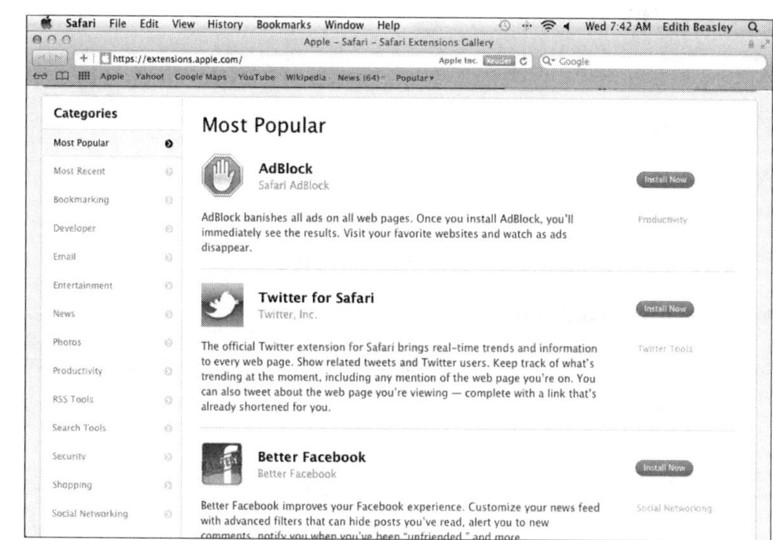

Figure 9.14 *You may have to scroll down to see the categories.*

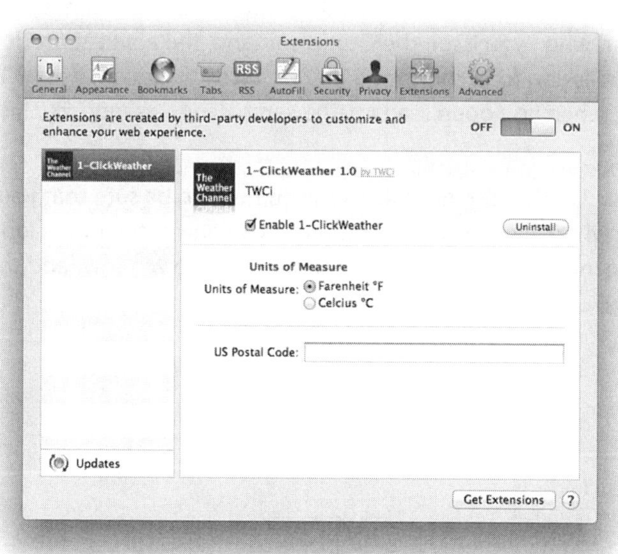

Figure 9.15 *The Get Extensions button provides another way to go to Apple's Extension Gallery page to download extensions.*

Uninstalling an Extension

If an extension is no longer needed or wanted, maybe it just didn't live up to what you expected, you can uninstall it. Follow these steps to uninstall an extension:

1. Click Safari in the menu bar and then click Preferences.
2. Click the Extensions tab, if necessary.
3. Select the extension in the sidebar and then click the Uninstall button. A confirmation dialog box opens. Click Uninstall again.

Instead of uninstalling an extension, you can just turn it off.

Quitting Safari

By this time, you know that you can quit an application by pressing Command-Q or by clicking the Quit Safari option from the Safari menu. If you have any windows open in Safari when you issue the Quit command, the application closes immediately without asking for a confirmation. Don't worry, though. If you close Safari accidentally, when you open it again, the same windows reopen. This is a new feature in Lion.

If you browse Safari using multiple tabs, you need to be sure that you don't close the window when you really only mean to close one of the tabs. Lion no longer asks you to confirm that you really mean to close the window (and therefore all the tabs) as Snow Leopard does.

This chapter shows you how to use the Address Book and iCal applications to keep track of your contacts and your schedule.

10

Using the Address Book and iCal

The Address Book and the iCal applications are two programs that can play a key role in keeping you organized, not only on your Mac, but with practically all your other sources of contact and scheduling information. With its syncing capabilities, Address Book can coordinate its contacts with the contact information that you have on other computers and devices, such as your iPod and iPhone, and in Internet address books, such as Google Contacts and Yahoo! Address Book. iCal also syncs across computers and devices, and you can set up CalDAV, Exchange Server, Google, and Yahoo! accounts in iCal to share calendars across multiple platforms.

This chapter covers the basic features and routines you need to know about these two applications: how to customize the Address Book template; how to add, edit, delete, and find contacts; how to add, edit, delete, and find events in iCal; and how to use the Reminder list.

Using the Address Book

The Address Book application holds information about your contacts and dispenses it to other applications. For example, the Address Book supplies email addresses to the Mail application and birthdays to iCal. Additionally, you can print your contacts in a list, on envelopes, labels, or in the form of a pocket address book. The printout can include all contacts or just the ones you select, and you can specify the particular contact information you want to include. Additionally, if you own an iPhone or iPod Touch, you can sync your Address Book to the address books on these devices.

To open the Address Book, click the Address Book icon in the Dock. As shown in Figure 10.1, if you have a new installation of Lion, Mac OS X automatically creates two address cards for you to start—one for Apple and one for yourself. You can close the Address Book by clicking the red Close button in the upper-left corner of the window. This is a new behavior introduced in Lion. In Snow Leopard, when you click the Close button in the Address Book, the window closes but the application continues to run.

In the two-page layout, shown in Figure 10.1, the left page shows the list of contacts and the right-hand page shows the information for the contact selected on the left page.

To see a longer list of contacts on the left page or more information about a contact on the right-hand page, drag the Address Book window longer.

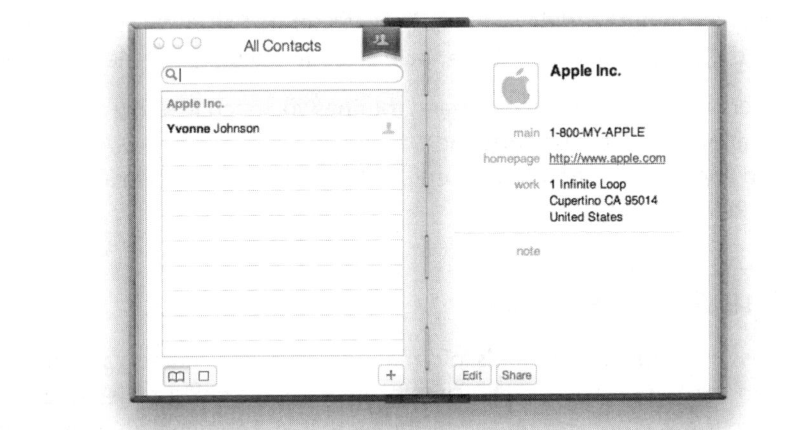

Figure 10.1 *The new Address Book interface now more closely resembles its icon in the Dock.*

Figure 10.2 shows the one-page layout. To change to the one-page layout, click the display mode button that shows one page. (It's in the lower-left corner beside the button for the two-page layout.) To change back to the two-page layout, click the display mode button with two pages on it.

Figure 10.2 *The display mode buttons toggle between a two-page and one-page layout.*

Creating Address Cards

Even though address cards can come into the Address Book from email, your iPhone, or other sources, you probably are going to have to type some address cards manually.

SHOW ME **Media 10.1—A Video about Creating a New Address Card**
Access this video file through your registered Web Edition at
my.safaribooksonline.com/9780132819091/media
or on the DVD for print books.

LET ME TRY IT

Creating a New Address Card

You can use address cards as the repository for all the information you have about your friends, business contacts, and anyone you might need to contact. To create an address card, follow these steps:

1. Click the Add button. (It's the one with a plus on it.)

2. Begin by typing the first name and then Tab to the next field and type the last name.
3. Tab to the Company field and type the text if a Company name is associated with the contact. If you want the contact to be listed (and therefore sorted) by company name instead of the individual's name, click the Company check box. If no company is associated with the contact, just Tab to the next field, which is a phone number.
4. At this point, the contact form starts to accommodate your needs automatically. If a contact has several different phone numbers, you can enter all the numbers, and the form will keep adding phone number fields until you finally skip the last phone number field. Of course, the labels that the form adds for each phone number might not be in the order you want, but you can always click the pop-up button on the label and change it.
5. Continue typing the text for each field and Tabbing to the next field. The form adds additional fields for you in each category just as it did in the phone number category. Additionally, you can click the pop-up button for any field label and select a different label. Again, when you finally skip the last field in the category, the form stops adding fields.
6. If you have a photograph of the contact or just a graphic you want to add, double-click the placeholder, click Choose, navigate to the file, and double-click it. Use the slider shown in Figure 10.3 to adjust the size of the picture. Drag the photo around in the box to position it. For a stylized effect, click the Apply an Effect button and click the effect you want. Click Set when finished.

> If the card to which you are adding the photo is your own, you can take your own picture after you double-click the photo box. Just click the button with the camera icon, look at the built-in camera's tiny camera lens, and smile. The camera counts down from three. Click Set if you like the picture or click Cancel and try again.

7. To add a field that doesn't appear on the form, such as the Birthday field, click Card in the menu bar, click Add Field, and click the field you want to add from the list shown in Figure 10.4.

> The Phonetic First/Last Name is a good field to add on cards with difficult name pronunciations that you might not remember. When you add this field, it appears at the top under the regular First and Last fields.

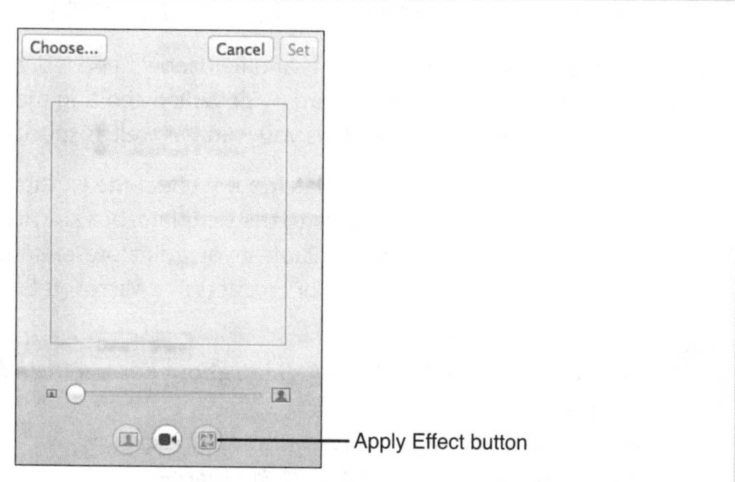

Figure 10.3 *Click Choose to access your image files.*

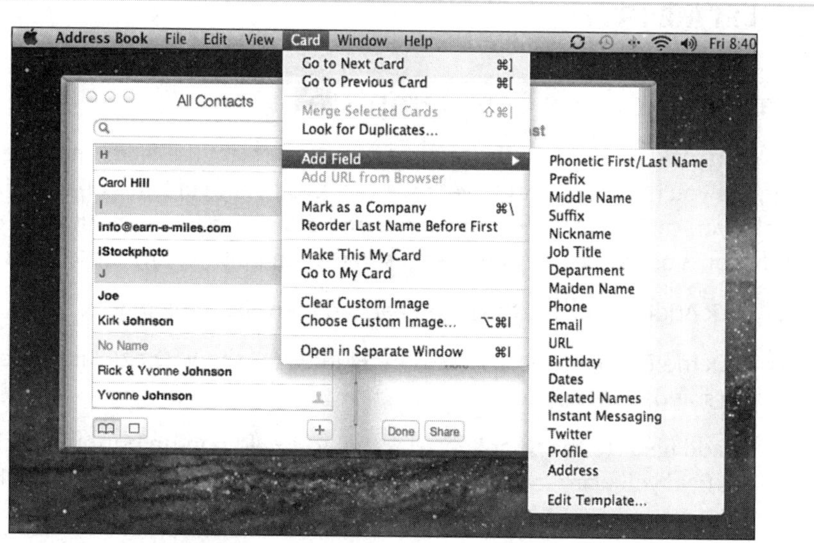

Figure 10.4 *This menu lists all possible fields you can add to a card.*

8. When finished creating the card, click the Done button to save the card and display it in final form. Notice that the fields you left blank do not appear on the completed card.

Customizing the Address Card Template

The standard template contains fields and field labels, and it determines where these fields appear on an address card by default. By editing the template, you can select the exact fields and field labels you want, as well as specify custom labels.

Any changes you make to the template do not affect the existing fields on cards that were created before the change to the template, but any new fields made available in the template will be available if you edit a pre-existing card. Also, custom labels are not applied to cards for contacts in a Microsoft Exchange account.

SHOW ME **Media 10.2—A Video about Editing the Address Card Template**

Access this video file through your registered Web Edition at
my.safaribooksonline.com/9780132819091/media
or on the DVD for print books.

LET ME TRY IT

Editing the Address Card Template

When you make changes to the template, you can select the fields and labels you want, but you have no control over the exact positioning of fields on a line. Additionally, you can't format the appearance of the card in any way, such as by changing the fonts or colors. To make changes to the template, follow these steps:

1. Click Address Book in the menu bar and then click Preferences.
2. Click the Template tab, if necessary. Figure 10.5 shows the default fields on the standard template.
3. To add fields to the template, click the Add Field pop-up button and click the field you want to add. Fields that already appear on the template have a check mark beside them on the pop-up menu.
4. To add more fields of a particular type, such as a Phone field, click the Add button (the green circle with the plus in it) beside the field. (Field types that do not have the Add button do not allow additional fields. The Birthday field is an example of this.)
5. To remove a field, click the Remove button (red circle with a minus in it) beside the field. You can delete all fields except First, Last, and Company name.

6. To change a field label, click the pop-up button beside the label and select the one you want from the menu or select Custom, type the label you want to use, and click OK.
7. Close the window when you are finished.

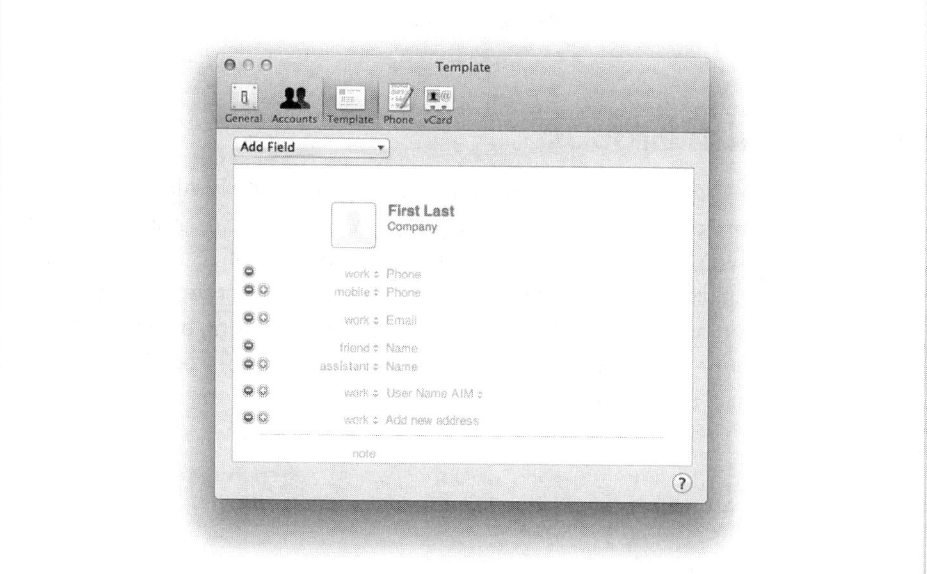

Figure 10.5 *The template starts out with these default fields.*

Using iCloud to Synchronize Contacts

In the fall of 2011, when iOS5 is released, Apple will also be releasing iCloud, thought of by some as the "huge hard disk in the sky." If you purchase iOS5 for your iPhone, iPad, or iPod Touch, iCloud is free. If you have a MobileMe account, it will be converted to an iCloud account—also for free. (That's right—the MobileMe subscription fee of $99 goes away!) If you don't happen to purchase a device that has iOS5 or have a MobileMe account, you still can get an iCloud account for free.

With iCloud all your contacts are synchronized automatically to all your iDevices and to all your Macs. So if you add a contact on your iPhone, it goes in the Address Book on the iPhone, of course, but it also goes to iCloud. Then iCloud pushes that information back down to your Mac, iPad, and iPod Touch. This all happens in the background, and you don't have to lift a finger!

Automatic synchronization doesn't stop with the Address Book. Mail and iCal also automatically send data to iCloud, and iCloud pushes that information down to all your iDevices and to all your Macs. All your information stays in perfect synch all the time. I nominate Steve Jobs for the Nobel Peace Prize!

See Chapter 16, "Keeping Your Mac Safe, Updated, and Backed Up," to learn more about iCloud.

Working with Groups

By default, the Address Book creates a group called All Contacts. All contacts that you add to your Address Book are in this group. To bring more organization to your Address Book, you can create additional groups, such as Family, Business, Soccer Team, and so on, and include cards of contacts that fit in the group. A single address card can belong to multiple groups unless you are using a Microsoft Exchange account. In an Exchange account, the groups are referred to as folders and a contact can be in only one folder.

The Mail application can email individual messages to all members in an Address Book group. It's called a distribution list in the Mail application.

Creating a Group

To create a group, click the Group button to go to the Group page or click View in the menu bar and click Groups. The Group button, which looks like a red bookmark with the outline of two people on it, doesn't display if you are using the one-page layout. When you are on the Groups page, click the Add button (the one with the plus on it). Type a name for the group and press Return. The new group appears under All Contacts on the left-hand page (even if the name of the group would come before "All" in the alphabet).

To rename a group, select the group on the left-hand page, press Return, type the new name, and press Return again.

Adding and Removing Names in a Group

To add names to a group, you can copy existing contacts or create new ones. To copy existing names, click the name of the group on the Groups page that has the contact you want to copy. All the contacts for the selected group display on the right-hand page. Drag the contact you want to copy from the right-hand page and drop it on the name of the group you want to copy it to on the left-hand page. To speed things up, select multiple contacts on the right-hand page by Command-clicking them.

To create a new card in a group, double-click the group on the Groups page to open it and then follow the procedure for creating a contact outlined earlier in "Creating a New Address Card." Adding a contact to a group also adds the contact to the All Contacts group. To remove a name from a group, select the name in the group and press Delete. Then click Remove from Group.

To return to the All Contacts grouping after you've switched to a different group, click the bookmark and click the All Contacts group.

If you need to know all the groups that a contact belongs to, go to the Groups page, select the contact on the right-hand page and then press the Option key. All the groups that contain the contact are highlighted on the left-hand page.

Deleting a Group

You can delete any group except the All Contacts group. To delete a group, select the group on the Groups page and press the Delete key. When asked to confirm the deletion, click the Delete button. The contacts that were in the deleted group still remain in the All Contacts group.

Performing Common Tasks with Address Cards

This section describes many of the common tasks that you perform with address cards. It also includes some not-so-common tasks because I just couldn't resist telling you about them.

Sorting Address Cards

By default the Address Book sorts contacts by first name. It also displays the first name before the last name. For many users, this just doesn't cut it. Fortunately, these are two defaults that you can change in the Preferences window.

LET ME TRY IT

Changing the Name Preferences in the Address Book

To change the display order of the first and last name and to change the sort order, follow these steps:

1. Click Address Book in the menu bar and click Preferences.
2. Click the General tab if necessary.
3. Click the option you want for Show First Name.

4. Click the Sort By pop-up button, as shown in Figure 10.6, and select whether you want to sort by First Name or Last Name.

5. Close the Preferences window.

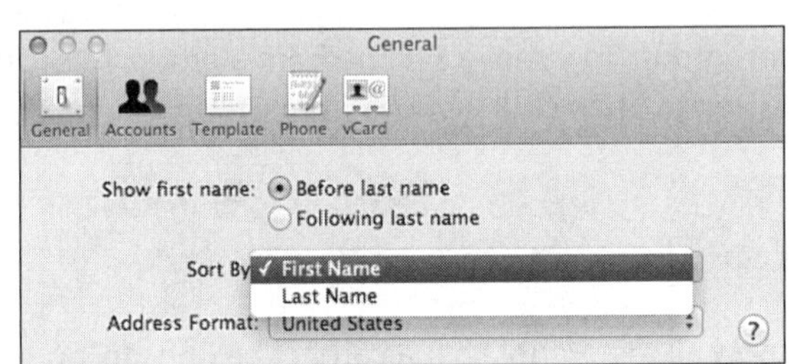

Figure 10.6 *If you have a large number of contacts with the same first name, you might want to sort by last name.*

Finding a Contact

To go quickly to a contact's card, select the group and type part of the contact's name or some information that you know is on the card in the Spotlight field. You could type the last name and the house address, for example. Cards that contain the search text display immediately. If you are on the Groups page, the contacts display in a list on the right-hand page. If you are using the two-page layout, all the names that contain the search text show in the list on the left-hand page. If you are using the one-page layout, the first name that contains the search text displays, and you must use the Next and Previous arrow keys to scroll through the contacts.

Editing a Contact

People move, they change their phone numbers, they get married. As these events occur, you need to edit address cards, but if this is a new installation for you, the first card you should edit is your own! Other applications, such as iCal, iChat, and Mail use information from your card so it needs to be correct and as complete as possible.

To edit a card, first you have to select it. To select your own card quickly and easily, click Card on the menu bar and click Go to My Card. This works from anywhere in any layout. Selecting any other address card is not quite so easy. If you are using the one-page layout, and you are not looking at All Contacts, you might be looking at a group that doesn't have the contact you want to edit. No amount of scrolling in the one-page view is going to display the contact. You have to click View in the menu bar, click Groups, and select the group if you know it or select All Contacts.

At this point, you should be able to find the contact on the right-hand page. Then you can click it to select it or double-click it to open it in a separate window.

If you have hundreds of contacts, which is not unusual in a corporate setting, you might want to search for the contact as explained in the previous section.

After selecting the correct contact, click the Edit button, make the necessary changes, and then click the Done button to save the changes. If you double-clicked the contact and opened it in a separate window, close the window.

It doesn't matter whether you originally selected the card from a group you have created or from All Contacts. Any changes that you make to the card appear on the card in all groups to which it belongs.

Printing Contacts

You have several options for printing the information in your address cards. You can print a pocket address book, mailing labels, or envelopes.

LET ME TRY IT

Printing a Pocket Address Book

If you think you will find yourself in a situation in which you cannot access your contacts, you can print the entire Address Book or a portion of it to take with you. To print your address book, follow these steps:

1. Select the contacts you want to include by selecting multiple contacts or selecting a group. (Use Shift-click to select a block or Command-click to select individual contacts.)
2. Click File in the menu bar and click Print.
3. Select the printer you want to use from the Printer pop-up list.
4. Your screen should look something like Figure 10.7. If it doesn't, click the Show Details button at the bottom of the window.
5. Select Pocket Address Book from the Style pop-up menu.
6. Check/uncheck the Attributes to include or exclude.
7. Select an option from the Flip Style pop-up menu.
8. Click the Set button to specify different font settings. Select the font attributes and close the window.

9. Set all other print options such as Copies, Pages, Orientation, and so on.
10. Click Print.

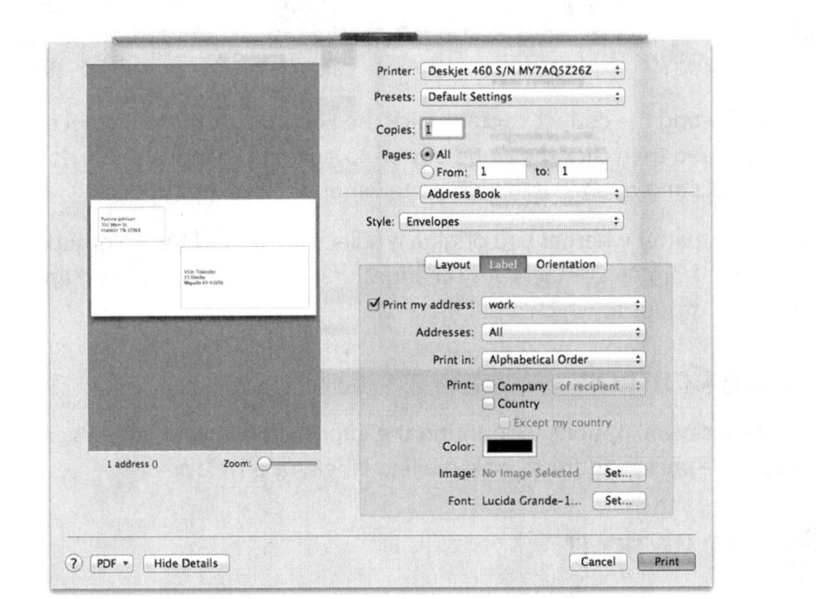

Figure 10.7 *The number of cards you selected is shown below the preview.*

LET ME TRY IT

Printing Mailing Labels

When printing mailing labels, you must consider the fact that some address cards have more than one address. When you print the labels, you must select the address that prints. Of course, if you are not truly going to use the labels for mailing, you can print all the addresses on the label. To print mailing labels, follow these steps:

1. Select the contacts you want to include by selecting multiple contacts (with Shift-click or Command-click) or by selecting a group.
2. Click File in the menu bar and click Print.
3. Select the printer you want to use from the Printer pop-up list and specify the number of Copies and the Pages.
4. Select Mailing Labels from the Style pop-up menu.

5. Click the Layout button and specify the label you are going to use.
6. Click Label and do the following:
    - Select the address you want to print from the Addresses pop-up menu.
    - Select the order in which you want to print the labels by making a selection from the Print In pop-up menu. (Your choices are Postal Code Order and Alphabetical Order.)
    - Select the Print options you want to use (Company, Country, Except My Country).
    - Click the Color field to open the Colors window. Click a color tab at the top, specify the color using the appropriate options for the color mode you have selected (the box of crayons is easy to use), and then close the Colors window.
    - Click the Set button beside the Image option. Navigate to an image you want to use on the label and double-click it.
    - Click the Set button beside the Font option to open the Font window. Select the font attributes and then close the Fonts window. At this point the labels should be ready to print. Figure 10.8 shows what the screen would look like if you had set all the options described in these steps.

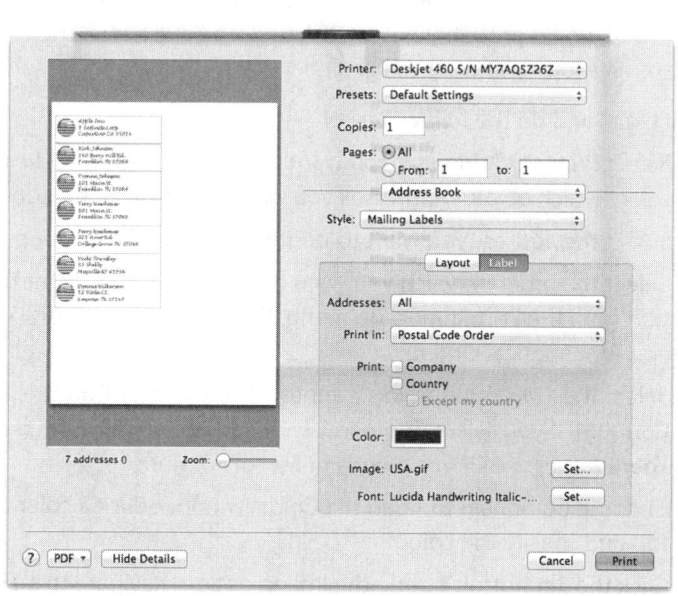

Figure 10.8 *Lion includes only contacts that have addresses from the cards you select, but it will include incomplete addresses so you should check them before printing.*

7. Click Print and close any open windows that you used to make settings for color or fonts.

Printing Envelopes

When you print envelopes addressed to your contact, you also can print a return address. The address comes from your own address card so be sure you have included this information on your card if you want it to print on the envelope. To print envelopes, follow these steps:

1. Select the contacts you want to include by selecting multiple contacts (with Shift-click or Command-click) or by selecting a group. Be sure the contacts you select actually have addresses!
2. Click File in the menu bar and click Print.
3. Select the printer you want to use from the Printer pop-up list and specify the number of Copies and the Pages.
4. Select Envelopes from the Style pop-up menu.
5. Click Layout and select a category of envelopes. (For most readers of this book, that would probably be North American Envelopes.) Then select the type of envelope you want to use.
6. Click Label and do the following:
   - Select Print My Address if you want to include a return address, and then select which of your addresses you want to use from the pop-up menu.
   - Select the address you want to print from the Addresses pop-up menu.
   - Select the order in which you want to print the labels by making a selection from the Print In pop-up menu. (Your choices are Postal Code Order and Alphabetical Order.)
   - Select the Print options you want to use (Company, Country, Except My Country). If you select Company, select an option from the pop-up menu. Your choices are Of Recipient, For Me, or For Both.
   - Click the Color field to open the Colors window. Click a color tab at the top and specify the color.
   - Click the Set button beside the Image option. Navigate to an image you want to use on the label and double-click it.
   - Click the Set button beside the Font option to open the Font window. Select the font attributes in this window.

7. Click Orientation and select Portrait or Landscape.

8. Click Print and close any open windows that you used to make settings for color or fonts.

Deleting a Contact

To delete a contact from all groups, select the All Contacts group, select the contact, and press the Delete key. When asked to confirm the deletion, click Delete. Oops! Deleted the wrong contact? Sorry! There's no Undo feature for deleted address cards so next time pay more attention to the confirmation dialog box.

To delete a contact from a particular group, select the group, select the card, and press the Delete key. When asked to confirm the deletion, click Delete. Don't think that just because you delete your brother-in-law from the Family group that you're rid of him. He's still in the All Contacts group and any other group he belongs to.

You also can select multiple cards in the same group to delete at the same time.

Sharing a Contact

Undoubtedly, as you have been working with address cards you have noticed the Share button at the bottom of the page. When you click this button, the Address Book opens a new email with a vCard attachment of the current address card. A *vCard* is a virtual business card that recipients can add to their own Address Books.

Before you start sending out vCards, you should view the settings for vCard Preferences and make any changes that you want. Click Address Book, Preferences, and click the vCard tab. Figure 10.9 shows the default preferences. You might want to deselect exporting notes if you have written anything personal in a contact's notes. Also, you might not want to include the photo. You should definitely enable the Private Me Card option so you can control what information you send out about yourself.

If you have enabled Private Me Card, your address card contains check mark boxes by each field that you have filled out on your card. These boxes only display while you are editing your card. You can uncheck any field that you do not want to include in a vCard.

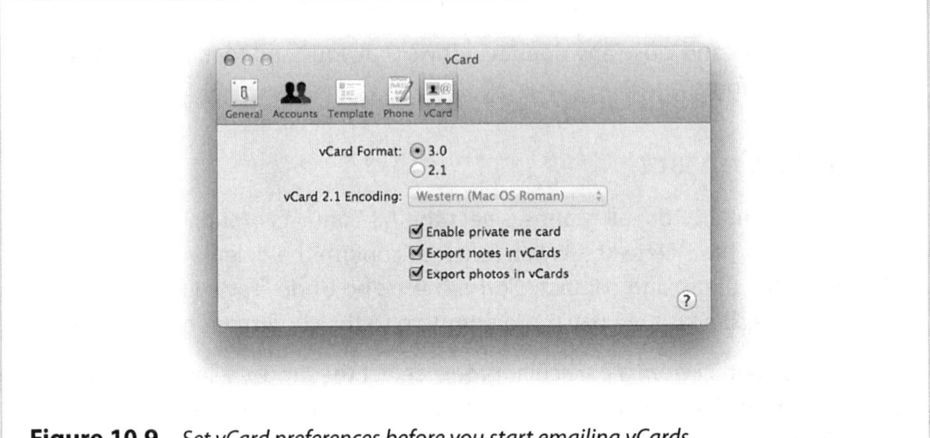

Figure 10.9 *Set vCard preferences before you start emailing vCards.*

Merging Duplicate Cards

If you bring contacts into your Address Book from different sources, you may end up with more than one card for the same contact. If the cards are exactly the same, you can just delete one of them, but if they are not the same, you may want to merge the two cards into one card. Follow these steps to merge the two cards:

1. Select the card that has the name and, if applicable, the photo you want to keep when the cards are merged.
2. Select the second card using Command-click.
3. Click Card in the menu bar and click Merge Selected Cards. Address Book merges the cards. The new card may contain new data in the Notes field. For example, if you merge the cards for Anthony Stewart (the first card selected) with the card for Tony Stewart, the new card has the word *Tony* in the Notes field.

Archiving the Address Book

Archiving your Address Book is a good way to back up its content. When you archive the Address Book, the addresses are exported to an archive file. You can also use the archive file to move your Address Book to another computer.

LET ME TRY IT

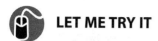

Making an Archive

To archive the Address Book, follow these steps:

1. Click File in the menu bar and click Export.
2. Click Address Book Archive.
3. Type a different name for Save As if you don't want to use the name provided.
4. Select a location for Where. Click the down-arrow beside the Save As field to expand the dialog box with the "mini-Finder."
5. Click Save.

Using iCal

iCal is Mac's equivalent of the Day-Timers that everyone used to carry around before electronic PDAs and smart cell phones took their place. (The new interface in Lion for the Address Book and iCal even remind you visually of the Day Timer binders.)

iCal keeps your schedule and your Reminders up to date and syncs them with your iPhone, iPad, iPod, and other calendars you may have on the web, such as Google Calendar. Additionally, you can publish your calendar on MobileMe (if you have paid for an account) or on a private web server.

When the free iCloud account replaces MobileMe, you will also be able to publish your calendar on that account.

TELL ME MORE **Media 10.3—A Discussion about Publishing a Calendar to the Web**

Access this audio recording through your registered Web Edition at ***my.safaribooksonline.com/9780132819091/media*** *or on the DVD for print books.*

Getting Familiar with iCal

To open iCal, click the iCal icon in the Dock. The calendar page on the Dock icon always displays today's month and date, and the calendar always opens to the current date. Figures 10.10 through 10.13 show the four different views available in iCal. The Day view has the events for the day listed on the left and the detailed schedule on the right. A mini calendar of the month is always visible, and you can use this calendar to navigate to another date.

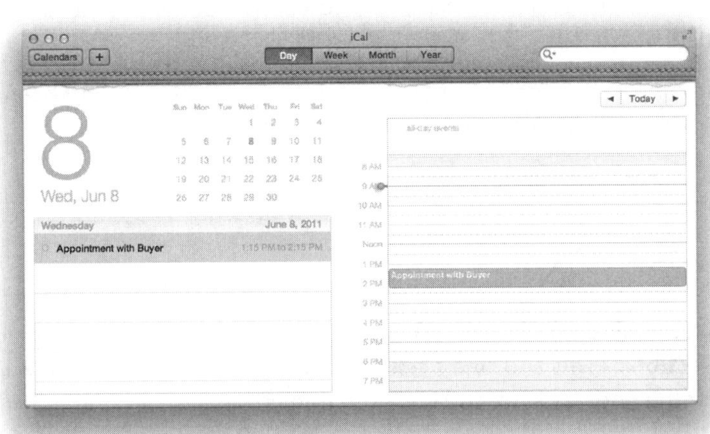

Figure 10.10 *The Day view marks the current time on the daily time schedule with the red indicator and gray line.*

The default week view gives you your schedule from Sunday through Saturday. If you change the setting for the first day of the week, the day you select, such as Monday, displays in the first column and Sunday then becomes the last day of the week. A time grid on the left helps you determine the start and end times for an event.

Figure 10.11 *The Week view also marks the current time with a red indicator and gray line.*

In the month view, the events for each day display in the block for the appropriate date. Due to space limitations, the start and end times for events do not display.

Figure 10.12 *The Month view shows five weeks including the days before and after the current month.*

The year view shows your daily activities with a heat map. Each day is colored with a color from shades of blue or red to indicate the least number of events (the blue range) to the most number of events (the red range).

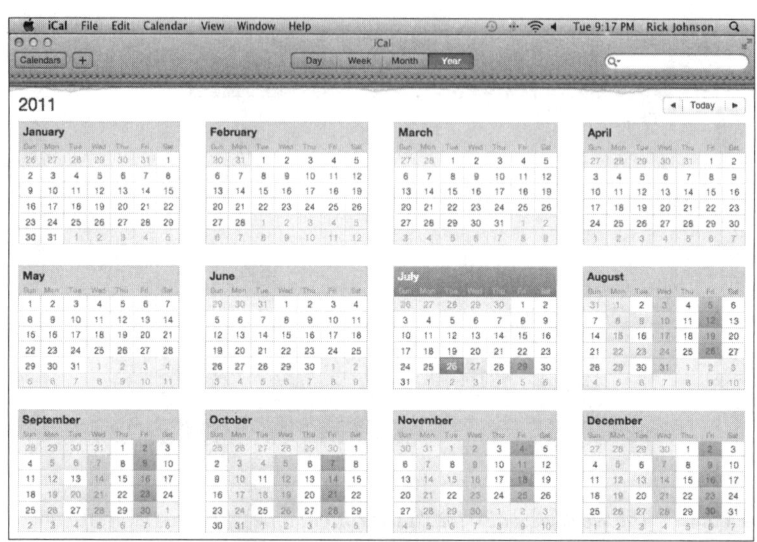

Figure 10.13 *The Year view does not show individual events.*

Notice that the Reminder list (the new name for the To Do list) displays on the right in all views. Additionally, by default, each view displays events from two calendars at once, the Home calendar and the Work calendar. These are the two default calendars that iCal gives you, but you can create additional calendars as well.

You can hide and display the Reminders pane. To hide it, click View in the menu bar and click Hide Reminders. To display the Reminders pane, click View, Show Reminders.

If you click the Calendars button in the upper-left corner, you can see the calendars for all your accounts. Figure 10.14 shows the default calendars for the default account called On My Mac. Both calendars are checked, which is why events from both will display. Notice the calendars are color coded so you can tell which events go with which calendar. All events for the Home calendar use a blue font with blue shading and the Work events use a green font and green shading.

If I added an account for my MobileMe (soon to be iCloud) service, it would also display a Home and a Work calendar in the Calendars' window.

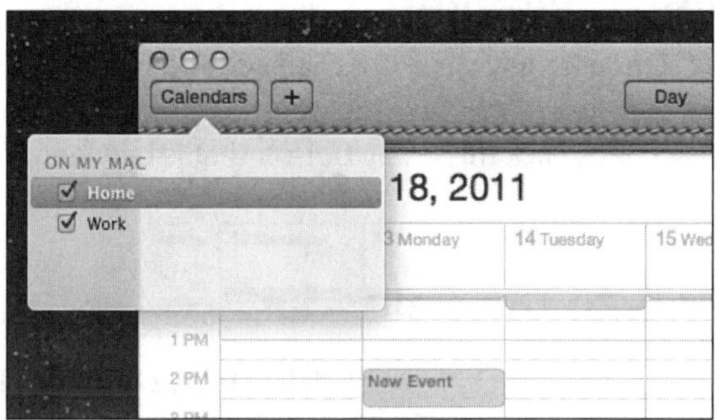

Figure 10.14 *Lion creates two calendars for you by default.*

The default iCal preferences dictate that the Week view has seven days, starting on Sunday. It also defines the start time for the day as 8:00 a.m. and the end time as 6:00 p.m. It also designates the Work calendar as the default calendar. To change any of these preferences, click iCal in the menu bar and click Preferences. The preferences I mentioned appear on the General pane, as shown in Figure 10.15.

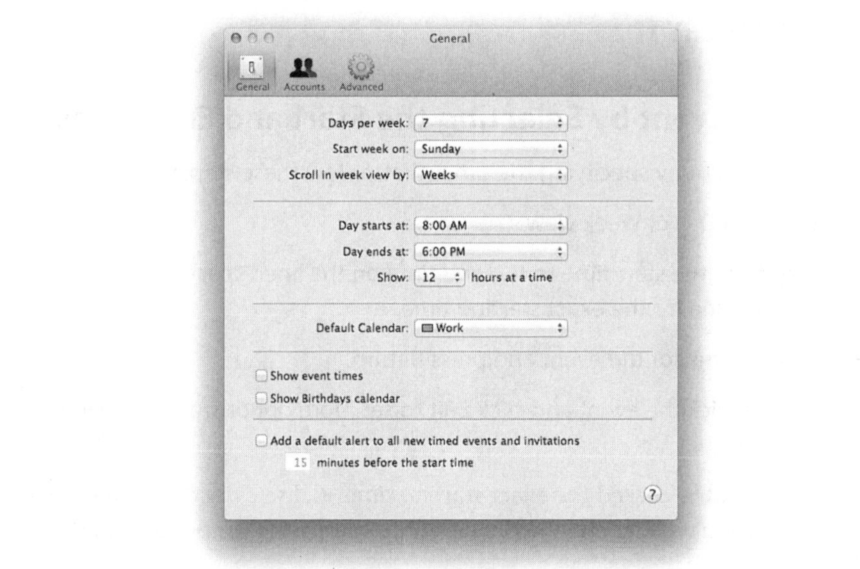

Figure 10.15 *Set the iCal preferences for when your day starts and ends on the General pane.*

Navigating the Calendar

To navigate the calendar in any view, use the Back and Forward buttons (see Figure 10.10) to go back or forward one day, one week, one month, or one year at a time. To return to today's date, click the Today button that is between the Back and Forward buttons.

Adding Events to the Calendar

An event is an item you put on the calendar. It can be a meeting, an appointment, a tickler, a ball game, and so on. If you have an event that repeats on a regular basis, you can specify the recurrence interval, and iCal automatically adds the event to dates in the future.

When you create an event, iCal assumes that the event belongs to the default calendar, which is the Home calendar, unless you have specified otherwise in the General pane of the Preferences window. If the default calendar is not the one you want to use, you might want to select the calendar before you create the event.

You can create new events in a few different ways, as shown in the following sets of instructions.

LET ME TRY IT

Creating an Event by Selecting the Start and End Times

To create an event by specifying the times first, follow these steps:

1. Switch to Day or Week view.
2. Drag from the start time to the end time on the lined spaces or double-click the line for the exact starting time.
3. Type a name for the event and press Return.
4. Double-click the event and click Edit to set more options, as shown in Figure 10.16.
5. If you double-clicked the exact starting time, iCal sets the duration for one hour. If you want to change the duration, specify the correct time in the To field.
6. Click the Done button when you are finished.

Figure 10.16 *Add details to an event using this dialog box.*

Creating an Event Using Quick Event

The Quick Event feature relies on four pieces of information to correctly place the new event on the calendar. To create an event using Quick Event, follow these steps:

1. Click and hold the Add button (see Figure 10.20).
2. Select the calendar for the event. The Quick Event box opens, as shown in Figure 10.17.
3. Type a name, a date, and a start time. Additionally, you can type an end time for the event. For example, you can type Logan's Birthday on April 28 from 1:00 pm–4:00 pm. (If you type only a start time, iCal automatically sets the duration for one hour.)
4. Press Return. The dialog box with the event details opens.
5. Set other options as desired.
6. When finished, click the Done button.

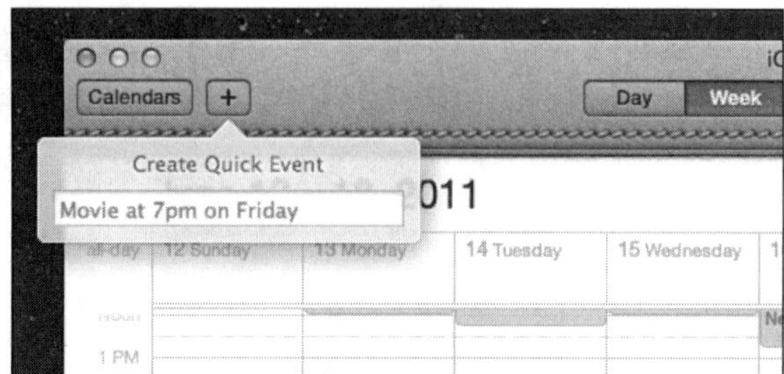

Figure 10.17 *The Quick Event box gives you a hint about what to type.*

LET ME TRY IT

Creating an Event in the Month View

When you create a new event from the Month view, iCal assumes that it is an all-day event. Of course, after you create the event, you can set the duration for anything you want. To create a new event from the Month view, follow these steps

1. Click the Month button and then scroll to the month you want.
2. Double-click the day of the month for the event.
3. Type a name for the event and press Return.
4. Double-click the event to open it and change or set other options as desired.
5. Click Done when finished.

LET ME TRY IT

Creating a Recurring Event

A recurring event is one that happens over and over again on a predictable schedule, such as the first Monday of every month. To create a recurring event, follow these steps:

1. Create an event using your preferred method.
2. Double-click the event, click the Edit button, and click the Repeat pop-up button.
3. Select a repeat time from the pop-up menu or select Custom.

4. If you select a standard repeat time from the menu, you're finished, so just click the Done button and skip step 5.
5. If you selected Custom in step 3, select a Frequency and then specify the other criteria. (Each frequency has its own set of criteria.) Click OK when finished. If desired, specify an End option. Click Done to close the event.

SHOW ME **Media 10.4—A Video about Setting Event Alerts**
Access this video file through your registered Web Edition at
my.safaribooksonline.com/9780132819091/media
or on the DVD for print books.

LET ME TRY IT

Setting Event Alerts

You probably have noticed the Alert option when creating or editing events. The default for this feature is None, so you may not have been using this handy feature. iCal can remind you of an event by displaying a message onscreen—with or without sound, sending you an email, opening a file, or running a script. In fact, you can set multiple alerts for different times if you are one of those *very* forgetful people. For example, you could set a message alert for the day before the event and one for two hours before the event. Additionally, you could send two email alerts to two different email addresses. To set an alert, follow these steps:

1. Double-click the event and click the Alert pop-up button.
2. Click the type of alert you want.
3. Supply additional information as needed (such as which email address to use or which file to open).
4. Click the pop-up button beside the time and specify a time for when the alert should occur.
5. Repeat steps 2 through 4 to set more alarms if you need them.
6. Click the Done button when finished.

If you are afraid you will forget to set an alert, go to the General page of the iCal preferences, and select Add a Default Alert to All New Timed Events and Invitations. Also specify the number of minutes you want the alert to display before the start time.

Performing Common Tasks with Events

Finding, editing, and deleting events are all tasks that you need to know how to do, because you'll do these things repeatedly. If your job or social life requires you to schedule meetings or events, you'll also need to know how to send out invitations.

Finding Events

After you have several calendars with many events, you might need to use the Spotlight to help you find a particular event. Using the Spotlight in iCal has a few more steps to it than usual.

LET ME TRY IT

Using Spotlight to Find Events

Follow these steps to use Spotlight in iCal:

1. Click the Calendars button and check all calendars that you want to search.
2. Click the Spotlight pop-up button and select an item to limit the search if you want. If you don't put any limiting factors on the search, iCal searches the entire content of all items (including Reminders).
3. Type text that appears in the item you want to find. The results appear in a pane at the bottom of the screen, as shown in Figure 10.18.

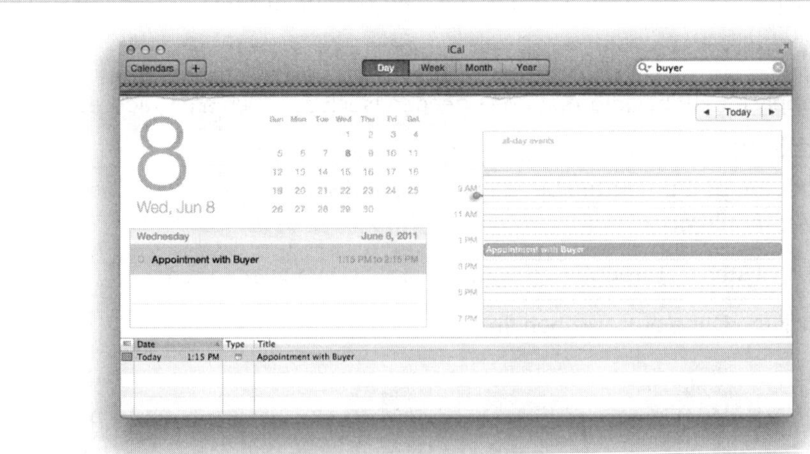

Figure 10.18 *The results of a Spotlight search display in the pane at the bottom.*

4. Double-click the item to open it.
5. To close the search results pane, click the x in the Spotlight field.

Editing Events

To make changes to an event, use an appropriate procedure from the following list:

- To change the start time, drag the event up or down in the Day or Week view. Note that the time changes in 15-minute increments.
- To change the end time, drag the bottom line of the event up or down in the Day or Week view.
- To change to a different date, switch to the Month view and drag the event to the new date or double-click the event, click Edit, type the new date in the From or To field, and click Done.
- To change the name of an event, double-click the event and click the Edit button. Type the new name and click the Done button.

Deleting Events

To delete an event, use one of the following two methods:

- To delete an event, click the event to select it and press the Delete key on the keyboard.
- Select the event, click Edit in the menu bar, and click Delete.

To undo the deletion of an event, click Edit in the menu bar and click Undo Delete Event.

Creating a New Calendar

If the Home and Work calendars are not sufficient for you, you can create additional calendars. To create a new calendar, click File in the menu bar and click New Calendar. If you have several accounts set up, select the account under which the calendar should be created. Type a name for the new calendar and press Return. iCal assigns a new color to the new calendar and all events and reminders for that calendar use the assigned color.

One very useful type of calendar that iCal can create for you is a calendar of your contacts' birthdays.

LET ME TRY IT

Creating a Birthday Calendar

iCal works in conjunction with the Address Book to create the birthday calendar, so before you start, you might need to open your Address Book and be sure you have listed all the birthdays you want to include on your calendar. To create a birthday calendar, follow these steps:

1. Click iCal in the menu bar and click Preferences.
2. Click the General tab if necessary.
3. Click the Show Birthdays Calendar check box.
4. Close the Preferences window.

> You may want to view only the birthday calendar sometimes. In these cases, click Calendars and deselect the check boxes for all calendars except Birthdays.

Working with Reminders

iCal provides a convenient To Do feature for you in a third pane. It works in conjunction with your calendar so you can attach due dates and alarms to your To Do items. To turn on the Reminders pane, click View in the menu bar and then click Show Reminders.

SHOW ME **Media 10.5—A Video about Creating a Reminder**
Access this video file through your registered Web Edition at
my.safaribooksonline.com/9780132819091/media
or on the DVD for print books.

LET ME TRY IT

Creating a Reminder

To create a Reminder, follow these steps:

1. Display the Reminders pane, if necessary, and double-click in the Reminders pane to create a new reminder.
2. Type a name for the item and press Return.
3. To make additional settings, as shown in Figure 10.19, double-click the reminder.

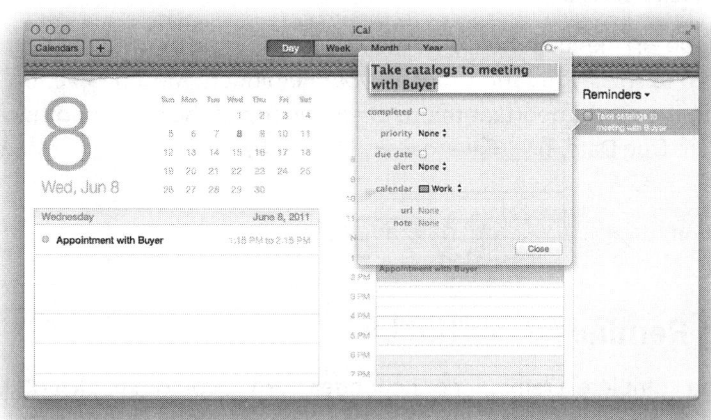

Figure 10.19 *Add additional details to a reminder using this dialog box.*

4. To set a priority, click the pop-up button and click a priority.
5. To set a due date, click the Due Date box and type a date.
6. To set an alert, click the Alert pop-up button and select the type of alert you want to set from the pop-up menu. If you select Email, Open File, or Run Script, supply the additional information that is needed. Repeat this step to set as many alerts as you want.
7. To attach the item to the appropriate calendar, click the Calendar pop-up button and then click the name of the calendar.
8. Click the URL box and type a web address that is somehow associated with the reminder if appropriate.
9. Click the Note field and type any text that you need to help you with this reminder.
10. When you are finished, click the Close button.

Editing and Deleting Reminders

To edit a reminder, double-click it in the list, make your changes, and then click the Close button.

To delete a reminder, select the reminder in the list and press the Delete key. If you delete a reminder by mistake, click Edit in the menu bar and click Undo Delete Reminder.

Sorting Reminders

Use the pop-up menu at the top of the Reminders pane (next to the word *Reminders*) to specify the sort order for your Reminders. Most people sort by priority so that the most important things are at the top of the list. Your other sort options are Due Date, Title, Calendar, and Manually.

> You also can drag reminders to different locations in the list.

Marking Reminders off the List

When you complete a reminder or no longer need it, you can mark it off the list by clicking the check box beside it in the Reminders list. Nothing is quite so satisfying as a Reminder list that is all checked off. At least, that's what I've been told.

> If you prefer that the reminder disappear after it is checked, you can set a preference for this in the Advanced pane of the Preferences window. You would set the preference to hide reminders 0 (zero) days after they have been completed. Of course, if you want to glory in your accomplishments and see the check marks for a while, set a value greater than zero for this option.

Printing the Calendar and Reminders

To print a calendar, click File in the menu bar and click Print. Select all the options you want in the Print window, shown in Figure 10.20. The view in the left pane reflects the options you select. Click Continue to open the Print dialog box. Select your printer and click Print.

> If you want to print a blank monthly calendar, create a new calendar just for this purpose. Don't schedule any appointments on it, of course.

To print only your list of reminders (whether or not they have due dates), select List for the View in the Print dialog box and deselect All-day Events and Timed Events in the Options section, as shown in Figure 10.21.

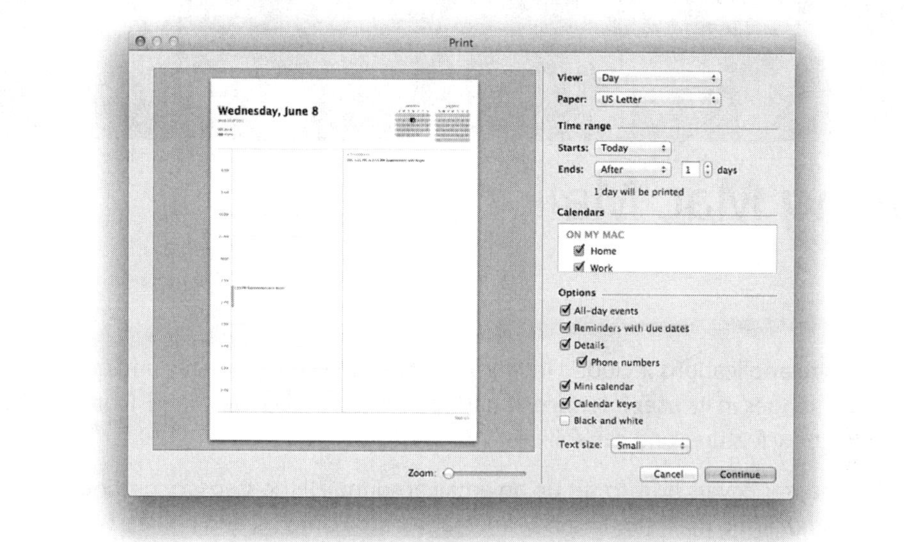

Figure 10.20 *The View option determines the layout of the printed calendar.*

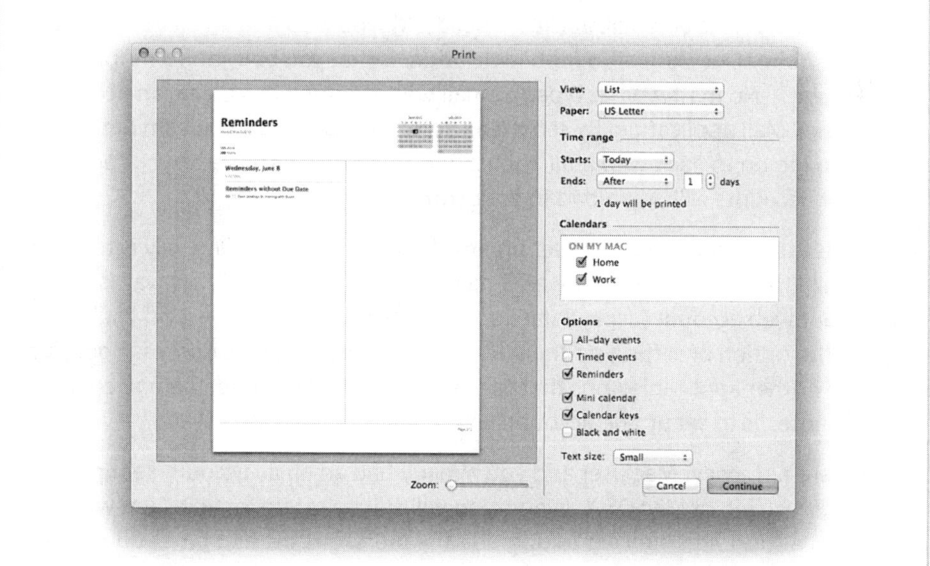

Figure 10.21 *Print your reminder list to take with you when you do your errands.*

This chapter gives you the ins and outs of using Mac Mail.

11

Using Mac Mail

Of all the applications included in Mac OS X Lion, Mail has probably undergone the most changes in its user interface. It has been completely redesigned. Lion has also added new features and capabilities.

This chapter covers how to set up an email account, all the steps for getting, viewing, and reading mail; sending new messages, attachments, and replies; filtering spam; finding, flagging, deleting, and archiving messages; creating mailboxes, creating notes, customizing Mail, and working with RSS feeds.

Getting Mail Accounts Set Up

You probably have an email address already. Maybe it's a free email address from Google, Yahoo!, or Hotmail, a MobileMe address that you bought from Apple, or one of each! No matter what type of email you have, you can create an account for it in Mac's Mail application. By setting all accounts up in Mail, you eliminate the need to log on to each web mail application separately because all your email from all your accounts will download to your computer in Mail.

There is more than one way to set up email accounts in Lion. One way is to open the Mail Preferences. In the case of Gmail, Yahoo!, and AOL, another way is to log into your web account (using Safari) after you have installed Lion, and you'll be given the option of setting up the web account with Mail, iCal, Address Book, iChat, and any other applicable apps that you have. The third method, the one covered in this chapter, is to set up the accounts in the Mail application.

If you are not a new Mac user and you already had an email account set up in a previous version of Mac OS X, everything will still be set up for you. Lion will just perform a short little process to upgrade the messages the first time you use Mail, and then you're good to go.

LET ME TRY IT

Setting Up Your First Email Account

If you have a new Mac and have not set up your email accounts before, follow these steps:

1. Click the Mail icon in the Dock. A dialog box like the one shown in Figure 11.1 opens to assist you in setting up your mail account.

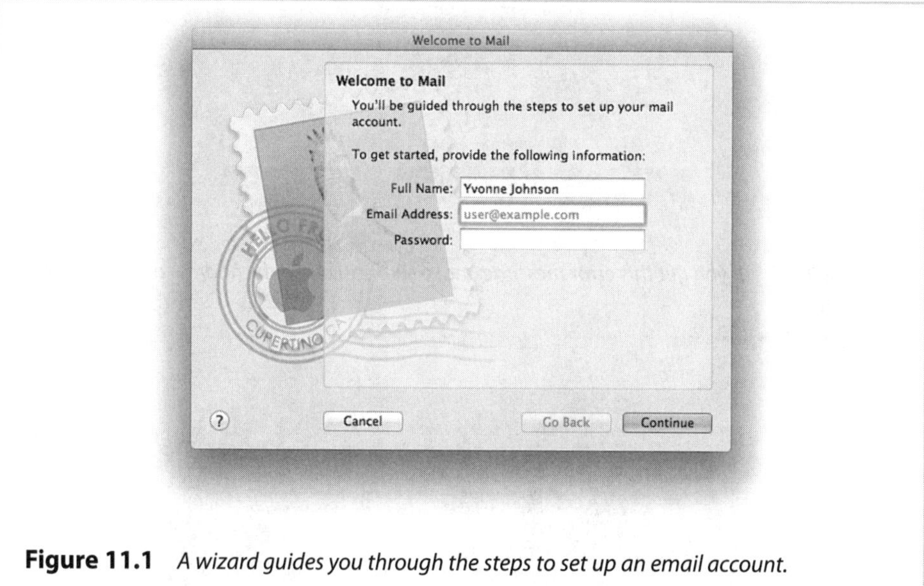

Figure 11.1 *A wizard guides you through the steps to set up an email account.*

2. If you want to change your full name, select the text and type the new text. This is the name that shows as the From name when someone gets an email from you.

You can use any name or nickname in the Full Name field.

3. Enter your email address and password and then click Create. Mac OS X connects to your email server and checks the information you have supplied. (Mac OS X knows the server to connect to based on your email address.) If your Mac has difficulty connecting or verifying your information, you see a message like the one shown in Figure 11.2. Correct your user name and/or password if you made a typographical error and click Continue. When everything checks out, a dialog box like the one shown in Figure 11.3 opens. If Mail cannot figure out your server name, it will display a dialog box for you to supply all the mail settings.

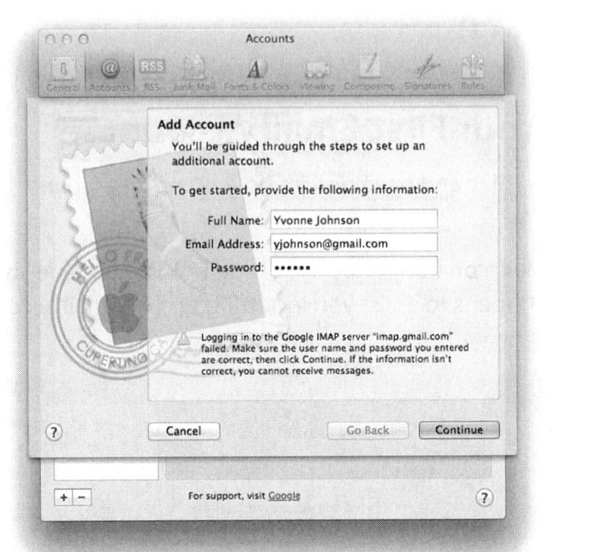

Figure 11.2 *If you get this error message, make sure you typed the address and password correctly.*

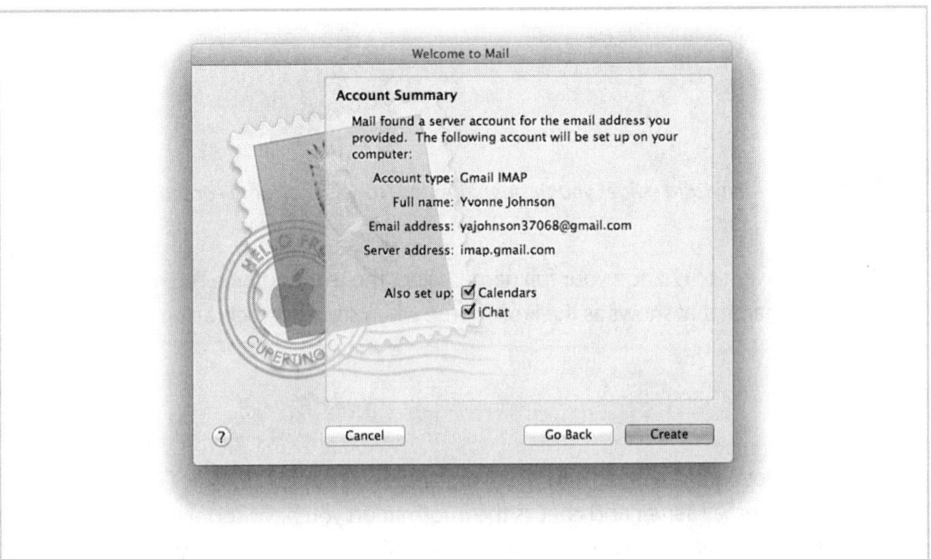

Figure 11.3 *Your Mac sets up your Mail account for you based on your email address.*

4. For some email account types, you can choose to have the setup wizard use your information to set up iCal and iChat. If you want to do that, select the appropriate options.

5. Click Create. The Mail window opens and Mail downloads any existing messages that you have. If you have quite a few messages on your mail server, downloading all the messages to your computer can take a little while.

If you want to receive messages from an additional email address that you have, click File in the menu bar, click Add Account, and then repeat the procedure just described. Email messages for both addresses display together.

Exploring the Mail Window

The Mail window has the typical window features at the top of the window—the title bar and the toolbar. A new feature in Lion, located just under the toolbar, is the Favorites bar. It has buttons for mail folders that people use most often.

The new design of the Mail window uses three panes. The pane on the left is the Message List pane. As you can guess from its name, it displays a list of messages. The right pane (the Message pane) displays the content of the email message that is selected in the Message List pane. To open the Mailbox List pane, click the Show button in the Favorites bar. Figure 11.4 shows all three panels open.

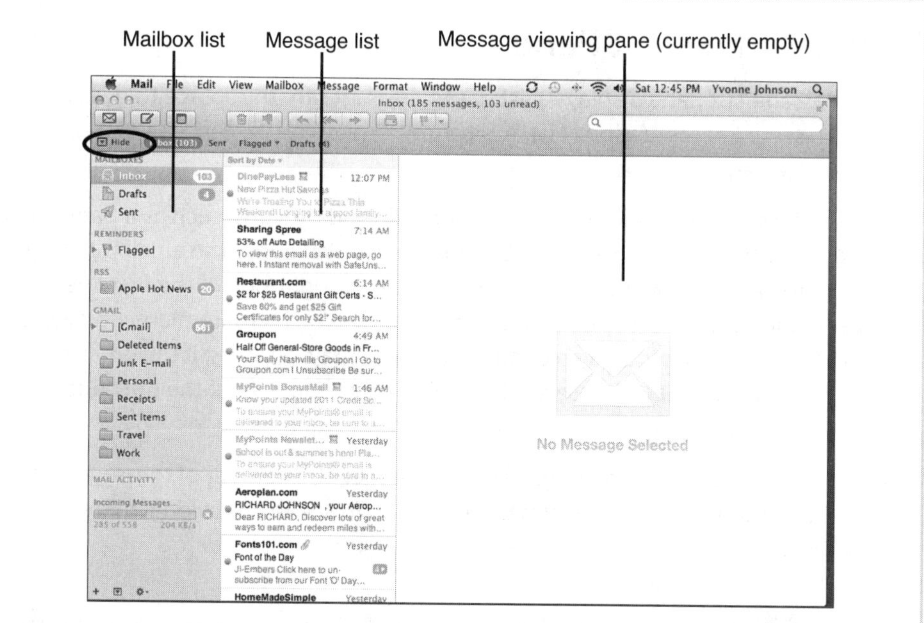

Figure 11.4 *When the Mailbox List is open, the Show button changes to the Hide button.*

If you upgraded to Lion, the first time you open Mail, you might see only the List pane. To reveal the pane on the far right, point to the right edge of the window and double-click the vertical bar. When you point to the bar, you should see a pop-up that instructs you to double-click to restore the previous location.

Exploring the Mailbox List

The Mailbox List has the following categories: Mailboxes, Reminders, RSS, and, in the case of Figure 11.4, Gmail. The Gmail category name is taken directly from the Description field in your account information. If you want to change the name of this category in the Mailbox List, open the Mail preferences window to the Account pane, edit the Description field, and save the change when prompted.

Selecting an item from one of the categories in the left pane displays the messages in that source in the List pane. For example, selecting Junk E-mail in the Mailboxes List pane displays all the email designated as junk in the List pane.

The number of messages that are unread in each mailbox displays to the right of the name in the Mailbox List.

Exploring the List Pane

The Message List pane displays a list of the messages for the source that is currently selected in the Mailbox List. A blue dot displays on the left side of any unread message.

The sender's name appears on the first line followed by icons, such as a paperclip if there is an attachment, a recycling bag for trash if Mail thinks the email is junk, a flag if you have flagged the email, and so on. At the right side of the first line appears the date or time the email was sent. If the email is more than two days old the date appears; if it is a day old, the word "yesterday" appears; if the email came today, the time appears. The second line displays the subject of the message, and the next two lines display a snippet (or preview) of your messages.

If there is more than one message from the sender, the number of messages displays in a button with a disclosure triangle on it. To see the individual messages, click the button.

You can hide the snippet by changing the number of lines to zero or increase the snippet to as many as five lines. Open the Mail preferences and click the Viewing tab to set the List Preview option.

Exploring the Message Pane

The Message pane displays the complete email message, including a photo of the sender if one exists for the sender in your Address Book. The header displays at the top, and you can view the details of the header or hide them by clicking Details or Hide. Figure 11.5 shows the difference.

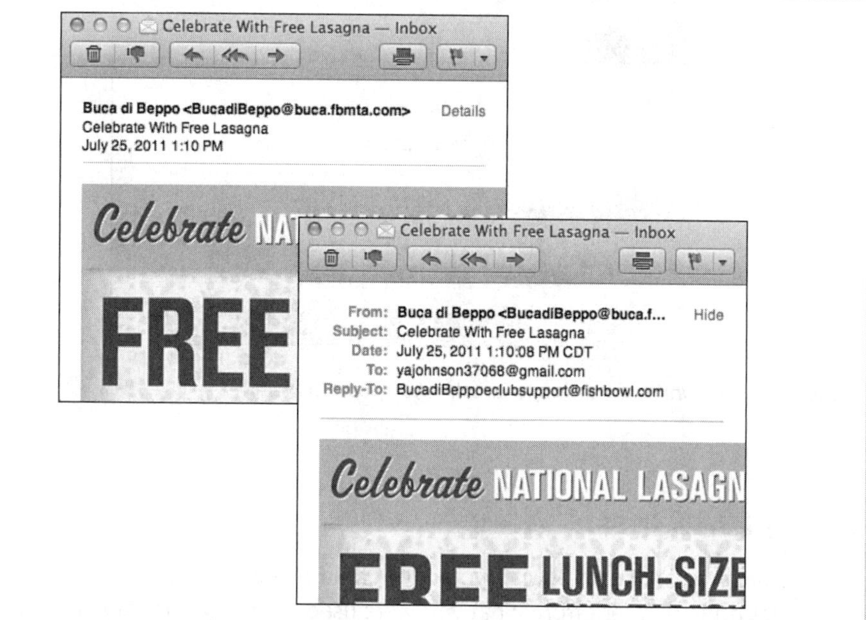

Figure 11.5 *The detailed header shows the labels for each heading plus the Reply to address.*

Another new feature in Lion is the four-button control that appears on a message's dividing line if you mouse over it (see Figure 11.6). These are called the *inline controls*. The same buttons, Delete, Reply, Reply All, and Forward, also appear on the toolbar, but this is another convenient place for the buttons, especially if you have the toolbar hidden.

Exploring the Favorites Bar

If you decide not to display the Mailbox List (to increase your mail viewing space), you can use the Favorites bar to select the folders you want to use. Just click the name of the folder to display it. Granted the Favorites bar has only a few of the folders listed in the Mailbox List, but you can add items to the Favorites bar by dragging them from the Mailbox List and dropping them in the Favorites bar. You also can delete items in the Favorites bar by dragging them off the bar. Of course, items on the Favorites bar are not the real deal. They are only links to the real folders, so deleting an item from the Favorites bar has no effect on the real folder. Finally, you can arrange items in the Favorites bar by dragging them left or right.

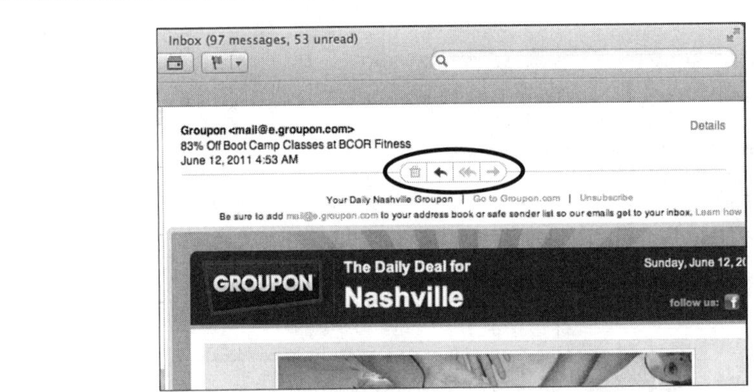

Figure 11.6 *Inline controls appear when you point to them.*

Using the Classic View

If you are a veteran user of Mail, you might be bowled over by the new look of Mail. It's quite different from what you were used to, but give it a try and see whether you like it. If you just can't get comfortable with it, you can change back to the classic look and still have the advantage of the other new features.

LET ME TRY IT

Switching to the Classic Layout

To switch to the classic layout, follow these steps:

1. Click Mail in the menu bar and click Preferences.
2. Click the Viewing tab, if necessary.
3. Select Use Classic Layout and close the preferences window. Figure 11.7 shows the classic layout.

The classic layout has a Mailbox List and a pane on the right that can be split horizontally into two panes. To split the pane, double-click the separator bar that appears at the bottom of the window. After it's split, the pane at the top displays a list of messages, and the one at the bottom displays the content of the message selected in the top pane. If you use this layout, I recommend dragging the divider line down so that you can see more messages at the top and just a few lines of the content at the bottom—enough to give you a preview of what's in the email.

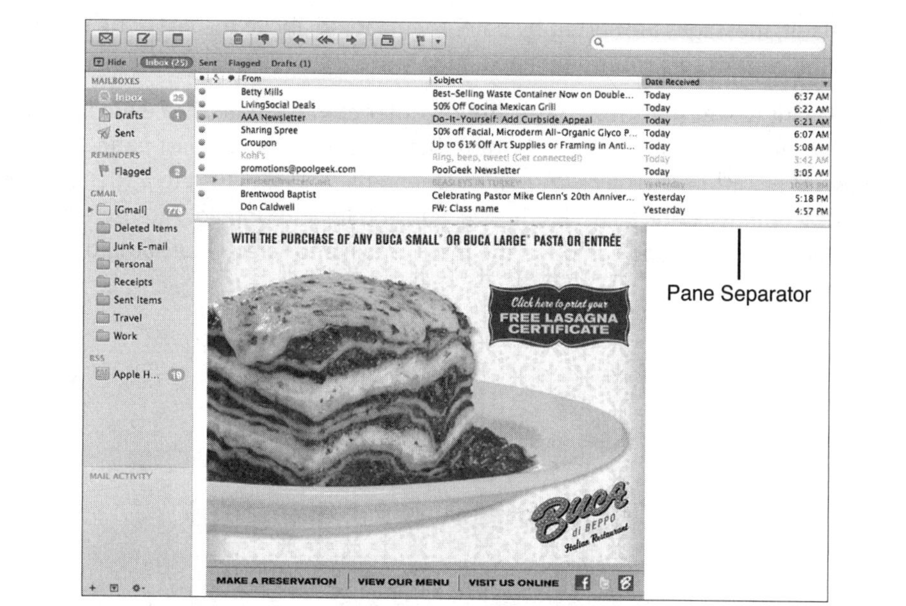

Figure 11.7 *The classic layout still has the Favorites bar.*

In the classic layout, you can decide which columns you want to see in the top-right pane and even arrange the order of the columns. To add or remove columns, click View in the menu bar and then click Columns. Click a column to select it, or click a column that has a check mark beside it to remove the column from view. To rearrange the columns, drag the column headings to the desired locations.

Getting, Viewing, and Reading Email

Before you can view or read your mail, you have to have some. By default, while you are online, Mail checks your mail server every five minutes. If new mail has arrived at the server, Mail pulls the messages down to your hard drive and puts them in your Inbox where you can view and read them any time (even when you're not online).

You can change the time interval for checking the server or manually check your mail. To change the interval, open the Mail preferences and click the General tab. Click the pop-up for Check for New Messages. Your choices are 1, 5, 15, 30, and 60 minutes. Any time you want to check for new mail, you can click the Get New Messages button in the toolbar. (It's the first button in the toolbar.)

Sorting Messages

By default, messages are sorted by date. The heading above the List pane tells you what the current sort criterion is and allows you to change the criterion.

If you want to sort messages by a criterion other than the date they were received, you can click the Sort By pop-up button that appears above the List pane, as shown in Figure 11.8 (or click View in the menu bar and click Sort By). Your choices are Attachments, Date, Flags, From, Size, Subject, To, and Unread. After selecting a criterion for sorting, you can open the menu again and select Ascending or Descending.

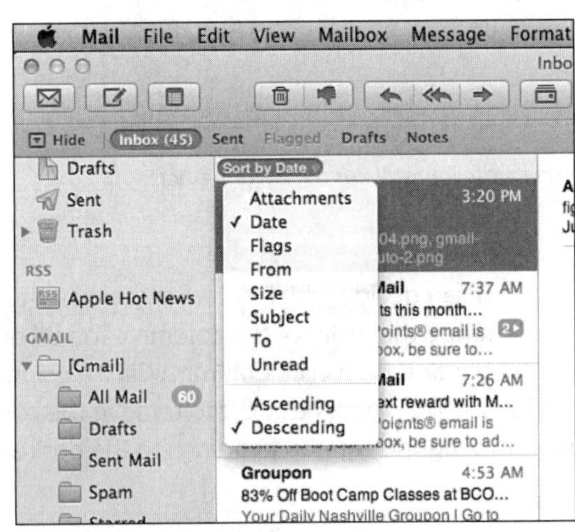

Figure 11.8 *Select a criterion to rearrange the order of the messages in the List pane.*

If you are using the classic layout, you also can sort on any column that is displayed by simply clicking the column heading. Click the column heading once to sort in one direction (ascending or descending) and click the column heading again to reverse the direction. When you click a column heading a triangle appears indicating whether the sort is ascending or descending. In the default layout, the sort order appears at the top of the column that shows all the emails.

Viewing Messages in a Conversation

By default, Mail groups messages in conversations (also called message threads). This is a redesigned feature in Lion, and it looks much better than it did in Snow Leopard (not to mention many other email applications)! Figure 11.9 shows a conversation in Mail. Each email is separated and numbered. The look is clean and uncluttered. If you want the traditional look shown in Figure 11.10, just click on the link under the signature that says See More from *<name of sender>*.

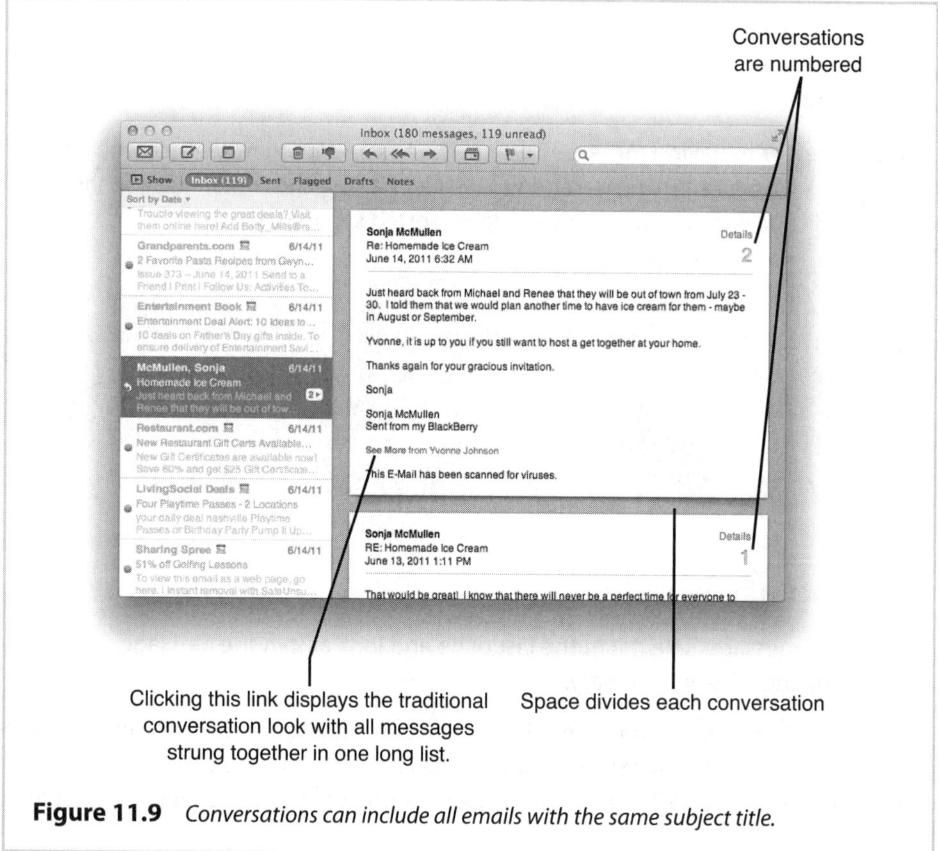

Figure 11.9 *Conversations can include all emails with the same subject title.*

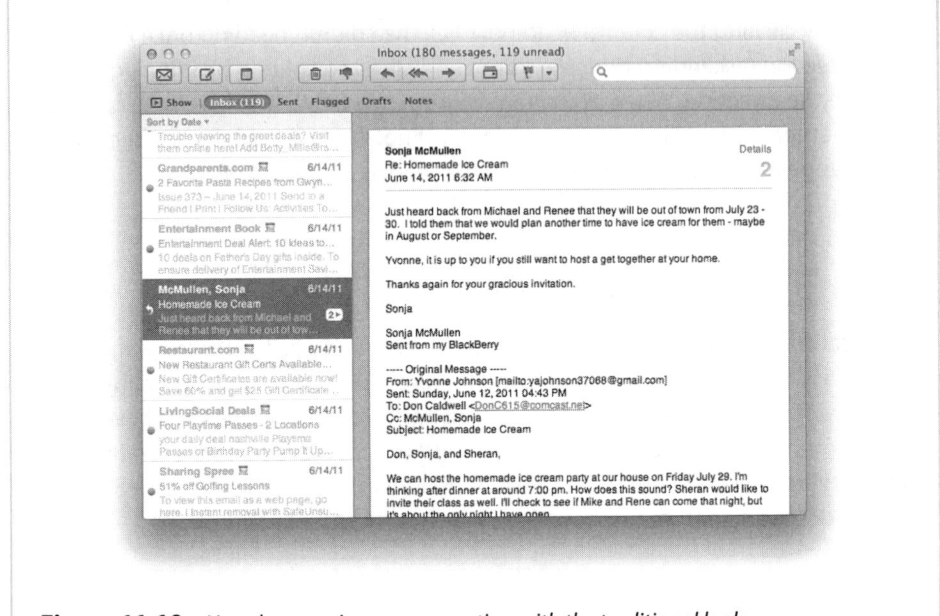

Figure 11.10 *You also can view a conversation with the traditional look.*

If you prefer not having messages grouped, you can click View in the menu bar and then click Organize by Conversation to deselect it. The check mark beside the option disappears and messages are again sorted separately.

By default, Lion includes only emails in the current mailbox in a conversation. If you want to include messages from other mailboxes, such as the Sent mailbox, in all conversations, you must set the preference Include Related Messages. You can find this preference on the Viewing tab in the Mail Preferences window. If you simply want to include related messages for a particular conversation, select it and click View in the menu bar and then click Show Related Messages.

Reading an Email

To read a message, select it in the List pane and look at it in the Message pane. Scroll the message if necessary.

When I read my email, sometimes I like to open a message in its own window. To do that, just double-click the message in the List pane. The advantage to this method is that you can have several messages open at the same time in different windows, and you can compare them or copy something from an open message and paste it in a new message or reply. The new window shows the default header information at the top and the body of the message under a thin dividing line.

If the message is a reply, you generally see the original message below the new message. If you don't see the original message, there's nothing wrong with your application; the sender has the option not to include original text in a reply.

When you receive a message from someone who is not in your Address Book, you can add that person to your Address Book by right-clicking the sender's email address in the From field and clicking Add to Address Book. In a similar manner, you can add email addresses, phone numbers, or addresses that appear within the body of an email message to the sender's existing card in the Address Book, or you can create a new card using the information. A feature called Data Detectors enables you to capture this information. Here's how. Just point to the data, click the pop-up button that appears, and select Create New Contact or Add to Existing Contact, as shown in Figure 11.11.

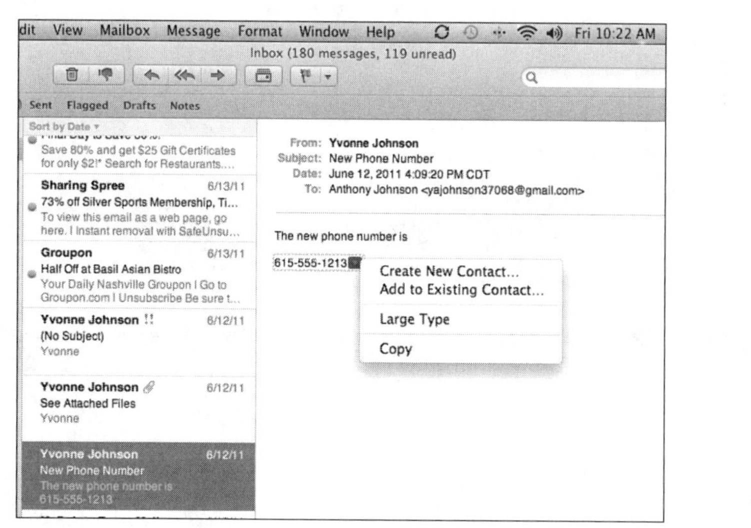

Figure 11.11 *Use pop-up menus in Data Detectors to supplement or create new contacts.*

Handling Attachments

Photos, documents, and other files that you send along with an email message are called *attachments*. If you receive a message with an attachment, the attachment information appears at the bottom of the header area, just above the dividing line, as shown in Figure 11.12. (Click Details if you do not see the information.) Some types of attachments, such as the one in Figure 11.12, can be viewed within the content of the message.

To quickly see the names of all attached files, click and hold the Save button in the header. To see the content of the attachment, click the Quick Look button in the header.

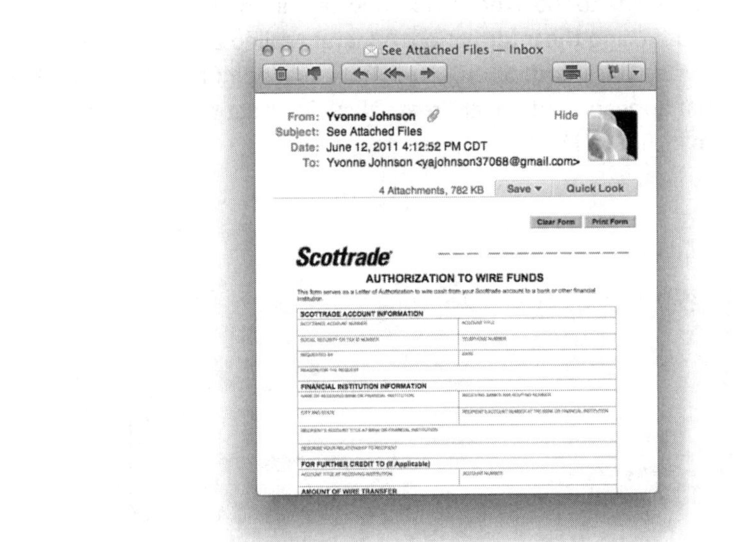

Figure 11.12 *Mail displays the number of attachments and the size in the header.*

LET ME TRY IT

Saving an Attachment in a Specific Location

To save all attachments to the Downloads folder at one time, click the Save button. If you want to decide where an attachment should be saved, follow these steps:

1. Click and hold the pop-up button on the Save button until you see the pop-up menu.

2. Click the name of the file. A dialog box opens, as shown in Figure 11.13. (If the Finder does not appear in the bottom portion of the dialog box, click the disclosure arrow to the right of the Save As box.)
3. Type a name for the file in the Save As box if you want to name it something else.
4. In the Finder, navigate to the location where you want to save the file.
5. Click Save.

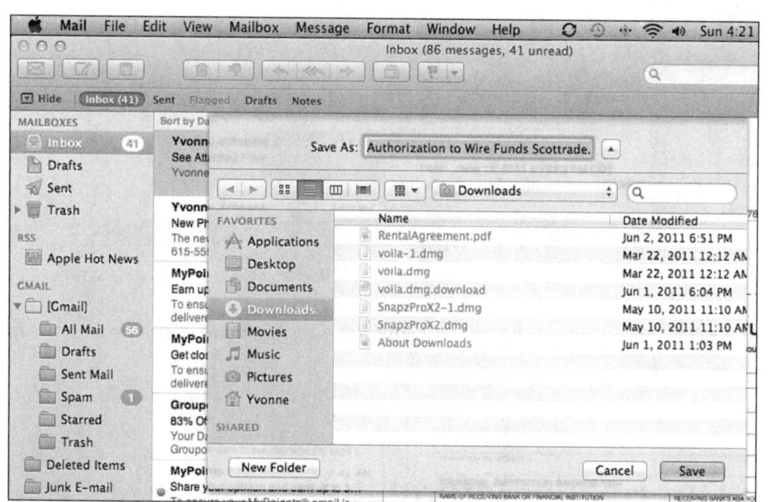

Figure 11.13 *Use the Finder to select the location where you want to save the attachment.*

For graphic files, you can click Add to iPhoto on the Save pop-up menu and import the files directly into iPhoto.

Sending New Messages and Replies

To send a new email message, click the New Message button in the toolbar (second button on the left). The message form opens in its own window, as shown in Figure 11.14.

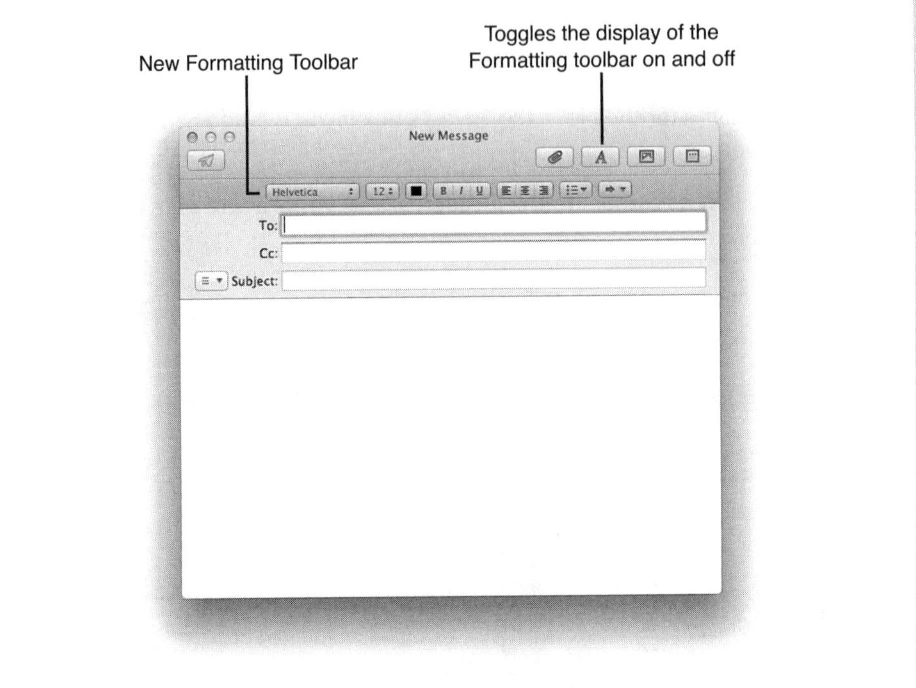

Figure 11.14 *The fields at the top comprise the message header. The body of the message is below the header.*

Filling Out Header Information

When preparing an email to send, you must at least fill out the To field in the header. Although not required, the other fields you can fill out are CC, Bcc, Reply to, and Subject, described here:

- **To address field**—Fill in the To line with the first recipient's email address. As you start typing, the auto-complete feature kicks in. If the recipient's name and email address are in your Address Book, auto-complete pulls the information from there and completes the address for you, encapsulating the address in a blue bubble. Type additional recipients in the To field if necessary. All recipients of your message will be able to see all the addresses you include in this field and the Cc field.

Auto-complete allows you to type the person's name (exactly as it appears in the Address Book) instead of an email address that is too difficult to remember. For example, you can type *Brad Harris* in the To field instead of *harris372.b.r@bestlittleinternetproviderintheworld.net*.

Additionally, auto-complete pulls information from the Previous Recipients List that Mail keeps for you. This list contains the email addresses you have sent messages to in the past. Most addresses on the list do not have a name, so Mail can only complete those without names if you start typing the actual email address. To refer to the Previous Recipients List, click Window in the menu bar and then click Previous Recipients.

- **Cc address field**—Fill in the Cc line with addresses of recipients who should receive a copy of the message. Auto-complete works here, too. All recipients of your message will be able to see all the addresses you include in this field and the To field. People in the Cc field may feel that they are not as important as the people in the To field or that they have no responsibility to take any action in regard to the subject of the email. They see a copied email as a simple FYI. You've been advised. Address accordingly.
- **Bcc address field**—The Bcc (blind carbon copy) field does not appear by default. To add it to the header, click the pop-up button to the left of the Subject line (see Figure 11.15) and then click Bcc Address Field. Fill in the Bcc line with addresses of recipients who should receive a copy of the email without the To and Cc recipients knowing it. Only recipients in the Bcc field will be able to see addresses in the Bcc field, but these recipients will be able to see everyone that you include in the To and Cc fields.

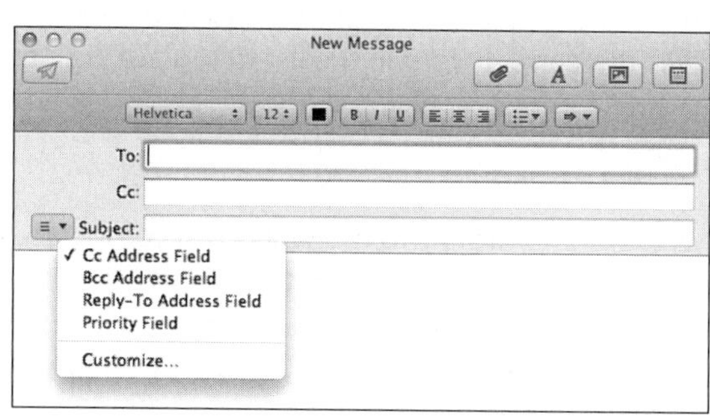

Figure 11.15 *Use this pop-up to display additional fields in the header.*

TELL ME MORE Media 11.1—A Discussion about Special Uses for the Bcc Field

Access this audio recording through your registered Web Edition at ***my.safaribooksonline.com/9780132819091/media*** *or on the DVD for print books.*

- **Reply-To address field**—This field also does not appear by default. To add it to the header, click the pop-up button to the left of the Subject line (see Figure 11.17) and then click Reply-To Address Field. Type one of your other email addresses in this field if you do not want replies sent to the address that originates the message.
- **Subject field**—Type a word or phrase that relates to the content of the message.

Instead of typing recipients in the To, Cc, or Bcc fields, you can drag them from the Address Book. Click the Show Addresses button in the toolbar to open the Address Book. To send email to a distribution list, drag a group from the Address Book.

Typing the Message

After you fill in the appropriate header information, click in the large white space below the header to start typing the message. As you type, Mail checks your spelling, marking misspelled words with a dotted red underline. You can right-click a misspelled word to display a pop-up menu with suggestions for the word you meant to type. Click the correct word in the list to replace your mistake.

Formatting Messages

Mail gives you two different formats to use when you compose a message—plain text and rich text. Plain-text messages cannot use formatting, but rich-text messages can use bold, italic, numbered or bulleted lists, different fonts, different font sizes, colors, stationery, embedded graphics, and so on. Email purists, however, prefer plain text for several reasons:

- Any type of email service that the recipient might have can read it.
- It's a safe format for recipients who are PC users, unlike rich text, which can be used to mask security threats and malware, causing many system administrators to bounce incoming messages in rich text format. (This is not a problem for Mac users who are using Mac Mail.)

- It's faster to send and uses less bandwidth.
- It opens faster for the recipient.

Although I almost always use plain-text emails, I use the rich-text format in some circumstances—if the recipient uses a Mac, or I need to make the message more readable by using bold text or formatted lists and I know the receiving mail server accepts rich text. If I need to use sophisticated formatting, I just create a document and attach it to the email. I hope you will follow my example and resist the urge to use ten different font colors and sizes, embedded pictures, and a colored background just to send the earth-shattering message, "Whassup?"

If you want to include some "light" formatting in a message, first click the Format menu and make sure that you are currently using Rich Text as the format. If Rich Text is the current format, the Format menu displays Make Plain Text. (I know. It seems backwards, but that's just the way it works. It's a toggle.) Then use the new Formatting toolbar (refer to Figure 11.14) to select the font, size, color, and emphasis (bold, italic, or underline), as well as the paragraph alignment, numbering, bulleting, and indent.

Setting a Message Priority

Assigning a priority to an email before you send it adds a visual cue for the recipient (see Figure 11.16). Different email applications use different symbols as visual cues. In Mail, a high-priority message has two exclamation points after the sender's name in the List pane.

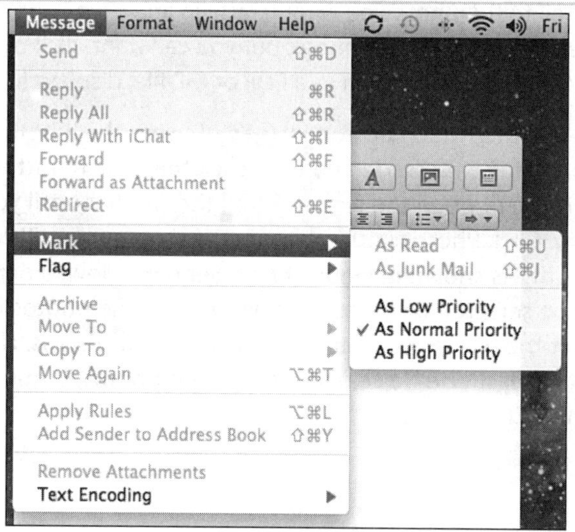

Figure 11.16 *Assigning a priority level to an email tells the recipient how important it is.*

Sending Attachments

As explained earlier in this chapter, attachments are files that you send with an email. Technically, you can attach and send any file, but many email servers have a limit on the size of a file you can send and receive. Most email servers only accept files under 5MB.

If you have a file that is more than 5MB, you can compress it before you attach it; however, don't bother compressing JPG, GIF, PDF, MP3, AAC, WMV, WMA, or MOV files because the compressed file won't be any smaller than the original. To compress a file, select the file in Finder, click File on the menu bar, and click Compress.

What can you do if you need to send a large file? Use a free service such as You Send It. You upload the file to You Send It, You Send It notifies the recipient by email that you have uploaded a file for them, and the recipient downloads the file from You Send It. If the file is too large for the free service offered by You Send It, try DropBox.

To attach a text file to a new message or a new reply, click in the body of the message (maybe at the end of the message under your name) and click the Attach button. Locate the file in the Finder that you want to attach and double-click it. The file appears as an icon with the name and size displayed under it.

The easiest way to attach a photo that is stored in iPhoto is to use the iPhoto Browser. To display the browser, click the Photo Browser button on the right side of the toolbar. Scroll to the photo you want to attach and drag it into the body of the message. It comes in as a full-size photo, but you can right-click the photo and click View as Icon. (Any graphic file, such as a PDF or GIF file, displays in full size.)

If you want to use the Attach button instead of using the iPhoto Browser, first click in the body of the message and then click the Attach button (the one with the paperclip on it) to open the Finder. Scroll the sidebar until you see the Media category. Click Photos in this category and then click iPhoto in the top pane on the right. As shown in Figure 11.17, Send Windows-Friendly Attachments should be selected by default. Scroll through the photos in the bottom pane and select the ones you want. To select adjacent photos, click the first one and Shift-click the last one. To select nonadjacent photos, Command-click each photo. Then click Choose File.

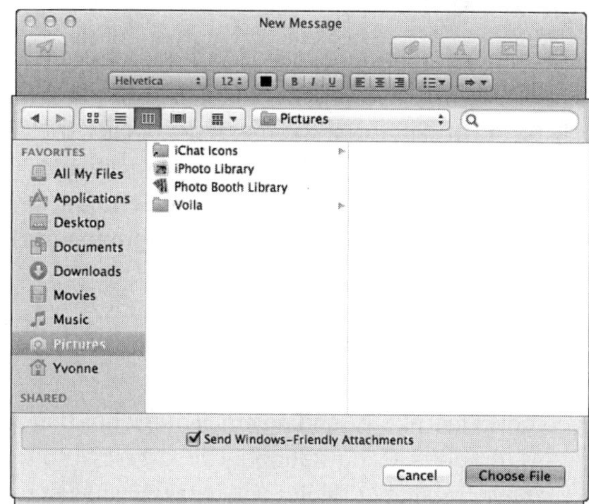

Figure 11.17 *Windows users may not be able to open your attachments if you don't send "friendly" ones.*

Sending a Message

When you are finally ready to send the message, click the Send button (the button with the paper airplane on it). If you are online, the message goes out immediately. If you are offline, the message goes into the Outbox and waits until you are online again to be sent.

Saving a Message as a Draft

If you want to stop typing a message and finish it later, click the red Close button and then click Save. Lion saves the message in the Drafts folder. Then when you have time, click the Drafts folder in the Mailbox List, double-click the draft message, type the rest of the message, and click the Send button. (If you are a new user, you will not see a Drafts folder in the Mailbox List until you actually save a message as a draft.)

Opening Mail and sending a new message is not the only way to send an email. You can originate emails from other applications as well, including Address Book, iCal, iPhoto, Safari, TextEdit, and so on. Lion also provides one new way to send an email. In the Finder, you can right-click a file and click New Email with Attachment. This seems like a little feature, but I bet many people out there like me have wanted this feature for a long time.

Replying to a Message

To reply to a message that you have received, click the message in the Message List pane to select it or double-click it to open it in its own window. Click the Reply button to send a reply to the originator of the message, or click the Reply All button to send a reply to the originator and the original copied recipients. If you want to, add additional recipients. Type the message and click the Send button. After you have replied to a message, a curved arrow icon appears before the message to let you know you have sent a reply.

Using Stationery

I've already told you how I feel about sending email messages that are bloated with formatting and useless graphics. Using stationery *almost* falls into this category, and I personally don't ever use it, but I'll give you a pass if you just use it for special occasions—which is its intended purpose. Mail provides stationery templates in the following categories: Birthday, Announcements, Photos, Stationery, and Sentiments.

All you have to do to use stationery is create a new email message, click the Show or Hide Stationery Panel button in the toolbar, click the category, and click the template you want to use. Figure 11.18 shows the panel with templates.

If the template contains photo placeholders, drag your own photos to the placeholders. Select the text and replace it with your own. Address and send the email as you normally would.

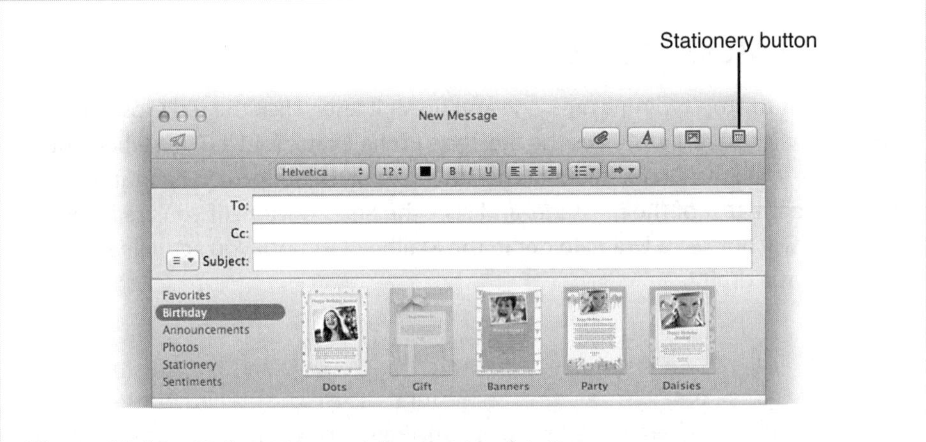

Figure 11.18 *Mail provides several categories of stationery.*

Filtering Spam

Spam is another one of those terms that needs no explanation. You know what it is whether it's fried and put on your plate or sent to your email address. Most mail servers have spam filters that they apply to incoming mail, and Mail has its own filters as well. So in all likelihood, you are doubly protected.

When you first start using Mail, you have to train it for a while to help it identify true junk mail. By default, it flags a message as junk if the sender is not in your Address Book, if you have not sent mail to the sender recently, or if the email is addressed to just your email address and not your full name. These messages appear in the Inbox with brown text so you can recognize them and confirm that they are actually junk mail. If Mail flags a message that is not spam, you should click the Not Junk button so that Mail knows not to mark it the next time.

After Mail seems to be getting it right most of the time, you can tell it to start putting the junk mail messages in the Junk mailbox so they are not mixed in with your regular mail in the Inbox. This instruction is on the Junk Mail pane of the Mail preferences window shown in Figure 11.19. (Click Mail in the menu bar and click Preferences to open the window.)

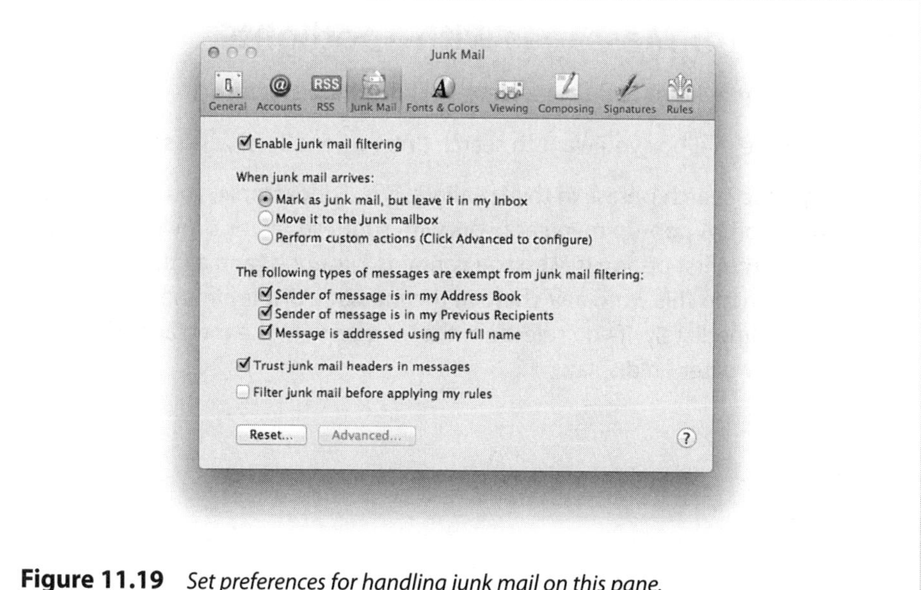

Figure 11.19 *Set preferences for handling junk mail on this pane.*

Finding Messages

Sorting messages in ascending or descending order is one method you can use to find a particular email (see "Sorting Messages" earlier in this chapter), but if you've read any other chapters in this book, you know that Spotlight is the go-to guy for finding anything. Lion has added new capabilities to the Spotlight feature in Mail, making it even more powerful than before. Now, when you type a search word or phrase, Lion makes suggestions for you to choose from based on the actual messages in your Inbox. Additionally, you can type more than one search phrase in the Spotlight search field. So, for example, you can specify a sender name, a date, and some words in the subject.

SHOW ME **Media 11.2—A Video about Searching for Emails and Creating Smart Mailboxes**

Access this video file through your registered Web Edition at
my.safaribooksonline.com/9780132819091/media
or on the DVD for print books.

Searching for Messages with Spotlight

To search for messages and save a search, follow these steps:

1. Click the mailbox you want to search (Inbox, Sent, Trash, and so on).
2. Type the search phrase in the Spotlight box. For example, you might type "groupon." A pop-up menu appears with suggestions, as shown in Figure 11.20. The first option is Message contains "groupon," and all the messages that contain this word anywhere in the message display in the Mail window immediately. If you select another suggestion, the messages that fit the new criterion display.

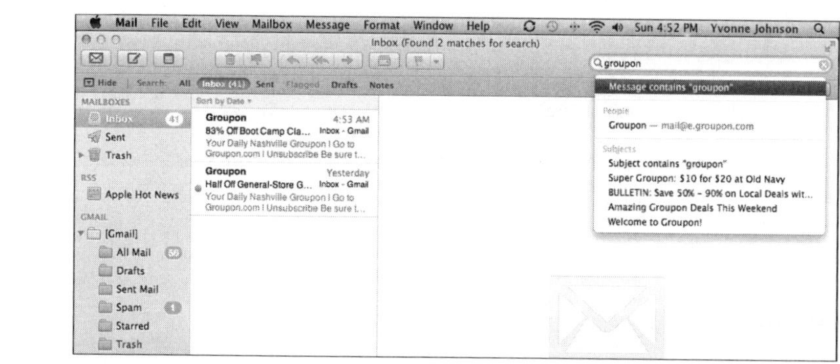

Figure 11.20 *Suggestions provided are based on your actual emails.*

Mail even searches the names and content of attachments—a new feature in Lion. If the word or phrase you type in the search box is contained in an attachment name or its content, a suggestion appears in the list for Attachments.

3. After you select a suggestion, the search field generally displays a search token followed by the suggestion, as shown in Figure 11.21. Sometimes the search token has a pop-up button that allows you to change the scope of the token. To change the scope, click the pop-up button (if there is one) and make a different selection. For example, if the search field has a From search token, you can click it and then select To or Entire Message. The messages that display change again to fit the scope of the new criterion.

Figure 11.21 *This search token has a pop-up button.*

4. Repeat steps 2 and 3 to continue adding search criteria. The messages that display must match all the criteria. Figure 11.22 shows two criteria. I am looking for all messages I received from Groupon.com yesterday.
5. To change the scope of the search, select All in the Favorites bar or click a different folder. Messages that meet your complete criteria appear instantaneously, and you can double-click a message to open it.

Figure 11.22 *Being able to specify more than one search item in the search box is a new feature in Lion.*

LET ME TRY IT

Saving a Spotlight Search in Mail

You can search your mailboxes on a case-by-case basis, as described in the previous set of steps, or you can save a search to use it over and over again. A saved search is referred to as a *Smart Mailbox*. To save a Spotlight search, follow these steps:

1. Type the criteria in the Spotlight as explained in the previous set of steps.
2. Click Save in the Favorites bar (located on the far right side). The dialog box shown in Figure 11.23 opens.

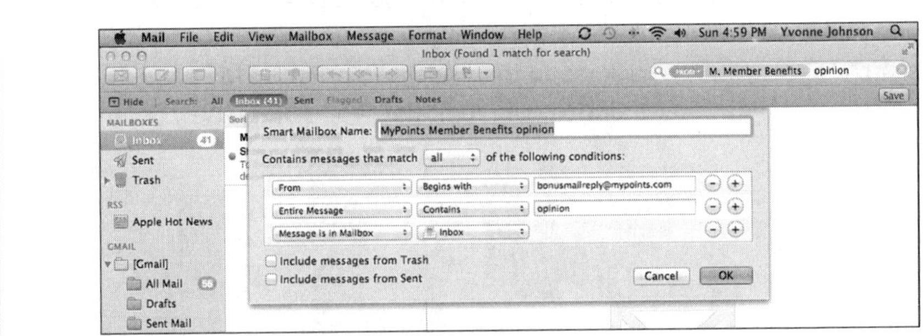

Figure 11.23 *Change the default Smart Mailbox Name if you want to.*

3. Type a name for the Smart Mailbox if you don't like the one that is supplied for you. This is the name that appears in the Mailbox list when the Smart Mailbox is saved.
4. Select the appropriate option for Contains Messages that Match <All> or <Any> of the Following Conditions. If you select All, the default, only messages that meet all the conditions display. If you select Any, all messages that meet any one of the conditions display.

5. Make any changes you want in the criteria that are listed or delete an existing criteria by clicking the Remove button beside it (the button with the minus).
6. Add another criterion by clicking an Add button (the button with the plus). The new criterion fields display on the line under the line with the Add button that you clicked. Specify the options for the new criterion.
7. If you want the results of your search to include messages in the Trash or Sent folders, check mark the appropriate option.
8. Click OK when all conditions are defined. The Smart Mailbox appears in the Mailbox list and you can click it at any time to see the latest content.

To clear the results of the search, delete the text in the Spotlight box by pressing Esc or clicking the X in the Spotlight search field.

Flagging Messages

Mail provides seven different-colored flags that you can attach to messages. You can attach your own personal significance to each color. For example, you might flag all your most urgent messages with a red flag and all your messages that are on the verge of being deleted with a gray flag.

When you apply a flag to a message, Mail creates a folder named for whatever color you use for the flag, such as Red. The new folder appears under the Reminders category in the Mailbox List and all messages with that color flag are accessible from the folder.

These are the actions you can take with flags:

- To attach a flag, select the message (or multiple messages), click the Flag pop-up button in the toolbar, and click the flag color.
- To see all your flagged messages listed together, click the Flagged button in the Favorites bar.
- To clear a flag, select the message (or multiple messages), click the Flag pop-up button in the toolbar, and click Clear Flag.
- To search for a flagged message in Spotlight, use the color of the flag as a criterion (see Figure 11.24).

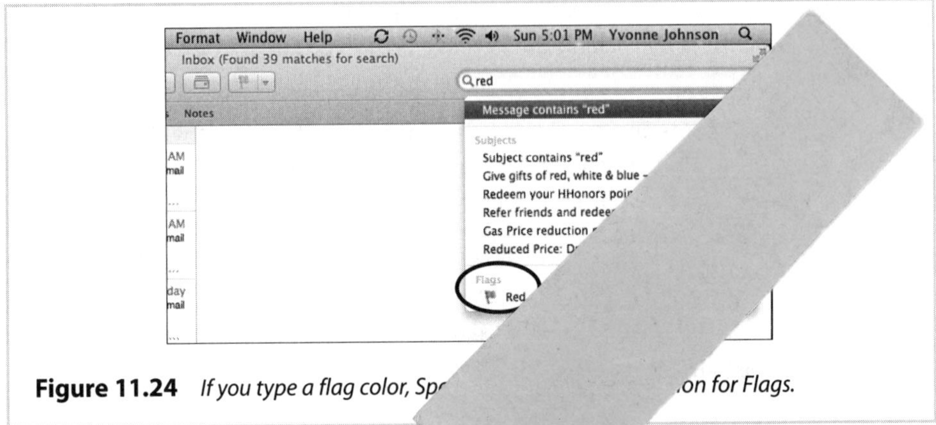

Figure 11.24 *If you type a flag color, Sp ... on for Flags.*

Archiving Messages

An archived message is one that has been removed from the Inbox and stored in the Archive folder. It remains in the Archive folder until you delete it. To archive a message, select the message, click Message in the menu bar, and click Archive. It's that simple. Just two clicks! Want to cut your work in half? Add the Archive button to the toolbar and you can archive with one click! See "Customizing Mail" later in this chapter.

Deleting Messages

Keeping up with email and deleting messages that you no longer need or want can be like bailing water on the *Titanic* with a teacup. I personally have hundreds of email messages in my Inbox this very minute and I haven't read 80 of them. I'm sure that at least half of those messages should be deleted. If you are diligent and delete messages right away instead of letting them pile up, all you have to do is click the Delete button in the toolbar after you read the message.

If you procrastinate or you get tons of email every day like I do, then you need a better method than deleting messages one by one. When I have time to go on a cleaning binge, I sort the Inbox by sender, and then I delete all the messages from my friend Betty Lou and my Aunt Eunice because neither one of them ever send me anything but the latest joke, the cutest animated picture of a dancing frog, or the world's stupidest home video. Then I delete all the automatic bill reminders, the newsletters that I haven't had time to read, and the expired notifications of weekly specials at Costco. To delete messages in bulk, click the first message in the group and Shift-click the last message to select the entire group. Then click the Delete button in the toolbar.

Another method of deleting multiple emails is to group messages by conversation. If you no longer need all the emails associated with last Christmas' Secret Santa party, you can delete them all at once by first grouping by conversation and then deleting the most recent message in the conversation. Note, however, that related messages, those in other mailboxes, are not deleted.

Creating Mailboxes

Because the Spotlight feature can find anything for you, you could just leave all your mail in the Inbox in one gigantically long list, but wouldn't you feel more in control if you could put your messages in folders like files? Well, actually you can. You don't really put them in folders; you put them in mailboxes, but for all intents and purposes, it's the same thing. To create a mailbox, click Mailbox in the menu bar and then click New Mailbox. Select the location, name it, and click OK. Then drag messages from the Inbox to the new mailbox.

Customizing Mail

Beyond selecting a layout to use for the Mail window (the new layout or the classic layout), you can make some additional customizations in the Mail Preferences window. For example, you can specify the fonts and colors you want to use on the Fonts & Colors tab, and you can create different signatures to use for different purposes on the Signatures tab.

Other customizations you can make include adding buttons to the toolbar and setting limits on email usage with parental controls.

SHOW ME **Media 11.3—A Video about Customizing the Mail Toolbar**
Access this video file through your registered Web Edition at
my.safaribooksonline.com/9780132819091/media
or on the DVD for print books.

LET ME TRY IT

Customizing the Mail Toolbar

A large number of buttons are available to the Mail toolbar. To add or delete buttons in the toolbar, follow these steps:

1. Click View in the menu bar and click Customize Toolbar. The dialog box shown in Figure 11.25 opens.

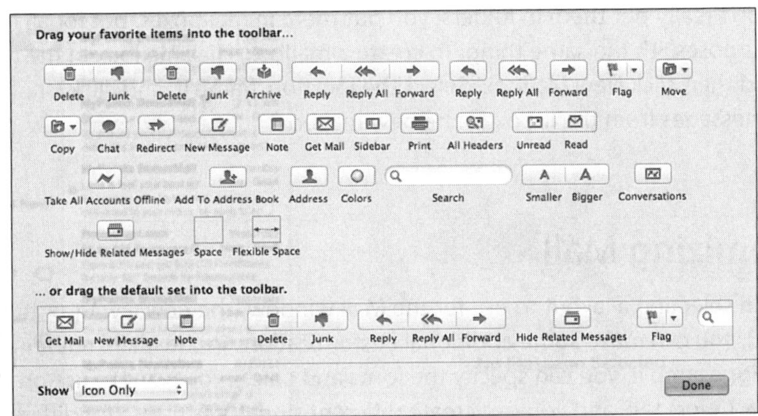

Figure 11.25 *Customize the Mail toolbar by adding buttons for menu commands you use frequently.*

2. Drag the buttons that you want onto the toolbar and drop them in the positions you want them to occupy. I recommend adding the Print button and the Conversations button.
3. Drag the buttons you don't want off the toolbar.
4. Even if you don't make any changes to the buttons on the toolbar, I recommend that you select Icon and Text for the Show option in this dialog box.
5. When finished, click Done.

SHOW ME **Media 11.4—A Video about Setting Parental Controls in Email**

Access this video file through your registered Web Edition at
my.safaribooksonline.com/9780132819091/media
or on the DVD for print books.

LET ME TRY IT

Setting Parental Controls in Email

Using parental controls you can specify all the email addresses with which an account can exchange email. Additionally, you can set an option to have an email sent to you whenever the user attempts to exchange email with a contact not on the list. To set these controls, follow these steps:

1. Click the System Preferences icon in the Dock and click Users & Groups.
2. Click the lock icon and type your password. If you do not have an Administrative account, you must enter the name and password of an Administrative account. Click Unlock and the padlock opens, allowing you to make changes.
3. Select the user account in the sidebar and click Enable Parental Controls if it is not already selected.
4. Click Open Parental Controls and click the People tab.
5. Click Limit Mail, as shown in Figure 11.26.

Figure 11.26 *Use Parental Controls to limit email.*

6. Click the Add button (the plus sign) in the right pane. The dialog box shown in Figure 11.27 opens. Enter the first and last name and the email address of the approved person.

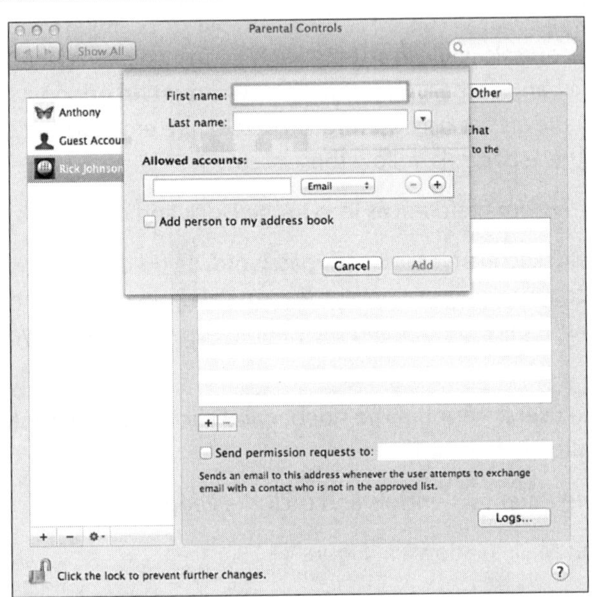

Figure 11.27 *Specify names that you will allow the user to send emails to and from.*

7. Click Add Person to My Address Book if you want and then click Add.
8. Repeat steps 6 and 7 for all persons on your approved list.
9. Close the Preferences window and Lion locks the padlock for you automatically.

Synchronizing Email on All Your Devices

Because Mail is a program that has to operate with a mail server, usually no problem occurs keeping your email messages synchronized across devices. The server usually does this for you automatically. So if you set up your email account on your Mac as well as on your iPhone, and you delete an email message using your iPhone, the iPhone sends that information to the server. The next time you check email on your Mac, the server deletes the message on your Mac that you deleted from the iPhone.

Even more robust and more automatic synchronization for Mail will be available in the fall of 2011, when iCloud is available. If you purchase iOS5 for your iPhone, iPad, or iPod Touch, or OS X Lion, iCloud is free.

If you have been paying the yearly $99 fee for a MobileMe account, you'll be able to move your MobileMe email address to the iCloud for free and within a year (June 30, 2012), MobileMe will no longer be available.

See Chapter 16, "Keeping Your Mac Safe, Updated, and Backed Up", to learn more about iCloud.

Quitting Mail

When you quit Mail using any of the standard methods (clicking Mail, Quit Mail; pressing Command-Q; and so on), Mail closes all open windows. If you have email messages open in their own windows, it closes those. If you have started new messages or replies, it saves them in the Drafts folder and closes them. When you start Mail again, the same windows open.

This chapter covers the features of the two communication applications—iChat and FaceTime—including making presentations in video chats and screen sharing.

12

Using iChat and FaceTime

iChat and FaceTime are two applications that you can use to communicate with other users in real time. Although iChat has a more extensive reach, FaceTime is more cutting edge. In iChat, you can communicate with a wider range of people, and you do have video capabilities, but you can't communicate with iPhones as you can with FaceTime.

Using iChat

Instant messaging has come a long way baby—from typed messages with "emoticons" to full-scale audio and video—and Mac's iChat application provides it all. It is also compatible with the major IM accounts offered by Yahoo!, AOL, MobileMe, Google and other services that use Jabber. All you need is an instant messaging account, and you are ready to chat with your friends.

Opening iChat the First Time

If you have a Gmail or Yahoo! email address, the first time you open the account in Safari using the new Lion operating system, you are given the opportunity to set up Mac Mail and iChat automatically. This is the easiest way to set up both applications. If you decide not to do this, then, of course, you can set up the applications when you open the programs for the first time on your Mac. Additionally, if you set up Mac Mail first, you have the option to have Mail set up iChat for you.

If you haven't set up iChat automatically, before you open iChat for the first time, be prepared. You need to have an IM (instant message) account. If you don't have one, or you don't have time to set one up, don't even bother opening iChat. When you have the time to set up an account, then open iChat and let it guide you through the process. Naturally, you must be online to complete this process.

If you haven't set up iChat, then the first time you open it, a welcome screen opens and gives you an overview of what you can do with iChat, your "personal videoconferencing system." Click Continue to move on. In the next dialog box, shown in

Figure 12.1, you must supply your IM account type, the name associated with your account, and your password. After filling in all the information, click the Continue button, and then click the Done button to start using iChat.

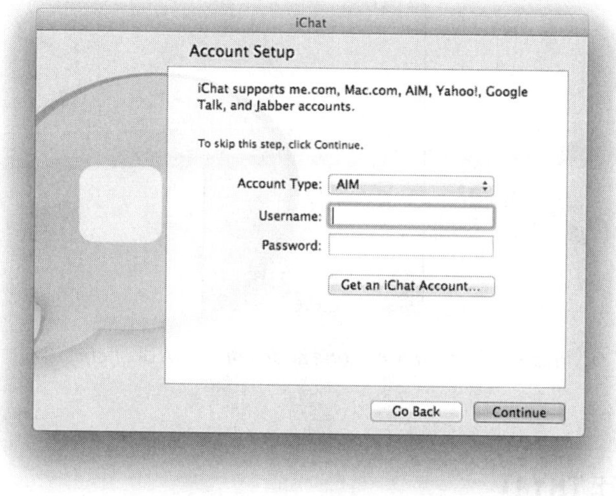

Figure 12.1 *If you don't have an IM account, you can get an AOL account or an Apple ID account by clicking Get an iChat Account.*

If you have set up iChat through the web or through Mac Mail, the first time you open iChat, you will be offline. Click iChat in the menu bar and click the option to log in. Enter your password and press Return.

Your buddy list window opens immediately. As shown in Figure 12.2, your name is listed under the title bar. If you have added a photo or graphic image to your address card, that image displays beside your name as well. Otherwise, a generic icon displays. Your buddy list may have buddies in it if you have contacts with accounts for the same chat service.

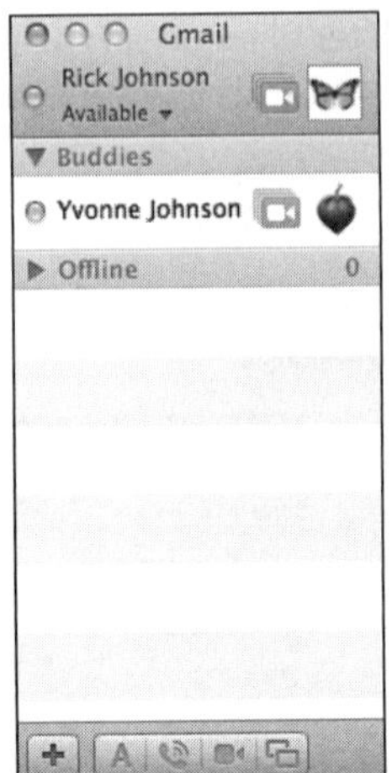

Figure 12.2 *My husband Rick only has one buddy and I am online!*

Changing Your Picture

If you have not selected a picture for yourself in the Address Book, or you just want to use a different picture in iChat, you can change your picture in iChat without affecting the Address Book. To change your picture, follow these steps:

1. Click iChat in the menu bar and click Change My Picture. The dialog box shown in Figure 12.3 opens.
2. Use one of these three methods to acquire your picture:
   - Click the button with the camera, look at your built-in camera lens and smile. The camera counts down from three. Repeat this step if you don't like the photo.
   - Click the pop-up button for Recent Pictures and click one of those.
   - Click Choose, navigate to the picture you want to use, and double-click it. (If you click Pictures in the sidebar and click iChat Icons you will find nine different folders with icons you can choose.)
3. To zoom in or out on the picture, drag the slider to the right or the left. If you zoom in, you can then point to the picture and drag the part of the picture you want to use into the frame.

4. To add a special effect to the picture, click the Apply an Effect button under the slider. The effects dialog box opens. Click the right arrow button in the lower-right corner of the dialog box to see more effects. Click the effect that you want.

5. Click Set.

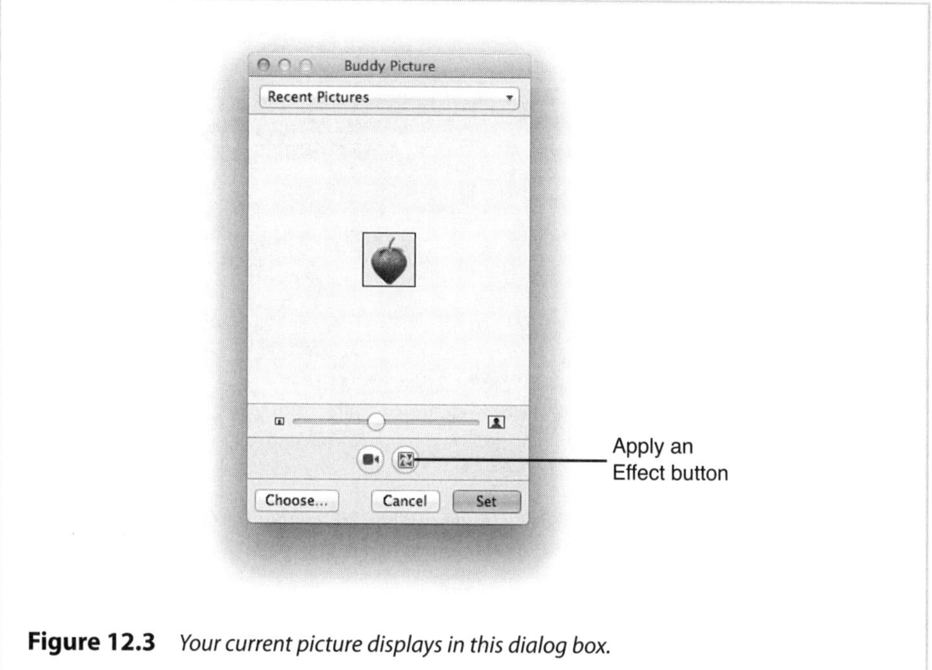

Figure 12.3 *Your current picture displays in this dialog box.*

LET ME TRY IT

Setting Up Additional Accounts

Setting up the right type of chat account is key. If all your friends have Google Talk accounts, and you have a MobileMe account, you'll have to set up a Google Talk account to chat with them. With these two accounts you can chat with people who have a me.com account, mac.com account, AOL account, and a Gmail account. But what about your Yahoo! friends? Well, you'll have to get a Yahoo! account to talk with them. Fortunately, if you have more than one account for chatting, you can set up all your accounts in iChat. To set up additional chat accounts, follow these steps:

1. Click iChat in the menu bar and click Preferences.

2. Click the Accounts tab, if necessary.

3. Click the Add button (+) at the bottom of the Accounts list (shown in Figure 12.4).

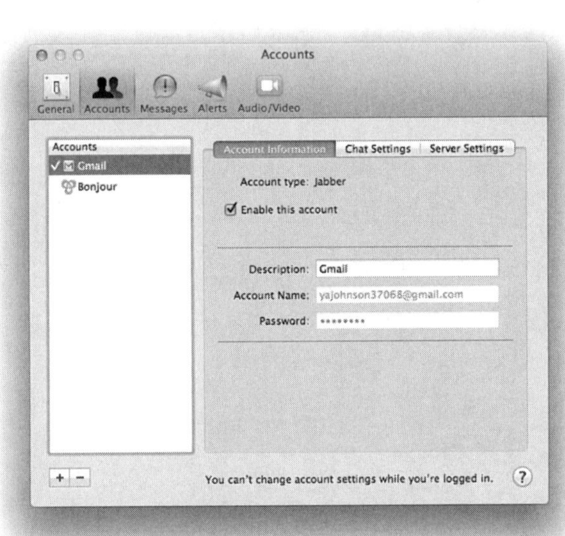

Figure 12.4 *The Bonjour account listed under Accounts is a default account that is not enabled until you set it up.*

4. Select the account type and type your name and password.
5. When finished, click Done.

Working with the Buddy List

In previous versions of Mac OS X, you had to maintain separate buddy lists for different chat services. In Lion, your buddy list unifies all chat services in one list by default. So, for example, if you have a GoogleTalk account and a MobileMe account, buddies from both lists appear in your iChat buddy list. If you want separate lists for different services, you can open iChat preferences and deselect Show All My Accounts on One List on the General tab.

By default, the buddy list uses groups to categorize your buddies. The groups available are Buddies (a generic group), Family, Friends, and Co-Workers. You can add your own groups by clicking the Add button (+) at the bottom of the buddy list and clicking Add Group. Type the name of the group and click Add. You can delete a group by right-clicking it in the buddy list and clicking Delete and confirming by clicking Delete again.

SHOW ME **Media 12.1—A Video about Adding a Buddy**
Access this video file through your registered Web Edition at
my.safaribooksonline.com/9780132819091/media
or on the DVD for print books.

LET ME TRY IT

Adding a Buddy

To add a name to the buddy list, follow these steps:

1. Click the Add button in the bottom-left corner of the buddy list (it has a plus on it).
2. Click Add Buddy.
3. If you have more than one type of chat account, select the account list the buddy should be added to.
4. Enter the email address for the account. If the email address is in your Address Book, the address fills in automatically.
5. If you don't want to categorize the new buddy in the generic Buddies group, click the pop-up button for Add to Group and select a different category.

You can recategorize buddies right in the buddy list by dragging a buddy name and dropping it on the category you want to move it into.

6. Enter the First and Last Name. (If the name is in your Address Book, the fields are filled in for you.)
7. When you are finished, click the Add button. If the person you just added is not currently online, the name appears in the Offline category in your buddy list. If the person *does* happen to be online, the name appears in its related category with an available status. (To see names in a category, click the disclosure triangle to the left of the category.) Additionally, certain types of chat accounts, such as Gmail, will say "Waiting for Authorization," as shown in Figure 12.5.

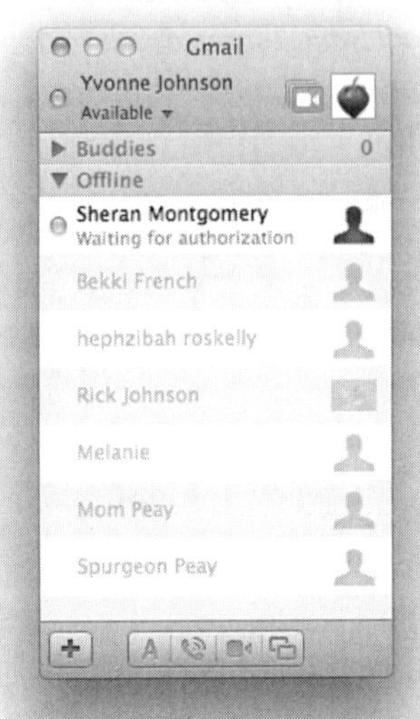

Figure 12.5 *The buddy list shows the names of buddies that have still not accepted you.*

If the buddy you want to add has a Google Talk or Jabber account, he receives an authorization notice that he can accept or decline. If he accepts, he's added to your list and you then receive an authorization notice that you can Accept or Decline to be added to his list. If he declines, you aren't added to his list, but you still will be able to chat with him. You might want to contact your buddies directly to alert them you want to be "accepted" before you try adding them to your buddy list.

Deleting a Buddy

It's sad, but sometimes you fall out of buddyship with one of your buddies and have to delete the buddy from your list. To delete a buddy, select the buddy in the list and click Edit in the menu bar. Click Delete and then click Remove to confirm the deletion. Alternatively, you can select the buddy in the buddy list and click Buddies in the menu bar. Then Click Remove Buddy *<buddy's name>* and click Remove to confirm.

Showing Your Status

When you launch iChat, your status, shown in the buddy list window, is automatically set to "Available." You can change your status at any time by clicking the pop-up button and selecting a status from the menu shown in Figure 12.6. The option you choose from the menu tells your AIM buddies what you're doing (even what iTunes song you are listening to, if they really care) because they see your status on their buddy lists. (Buddies on other networks don't see quite the same status descriptions, but they know whether you are online or idle.)

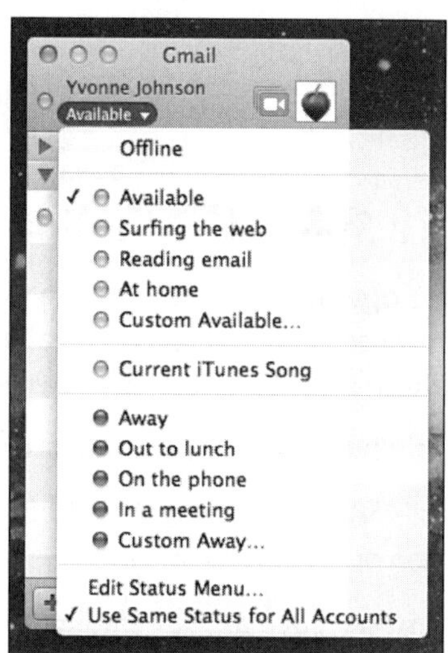

Figure 12.6 *Green dots denote Available statuses and red dots denote Away statuses.*

By default, when the computer is inactive, iChat automatically changes your status to "Away." When you are active on the computer again, a message asks whether you want to change your status back to Available. You can click Change, and iChat changes your status back to Available (or whatever you had selected from the menu), or you can click Don't Change if you just don't want to be bothered for a while. When the time is convenient for you to chat, you can change your status manually by selecting a status from the pop-up menu.

If you select Offline for your status, iChat disconnects itself from your Internet connection, but it doesn't disconnect you from the Internet. When you change your status to anything else, iChat reconnects again. If you want iChat to remain connected but give the appearance that you are offline, select the Invisible status. (Note that the invisible status is available if you have a MobileMe account.)

In Lion, you now have the ability to show the same or a different status for each chat service for which you have an account. To set this option, open the status menu on your buddy list and select or deselect Use the Same Status for All Accounts (refer to Figure 12.6).

SHOW ME **Media 12.2—A Video about Creating or Deleting a Status Description**

Access this video file through your registered Web Edition at
my.safaribooksonline.com/9780132819091/media
or on the DVD for print books.

LET ME TRY IT

Creating or Deleting a Status Description

If none of the default status options fit, you can delete the ones you don't want and create your own status description, such as "Available for Emergencies Only" or "Gone Shopping." Follow these steps to create your own status description:

1. Click the status pop-up button and click Edit Status Menu.
2. Click Custom Available or Custom Away. A text box opens at the top of the buddy list with a green or red dot beside it.
3. Type the text for the status, such as "Day Trading," and press Return. The new status automatically becomes your status.
4. Repeat steps 2 and 3 to create as many new descriptions as you want.
5. To delete a description, click the status pop-up button and click Edit Status Menu. Select the description in the Available or Away column and click the corresponding Remove button (–), as shown in Figure 12.7.
6. Click the OK button when you are finished.

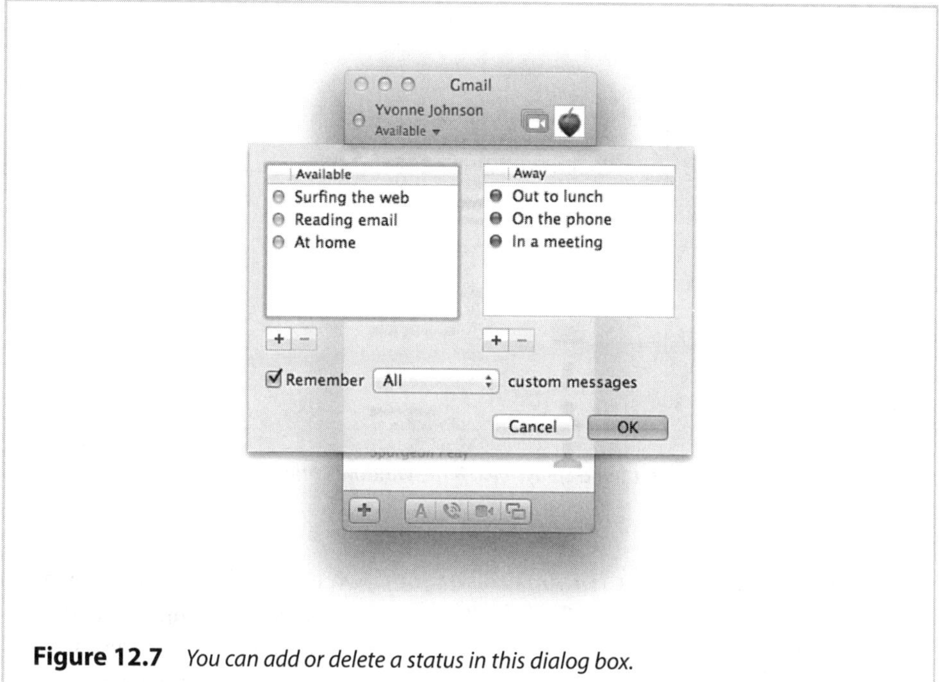

Figure 12.7 *You can add or delete a status in this dialog box.*

Chatting with Text

To start a text conversation with a buddy, double-click the buddy's name in the buddy list. (The list must show that the buddy is available.) A Chat window opens, as shown in Figure 12.8. If your buddy has multiple accounts, click the disclosure triangle in the Recipient bar and select the account you want to use. (If you don't see a disclosure triangle, the Recipient bar is probably hidden. Click View, Show Recipient Bar.)

Now that the buddy lists are combined, you might have a really long list. To help you find your buddy in the list, press Command-F, type part of the buddy name, and the buddy list filters out names that don't match.

Type your message in the box at the bottom of the Chat window. (Type something like "Hey, Judy.") Soon you will see a response on your screen from Judy if she types something and presses Return. When she responds, you know you are connected, and you can start typing messages back and forth to each other. You can even insert smiley faces for all occasions (Edit, Insert Smiley), but if you want to use some of the standard smiley faces, you can just type them in and iChat will convert them for you.

Figure 12.8 *The Recipient bar displays below the window's title bar.*

While you are chatting, both of you can see your own text on the screen and the responses of the other person. By default, the text messages show up in "talking balloons" that use different colors. To change the background and font color that your messages use, open the iChat preferences and go to the Messages pane. Additionally, you can change the appearance of the text by clicking View, Messages and choosing Show as Boxes, Show as Compact, or Show as Text.

To start a text chat with someone who is not in your buddy list, click File, New Chat. Type the IM account name in the To field and click Chat.

SHOW ME **Media 12.3—A Video about Using Graphics in Buddy Accounts**

Access this video file through your registered Web Edition at
my.safaribooksonline.com/9780132819091/media
or on the DVD for print books.

LET ME TRY IT

Using Graphics in Buddy Accounts

An identifying photo or, in the absence of a photo, a generic icon (such as a light bulb for Google Talk and other types of Jabber accounts) appears beside your comments and those of your buddy in the Chat window. If your buddy has added a photograph or graphic to his *own* IM account, you see that photo or graphic beside his comments. If you have a graphic of your buddy you want to use instead of what he uses, you can override his graphic by adding your graphic as his picture in your Address Book. Follow these steps to add a photo without even leaving iChat:

1. Right-click the name in the buddy list and click Show Info.
2. Click the Address Card tab.
3. Open iPhoto if it's not already open and navigate to the photo you want to use.
4. Drag the photo and drop it on the Picture box. (This is a new capability in Lion.)
5. Select Always Use This Picture.
6. While the window is open, you can add any additional information you have, such as the nickname or additional chat accounts.
7. Close the window when finished.

Responding to an Instant Message

If someone initiates a chat with you by sending you an instant message, a Chat window opens with the buddy's name in the title bar, the graphic that represents your buddy, and the text typed. To respond, click the window to select it, type something in the box at the bottom of the window, and click Accept or press Return (see Figure 12.9). To reject the message, click Decline.

Figure 12.9 *Clicking Accept or pressing Return immediately sends the reply.*

While connected on iChat, you can send a file to your buddy by dragging the file's icon from the Finder into the box where you normally type.

Keeping Up with Multiple Chats at the Same Time

Lion has a new feature that allows you to organize your chats. In the Chat window, you can rearrange your tabs by dragging them up or down. You can even drag a tab out of the chat window to create a new chat window or drag tabs from one window to another to merge the windows. Figure 12.10 shows the window with multiple tabs.

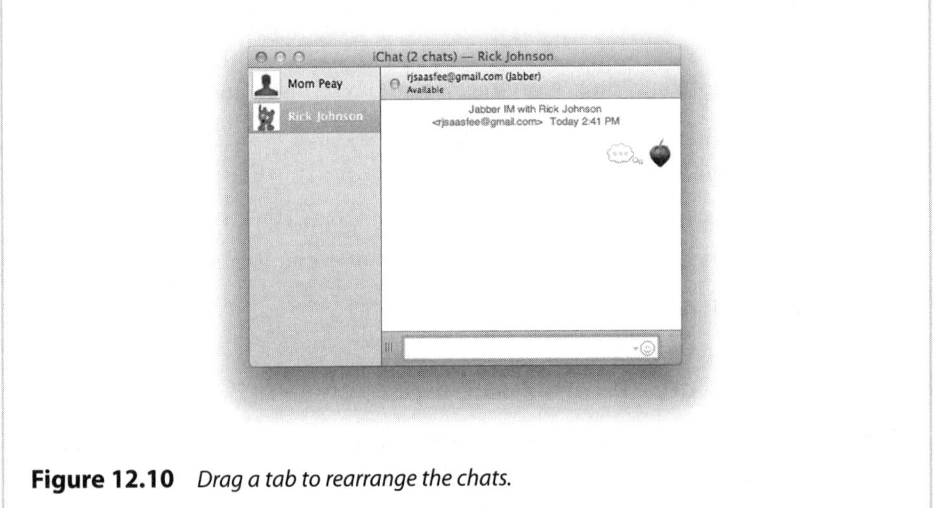

Figure 12.10 *Drag a tab to rearrange the chats.*

Chatting with Audio

Sending your mom who lives in another state an invitation to an audio chat is equivalent to making a free long-distance call! Of course, the catch is that you both have to have a microphone. You're using a Mac, so you have a microphone. Now you just need to make sure your mom has one. If she does, a telephone icon should appear beside her name in the buddy list.

To start an audio chat, click the telephone icon next to the buddy's name or right-click the buddy's name and click Invite to Audio Chat. The buddy must accept your invitation and then you can start talking. You can talk to each other just as you would on the phone; that is, you can hear and speak at the same time. Depending on the speed of your connections, there may be a slight delay, however. When you are finished talking, close the audio window.

A meter showing your sound level displays while you are chatting. This lets you know that your microphone is working.

Chatting with Video

Video chats require both parties to have a broadband connection. To start a video chat, click the camera icon next to the buddy's name. A preview window opens on your screen showing you "live and on camera." This is what your video buddy will see when he accepts, only in a larger window. A window showing your video buddy opens on your screen when he accepts the video invitation. Now you can talk to each other "face to face." The preview window you are in reduces to a small window inside of the larger window that displays your buddy. If you don't want to see your preview, click Video in the menu bar and click Hide Local Video. When you are finished, close the video chat window.

If you receive a video invitation, click the invitation and then click the Decline or the Accept button. If you accept, a large window showing the sender opens on your screen and your preview window showing you appears in the lower-right corner of the larger window.

Making Presentations with iChat Theater

Using iChat Theater, you can make presentations with iPhoto slideshows, iPhoto albums, or just about any type of file on your computer. Now, in Lion, you also can share a webpage. You don't even need a video camera to use iChat Theater, but everyone on the chat must be using the same service (that is, MobileMe, AIM, Google Talk, or Jabber).

LET ME TRY IT

Making a Presentation

If you are already in a video chat, you can start presenting immediately, but you don't have to start the video chat first if you don't want to. You can take your time and get everything ready first. To use iChat Theater to present a slideshow, follow these steps:

1. Click File in the menu bar.
2. Click Share a File with iChat Theater. If you are not already on a video chat, a dialog box opens saying that iChat Theater is ready to begin, but you need to invite a buddy.
3. Double-click the buddy in your buddy list. When the buddy accepts, iChat opens Quick Look on your screen.
4. Use the navigation keys to move through the file.

5. When the presentation is finished, close the Quick Look window.
6. End the video conference when you are ready by closing the video chat window.

Sharing Your Computer

One other feature that iChat provides is the ability to share another Mac user's screen and have full control of his computer or share your own screen and give your buddy complete control. You connect with the user via iChat and then set up the screen sharing. When you are sharing the user's screen, his screen replaces your screen, and your screen reduces to a small window in the lower-right corner of your display. You can toggle between the two. This feature is good for troubleshooting a friend's problem or demonstrating how to do something on the Mac, but it only works for two computers that have OS X 10.5 (Leopard) or later.

To share your screen, right-click the name of the buddy you want to share your screen with in the buddy list. Click Share My Screen with *<buddy name>*. When your buddy accepts the invitation, the sharing begins.

When sharing your screen with another user, be sure you are sharing with a trusted person because the other person really does have complete control of your computer.

To request a sharing session with another user, right-click the user in your buddy list and click Ask to Share *<buddy name>*'s Screen. When your buddy accepts the invitation, his screen becomes available to you.

To quit a sharing session, click the X in the upper-left corner of the small desktop window.

Using FaceTime

The FaceTime application makes video calls. The application is similar to Skype, but the recipients of the video call are limited to users of other Mac computers (must be Intel-based), an iPad 2, an iPhone 4, or the fourth-generation iPod Touch (or newer).

Activating FaceTime

The first time you use FaceTime on any of your Macs, you must activate the software. This is a simple procedure of signing in and receiving validation.

LET ME TRY IT

Setting Up the FaceTime Application

The first time you open FaceTime, you will be guided through the procedure to activate the application. Follow these steps:

1. Click the FaceTime icon in the Dock.
2. Enter your Apple ID username and password and click Sign In.
3. Enter the email address that people will use to call you (if it does not already appear in the Address box).
4. Click Next. The system verifies the address and then displays all your contacts from your Address Book. You can now start to make video calls to people in your Address Book, as described next.

Getting Connected

To call someone with FaceTime, the person must be listed in your Address Book. FaceTime is fully integrated with Address Book, so if the person you want to call is not in your Address Book, you can add the contact for the person right in FaceTime. All you have to do is click the Add button (the one with the plus, at the top-right corner of the screen) and fill in the appropriate fields. You are given just a minimum number of fields in FaceTime, but you can always add more information to the contact card in the Address Book later.

If the person you want to call has a contact card in the Address Book, but the contact card doesn't have an email address or phone number that you can use in FaceTime, you can edit the contact and add the information if you have it. To edit a card, select the card in the list and click the Edit button (at the top-right corner of the window). The dialog box shown in Figure 12.11 opens. Add the information and click Done when finished.

LET ME TRY IT

Making a Video Call to a Mac, iPad 2, iPod Touch, or iPhone 4

To make a video call to someone in your Address Book, follow these steps:

1. Click the contact in the list to open it. (If you have a very long list of contacts, you might want to type a name in the Spotlight search box to quickly find the contact.) Alternatively, if the contact is someone you call

frequently, click the Recents button and click the name in the list. (The Recents feature is just like the Recents feature on the iPhone 4.)

Figure 12.11 *Notice that you also can delete a contact.*

> If you have more than one input source for sound, that is, you have a microphone connected to the Mac in addition to the internal microphone, be sure the correct microphone is selected before you make the call. (Click Video and select the microphone.)

2. When the contact is open, you can click Add to Favorites before you click the email address or phone number for the person.
3. To call another Mac, iPad 2, or iPod Touch, click the email address. To call an iPhone, click the phone number. The call is initiated.

> The email address must be associated with the user's Apple ID.

4. If the user you are calling accepts the call, the call goes through and you can see the user in your FaceTime window. Your face shows in a smaller window at the bottom-left corner of the screen. If the user you are calling declines the call or simply is not available, the call does not go through and a message appears at the top of your screen telling you that the user is not available for FaceTime. You can click the Call Back button to try again or click Cancel.
5. To end a call that went through, click the End button.

Receiving a FaceTime Call on the Mac

When someone calls you on FaceTime, your Mac rings (just like a phone) even if FaceTime is not open. In fact, every Mac you own rings when a call comes in as long as you are signed into FaceTime on that computer. On the other hand, your Mac will not ring if you have FaceTime turned off as described in the next section. So when the call comes in, click Accept in the call window. To reject the call, click Decline.

FaceTime and iChat are very similar when it comes to availability. You launch both programs to be available. Calls that you get in FaceTime when the program is not launched show up as missed calls.

Turning FaceTime Off and On

If you don't want to be bothered with FaceTime calls for a period of time, you can turn FaceTime off. Basically, this is like turning off your phone. When you want to be available for FaceTime calls again, turn FaceTime back on. The commands to turn FaceTime off and on are on the FaceTime menu, as shown in Figure 12.12.

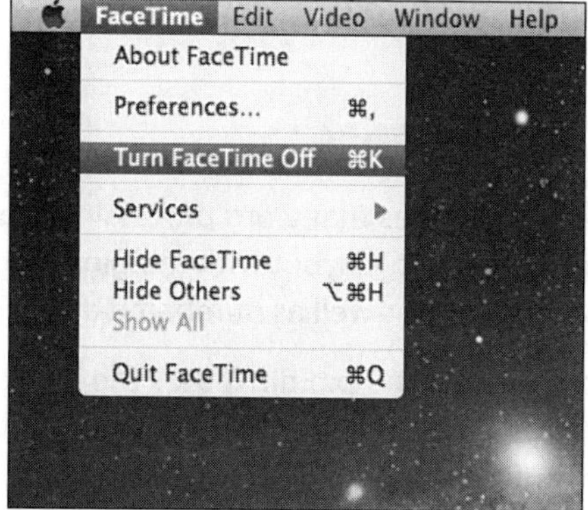

Figure 12.12 *Turn FaceTime off and back on again from the FaceTime menu.*

This chapter gives you enough information about using TextEdit that you may not need any other word processing program.

13

Using TextEdit

Chances are, if you've been using any kind of computer for any length of time, you are familiar with Microsoft Word. For years, it has been the universally accepted standard in word processing software. All other word processing programs must be compatible with it to survive, and Mac's word processing application, TextEdit, is no exception.

TextEdit is a cross between the old text-editing window that programmers used to use and a scaled-down version of a sophisticated word processing application. If your word processing needs are modest, you could use TextEdit as your only word processing program because it has most of the basic features of more sophisticated applications. For example, you can include graphics, use tables, use styles, format text, create numbered lists, and so on. On the other hand, if basic word processing is not going to get you by, then you might want to invest in the Mac version of Word or Apple's own Pages.

Working with Documents

People usually refer to the text files that word processing programs create as *documents*. A document has a page layout with margins and tabs. It can include tables, formatting, and graphics, as well as numbered and bulleted lists.

When you create a document with TextEdit, it uses the New Document preferences shown in Figure 13.1 to determine the format of the new document. By default, TextEdit is set up to operate as the "old text-editing window that programmers used," which I mentioned previously. If you intend to use TextEdit for all your word processing needs, I recommend that you change the preferences so TextEdit behaves like its better half, the scaled-down, sophisticated word processing program. The rest of this chapter assumes that you have made this change.

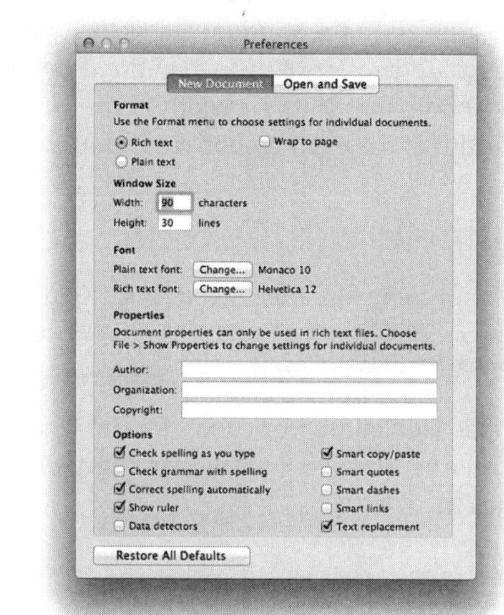

Figure 13.1 *TextEdit uses these preferences in all new documents.*

Setting New Document Preferences

You just need to make one small change to the New Document preferences to make the "programmer window" behavior go away. While you're setting preferences, there are a few more that I recommend you set to raise the sophistication level. Follow these steps to set the preferences for new documents:

1. Click TextEdit in the menu bar and click Preferences.
2. On the New Document pane, click Wrap to Page.
3. Under Options, check the boxes for the following:
    - **Data Detectors**—Turns on a pop-up menu for dates, addresses, and phone numbers that allows you to manipulate the data in various ways, such as add a phone number to an existing contact
    - **Smart Quotes**—Converts straight quotes to curly quotes
    - **Smart Dashes**—Converts two hyphens to an em dash
    - **Smart Links**—Converts a web address to a clickable link
4. Close the window.

To see the change that has come over TextEdit, create a new document and notice the rectangle that now appears in the window. This is the typing area, and text wraps within the rectangle regardless of the size of the window. When TextEdit is in "programmer-window" mode, changing the width of the window causes the text to rewrap to fit the new width of the window. You really don't want that!

Creating a Document with TextEdit

After you have TextEdit behaving like a real word processing program, you are ready to start creating your documents. To create a new document, follow these steps:

1. Click the Launchpad icon in the Dock and click the TextEdit icon. (You may have to scroll to another page to find the icon.) TextEdit creates a new document automatically.

> If TextEdit is already open, you can create a new document by clicking File in the menu bar and clicking New. To open an existing document, click File in the menu bar and click Open. Select the document in the Finder and double-click it. If you want to work on a document that you have opened recently, click File, Open Recent. Click the document you want from the list of documents that displays.

2. Click File in the menu bar, and click Save.
3. Type a name for the document and select a location where you want to store it. The default file type is rtf (Rich Text Format) and the default folder is Documents. The name you give the document appears in the title bar at the top of the window. The insertion point (text cursor) is blinking on the first line waiting for you to begin typing.
4. Begin typing the document. The insertion point follows the last character you type, marking the location where you can type new text. Additionally, as soon as you type the first character, you will see the word *Edited* following the document name in the title bar. This is an indication that you have edited the document since the last version was saved.
5. Continue typing until finished, but don't worry about saving periodically. That's a thing of the past with the new feature in Lion that saves versions of your document as you go along.

A new feature in Lion allows you to add diacritical marks to letters quickly and easily. For example, to add a tilde over an "n," press and hold the N key until a list of n's with different diacritical marks appears above the line where you are typing. Click the one with the tilde and Lion inserts it in the document.

6. When finished, you can close the document by clicking the Close button or just quit TextEdit by clicking TextEdit, Quit TextEdit or pressing Command-Q. That's right! There's no mistake here. As long as you have saved the file at least once, you don't have to save one last time before you close the file or quit. In fact, if you leave the file open and quit TextEdit instead, the next time you launch TextEdit, the file will open and it will be just as you left it. Even the text insertion point will be in the same location. If you had any inspectors open when you quit, such as the Fonts window, they will open and return to the same position on the screen where you last placed them.

TextEdit saves versions of your work at intervals. If you are working on the document diligently, adding more and more content, TextEdit saves more often. Periodically, TextEdit deletes some of the hourly versions that it saves to make browsing the versions a little easier. Each hourly version that it keeps, it keeps for 24 hours. Then versions are available on a daily basis until they are a month old, when they are then available on a weekly basis.

When you have a document just the way you want it, you can lock it so that no additional changes can be made. If you don't lock a document, Lion automatically locks the document for you two weeks after the last edit. To lock the document, click the pop-up button in the title bar. If you don't see the button, point to the right of the document name. Click Lock. If you try to make a change to a locked document, a confirmation dialog box opens asking whether you want to unlock or duplicate the document.

For more information about the Versions feature, such as how to browse through the versions or revert to a different version, see Chapter 8, "Managing Applications."

You also can save a TextEdit document in PDF format by clicking File in the menu bar and clicking Export as PDF. This format can include paragraph and font formatting, tables, graphics, and lists. It is the standard format used for printable files on the web.

Navigating and Editing Text

Seldom, if ever, do you type a complete document, then go back, and edit it. It's a mixed process. You type new text and edit as you go. As you are creating and editing, you have to move back and forth in the document, sometimes to enter new text, sometimes to find text you have already entered and edit it.

Navigating in a Document

To edit text, you must position the I-beam-shaped insertion point (text cursor) in the right place. Certainly, you can use the mouse to position the I-beam, but because you are generally typing in a document, learning the keystrokes that help you move around in a document as well just makes sense. Table 13.1 lists some of the common keystrokes used to navigate in a document.

Table 13.1 Navigation Techniques

To Move To:	Press:
The beginning or end of a line	Command-Home or Command-End
The top or bottom of the document	Command-Up Arrow or Command-Down Arrow
The beginning or end of a word	Option-Left Arrow or Option-Right Arrow
The beginning of a word	Option-Left Arrow
Up or down one line	Up Arrow or Down Arrow

Using the Find Command

Another way to navigate in a document is to use the Find command. This feature has been completely reworked in the Lion version of TextEdit. Instead of typing the search text in a dialog box and using the Next button to go to each one in the document, now you type the search text it in a Spotlight field. To open the Spotlight bar, click Edit in the menu bar, and then click Find, Find. After you type the search text, TextEdit highlights all the occurrences for you inline. Use the Next and Previous buttons in the bar to go to each one. Click Done when finished.

Editing Text

Editing text requires inserting text; deleting text; and copying, cutting, and pasting text. Table 13.2 lists some of the most common editing commands and shortcuts.

Table 13.2 Editing Techniques

To:	Do this:
Insert text.	Click the cursor where the new text should go and type the text.
Delete the character to the left of the text cursor.	Press Delete.
Delete the character to the right of the text cursor.	Press Fn-Delete.
Delete a complete word.	Double-click the word and press Delete.
Delete a complete line.	Triple-click the line and press Delete.
Delete a section of text.	Drag the cursor through the text and press Delete.
Copy text.	Drag the cursor through the text and click Edit, Copy or press Command-C.
Cut text.	Drag the cursor through the text and click Edit, Cut or press Command-X.
Paste text.	Click the cursor in the new location and click Edit, Paste or press Command-V.

If you make a revision in a document that you'd like to take back, press Command-Z. (The menu command is Edit, Undo.) You can undo changes in a document until the cows come home—all the way back to the way the document was when you first opened it. The opposite of Undo is Redo (Shift-Command-Z). The Redo command reverses an Undo action.

Correcting Spelling

As you type, you may notice that TextEdit corrects some of your typographical or spelling errors for you and underlines others with a dotted red line. This occurs because Correct Spelling Automatically and Check Spelling As You Type are the default settings in the New Document preferences. To correct a misspelling, right-click the word with the red underline and click the correct spelling in the list that appears at the top of the shortcut menu.

SHOW ME **Media 13.1—A Video about Using the Spelling and Grammar Checker**

Access this video file through your registered Web Edition at ***my.safaribooksonline.com/9780132819091/media*** *or on the DVD for print books.*

LET ME TRY IT

Using the Spelling and Grammar Checker

If you want to correct all misspellings at once, just wait until you have finished typing the document, and follow these steps:

1. Click Edit in the menu bar.
2. Click Spelling and Grammar, Show Spelling and Grammar. This opens TextEdit's full-blown spell checker, as shown in Figure 13.2.

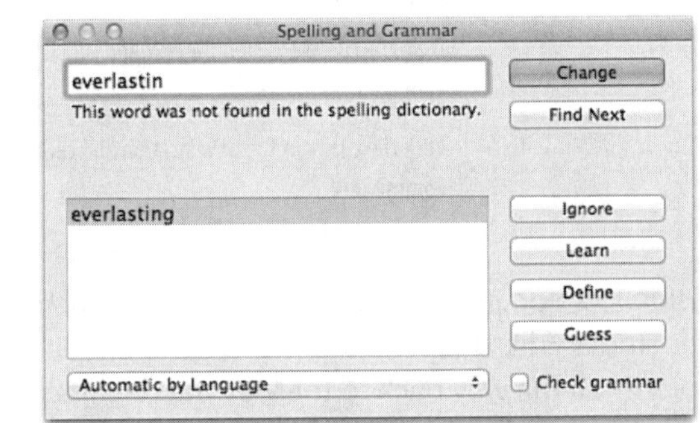

Figure 13.2 *Misspelled words appear in the box at the top and suggested spellings appear in the box at the bottom.*

3. The first word not found in the dictionary appears in the box at the top and one or more suggestions appear in the box at the bottom. (It is also possible that no suggestions appear.)
4. If the word is not misspelled, click Ignore or click Learn to add it to your personal dictionary. If it is misspelled, select the correction you want if it appears and click Change. If the correct spelling does not appear as a suggestion, edit the misspelled word in the top box and click Change.
5. To continue without making a change, click Find Next.
6. When no more words display in the box at the top, the spelling check is finished and you can close the window.

If you accidentally add a word to your personal dictionary that is misspelled, right-click the word in the document and click Unlearn Spelling.

Finding and Replacing Text

Sometimes you need to make global revisions in a document; that is, you need to change the same word or phrase that appears multiple times in the document. TextEdit not only can find each occurrence for you, but can replace it for you as well. The Find and Replace feature, built on the redesigned Find feature, also uses the Spotlight bar to search and replace text inline.

SHOW ME **Media 13.2—A Video about Finding and Replacing Text**
Access this video file through your registered Web Edition at
my.safaribooksonline.com/9780132819091/media
or on the DVD for print books.

LET ME TRY IT

Using the Find and Replace Command

The Find command can locate the text that you specify even if the text is in the middle of a word or just at the beginning of a word. To find a particular word or phrase and replace it with something else, follow these steps:

1. Click Edit in the menu bar and then click Find, Find and Replace. The Spotlight panel opens just below the ruler at the top of the screen.
2. Type the word you want to find in the Find field.
3. Type the word you want to replace it with in the Replace field, as shown in Figure 13.3.
4. Click All if you want to replace all occurrences of the text.
5. If you don't want to change all occurrences of the text, click the Next button in the Spotlight panel to find the next occurrence that appears in the document after the point of the cursor.
6. Click Replace to replace the currently selected text and move to the next occurrence.
7. To skip an occurrence, click the Next button.
8. Continue replacing or skipping until all occurrences are processed.
9. Click Done in the Spotlight panel when finished.

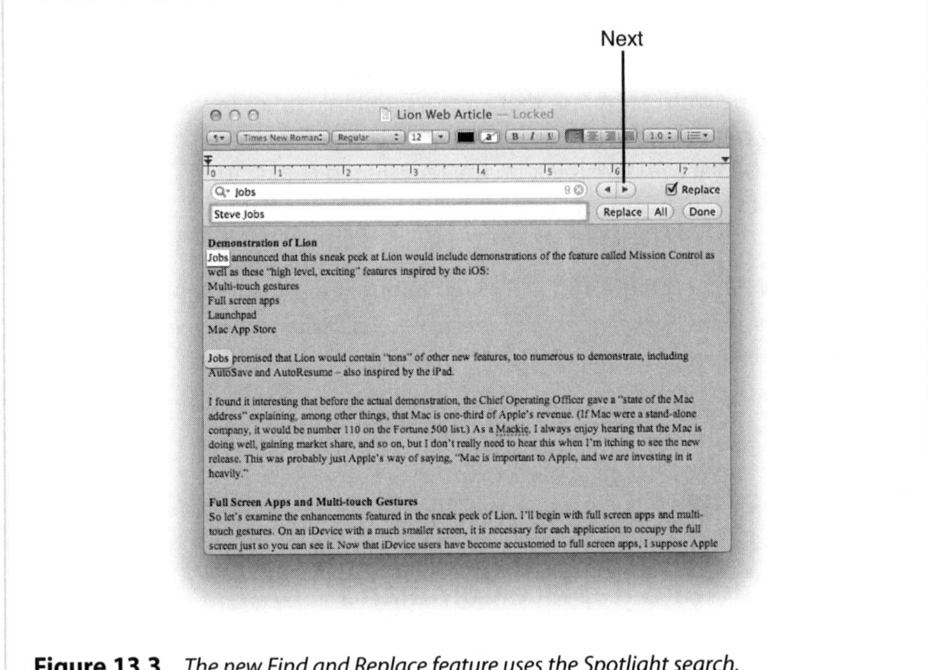

Figure 13.3 *The new Find and Replace feature uses the Spotlight search.*

Inserting Page Breaks

Eventually, you will fill up a page, and TextEdit will insert a page break automatically. If you want a page to stop before it fills up, you can insert a page break yourself by clicking Edit in the menu bar and clicking Insert, Page Break.

Setting Margins and Tabs

TextEdit sets margins for you on all sides (top, bottom, left, and right) at one inch. Changing the margin settings using formatting commands or printing commands in the application is impossible, but one-inch margins are probably adequate for 75% to 90% of the documents most home users create.

Figure 13.4 shows the ruler where margins and tabs are set. The first line indent and left indent icons are set at the same place initially, but the figure shows the left indent icon moved to the right so you can see both icons separately.

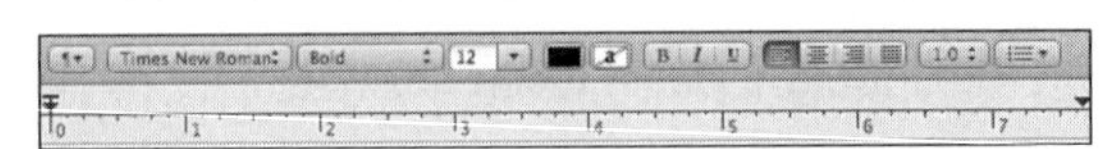

Figure 13.4 *If you do not see a ruler on your screen, click Format, Text, Show Ruler.*

Setting the Margins

"Wait a minute. There must be some mistake," you say. "You told us we couldn't change the margins. So why is this topic in here?" Simple. I said you couldn't change margins with any formatting or printing commands, and that's true, but there *is* a way to change margins. Very few people seem to know about this method, so maybe it's a little Mac OS X secret.

Changing the Margins

The secret to changing the margins is to display some normally hidden codes and change them. To do this you have to create a document, close it, and then reopen it. It's a bit "clunky," but it works! To change the top, bottom, left, or right margin of the current document, follow these steps:

1. Create a new document. Save it and then close the document.
2. Click File in the menu bar, click Open and select the document you just saved and closed.
3. Select the option Ignore Rich Text Commands at the bottom of the dialog box.
4. Click Open.
5. Find the following text: \margl1440\margr1440. These are the Rich Text Commands for the left and right margins, respectively. The value 1440 equals one inch. So 720 would equal half an inch, 1960 would equal an inch and a half, and so on.
6. Change the value of 1440 to the value you want.
7. Add the commands for the top and bottom margins (\margt and \margb, respectively) including the values that you want. When you are finished revising the margins, the commands would look like this if you set half-inch margins all the way around:

   ```
   \margl720\margr720\margt720\margb720
   ```

8. Save the document and close it. Reopen it without the Rich Text commands this time and type the document.

Being able to set margins means that you can create mailing labels and many other documents that might have been too much trouble or impossible to create otherwise. Consider this your "Get Out of Jail Free" card.

Setting Tabs

By default, TextEdit places a left tab every half inch on the ruler. These tabs are always there for you while you are typing, and they come in quite handy. If you need to type text that uses different kinds of tabs, however, as shown in Figure 13.5, the left tabs just get in your way, and you need to delete them. To remove any type of tab that has been set on the ruler, drag the tab icon off the ruler. To set a tab, click the point on the ruler where you want the tab. TextEdit sets a left tab. To change to a different type of tab, double-click the tab repeatedly to cycle through the tabs (right tab, center tab, decimal tab, and finally back to the left tab). To change the location of a tab, drag it to the desired location on the ruler. The exact location displays in a box above the tab as you drag it.

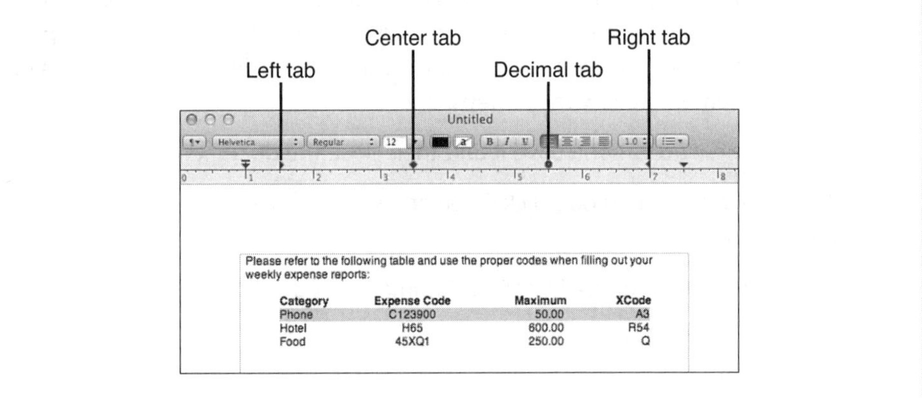

Figure 13.5 *This table shows text aligned on all four types of tabs.*

Formatting Text

The purpose of changing the appearance of text in a document is to make the document more readable and understandable. For example, if you want to let the reader know that a word or phrase is very important, you could make it bold or red. To differentiate headings from regular paragraph text, you could make the headings a different font and a larger size than the regular paragraph text.

Additionally, you can change some of the typesetting attributes of a font such as kerning, use of ligatures, and position of the baseline. Kerning adjusts the space between characters, and you might use this feature to lengthen or shorten a headline to fit a specific space. Ligatures are archaic, and I doubt you would ever need to use them. They are combinations of characters, such as *f* and *i*, and they are not even available in most fonts. Adjusting the position of the baseline allows you to create a superscript or a subscript. I don't have space in this book to explain the typesetting attributes in detail, but you can find them on the Format, Font menu.

Adding Emphasis

You can apply the following types of emphasis to text: bold, italic, underline, outline, and color. To add bold, italic, or underline, select the text and then click the appropriate button in the new Formatting toolbar. If you memorize the keyboard shortcuts, Command-B, Command-I, Command-U, you can use them as you type. For example, if you know you want to make a word bold, you press Command-B, type the word, and press Command-B again. In other words, turn on the attribute before typing the text and turn it off after you type the text.

If you want to make a font use an outline, then select the text, click Format in the menu bar, and then click Font, Outline.

If you want to use color in a document, select the text and click the button for color in the toolbar—it's the one right after the font size. Select the color from the color palette that displays in the popup or click Show Colors to open the Color window. If using the Color window, click the type of color palette that you want to use by clicking an icon in the toolbar. As you can see in Figure 13.6, I selected the Crayons palette.

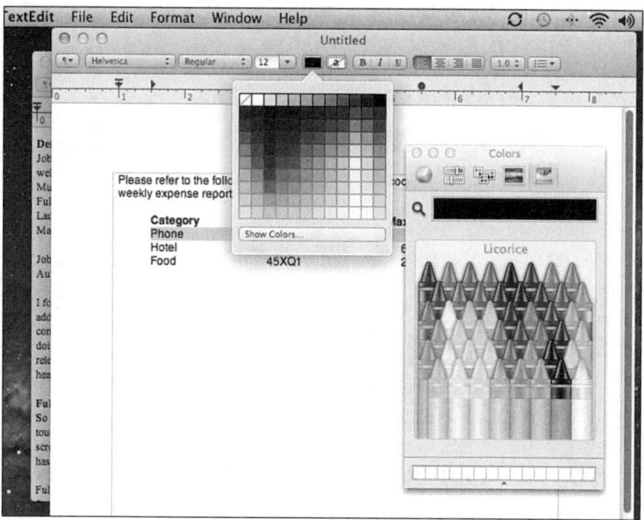

Figure 13.6 *You can keep the Colors window open and use it again or click a color from the Color popup.*

Selecting a Font Type and Size

Each new document you create in TextEdit uses the default font specified in the New Document preferences. In Figure 13.1, you can see that the default font for Rich Text Format documents is 12-point Helvetica. You can apply several different font attributes from the new Formatting bar, but to change several font attributes at the same time, select the text and open the Fonts window by clicking Format in the menu bar and then clicking Font, Show Fonts. In the Fonts window, you first select the font collection, and then you can select the family, the typeface, and the size.

The Fonts window also has buttons to apply underlines, strikethroughs, font color, and page background color.

Formatting Paragraphs

The paragraph formatting buttons appear on the right side of the new Formatting toolbar. If you start looking for a Paragraph command on the Format menu, you won't find it because TextEdit lists all paragraph-formatting options on the Text submenu, as shown in Figure 13.7. They include paragraph alignment and spacing options. By default, a new paragraph always has the same alignment and spacing options as the one before it.

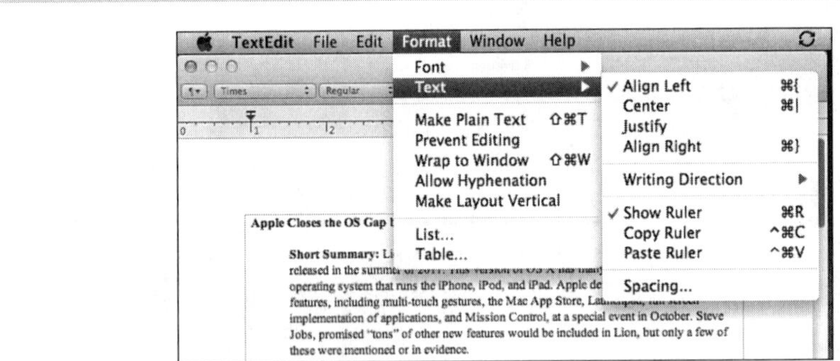

Figure 13.7 *Paragraph formatting commands are listed on the Text submenu.*

Setting Alignment

The paragraph alignment options include the following: Align Left (left margin straight, right margin ragged), Center (all lines centered), Justify (left and right margins straight), and Align Right (left margin ragged, right margin straight). To apply any of these alignments to an existing paragraph, click anywhere in the paragraph, and click the appropriate button on the Formatting toolbar or click Format in the menu bar, click Text, and then click the alignment you want.

Setting Spacing Options

Spacing options include line height multiple (single space, double space, and so on), line height, interline spacing, and paragraph spacing (space before and after paragraphs). To set spacing options in an existing paragraph, click in the paragraph you want to format, click Format in the menu bar, and then click Text, Spacing. The dialog box shown in Figure 13.8 opens. Set all the options that you want and click OK.

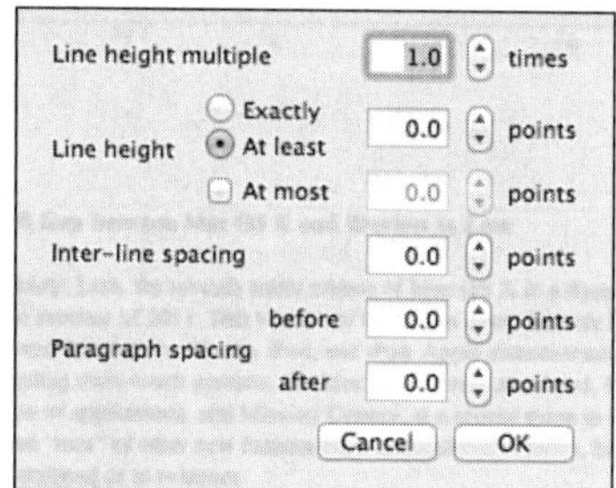

Figure 13.8 *You can set all paragraph spacing options at once in this dialog box.*

If you just want to set the line height multiple, click the pop-up button for the Line and Paragraph Spacing button on the Formatting toolbar and click the multiple you want.

TELL ME MORE **Media 13.3—A Discussion about Using Paragraph Spacing**

Access this audio recording through your registered Web Edition at ***my.safaribooksonline.com/9780132819091/media*** *or on the DVD for print books.*

Exploring Other Formatting Features

TextEdit has several other powerful formatting features that I want to cover very quickly. This section lists the bare-bones steps for each.

LET ME TRY IT

Creating a Numbered or Bulleted List

To create a numbered or bulleted list, follow these steps:

1. Select the paragraphs to be numbered or bulleted and click the List Bullets and Numbering button on the Formatting toolbar.
2. Select the bullet or numbering style you want.

You can perform step 2 before you type any text and the line where the insertion point is positioned will be numbered or bulleted. When you press Return, the next line is automatically numbered or bulleted. Pressing Return twice at the end of the list turns off the automatic numbering or bulleting.

SHOW ME **Media 13.4—A Video about Creating a Table**
Access this video file through your registered Web Edition at
my.safaribooksonline.com/9780132819091/media
or on the DVD for print books.

LET ME TRY IT

Creating a Table

To create a table, follow these steps:

1. Click Format in the menu bar and click Table. A table is inserted at the position of the insertion point and the Table inspector opens, as shown in Figure 13.9.
2. To create additional rows or delete rows before you begin typing in the table, increase or decrease the number in the Rows box.

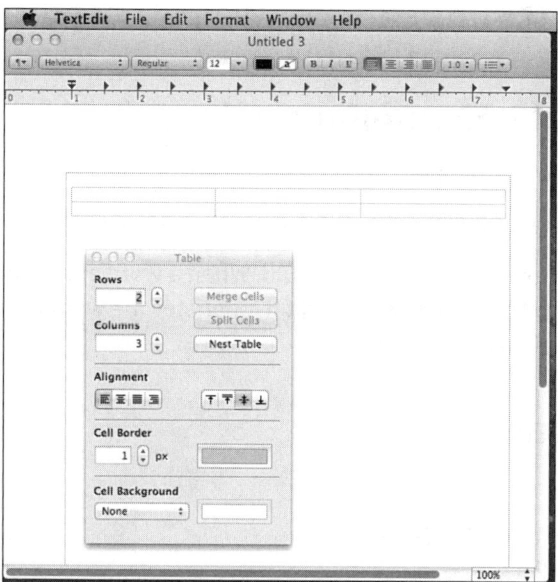

Figure 13.9 *Leave the Table window open as you type the table so you can format as you type.*

3. To create additional columns or delete columns before you begin typing in the table, increase or decrease the number in the Columns box.
4. To set options for individual cells (with or without data in them), select the cell(s) and do any of the following:
   - Click the appropriate button for horizontal and vertical alignment.
   - Specify the size of the cell border and specify the color of the border by clicking the shaded box to the right of the Cell Border control. Select the color from the Colors inspector.
   - Select the Cell Background (None or Color Fill). If you select Color Fill, click the box to the right of the Cell Background control and select the color from the Colors inspector.
5. Move to the next or previous cell using the Tab and Shift-Tab keys and type the text. If you leave the Table inspector open while you work on the table, you can continue formatting cells as you go along.

To make changes to the format of an existing table, click anywhere in the table, click Format in the menu bar, and click Table. The Table inspector opens.

LET ME TRY IT

Automatically Hyphenating Words

To turn on automatic hyphenation in a document, follow these steps:

1. Click Format in the menu bar and click Allow Hyphenation.
2. Type the text as you normally would. When a word at the end of the line is too long to fit on the line, TextEdit hyphenates the word if it can, based on the rules of syllabication.

LET ME TRY IT

Using Data Detectors

Data detectors, as explained earlier in the chapter, can add dates to iCal and phone numbers and addresses to the Address Book. Follow these steps to use a data detector:

1. Point to a date, phone number, or address. The data detector outlines the data and displays a pop-up button.

> If you don't see an outline when you point to the data, turn on the Data Detector option on the New Document pane of the TextEdit preferences.

2. Click the pop-up button to display a pop-up menu. The menu is different for each type of data.
3. Select the option you want from the menu and use your good sense from there.

LET ME TRY IT

Transforming Capitalization

To change the case that text uses, follow these steps:

1. Select the text you want to transform.
2. Click Edit in the menu bar and click Transformations.
3. Click one of the following: Make Upper Case, Make Lower Case, or Capitalize.

If you select Capitalize, TextEdit capitalizes all words, even words that you normally would not capitalize, such as *a, an, the, of, in,* and so on.

Printing

By default, TextEdit formats a page for printing on 8.5 by 11-inch paper in portrait orientation at 100% scale. If you want to change any of these settings, click File in the menu bar and click Page Setup. To print a document, click File in the menu bar and click Print. Select your printer and the other options that apply. Scroll through the pages in the preview on the left to be sure the document looks the way you want it to and then click Print.

If the Print dialog doesn't contain all the options you want, click the Show Details button at the bottom of the dialog box.

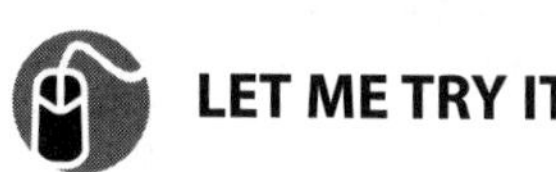

Printing the Document Info in the Header and Footer

Although you cannot specify the exact text to print in the header and footer, you can print the default document information. The header prints the name of the document file on the left and the date and time on the right. The footer prints the page number and total pages, such as "Page 1 of 1." To print a header and footer with the text of the document, follow these steps:

1. Click File in the menu bar and click Print.
2. Click Print Header and Footer. If you do not see this option, click the Show Details button.
3. Set other print options as needed and click Print.

This chapter deals with many of the valuable "little" applications that can increase your efficiency and make your life on the computer so much easier, such as widgets, Preview, Dictionary, Calculator, and more.

14

Using Widgets and Other Applications

Whereas other chapters concentrate on major Mac OS X Lion applications such as Safari, Mail, and TextEdit, this chapter concentrates on the applications that can assist you in small ways while you are working in the major applications. In this chapter, I explain how to select the widgets you want to use, how to download more widgets, and even how to create your own web widgets. Additionally, the chapter covers using Preview, looking up words in the dictionary, creating sticky notes, using the calculator, and using the Color Meter.

Using Widgets

Widgets are mini-applications that perform functions such as getting news and scores from ESPN, monitoring your stocks, checking the weather, or telling the time in any part of the world. Widgets "live" in the Dashboard. When you launch the Dashboard (click Launchpad in the Dock and then click Dashboard or, if you upgraded to Lion, just click the Dashboard icon in the Dock), it slides onto the screen from the left, as if it has just been waiting in the wings for you to call on it. When you finish with the Dashboard, press Esc, and it slides back to the left. Several default widgets appear on the screen, but many more installed widgets are waiting for you to discover them and even more widgets are waiting for you to install them.

TELL ME MORE Media 14.1—A Discussion about Exploring Default Widgets

Access this audio recording through your registered Web Edition at ***my.safaribooksonline.com/9780132819091/media*** *or on the DVD for print books.*

Managing Widgets

The default widgets that appear on the Dashboard may be just the ones you want to use, but you might also want to select some additional widgets. If you don't need some of the default widgets that Lion selected for you, you can disable them and select different widgets. When you disable a widget, it closes on the Dashboard, but it's still available for use in the future.

Many widgets depend on the Internet for data, so keep that in mind when you select them. Additionally, some widgets need additional information from you in order to perform their functions. For example, you must supply a Zip code or geographic location for a weather widget.

LET ME TRY IT

Configuring the Dashboard

Configuring the Dashboard involves enabling and disabling widgets, arranging them on the Dashboard, and supplying additional information to widgets that require it. To configure your own selection and arrangement of widgets on the Dashboard, follow these steps:

1. Open the Dashboard using one of these methods:
   - Click the Launchpad icon in the Dock and click the Dashboard icon.
   - Use the two-finger swipe from left to right on a Magic mouse.
   - Use the four-finger swipe from left to right on a Magic trackpad.
2. Click the plus icon in the bottom-left corner of the screen to display a bar with the installed widgets (see Figure 14.1).

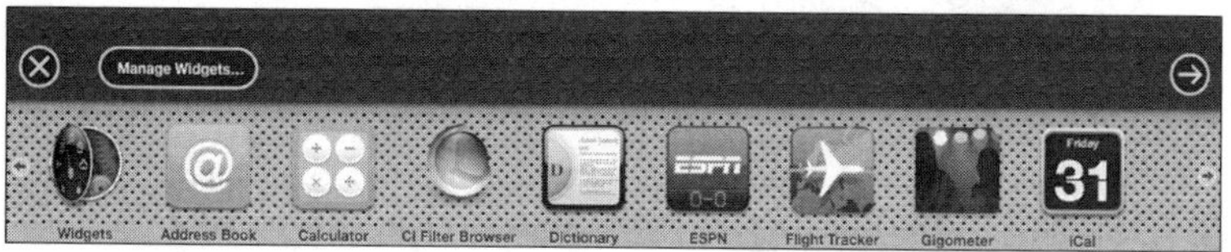

Figure 14.1 *The Widgets icon and the Manage Widgets button both open the same dialog box.*

3. Click the arrows at the right and left of the bar to scroll the widgets, and click each widget in the bar that you want to add to the Dashboard.

4. Point to any part of a widget that you have added and drag it to the location you want it to occupy on the screen.
5. Point to the bottom-right or bottom-left corner of the widget to see whether it has an information button. If it does, click it to flip the widget over to the back side. Complete additional information or make selections as required, and click Done.
6. Click the X in the upper-left corner of any widget that you want to disable.
7. When you are finished configuring the Dashboard, click the X just above the left side of the widget bar.

Downloading More Widgets

Tons of free widgets await your download on the Apple website. For the serious crowd, widgets are available that give you Mac tips and tricks, convert currency, and keep track of the hours you've worked. For the fun crowd, widgets exist that take you on a nonstop rollercoaster ride, count down to Christmas with the Grinch, and list upcoming gigs and events (called the *Gigometer*, of course). To access these widgets, click the Manage Widgets button (refer to Figure 14.1) and click the More Widgets button at the bottom of the dialog box. This button takes you directly to the page on Apple's website where you can download all the widgets your little heart desires. After the widget downloads to your computer, just click Install to install it in the Dashboard and then click Keep.

Creating Your Own Web Clip Widget

The purpose of about half a dozen of the default widgets is to deliver real-time information from the web, such as weather, sports, and stock prices. If your interests lie elsewhere, you can go to a website that has the information you want and create your own widget by clipping a frame from the site. Then, instead of going to the website, you can check the data you want to see in the web clip widget on your Dashboard.

SHOW ME **Media 14.2—A Video about Clipping a Widget from the Web**

Access this video file through your registered Web Edition at ***my.safaribooksonline.com/9780132819091/media*** *or on the DVD for print books.*

LET ME TRY IT

Clipping a Widget from the Web

Some websites have features on them that are always located in the same place on the page. These sites are good candidates for clipping a web widget. Follow these steps to create a web clip widget:

1. Open Safari and navigate to the page that has the content you want—the daily deal on eBay or the "I'm shopping for" box on Shopzilla, for example.
2. Right-click the web page and click Open in Dashboard. The screen dims and a rectangle appears.
3. Move the cursor so that the rectangle is over the information that you want to clip and click to anchor the rectangle (see Figure 14.2).

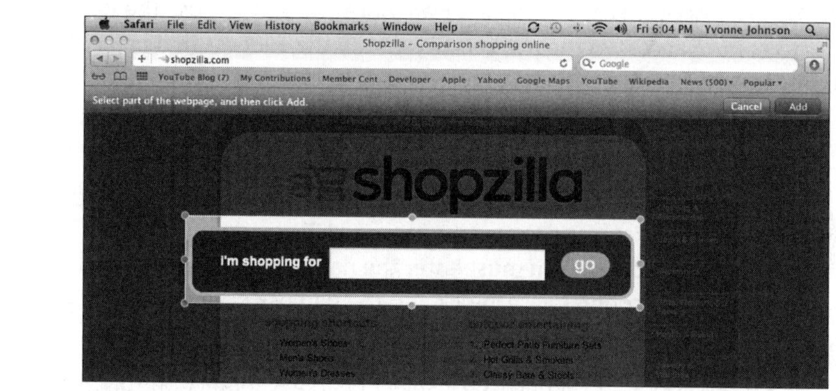

Figure 14.2 *The Add button sends the clip to the Dashboard.*

4. If necessary, drag the circular handles to adjust the size of the rectangle so it fits the size of the item you want to clip and then click Add (in the purple bar close to the top of the screen). The Dashboard opens and the clip starts loading. When finished loading, the clip appears on the Dashboard.
5. Drag the clip anywhere on the Dashboard that you want to put it.

After you create a widget, test it to see whether it really works. For example, if you clipped a log-in area, in all probability, it won't work. If your web clip is working and you really like it, avoid removing it from the Dashboard because you'll lose it. If you accidentally remove a clipped widget or one gets ruined because the web page design has changed, you can always create a new one.

Limiting Access to Widgets

Maybe you have downloaded the widget called Dreadtime Stories—an old-style radio horror podcast—and you don't want to expose your 10-year-old to it because he's going through the nightmare stage. Fortunately, you can control a user's access to all the widgets.

LET ME TRY IT

Controlling Access to Widgets

If you don't have a user account for your son, create one for him (see Chapter 3, "Setting Up User Accounts and Installing Hardware") so you can use the Parental Controls to control access to the widgets. To specify the widgets that an account can access, follow these steps:

1. Click the System Preferences icon in the Dock.
2. Click Users & Groups in the fourth row.
3. Click the padlock icon and type your password. If you do not have an Administrative account, you must enter the name and password of an Administrative account. Click Unlock and the padlock opens, allowing you to make changes.
4. Select the account and, if necessary, select Enable Parental Controls and then click Open Parental Controls.
5. Click the Apps tab, if necessary.
6. Select Limit Applications and click the disclosure triangle beside Widgets to see all the installed widgets, as shown in Figure 14.3.
7. Deselect the widgets you do not want the user to access.
8. Close the window when finished, and Lion closes the padlock for you automatically.

Figure 14.3 *All widgets are selected by default.*

Using Preview

The Preview application is a graphics-editing program that has joined forces with an Adobe Reader clone. Most Mac users don't utilize all the capabilities of Preview for several reasons:

- iPhoto duplicates some of its graphic capabilities (for example, cropping and adjusting exposure, brightness, and color).
- Users rarely need to edit or annotate PDF files.
- Users don't know what the full capabilities of the program are.

Normally, Preview opens automatically when you double-click certain types of files, but you can open the application *on purpose* from Launchpad or from its icon in the Dock.

You can use two new multi-touch gestures in Preview—a one-finger swipe left or right on a Magic mouse "turns the page" (a two or three-finger swipe on a Magic Trackpad) and a double tap zooms in on text or images.

One new feature in Preview is the Magnifier. This feature allows you to magnify a portion of a page so you can get a closer look, as shown in Figure 14.4. To turn on the Magnifier, click Tools in the menu bar and click Show Magnifier. To turn it off, go back to the Tools menu again and click Hide Magnifier. If you like this new tool, you can add the Magnifier button to the toolbar.

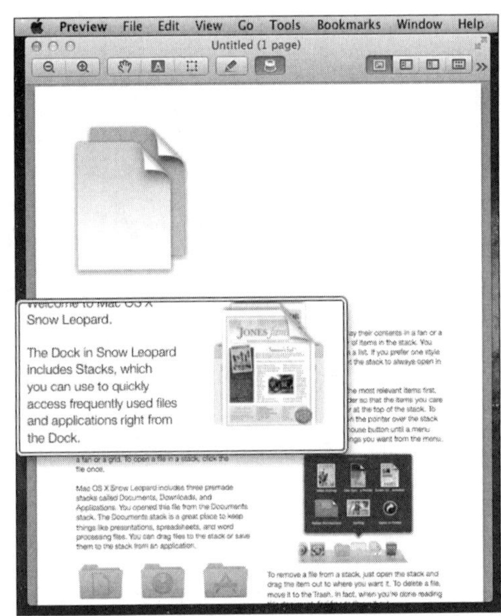

Figure 14.4 *The size of the magnification window adjusts automatically.*

To customize the toolbar, click View, Customize Toolbar and drag the button onto the toolbar in any position. Click Done when finished.

Working with PDF Files in Preview

As a PDF reader, Preview is awesome. It's not only a "reader," it's a "writer." It lets you search PDF documents; select and copy text from them; highlight, underline, or strike through text; click hyperlinks and add your own links; draw arrows, circles, and rectangles; add your own comments about the text and add text boxes to the text; format the text of your comments and text boxes; bookmark your place in the file; email the file; crop and rotate pages; and take a screenshot of the file.

The Annotations toolbar, which displays under the regular toolbar when you click the Annotate button, provides much of the functionality of Preview. Tools on the left side perform various actions in the file, and tools on the right perform formatting functions. A new tool on the Annotations toolbar lets you add your signature to a document by taking a picture of your signature with the built-in camera.

LET ME TRY IT

Searching in a PDF

If you are looking for a word or phrase in a PDF document, the new search feature in Preview provides new methods for finding exactly what you are looking for. Follow these steps to search a PDF file:

1. Click in the Spotlight search field and type the text. Preview immediately opens a sidebar listing the pages that contain the text and how many matches it finds on each page, as shown in Figure 14.5. It also shows all the occurrences highlighted in yellow in the right pane.
2. To sort the results, click the Page Order button or click the Search Rank button.
3. Click a page in the sidebar to go to the page in the right pane.

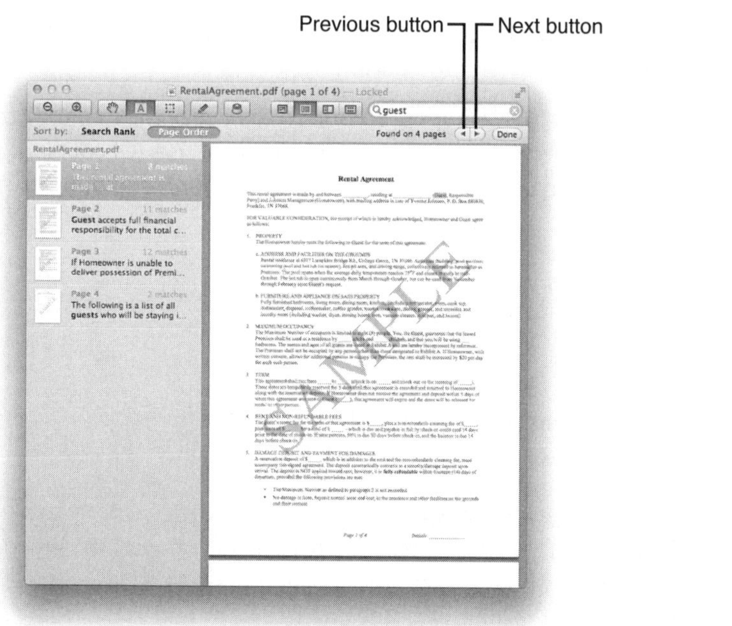

Figure 14.5 *The text that contains the first occurrence on the page is shown below the page number.*

4. Click the Next and Previous buttons to go to each occurrence.
5. Click Done when finished.

SHOW ME **Media 14.3—A Video about Drawing Shapes in Preview**
Access this video file through your registered Web Edition at
my.safaribooksonline.com/9780132819091/media
or on the DVD for print books.

LET ME TRY IT

Drawing a Shape

Quite often, when I'm reading something on a printed page, I get my red pen out and circle something to call attention to it. Essentially, you can do the same thing on the page of a PDF file. In addition to circles, you can draw rectangles, straight lines, and arrows. To draw a shape on the page of a PDF file, follow these steps:

1. Click the Annotate button in the toolbar.
2. Click the Shape pop-up button in the Annotations toolbar and click the shape you want to draw. If the button already displays the shape you want, then just click the button.
3. Click the Color Menu pop-up button to display the menu shown in Figure 14.6. Select the color you want the shape to use. (Of course, if the color you want to use already displays on the Color Menu button, you can skip this step.)

You also can draw the shape first and select a color afterwards. Just select the shape and then select the color.

4. Drag the cursor to draw the shape.

Press Shift after you start drawing to make a rectangle a perfect square, an oval a perfect circle, a line or arrow perfectly horizontal or vertical. When using Shift, when you are finished drawing the shape, be sure to release the mouse before you release the key. Otherwise, the shape may not be so perfect!

After drawing a line or arrow, you can set the thickness of the line by selecting the shape, clicking the pop-up button on the Line Width menu button, and clicking the thickness you want. You also can change the arrow to a double-headed arrow from this menu.

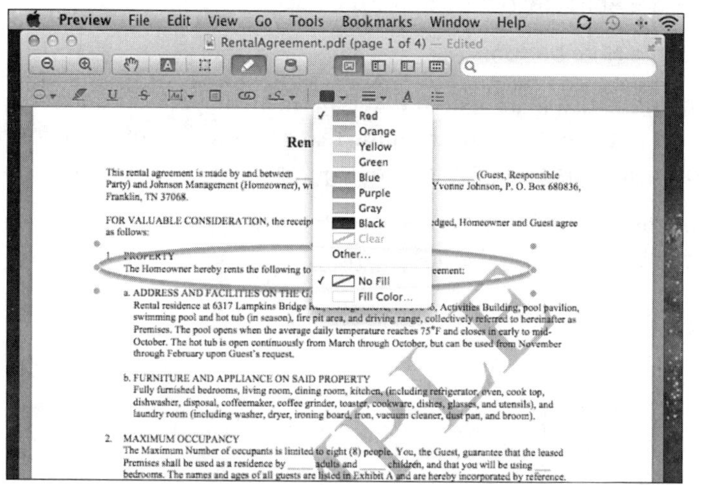

Figure 14.6 *Select the color you want to use from this menu.*

LET ME TRY IT

Highlighting, Underlining, or Striking Through Text in a PDF

To add any of these text attributes to text in a PDF file, follow these steps:

1. Click the Annotate button in the toolbar.
2. Before applying the attribute to text, make sure the attribute is the color you want to use. If the Color Menu button displays the color you want, you're good to go. Otherwise, select the color you want from the Color pop-up menu.
3. Click the Highlight button, the Underline button, or the Strikethrough button in the Annotations toolbar.
4. Drag the pointer over the text.

Adding a Note

To make a comment about something or add a note to a page, follow these steps:

1. Click the Annotate button in the toolbar.
2. Click the Note button.
3. Click in the text in a location that is germane to your comment or note. A yellow note symbol appears in the text and a comment space for you to type in appears to the left of the page, as shown in Figure 14.7.
4. Type the text and click the close button. The typing space closes and a yellow note icon displays in the document.

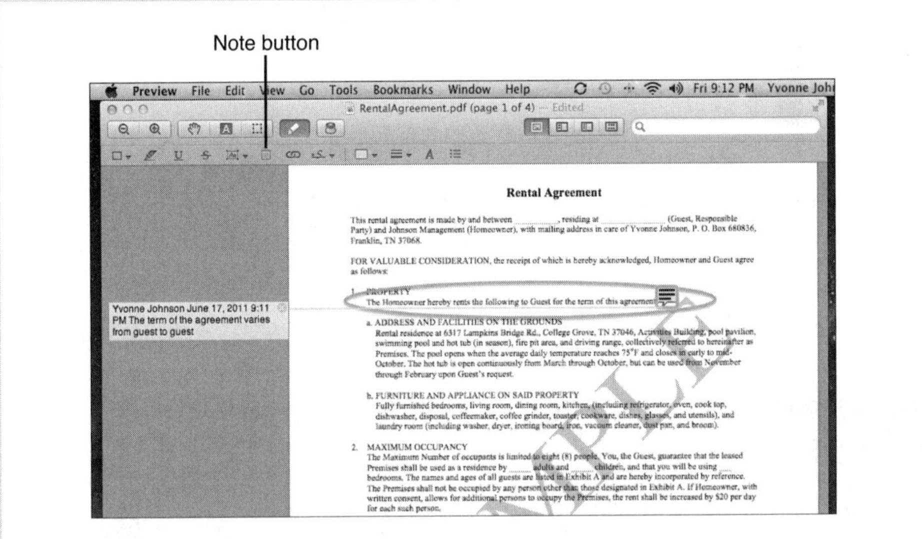

Figure 14.7 *Click a yellow icon to open and read the note.*

To read a note, just click the yellow icon that appears on the page using the Text pointer or the Select pointer.

Creating and Adding Your Signature to a File

Previously, if you wanted to add your signature to any type of document, you had to create a graphic file by scanning your signature and then inserting the graphic in the file. The new signature feature in Lion adds your signature by taking a picture of it. To add your signature to a document, follow these steps:

1. For best results, sign your name using a fine-tip black ink pen on a piece of white paper. I recommend using an 8.5 by 11- inch paper folded in half and signing it in the middle of the page. This gives you enough paper to hold on to without showing your hand in the photo. Make your signature a little smaller than you would write it on a check.
2. Click the Annotate button, if necessary to display the Annotate toolbar.
3. Click the Stamp/Signature pop-up button and click the option to create the signature from your camera. The option might be Create Signature from Built-in iSight or Create Signature from FaceTime HD Camera (Built-in). The Signature Capture dialog box opens and you see yourself in the picture box. The option to save the signature after you quit Preview is checked.
4. Hold the paper up in front of the camera so your signature rests on the blue line. This is the tricky part! Try to keep the paper as still as possible and try not to tilt the paper at an angle to the camera lens.
5. When the signature is lined up on the blue line and the white paper fills the entire picture box without showing you or your hand or any background, click Accept.
6. Click the Signature pop-up button and select your signature.
7. Click the location where you want the signature to appear.

Working with Graphics in Preview

As a graphic viewer, Preview can open practically any graphic format. In addition to viewing a graphic file in Preview, you can use annotation tools (described in the previous section) to draw rectangles, ovals, lines, or arrows and to add plain text or text in a speech or thought bubble. Figure 14.8 shows all three types of text added to a graphic.

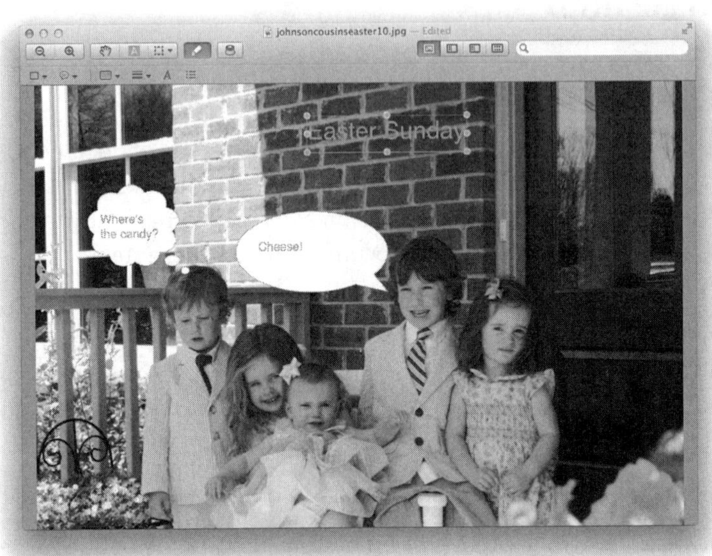

Figure 14.8 *When drawing a talking bubble, start at the mouth and drag away from the face.*

LET ME TRY IT

Reducing a Graphic File's Size

One other useful function that Preview can perform on a graphic is changing its dimensions and resolution. You might use this feature to reduce the size or resolution of a photo that is too large to email. (Reducing the dimensions and resolution automatically reduces the file size.) To reduce the size of a graphic file, follow these steps:

1. Open the graphic file in Preview.
2. Click Tools in the menu bar and click Adjust Size. The dialog box shown in Figure 14.9 opens.
3. Make desired changes in width, height, and resolution and click OK.

To reduce file size, not dimensions, reduce the resolution and select Resample Image.

4. Save the file.

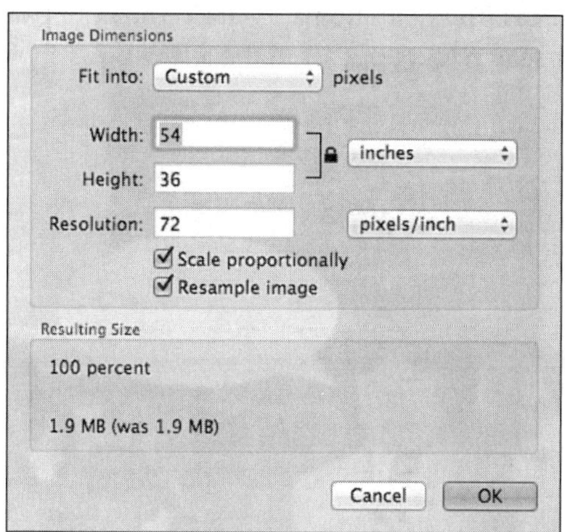

Figure 14.9 *Select Scale Proportionally so you don't distort the photo.*

Working with Versions

As you annotate a PDF file or a graphic file, Preview saves versions of the file for you using the Autosave feature. It saves the versions in the same file, and you can go back to an earlier version of the file at any time by browsing the versions that Lion saved for you. Additionally, you can save your own versions, delete a version, save a version as a new document, and lock the file so no additional versions can be saved. To learn more about versions, see Chapter 8, "Managing Applications."

Consulting the Dictionary

At my house, we use the Dictionary on my MacBook Pro all the time when we play Scrabble. It's much easier than using the two-ton, unabridged version, and it's much more up to date. We play so often that I've actually put the Dictionary in the Dock, but you can open it from the Launchpad.

Another quick way to open Dictionary is to click the Spotlight and type **Di**. Then click Dictionary in the list of results.

The Dictionary application actually has three separate dictionaries and a thesaurus: the complete *New Oxford American Dictionary*, the Apple Dictionary, Wikipedia, and the complete *Oxford American Writers Thesaurus*. Of course, the Wikipedia dictionary is actually online, and Dictionary just searches it for you. When you type a word, phrase, or part of a word to look up, you can click the All button at the top or just click one of the sources. The definition appears in the right pane, and a list of words that start with your search text appears in the left pane as shown in Figure14.10.

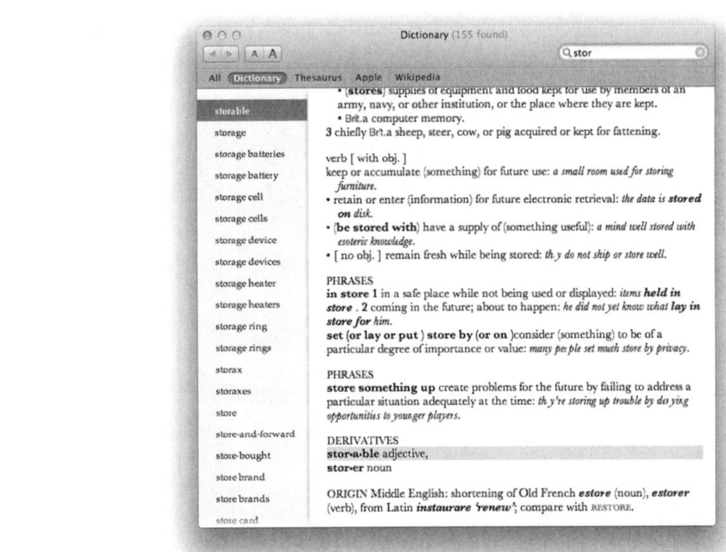

Figure 14.10 *Click an item in the sidebar to see its definition in the right pane.*

To quit Dictionary, click Command-Q or right-click the icon in the Dock and click Quit. Dictionary remembers which source you have selected when you quit, and it selects the same source the next time you open it.

The Dictionary widget in the Dashboard uses the same dictionaries and thesaurus but does not include Wikipedia.

Using Stickies

The Stickies application is the equivalent of the famous Post-It Note™, which my husband actually has stuck all around the perimeter of his screen because he doesn't know how to use this application. The Stickies application is not on the Dock by default, so open the Launchpad and click Stickies.

When you first open Stickies, you see two sticky notes, as shown in Figure 14.11. The two notes give you helpful information about creating and formatting stickies.

After you read them, you can save the content or delete them as explained later in this section.

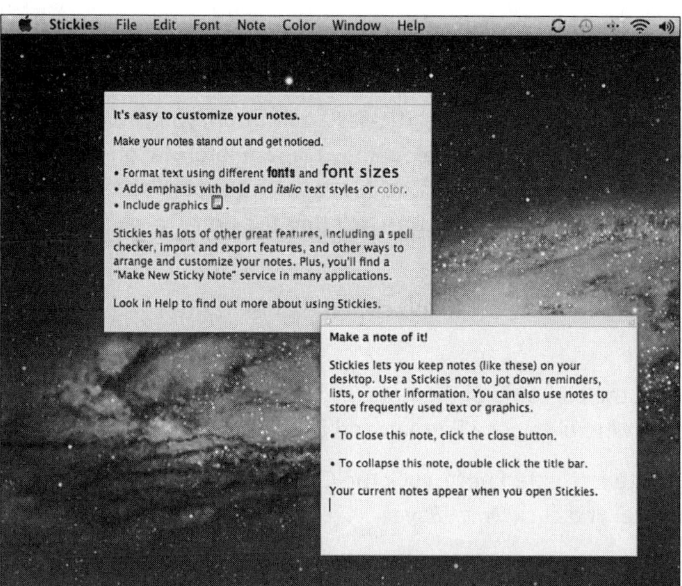

Figure 14.11 *These two standard sticky notes display the first time you launch Stickies.*

To create a sticky note, click File in the menu bar and click New. You can type text, paste or drag it from another file, or import it. Additionally, you can paste or drag graphics, movies, or sounds, and you can add web links. By default, notes are yellow, but you can click Color in the menu bar and select from five other colors in the pop-up menu.

The Stickies program is not like other applications that create files, such as Word. The sticky note is not actually an individual file. It only exists within the Stickies application; therefore, the only way to see a sticky note is to have the Stickies application open.

SHOW ME **Media 14.4—A Video about Saving or Deleting a Note**
Access this video file through your registered Web Edition at
my.safaribooksonline.com/9780132819091/media
or on the DVD for print books.

LET ME TRY IT

Saving or Deleting a Note

When a sticky note is outdated or no longer needed, such as the two notes that appear the first time you use the Stickies application, you can delete them. Sometimes a note that you want to delete may contain information that you want to save in an actual file on your disc. In this case, you should save the data in some format, such as a TextEdit file, before deleting the note. To save and delete notes, follow these steps:

1. Click the note to select it and click the Close button in the upper-left corner.
2. To save the contents of the note, click Save. Type a name for the file, specify Where, select a Format, and click Save.
3. To delete a selected note, click the Close button (in the upper-left corner of the note) and click Don't Save.

The Dashboard has a Sticky widget also, but it is not as robust as the Stickies application.

LET ME TRY IT

Positioning Stickies on the Screen

You can drag a sticky note to any location on the screen, and you can make it float on top of other windows that are open. Additionally, you can make a note translucent so that you can read what might be under the note. To position notes and change their appearance, follow these steps:

1. Point to the title bar at the top of the sticky note and drag the note anywhere on the screen.
2. If windows are covering some of your notes, click Window in the Stickies toolbar and click Bring All to Front.
3. To ensure that a sticky is always on top of other windows, click the note, click Note in the menu bar, and click Floating Window.
4. To make a note translucent so you can see what's underneath it, click the note to select it, click Note in the menu bar, and click Translucent Window.

5. To apply the floating and translucent settings to all notes, click the note that has had both settings applied, click Note in the menu bar, and then click Use as Default. Figure 14.12 shows a translucent note.

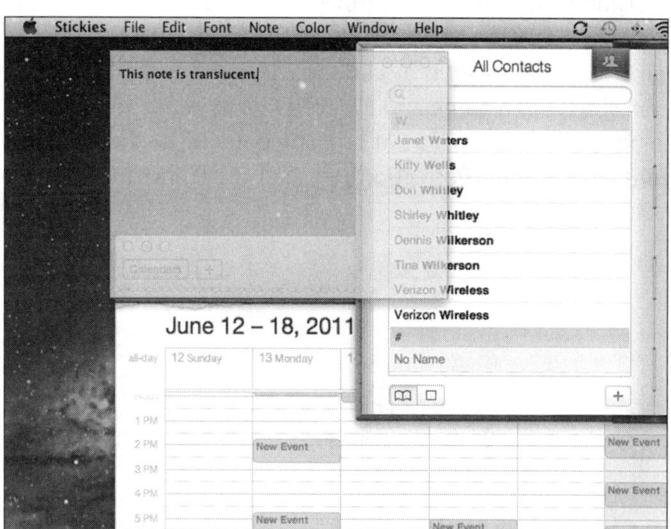

Figure 14.12 *Make your notes translucent so they can be on top of other windows and not obscure them.*

If you get too many notes on the screen, you can collapse them to one line by double-clicking the title bar. Expand them by double-clicking again.

6. Press Command-Q to quit Stickies. This closes all the notes, but the next time you open Stickies, the notes display again.

Using the Calculator

Every one needs a calculator occasionally, and Lion has a great calculator application with both a Scientific and a Programmer mode. Suppose after watching HGTV all day, the lady of the house decides that the driveway would look great with big pink circles painted all over it. She uses a piece of chalk and a string that is 1.75-feet long to scribe circles—10 of them—at random on the driveway. Now she needs to know how much paint to buy.

She remembers the formula for the area of a circle from her high school geometry class is pi times the radius squared (πr^2), but she doesn't remember the value of pi. No problem. She launches the calculator from the Launchpad and switches to

Scientific mode (shown in Figure 14.13) by clicking View, Scientific. Then she clicks in the formula. She clicks the π key; then the multiply key (refer to Figure 14.13); then she clicks 1.75 (the radius of the circle); and finally she clicks the x^2 key. This gives her the area of one circle. Then she continues and multiplies by 10 (the number of circles) and finally by 2 (the number of coats of paint) to find out that the total area that she has to cover with the paint is 192 square feet. As a reminder, she saves the tape of her calculation by clicking File in the menu bar and clicking Save Tape As. Then she types a name and clicks Save and prints the file. The next day she goes to the paint store with her print out. She determines that she only needs a quart of paint (Pink Petunia Perfection), so she buys it and goes right to work on her masterpiece.

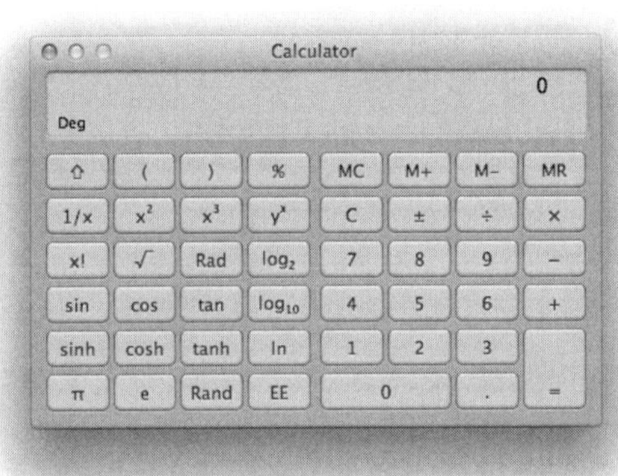

Figure 14.13 *To turn on the scientific mode shown here, click View, Scientific.*

When her husband comes home from work and sees the driveway, he uses the calculator to calculate the amount of blacktop sealer it will take to resurface the driveway. He quits the calculator by clicking the Close button, and then he calls the cable company to drop HGTV from their entertainment package. Bada-bing, bada-boom!

Well, that's an example of the Scientific mode. This mode also does calculations with logarithms, sine and cosine, tangent, square roots, and so on. If your work requires you to calculate angles, and radians, the square root of the length of the hypotenuse, and so on, you will know exactly how to use the Scientific mode.

The calculator also has a Programmer mode that you can switch to by clicking View, Programmer mode. If your work requires you to convert ASCII code to hexadecimal values, take 2's complement of X, shift bytes to the left or right, flip bytes, and so on, you will know exactly how to use the Programmer mode, shown in

Figure 14.14. Notice in the figure that the keys consist of 0 – 9, A – F, FF, and 00. These are all the characters you can use for a hexadecimal value. (Refer to Chapter 3 for examples of an ASCII password and a hexadecimal password for an ad hoc network.)

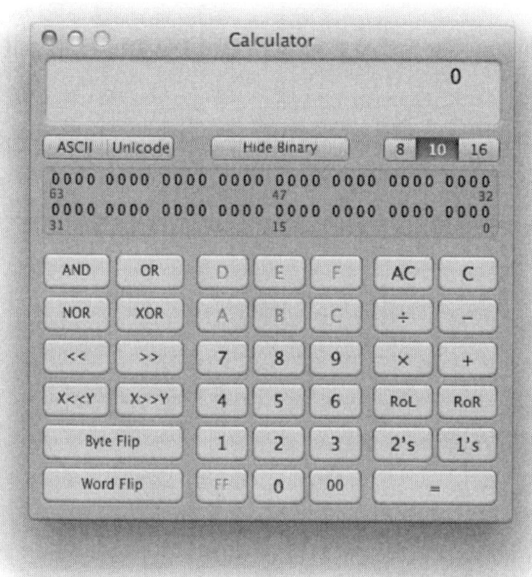

Figure 14.14 *Paper tape and memory are not available in the Programmer mode.*

The calculator's Basic mode is just what you would expect from a simple calculator. It has addition, subtraction, multiplication, division, and you can store values in memory. In Basic mode, the calculator is just like the widget calculator on the Dashboard.

In the Basic or Scientific modes, you also can use the calculator to perform conversions. The conversion categories include Area, Currency, Energy or Work, Length, Power, Pressure, Speed, Temperature, Time, Volume, and Weights and Masses.

LET ME TRY IT

Performing Conversions

When you use the calculator to perform a conversion, the calculator remembers the types of conversions you perform and stores them for later use. To perform a conversion, follow these steps:

1. Open the Launchpad and click Calculator.

2. Make sure you are not in the Programmer mode and enter the number you want to convert in the calculator, such as 48 (from the kilometer-to-mile conversion example). You can click the numbers on the screen or use your numeric key pad to enter the numbers.
3. Click Convert in the menu bar and select the appropriate category, such as Length. A dialog box opens.
4. Select the appropriate From and To options, such as From Kilometers and To Miles.
5. Click Convert. The dialog box closes and the answer appears on the calculator. Billy Joe Bob finds out that it is only 29.82 miles from the airport to his hotel. Now he just needs to find out how many gallons of gas are in a liter!

As you perform different conversions, the From and To parameters are stored on the Recent Conversions menu so you can go back to them quickly. The next time you want to convert kilometers to miles, you can click Convert, Recent Conversions, Kilometers to Miles.

Using the DigitalColor Meter

The DigitalColor Meter is a utility that tells you the RGB (red, green, blue) values for a color you see on your screen. "What? Are you crazy? Why would I possibly want to know that?" you say. Imagine this. You are surfing the Web and go to a website that has a logo with a color that you want to use in your own logo. Or maybe you have a website that needs redesigning and you want to use the color as the new background color of your navigation bar. If you get the RGB values using the DigitalColor Meter, you, your graphic designer, or your web designer can duplicate the color that you've found and fallen in love with.

RGB color values are for screen colors only, but they are easily translated into CMYK values (cyan, magenta, yellow, black), which are used in four-color process printing. So if you find a color you like on a website, and you want to use it in a printed brochure, just translate the RGB values. A special utility in Lion can do this for you. See Chapter 15, "Using System Utilities."

Because color you see on your screen is produced by mixing light and color you see on a printed page is produced by mixing pigment, you will never get exactly the same color for a color value when using two different media.

LET ME TRY IT

Determining the RGB Values of a Point on the Screen

To get the exact color of a pixel or an area on the screen, follow these steps:

1. Click the Launchpad icon on the Dock.
2. If necessary, navigate to the page that contains the Utilities folder and click its icon to open the folder.
3. Click the icon for DigitalColor Meter. Figure 14.15 shows you the application.
4. Adjust the aperture to the size you need.

> If you make the aperture as small as possible, you sample a single pixel on the screen. If you make the aperture larger, the color values of all the pixels in the aperture are averaged.

5. Point to the color on the screen and watch the box on the left to make sure you have the area selected that is the color you want. The RGB values display on the right.

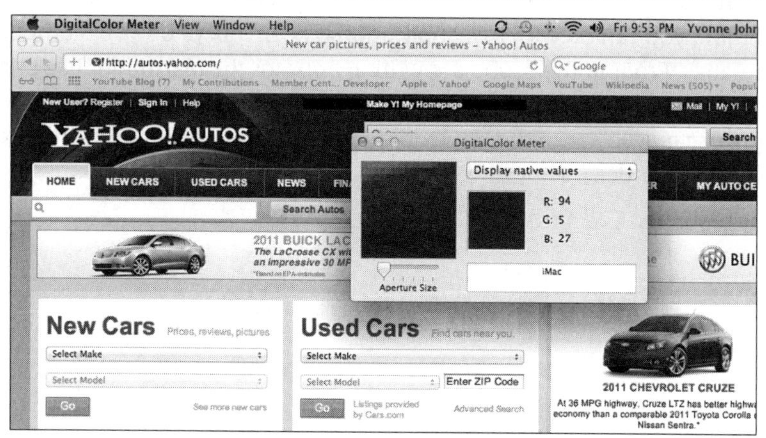

Figure 14.15 *The DigitalColor Meter reads color values for red, green, and blue.*

This chapter covers the system utilities that are bundled in Lion.

15

Using System Utilities

This chapter introduces you to the majority of the system utilities that come with Lion, those little applications that are grouped together in the Utilities folder on the Launchpad. If you are an average Mac user, you probably will not use every one of the utilities covered in this chapter, but you should at least know what they are and what they do just in case you have a need for them in the future. So for the utilities that are not used by many people, this chapter provides a brief description, and for the utilities that are used most often, it goes into more detail. The topics in this chapter are arranged alphabetically by utility name.

Activity Monitor

The Activity Monitor gives you information about the processes that are currently running on your computer and what percent of the CPU resources they are using. Additionally, the application gives you information about your CPU (computer processing unit), system memory, disk activity, disk usage, and network. The most useful thing you can do with this application is keep an eye on your computer's performance. Programmers who are writing apps for the Mac might use this utility to see how efficiently their programs run. Figure 15.1 shows the Activity Monitor. As you can see in the figure, the processes that are running are listed in alphabetical order.

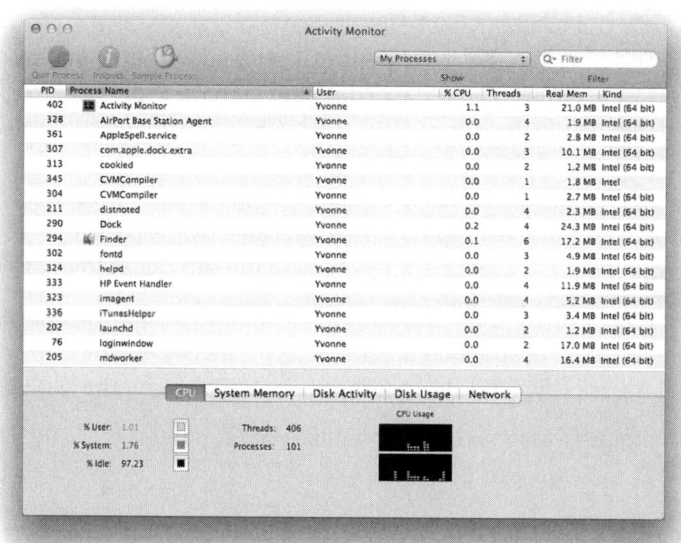

Figure 15.1 *The Dock is using only .2% of the CPU resources.*

Using the AirPort Utility

You use the AirPort utility to configure the wireless connection from an AirPort Base Station or Time Capsule to your computer. The AirPort Base Station and the Time Capsule are connected directly to the Internet to provide Internet service to all your Apple computers that are Wi-Fi–enabled and in range. If you don't have either of these devices, then you'll never use this utility.

Using the AppleScript Editor

The AppleScript Editor is the application you use to write, run, debug, and compile AppleScripts. An AppleScript is a file that contains commands written in the programming language by the same name (AppleScript). A compiled script runs (that is, performs the commands within the script) if you double-click it in the Finder. If you know what a macro file is and what it does, then you can understand what an AppleScript does. This application is for use by programmers who want to extend the functionality of Lion by creating automated routines.

Using Audio MIDI Setup

The Audio MIDI Setup utility configures the input and output of audio and MIDI (Musical Instrument Musical Interface) devices you have connected to your computer, both the built-in devices, such as the built-in microphone, as well as devices attached via FireWire, USB, Bluetooth, PCMCIA, and PCI, such as headphones. The configuration of audio devices may include setting options for volume, clock source, sample rate, and bit depth if made available by the particular device. For example, your device may not permit changing the setting for the sample rate.

For MIDI devices such as keyboard controllers or synthesizers, the utility shows a visual representation of your equipment, and you specify exactly how things are connected. You specify things like the inputs and outputs for the cables.

Musicians who use a Mac to record and mix audio soundtracks are the likely users of this utility.

Using Bluetooth File Exchange

The Bluetooth File Exchange utility sends a file from your Mac to a Bluetooth device that is in range and discoverable. For example, you can send a file from your iMac to your MacBook Pro using this utility. When you send the file, the two devices have to be paired so there is a pairing request and a password involved, but after the computers are paired, the file is sent. It's less trouble than copying files between computers using a flash drive.

LET ME TRY IT

Sending a File from One Mac to Another Using Bluetooth

The average user might find this utility useful, so here are the steps:

1. Before trying to send a file, you must make sure Bluetooth Sharing is activated on the receiving computer. Open System Preferences, click Bluetooth, and click Sharing Setup. Select Bluetooth Sharing, as shown in Figure 15.2. Set options as desired and close the System Preferences window.
2. On the sending computer, click the Launchpad icon in the Dock.
3. Click the Utilities folder.
4. Click Bluetooth File Exchange. The Select File to Send dialog box opens, as shown in Figure 15.3.

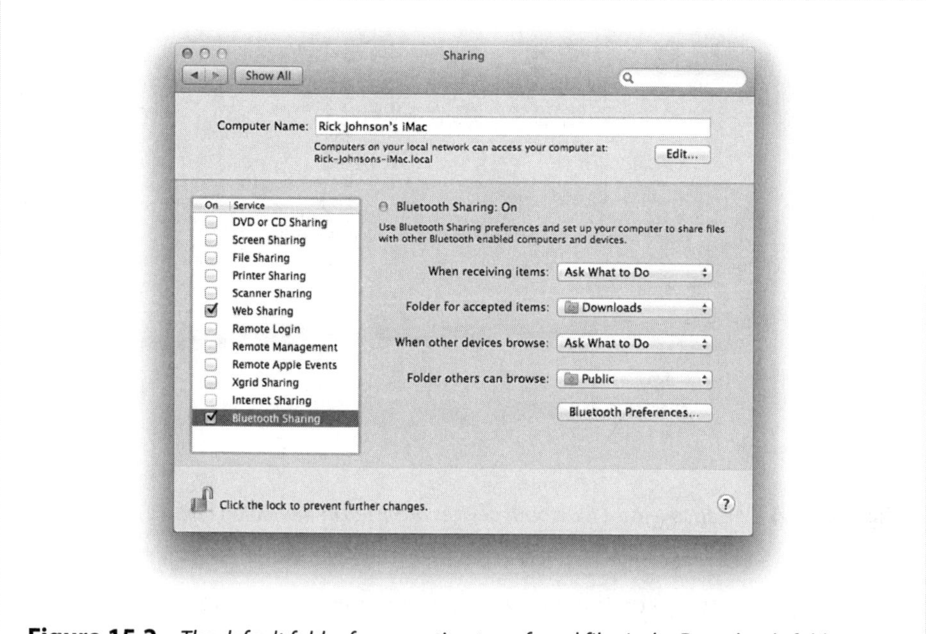

Figure 15.2 *The default folder for accepting transferred files is the Downloads folder.*

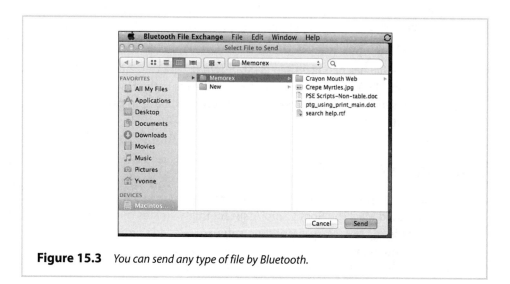

Figure 15.3 *You can send any type of file by Bluetooth.*

5. Navigate to the file you want to send and double-click it. The Send File dialog box opens, as shown in Figure 15.4.
6. Select the computer to which you want to send the file and click Send.

Figure 15.4 *All discoverable Bluetooth devices are listed in this dialog box.*

7. Enter a password on the receiving computer and then enter the same password on the sending computer. (You only have to do this once to pair the devices so you don't have to remember the password.)
8. On the receiving computer, click the Accept button in the Incoming File Transfer dialog box. Or, if you have changed your mind about transferring the file, click Decline.
9. When the file has been completely transferred, click the Show button in the Incoming File Transfer dialog box to select the file in the Finder. At this point, you can send more files if you want and you won't have to pair the computers again.

Using Boot Camp Assistant

A few years ago, Apple made it possible to install Windows in a separate partition on an Intel-based Mac. The Boot Camp Assistant utility creates the partition for you and downloads any necessary supporting software needed to run Windows. Then it starts the Windows installer. Of course, you must own a copy of Windows to install, and as of this writing it's not available in the App Store.

Using the ColorSync Utility

The ColorSync utility checks and repairs ICC profiles (International Color Consortium). An ICC profile is a color management system that describes the color attributes of a particular device by mapping the device to a profile connection space. In simpler terms, an ICC profile ensures that a color is rendered in a consistent way across different devices and different brands of devices, such as monitors, printers, scanners, digital cameras, and so on.

To see the profiles that are installed on your computer, launch the ColorSync Utility and click the Profiles tab, which is shown in Figure 15.5. To see the devices registered with ColorSync, click the Devices tab, which is shown in Figure 15.6.

Chapter 14, "Using Widgets and Other Applications," includes information about finding out the RGB (red, green, blue) values of a color on the screen by using the DigitalColor Meter. If you know the RGB values, you can easily translate the values into CMYK (cyan, magenta, yellow, black) values for color printing. The Calculator tab of the ColorSync Utility calculates these values (and others) for you. In Figure 15.7, you can see the values of a light blue translated from RGB to CMYK.

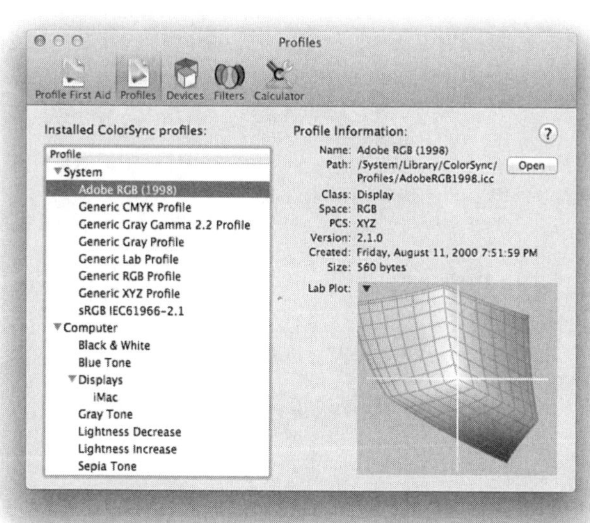

Figure 15.5 *Select a profile on the left to see the profile information on the right.*

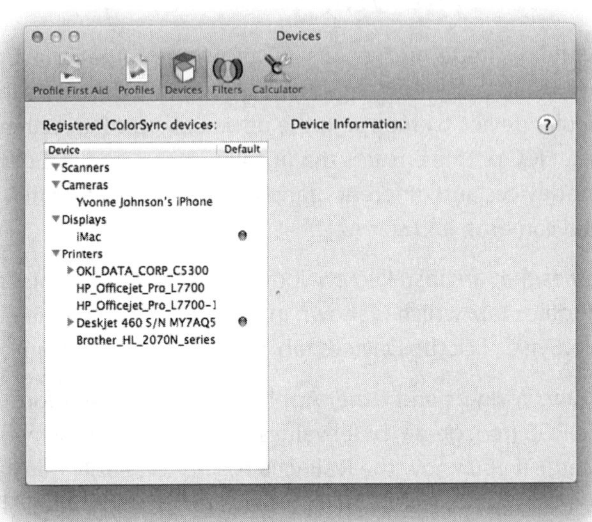

Figure 15.6 *Click the disclosure triangle to see the devices in each category.*

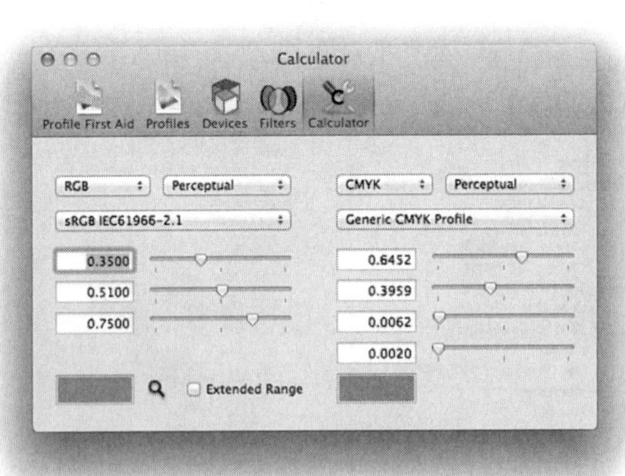

Figure 15.7 *Perceptual is selected for RGB because that is the type of profile the iMac display uses.*

Using Console

Stored away on your computer where you would never think to look, Lion keeps logs of internal messages about errors, alerts, events, and so on that are sent back and forth between applications and the operating system. These messages do not appear on your screen, but if a problem occurs a technician can view these messages and possibly find the cause of the problem.

If you ever have a problem on your computer, you may see a dialog box that asks whether you want to send information about the problem to Apple. The information kept in these logs is the information the dialog box is talking about. I always opt to send the information because it helps Apple improve its applications. Now, if you really want to look at this information yourself, you go ahead and open Console, but using this utility is way beyond what an average user would do or even *want* to do. Maybe you will just be satisfied with looking at Figure 15.8.

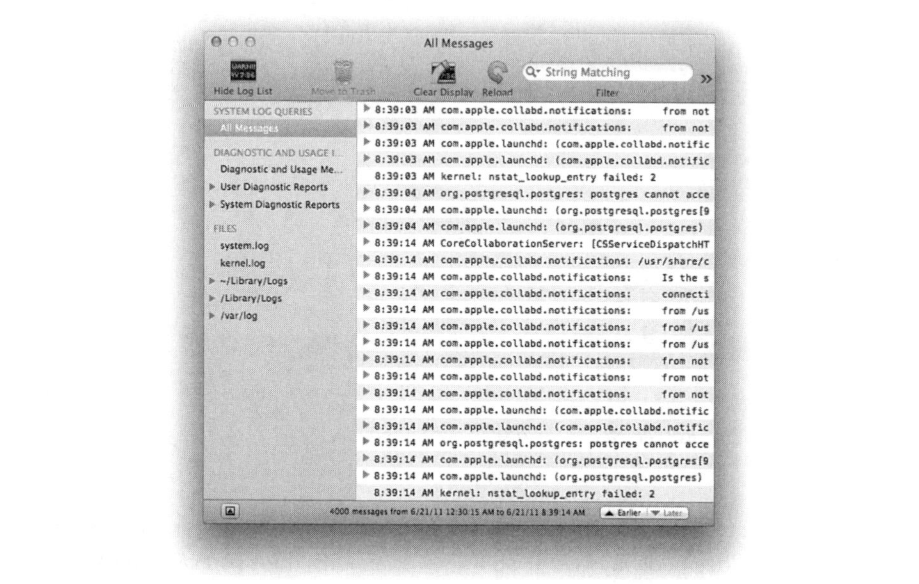

Figure 15.8 *This screen is constantly updating with the current messages.*

Using DigitalColor Meter

See Chapter 14 for information about this utility.

Using the Disk Utility

The Disk Utility is a utility I use on a regular basis to erase flash drives and rewritable CDs and DVDs. The Disk Utility has four possible tabs, depending on the type of disk. If the disk is not a hard disk, then you have First Aid, Erase, and Restore. If the disk is a hard disk, you have the additional RAID tab.

On the First Aid tab, you can verify a disk to see whether it needs repair. Figure 15.9 shows the message that opens on the screen when a disk has been verified and needs to be repaired.

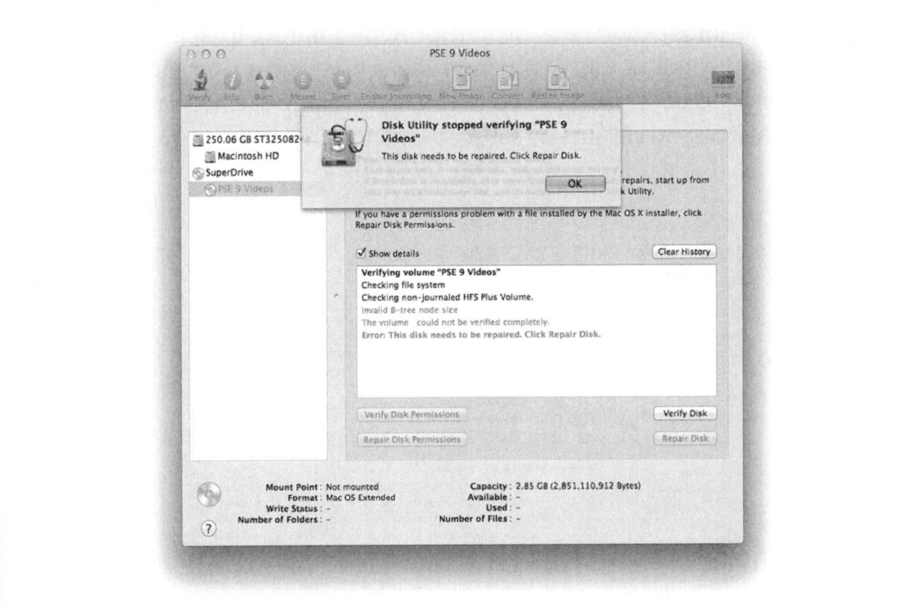

Figure 15.9 *The disk selected is the disk in the SuperDrive.*

If a disk needs to be repaired, you can select the disk in the sidebar and click Repair Disk. A repair doesn't always work, so if the repair fails, then you can go to the next tab and erase the disk so you can reuse it. Before erasing the disk, you can try to make a copy of its content, but sometimes a disk is completely unreadable.

SHOW ME **Media 15.1—A Video about Erasing Disks**

Access this video file through your registered Web Edition at ***my.safaribooksonline.com/9780132819091/media*** *or on the DVD for print books.*

LET ME TRY IT

Erasing Disks

The Disk Utility allows you to erase a disk in one of two ways—the fast way and the slow way. The fast way takes only a few minutes; the slow way could take as long as an hour. If a disk has been working reliably—no problems reading the disk, in other words, then you can use the fast method. This method doesn't really erase the disk, but it deletes certain file information on the disk so the optical reader will think the disk is empty and write over the data that really is still there. If you are having problems with the disk, use the slow method to completely erase and reformat the disk. If unusable sectors on the disk are causing the problem, the reformatting process will note the location of the sectors so an optical drive will not try to write new data to them.

To erase a disk, follow these steps:

1. Insert the disk.
2. Click the Erase tab in the Disk utilities window. Your screen should look something like Figure 15.10.

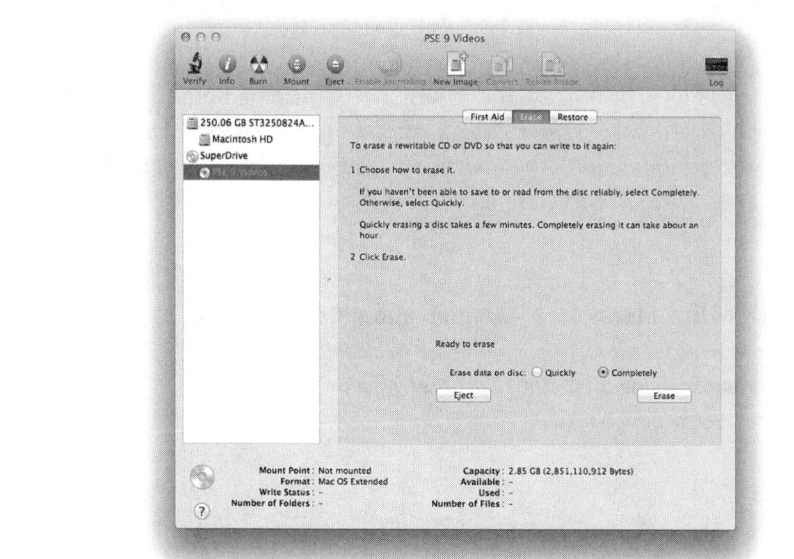

Figure 15.10 *Be sure you have the correct disk selected in the sidebar before you erase.*

3. Select the erase method you want to use: Quickly or Completely.
4. Click Erase. A confirmation dialog box opens asking whether you are sure. Read the dialog box carefully to be sure you have selected the correct disk to erase. If you have, click Erase. If you see that you have selected the wrong disk, click Cancel and start again.
5. When the process is finished, you see the dialog box shown in Figure 15.11 telling you that you have inserted a blank CD or DVD. Click Eject if you are finished, or click Ignore to leave the disk in the drive and continue working, or select an option from the pop-up menu and click OK.

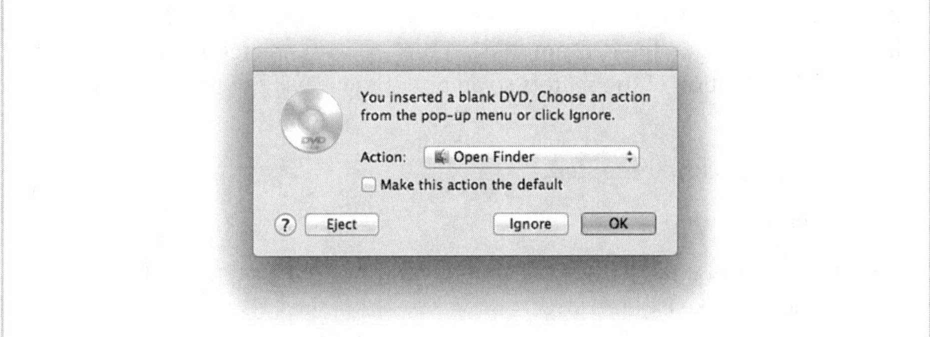

Figure 15.11 *Getting this message is a pretty good sign that the disk is usable again.*

If you have erased a CD or DVD several times, it may become unusable. Check the box the disks came in or refer to any documentation that came with them. Although a Mac can read a disk that has been used on a PC, if you erase the CD and try to burn data on it with your Mac, it may work and it may not.

SHOW ME **Media 15.2—A Video about Copying Disks**
Access this video file through your registered Web Edition at
my.safaribooksonline.com/9780132819091/media
or on the DVD for print books.

LET ME TRY IT

Copying Disks

The third tab in the Disk Utility window, Restore, can be used to copy a disk, just not a protected disk, such as a commercial music CD or DVD movie. When you copy a disk, the Disk Utility copies all the files on the disk to a .dmg file (a disk image file), which it saves on your hard drive. Then you can burn the .dmg file to a disc. To copy a disk, follow these steps:

1. Click the Restore tab of the Disk Utility.
2. Insert the disk you want to copy in the optical drive.
3. Click File in the menu bar and click New, Disk Image from <*disk name*>.
4. Type a different name for Save As if you don't want to use the name of the disk.
5. Select a format from the Image Format pop-up menu. The Compressed option creates a smaller image and the Read-Only option creates a disk more quickly and the copied disk opens more quickly.
6. Click Save. Disk Utility creates a copy of what is on the disk and lists it in the sidebar on the left, as shown in Figure 15.12. When you see the new disk image, you can eject the disk so you can insert the new disk. (Press the Eject button on your keyboard.)
7. Select the new image in the sidebar, click Images in the menu bar, and click Burn.
8. Insert a blank CD or DVD and click Burn.
9. One more time, click Burn. When the Disk is finished, a message displays telling you that the burn was successful and the disk is ejected.
10. Click OK.

Repeat steps 7 through 10 to make as many copies of the disk image as you want. When you don't need the disk image on your hard drive any more, you can delete it using the Finder.

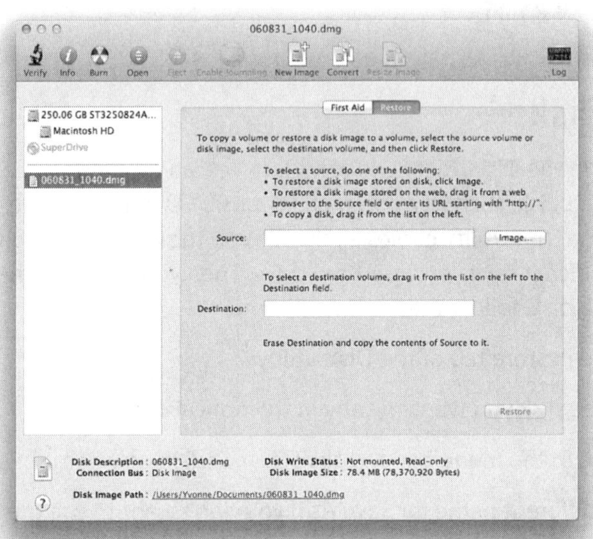

Figure 15.12 *The disk image file that was copied to the hard drive is listed under the dividing line in the sidebar.*

Using Grab

Grab is a screen capture utility. Both print and online writers often make use of screen captures in their work, including a book like this. Unfortunately, the images that Grab saves are not high enough in resolution for good quality printing, but they are fine for viewing on the web or on screen. You might use this utility to capture something problematic on the screen or an error message so you can show it to a technician. You might also use this utility to capture a web page that you see on your screen.

SHOW ME **Media 15.3—A Video about Capturing Screen Images**
Access this video file through your registered Web Edition at
my.safaribooksonline.com/9780132819091/media
or on the DVD for print books.

LET ME TRY IT

Capturing Screen Images

Using Grab you can capture the entire screen, part of a screen, or a window or dialog box. Additionally, you can take a timed screen capture. To take a screen capture, follow these steps:

1. Click the Launchpad icon in the Dock and click the Utilities folder.
2. Click Grab. The Grab icon appears in the Dock.

If you must capture several screenshots in a row, consider keeping Grab on the Dock for easier access. (Right-click the icon and click Options, Keep in Dock.)

3. Perform any steps necessary to display what you want to capture on the screen. For example, if you want a screenshot of the System Preferences window, click the System Preferences icon in the Dock.
4. Perform one of the following:
   - To capture the entire screen, click Capture in the menu bar and click Screen or press Command-Z. A dialog box opens with instructions. Click outside the dialog box.
   - To capture a window or dialog box, click Capture in the menu bar and click Window or press Shift-Command-W. A dialog box opens with instructions. Click outside the dialog box of instructions anywhere in the window or dialog box you want to capture.
   - To capture a portion of the screen, click Capture in the menu bar and click Selection or press Shift-Command-A. A dialog box with instructions opens. If the dialog box is in your way, you can move it. Drag over the portion of the screen you want to capture. If you include any part of the instruction dialog box, it will not be in the capture.
   - To do a timed capture, click Capture in the menu bar and click Timed Screen or press Shift-Command-Z. A dialog box opens. Click the Start Timer button. In ten seconds Grab will capture the entire screen as it appears at that time. During the ten seconds, you can perform any operations needed to display items on the screen.

5. The screen capture appears in a window so you can view it before saving it to a file. Click File in the menu bar and click Save. Give the file a name and select a location for it. Then click the Save button.

6. Close the window containing the screen capture.

Using Grapher

Grapher is a utility that creates graphs, as you would suspect. It graphs several types of algebraic equations in two and three dimensions. Most people who need to create graphs use Numbers or Excel, and most of those people are not graphing algebraic equations. Just thought you should know—doubt you'll use this one! It's an old feature that Apple promoted when marketing in the college sector.

Using Keychain

You definitely need to know about the Keychain, so see Chapter 16, "Keeping Your Mac Safe, Updated, and Backed Up," for details.

Using Migration Assistant

If you purchase a new MacBook Pro, and you want to transfer user accounts, files, and computer settings from your old MacBook Pro to your new one, then Migration Assistant is the utility you need to use.

LET ME TRY IT

Migrating from Another Mac to the Current Mac

Before you start using the Migration Assistant, you can close all other open applications. If you fail to close an application, the Assistant will do it for you during the process. To use the Migration Assistant in the scenario described earlier, follow these steps:

1. Click the Launchpad icon in the Dock, click the Utilities folder, and click Migration Assistant. The window shown in Figure 15.13 opens.

2. Click From another Mac, PC, Time Machine Backup, or Other Disk and click Continue.

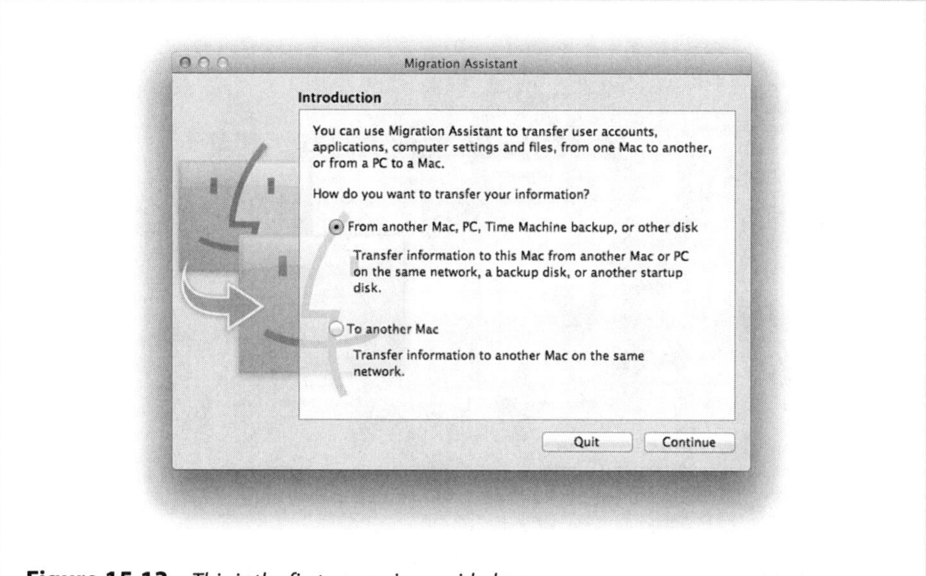

Figure 15.13 *This is the first screen in a guided process.*

3. Type your password and click OK.
4. Next you must select the Migration Method. If your computers are connected via a network, you can select From Another Mac or PC. If they are not networked, you can select From a Time Machine Backup or Other Disk.
5. When the wizard is able to detect data from another source, it displays a list of items you can migrate, as shown in Figure 15.14. Uncheck the items you do not want to migrate and click Continue. The Migration Assistant begins searching for and transferring the items. This can take a while and the Assistant will let you know approximately how long. Additionally, if you are transferring a user account and the same name is used on the new computer, you can choose to rename the incoming user, delete the user on the current Mac, or merge the two.
6. When the migration is finished, click Quit.

If any items in the transfer are incompatible, the Migration Assistant will not transfer them.

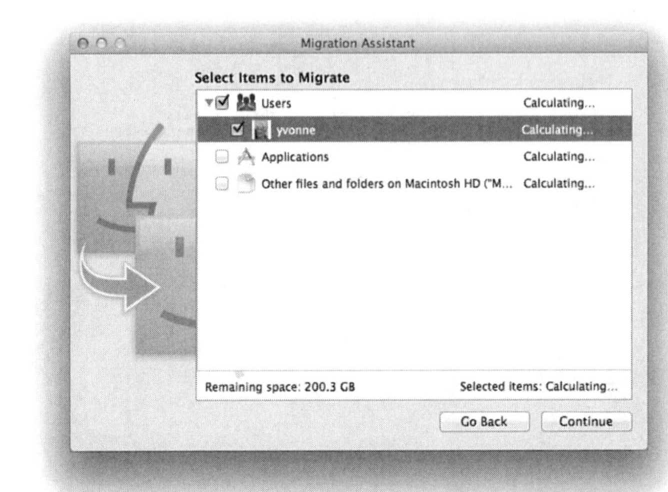

Figure 15.14 *The user home folder called Yvonne is selected to transfer.*

Using Podcast Publisher

The Podcast Publisher utility is a great place to get started if you're interested in podcasting on a very casual level. It records and publishes both audio podcasts and audio/video podcasts.

A podcast is a series of audio or video recordings or episodes generally about the same topic or a particular theme. For example, you could create a podcast about your hobby. You can add episodes to the podcast as often or as little as you want. Other people who are interested in the subject of your podcast can subscribe to it after it is published to the Internet, and new episodes you add will be downloaded automatically to the subscribers.

Using the Podcast Publisher to create the episodes is the easy part. Getting it published on the Internet will require some research on your part. When selecting a podcast host, you need to consider how much storage space your files will occupy and how much bandwidth will be used by your estimated number of downloads.

Using QuickTime Player 7

QuickTime Player 7 is included in the Utilities folder for backward compatibility. It is not the same program as the QuickTime Player in the Launchpad that is *not* in the Utilities folder. For information about using QuickTime Player, see Chapter 17, "Having Fun."

Using System Information

The System Information utility is a new utility that includes the old System Profiler utility from OS X Snow Leopard plus many more new features. You use this utility for such things as giving a technician your computer's serial number, checking the amount of storage you have left on your hard disk and what kind of files are taking up the most room, or checking how much memory is installed on your computer.

You can open the System Information utility from the Launchpad, but you also can open it from the Apple menu. Click About This Mac and click More Info. Figure 15.15 shows the Overview page.

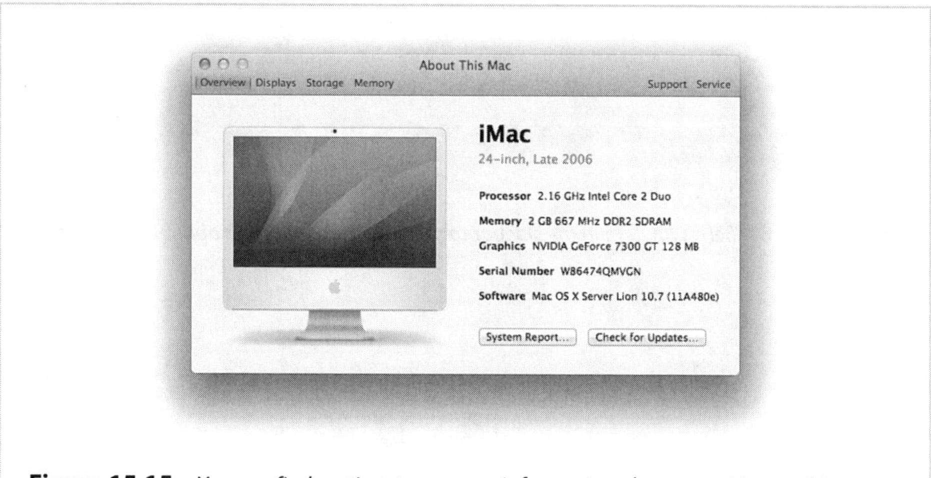

Figure 15.15 *You can find pertinent summary information about your Mac on this page.*

If you click the System Report button on this page, you will see the information shown in Figure 15.16. This is the same information that System Profiler gives you in Snow Leopard. This information tells you about every component of your computer.

The Displays page tells you what kind of monitor you have. If you click the Displays Preference button on this page you get the same window as you would if you clicked the System Preferences icon in the Dock and then clicked Displays.

Figure 15.17 shows you the Storage page, which gives you information about your hard disk and your optical drive. Clicking the Disk Utility button on this page opens the Disk Utility discussed previously in this chapter.

Click the Memory tab to find out how many memory slots are in your Mac and how much memory is actually installed, as shown in Figure 15.18.

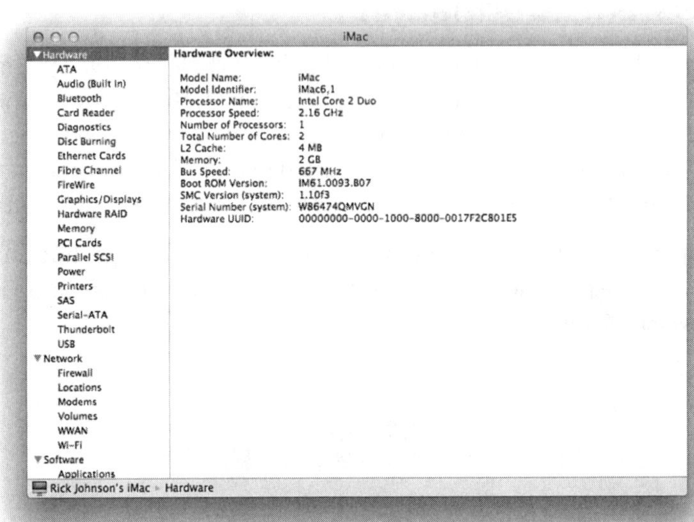

Figure 15.16 *Select an item in the sidebar to see specific information about it in the right pane.*

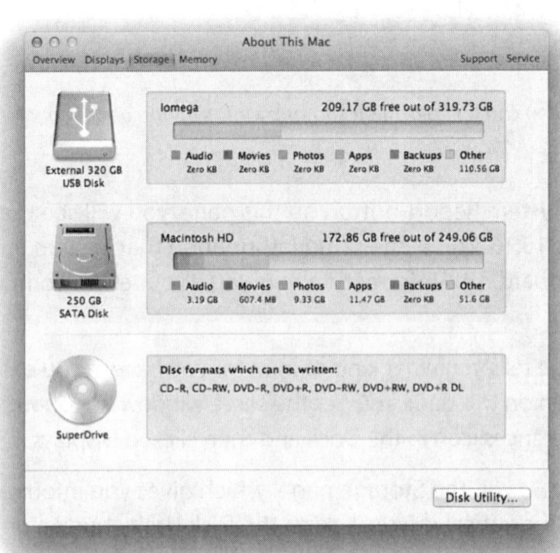

Figure 15.17 *The hard drive information lists the percentages that categories of files occupy.*

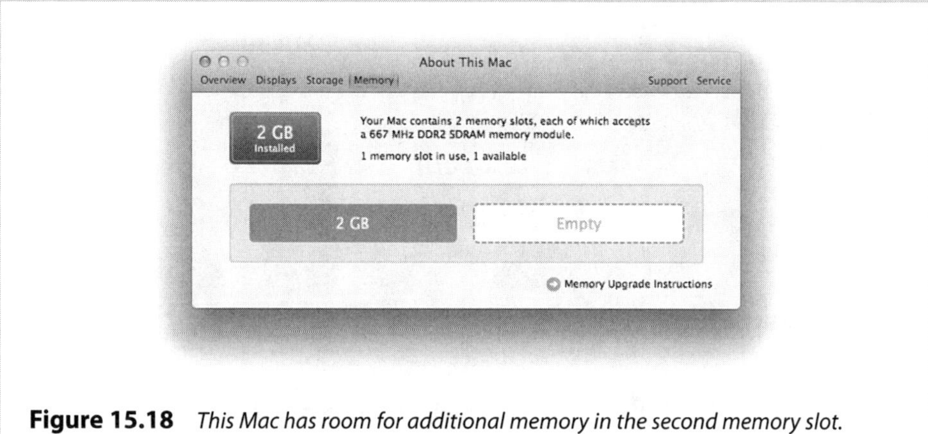

Figure 15.18 *This Mac has room for additional memory in the second memory slot.*

Click the Support tab for a list of links to various resources as shown in Figure 15.19.

Click the Service tab to gain access to your warranty information and repair records, as shown in Figure 15.20.

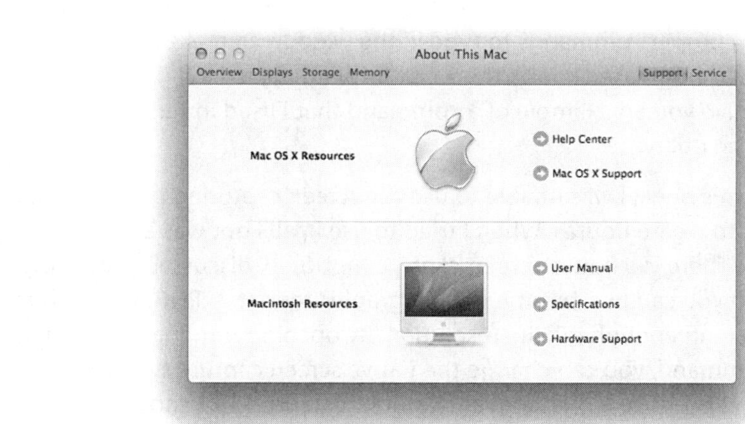

Figure 15.19 *Software support items are listed at the top and hardware support items are listed at the bottom.*

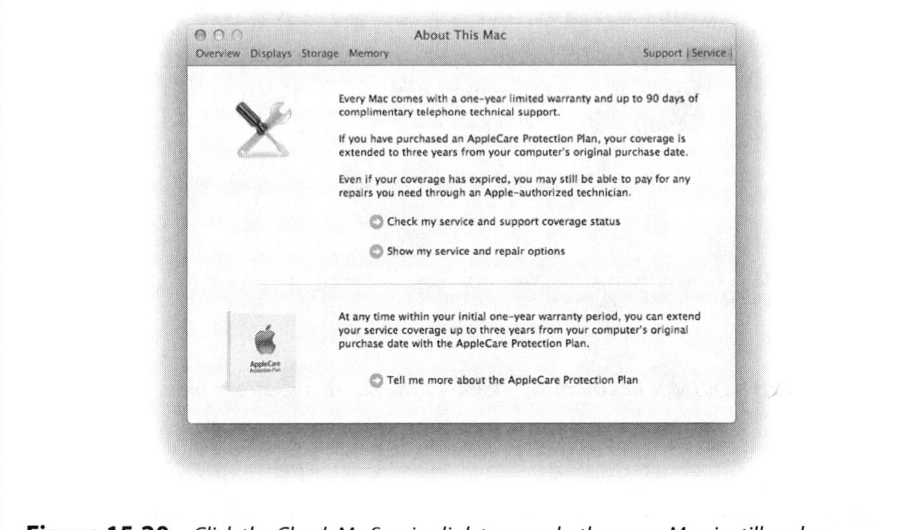

Figure 15.20 *Click the Check My Service link to see whether your Mac is still under warranty.*

Using Terminal

If you can remember back to the days of DOS on the PC, the Terminal window does not look too intimidating. It's similar to the old DOS window in that you must know the proper commands to type in the window to make anything happen. As an average user, I don't think you'll spend any time in Terminal, but I want to give you an example of a command that I used in Terminal so you get a feel for the utility.

While writing this book, I was unable to use the screen capturing program that I normally use to create figures. When I tried to use it, all I got was a picture of a black screen. There is a native screen capture (not Grab, discussed previously in this chapter) you can use, but the default graphic format is .PNG, which does not produce a high enough quality resolution. By opening Terminal and typing the correct command, you can change the native screen capture type to .TIFF, which *does* produce a higher quality graphic. Figure 15.21 shows the command.

If you want to hear about another terminal command that involves copying email addresses, listen to the audio file I've recorded for you.

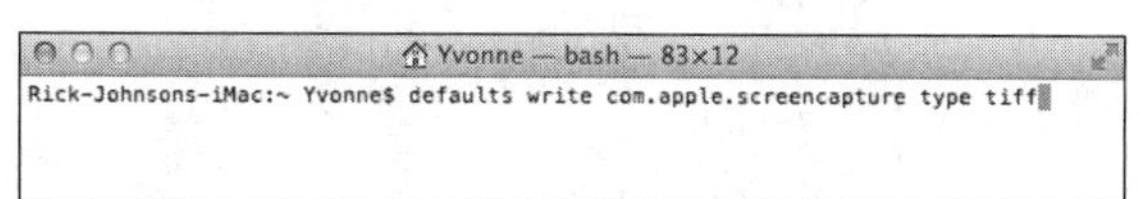

Figure 15.21 *The command starts after Yvonne$.*

TELL ME MORE **Media 15.4—A Discussion about a Terminal Command to Control Copying Email**
Access this audio file through your registered Web Edition at
my.safaribooksonline.com/9780132819091/media
or on the DVD for print books.

Using the VoiceOver Utility

The VoiceOver Utility assists a person who is visually impaired by reading aloud what is happening or what displays on the screen. For example, the VoiceOver feature can announce when the mouse cursor enters a window, speak the header when navigating across a table row, speak the text in a dialog box, and read text in a document including punctuation and word emphasis. This utility is highly customizable as you can see by looking at the Text page of the Verbosity category, shown in Figure 15.22.

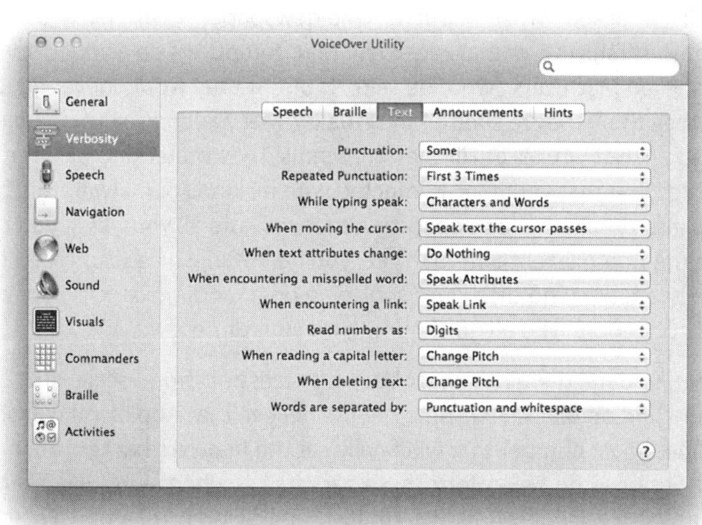

Figure 15.22 *This page specifies what VoiceOver will do when reading text.*

This chapter discusses the security features of your Mac, keeping your applications up to date, and backing up your entire system.

16

Keeping Your Mac Safe, Updated, and Backed Up

One of the reasons so many people love the Mac is because the operating system is so secure. There's very little you have to do to facilitate this—in most cases, just accept the default security settings and keep your software updated. Apple provides a safety net, though. In the unlikely event that some catastrophe wipes out all your data, you can use Time Machine backups to restore your entire system. This chapter covers the security settings for surfing the web, how to turn on the firewall, and the Keychain Access application that keeps your passwords. It also covers installing application updates and backing up and restoring with Time Machine.

Safely Surfing the Web

To date, there has never been a successful, broad-scale virus or spyware attack launched on Mac OS X. In May of 2011, a "so-called" virus named Mac Defender supposedly "attacked" Mac computers. One newspaper IT writer called it "one of the first, if not *the* first, virus or malware to hit Mac computers on a widespread scale," and he mocked Mac users, "who," he said, "thought they would never get a virus because they think they're special." In actuality, Mac Defender and a variant called Mac Guard are not viruses at all. They are scams. They pretend to be virus scanning software, tell you that your Mac is infected with all kinds of malware, and try to scare you into purchasing an application that will cure all your ills. If you voluntarily purchase the non-existent anti-malware, you voluntarily give your credit card number to the scammer who then goes shopping on your dime or sells your card number to lots of people who all go shopping on your dime.

So, I repeat, to date, there has never been a successful, broad-scale virus or spyware attack launched on Mac OS X. Some people believe that Apple's market share has reached the magic number that will finally set the malware hackers off in Mac's direction. Supposedly, heretofore, these hackers have been ignoring the Mac because it was too inconsequential. I'm just not buying it. Infecting a Mac would be the stuff that legends are made of in the dark netherworld of hackers.

In my opinion, and let me emphasize that this is just my *opinion*, I still think the Mac is secure because of its superior code and structure. If you look for anti-virus software in the Mac App store very little is there. If you are asking why there is anything there *at all*, my guess is that the application meets all the standards to be sold on the site but it's really a useless program. I could pay someone to look in my refrigerator every night for elephants, but that doesn't mean that the possibility exists that one will ever be found.

Here's one reason I don't think Mac users have anything to worry about. All the websites and applications you use in Safari are *sandboxed*, which means they do not have access to *any* information on your system. If you happen to surf to a site that has malicious code, the sandboxing feature restricts the code from doing any harm to your computer or capturing any of your personal data.

Having stated my very opinionate point of view, I want to acknowledge the fact that a day may come when a true virus or Trojan horse will be invented for the Mac. In the meantime, stay alert, make smart choices, and don't take any security risks. Additionally, if you are running Windows on a Mac, you should take every precaution possible just as you would on a PC. Any virus or Trojan horse that you get on the Windows partition can do damage to the Windows partition on your Mac, but it cannot cross over to the OS X partition.

Exploring Safari Security Settings

Safari's default settings for surfing the web securely are the best settings and you don't need to change them, but it won't hurt you to know what they are. To open the Security pane where these settings reside, click Safari in the menu bar, click Preferences, and click the Security tab, if necessary.

Following is an explanation of the Security preferences shown in Figure 16.1:

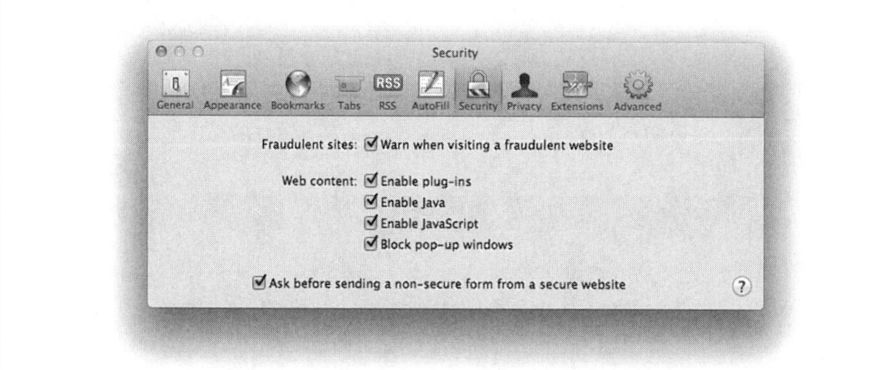

Figure 16.1 *Safari default preferences have the optimum settings.*

- **Fraudulent Sites**—Fraudulent sites often use various tricks to make their addresses appear to be the address of the site they are impersonating. Safari warns you when you land on one of these sites because it checks the site's certificate, which cannot be faked.
- **Web Content**—Plug-ins, Java, and JavaScript are all elements that websites may use to deliver content to you. If you disable any of these, a website may not function correctly. Most of the time you do not want to see pop-up windows, but occasionally a website may use a pop-up window for a legitimate reason. You can turn off the blocking while you are on that site by clicking Safari in the menu bar and clicking Block Pop-Up Windows to uncheck the option. When you leave the site, repeat the steps to start blocking again.
- **Ask Before Sending a Non-Secure Form from a Secure Website**—This preference is essential! *Do not change it.* Even if you are on a secure site, a form may not be secure. If Safari warns you that a form is not secure and it contains sensitive information such as your credit card or social security number, do *not* send the form.

Exploring Privacy Settings

Seeing exactly which websites are storing information on your computer—what they have stored and where they have stored it—is now possible in Lion. To see this information, open the Safari preferences and click the Privacy tab, if necessary. Figure 16.2 tells me that 87 websites have stored cookies or other data.

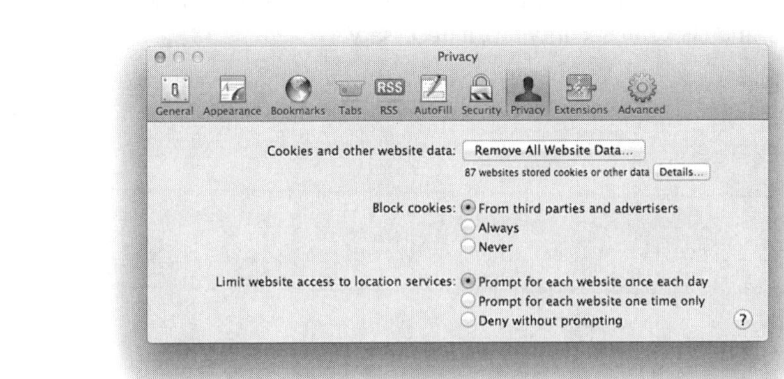

Figure 16.2 *Click Details to review and delete websites you don't want tracking you.*

If you click Remove All Website Data, Safari will clear the information that websites have stored on your computer to track you online. This button removes cookies,

Flash plug-in data, as well as information from databases, local storage, and the application cache. Instead of removing all the information, you should probably click Details and remove specific ones. Figure 16.3 shows the details. To remove a website's stored data, select the site and click Remove. Click Done when finished.

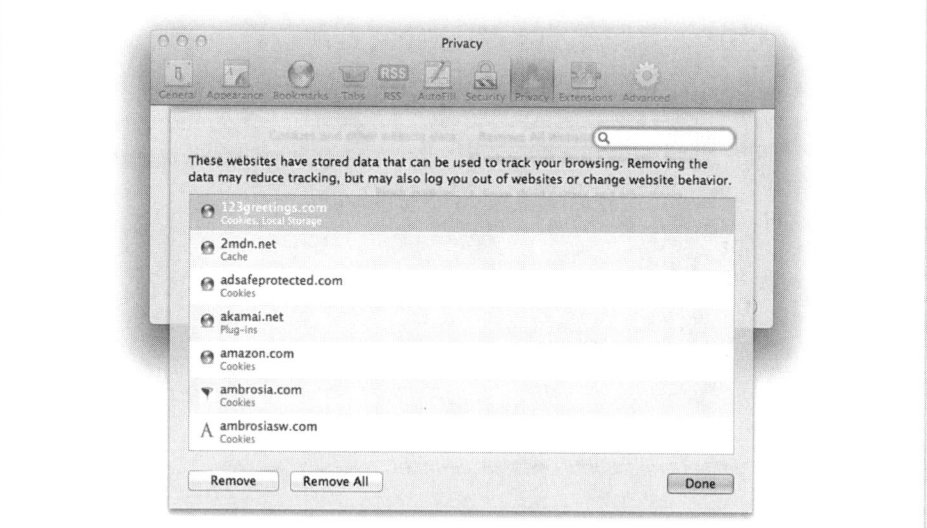

Figure 16.3 *The storage location of the information a website stores on your computer displays under the website name.*

Exploring System Security Preferences

Not only is your security and privacy guarded in Safari, it is guarded systemwide. Figure 16.4 shows the System Preferences window for Security & Privacy. Notice it has four panes.

Setting General Security Options

On the General pane, shown in Figure 16.4, you have several options to protect your computer while you are working. You can lock the screen after it goes to sleep or a screen saver starts, requiring a password to unlock it. Use this feature if you work on your computer around other people who should not mess with your computer if you step away for awhile without shutting it down. (This option is automatically turned on if you encrypt your data with FileVault.) If you select this option to lock the screen, you might also want to enter a message that displays on the screen when it is locked.

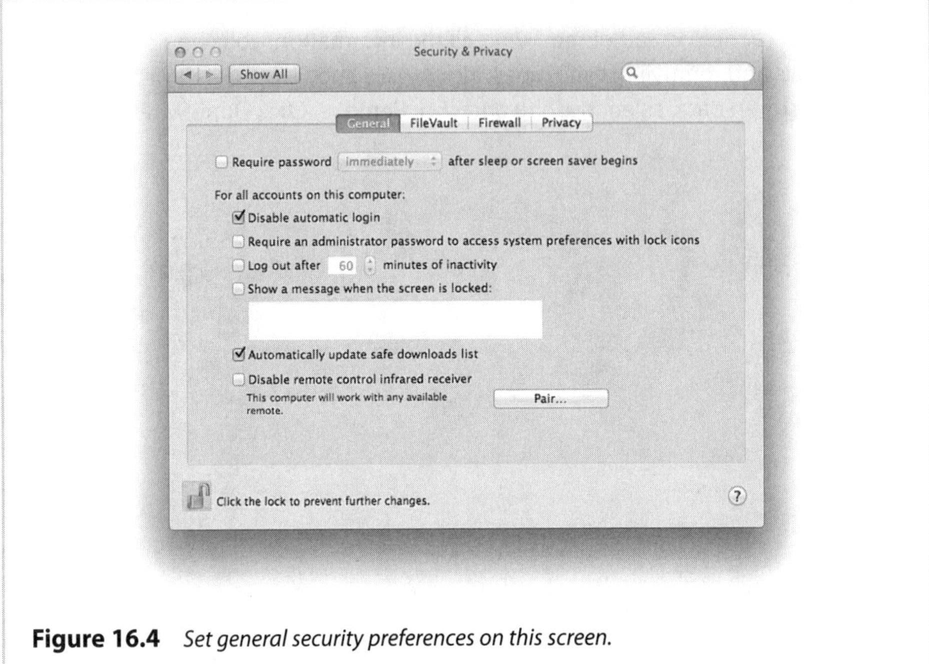

Figure 16.4 *Set general security preferences on this screen.*

Automatic login is disabled by default. If you have more than one person using your computer with separate user accounts, you definitely need to keep this disabled. If you want to use automatic login, be aware that anyone will be able to turn the computer on and get in on your automatic login.

Using FileVault 2

In Lion, FileVault 2 now encrypts the entire drive on your Mac. It uses XTS-AES 128 encryption to keep your files from being seen or copied unless the login password is entered. The encrypting and decrypting is so rapid that the impact on your computer's performance is virtually imperceptible. The initial encryption is also very fast, but more importantly, it is non-intrusive, allowing you to continue working while your entire hard drive is being encrypted.

SHOW ME **Media 16.1—A Video about Encrypting Data**
Access this video file through your registered Web Edition at
my.safaribooksonline.com/9780132819091/media
or on the DVD for print books.

Encrypting Your Data

To encrypt your data, follow these steps:

1. Click the System Preferences icon in the Dock, click Security & Privacy, and click the FileVault tab.
2. Click the padlock and type your password. If you do not have an Administrative account, you must enter the name and password of an Administrative account. Click Unlock and the padlock opens, allowing you to make changes.
3. Click Turn on FileVault. The list of users who have accounts on the Mac appears. Enable each user who should be able to unlock the disk and click Continue.
4. You are given a recovery key that you can use to unlock the data if you forget your login password. (Refer to Figure 16.5.) Write this key down and keep it in a safe place. Click Continue.

The recovery key is a "safety net" which can be used to unlock the disk if you forget your password.
Make a copy and store it in a safe place. If you forget your password and lose the recovery key, all the data on your disk will be lost.
UXCF-6PEX-RJOM-DQCO-P23Q-VGMY
Cancel
Back
Continue

Figure 16.5 *The recovery key cannot be accessed from your computer if the data is locked so write it down somewhere.*

5. In the next dialog box that appears, select Store the Recovery Key with Apple, or select Do Not Store the Recovery Key with Apple. Click Continue.
6. Click Restart to restart your Mac. The encryption process will begin when it reboots. It's not too late to back out. You can also click Cancel at this point. After the process starts, you still can stop it if you return to the FileVault page in System Preferences.

Using a Firewall

Your Mac provides a firewall for you to block unwanted incoming connections from other computers on a network or the Internet. Whereas in Snow Leopard, the firewall was turned off by default, in Lion it is turned on by default.

LET ME TRY IT

Turning the Firewall Off and On

When the firewall is turned off, your Mac accepts all incoming connections from other computers on networks or the Internet. Though generally not a good thing, sometimes turning the firewall off is necessary just so something that is having trouble getting through can make the connection. After you accommodate that little problem, you need to run, as fast as you can, to the Firewall preferences and turn the firewall back on. Follow these steps to turn the firewall off and on:

1. Click the System Preferences icon in the Dock.
2. Click Security & Privacy, and then click the Firewall tab.
3. Click the padlock icon and type your password. If you do not have an Administrative account, you must enter the name and password of an Administrative account. Click Unlock and the padlock opens, allowing you to make changes.
4. Click Start to turn on the firewall. Now the Mac allows only connections by software and services that have a signed, trusted certificate. Click Stop to turn the firewall off. Now any connection can get through.
5. Close the window and Lion locks the padlock for you automatically.

TELL ME MORE **Media 16.2—A Discussion about Signed Certificates**
Access this audio recording through your registered Web Edition at
my.safaribooksonline.com/9780132819091/media
or on the DVD for print books.

Setting Privacy Options

The Privacy page, shown in Figure 16.6, allows you to make a decision about sending diagnostic information to Apple about your computer. It also lists any applications that have requested your GPS coordinates in the last 24 hours. The location services are enabled by default. To disable these services, clear the check mark for the option.

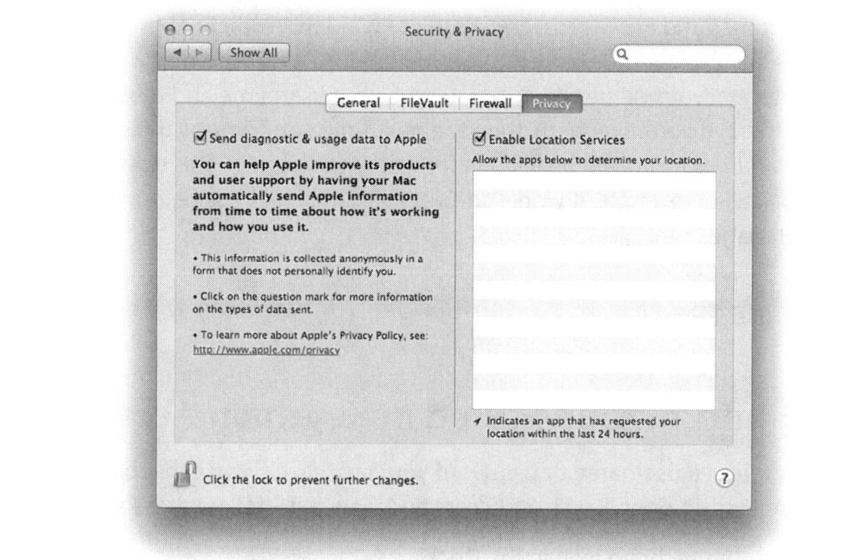

Figure 16.6 *Apple would like your help but understands if you don't want to send it information about your computer.*

Working with Keychain Access

Keychain Access is an application that stores your usernames and passwords. Using passwords is an integral part of using your Mac in a secure way. If you're one of those people who use the same login name and password for everything (not a good idea) because remembering a slew of different passwords is too difficult, you'll love the Keychain Access feature. It remembers your login names and passwords and can even enter them for you automatically in some cases. Before you throw away your little black book of passwords, however, realize that Keychain Access is on *your* hard drive. If you use another computer to log in to a password-protected site, you have to know your login name and password (or have your little black book with you).

Many applications and web pages work with Keychain Access by using a dialog box that asks whether you want to save your login name and password. The dialog box might say something like, "Would you like to save this password?" or "Remember this password in my keychain." Safari displays this type of dialog box on "cooperating" web pages if you set the AutoFill preference that triggers it. To set the preference, click Safari in the menu bar and click Preferences. Click the AutoFill tab, click User Names and Passwords, and close the window. If you enable AutoFill for usernames and passwords, the next time you log into a website that works with Keychain Access, you will be prompted to save your username and password after you enter them. If you save them, then the next time you come to the site, your username and password will be filled in for you automatically. This doesn't work on every website. For example, it works on Google's Gmail login page, but not on Citicard's login page.

LET ME TRY IT

Viewing Information Stored in Keychain Access

If you ever forget a username or password you have saved, you can look it up in Keychain Access. To open Keychain Access and view data, follow these steps:

1. Click the Launchpad icon in the Dock.
2. Click the Utilities folder and then click Keychain Access. A window similar to the one shown in Figure 16.7 opens.

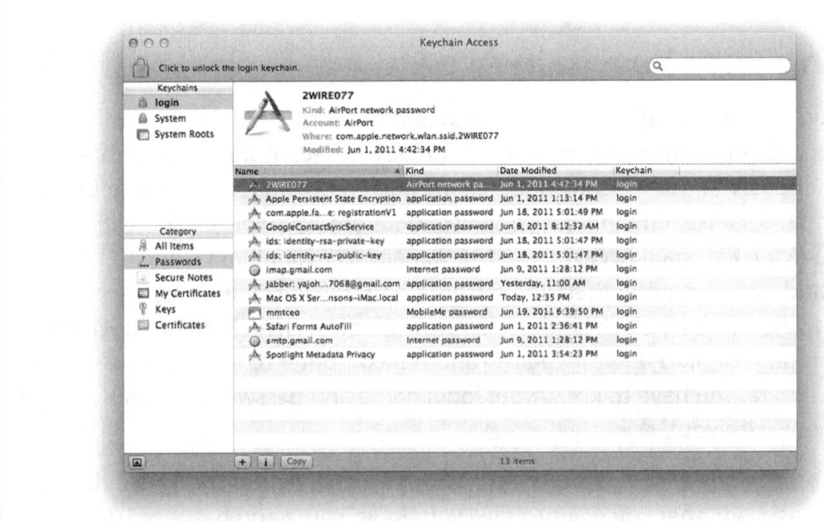

Figure 16.7 *The information in the right pane is different for every computer.*

3. Click the padlock in the upper-left corner, type your login password, and click OK. The padlock opens.
4. Click login under Keychains in the sidebar on the left and click Passwords under Category in the sidebar.
5. Double-click an item in the list in the right pane. A window like the one shown in Figure 16.8 opens.

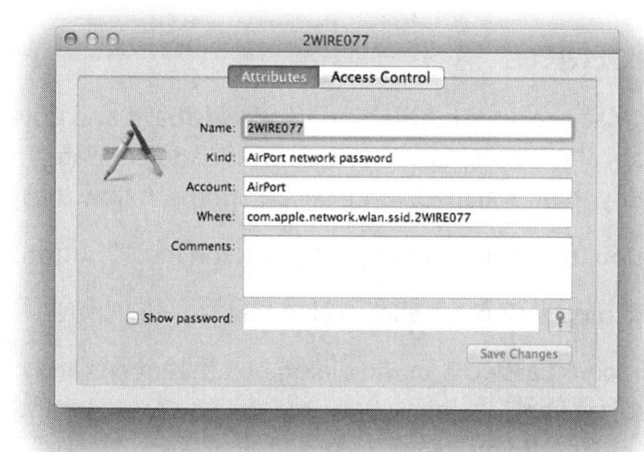

Figure 16.8 *To show the password for the item, you must enter your login password.*

6. To see the password, click the Show Password check box, enter your login password, and click Allow. The password is visible in the Show Password field.
7. Close the window.
8. Click the padlock icon in the upper-left corner and quit the application.

This is one padlock Lion doesn't close for you automatically.

TELL ME MORE **Media 16.3—A Discussion about Using the Keychain**
Access this audio recording through your registered Web Edition at ***my.safaribooksonline.com/9780132819091/media*** *or on the DVD for print books.*

Getting Software Updates

After the release of a major version of any Mac application, Apple releases updates that solve problems or add functionality. Updates are free, and you should always install them.

LET ME TRY IT

Installing Updates

By default, your Mac checks for updates on a weekly basis and downloads the updates automatically. When Mac OS X has downloaded updates, it notifies you that they are ready to be installed. To install an update, follow these steps:

1. When an update notification appears, click the Install button.
2. If licensing information appears, click Agree.
3. Enter your login password in the dialog box that opens and click OK. (If you do not have an Administrative account, you must enter the name and password of an Administrative account.)

> You can never install an application or an update without confirming that it is okay to do so by filling in this dialog box. This is one of OS X's many safety features.

4. When the installation is finished, you may have to restart the computer or simply click OK and then Quit.

If you don't want to wait for the weekly check, you can click the Apple menu and click Software Update to see whether there are any updates to install. If there are none, Lion displays a message telling you that your software is up to date. Click Quit.

Backing Up with Time Machine

How would you like to be in the Mac Minority Club? It's the exclusive club made up of all Mac owners who back up their Macs. The one-time membership fee is as low as $65, the price of a 500GB USB external drive from newegg.com. Membership benefits include perpetual peace of mind, uninterrupted sleep, and a complete backup of your entire system. Who could resist such a deal? Join today!

I'm sorry—did I lose you with that introduction? Here's the translation: Statistics show only a small minority (probably less than 10%) of Mac users back up their systems. This is *unbelievable* when you can buy an external hard drive for as little as $65 and use Mac's stellar backup application, Time Machine, to back up your entire computer. In the days before Time Machine, figuring out how to back up your system and then remembering to do it on a regular basis might have been somewhat daunting, but that's all ancient history. Time Machine is so simple and so automatic that you can literally "set it and forget it." There is absolutely no excuse for not using Time Machine to back up your system.

Creating Full Backups

A second hard drive is recommended for use with Time Machine. The second hard drive should be larger than the hard drive you're backing up, and it should be formatted for a Mac. (Many new drives come formatted for Windows only, but you may be able to reformat them for the Mac. Just make sure before you buy!) For most users, a 500GB drive should be adequate.

As soon as you install or plug in the additional drive, Mac OS X asks you whether you want to use it to back up with Time Machine. Click Use as Backup Disk. The Time Machine pane of System Preferences opens and the backup starts immediately.

If Lion is unable to determine whether the external drive you connected should be used for back up, you can set it up manually. Open the Time Machine in the Launchpad and click the Select Disk button. Select the external drive and click Use Backup Disk.

You also can click Options to exclude items from being backed up.

After the backup starts, Time Machine backs up everything on your hard drive, all your data and preferences, all the other users' data and preferences, all your applications, and the operating system. The first back up can take hours, depending on how much data is stored on the computer, but you can continue to work during that time. You may notice some slowness, but only during this initial backup. As long as the drive is attached to the Mac, Time Machine checks your computer for changes every hour and backs them up. It keeps multiple backups of your system, allowing you to restore from a particular date or time.

Eventually your backup drive will fill up and Time Machine will start deleting the oldest backups to make room for the newest backups.

Restoring Data

Time Machine can restore single or multiple data files, entire folders, applications, or the entire system to the Finder. Additionally, it can restore an item to iPhoto, an entry to the Address Book, or an item to Mail.

SHOW ME **Media 16.4—A Video about Restoring a File with Time Machine**

Access this video file through your registered Web Edition at ***my.safaribooksonline.com/9780132819091/media*** *or on the DVD for print books.*

LET ME TRY IT

Restoring a Deleted File to the Finder

Suppose you have a folder in the Finder that is missing a file. Maybe you deleted the file thinking you didn't need it any more, and you also emptied the Trash. Time Machine has a copy of the file that you can restore. Here's how you do it:

1. Open the Finder or select an open Finder window so Time Machine will know that is the application that needs to have an item restored.
2. If you know the folder where the file was stored, select it.
3. Open Time Machine from the Launchpad. The Finder window travels through time and space (on the screen only) and appears in Time Machine with windows of multiple backups behind it, as shown in Figure 16.9.
4. From this point, you have multiple ways to look for the file you want to restore: Click one of the Finder window title bars in the stack, click a date in the date line on the right, or click the flat arrow that is pointing away from you. If you do not know the exact location of the file, you can perform a search in the Spotlight search box.
5. When you think you have found the file you want to restore, select it and press the spacebar to view the content of the file. (Some files, such as .dmg files, cannot be viewed this way, but most can be verified with this method.)
6. If the file you found is the one you want to restore, click Restore in the bottom-right corner of the screen. (If you have multiple items selected, click Restore All.) The Finder window appears to travel back to the present and makes a landing on the desktop with the file restored to its original location.

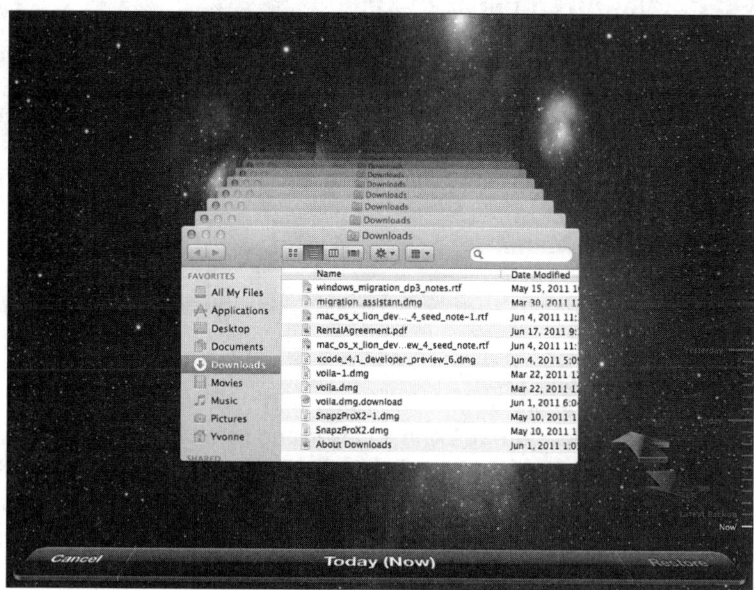

Figure 16.9 *The hash marks on the right side of the desktop represent the daily incremental backups.*

To restore items to iPhoto, the Address Book, or Mail, open the appropriate application first and then open Time Machine. Select a backup that contains the item and then follow the earlier steps to restore it. In the Address Book, you must confirm you want to add a card back to the book. In Mail, the recovered message goes into a folder called Recovered Messages listed under Time Machine in the sidebar.

Being Diligent

If you use an external drive for Time Machine's backups and you unplug it, Time Machine cannot perform its backups; however, the next time you plug in the drive, Time Machine starts backing up again. It does this automatically without your prompting. So the only thing you have to do to keep your backups current is keep the drive plugged in. If that's a problem for you, consider buying the pricier wireless Apple Time Capsule. It costs $299, but it holds 1TB of data (also available in 2TB), and it's a Wi-Fi base station.

This chapter is your entertainment guide for using DVD Player, QuickTime Player, iTunes, Photo Booth, and playing games.

17

Having Fun

When there's time to have some fun, Mac OS X provides some very good audio and video entertainment applications. This chapter tells you how to watch movies on DVD Player, look at videos on QuickTime Player, and listen to music in iTunes. Macs are very short on games that come with the system, but this chapter does show you how to play a game of chess with a friend or with your Mac and how to get more games from the App Store.

If you were also expecting instructions on how to use Front Row in this chapter, you will not find them. Sadly, Front Row is no longer included in Lion. It was a great way to watch DVDs, listen to music, and watch podcasts!

Using DVD Player

Did your two-year-old who loves all your remote controls somehow open the drive on your $300 DVD player and break it? Until you can rectify the situation, you can always fall back on your Mac.

By default, when you insert a DVD in the DVD drive, Mac OS X launches DVD Player and begins playing the DVD immediately. The video plays in full-screen mode. To display the controls, shown in Figure 17.1, point to the bottom of the screen.

If you click the Exit Full Screen button, you see the video in a window and the onscreen remote control is visible (see Figure 17.2). Use the mouse to click the controls on the remote. When you are finished, click the eject button in the onscreen controls and press Command-Q to quit DVD Player.

By the way, if for some reason you don't want the DVD player to start playing the movie immediately when you insert the DVD, open System Preferences, click CDs & DVDs, and select a different option for When You Insert a Video DVD.

Figure 17.1 *You can hide controls when you are not using them.*

Figure 17.2 *Use this virtual remote when viewing in less than full-screen mode.*

Using QuickTime Player

QuickTime Player is yet another application that plays movies, but not the movies that you view with DVD Player. You use QuickTime Player to view short videos like you see on YouTube. QuickTime Player can also record movies, record audio only, and record action on your screen. If that's not enough for you, QuickTime Player also can do some video editing, such as splitting, adding, and trimming clips.

Playing a Video on QuickTime Player

Like me, you probably have friends who send you funny and interesting videos in email messages. To play one of these videos, double-click the file and, if the video is in a format QuickTime Player can read, QuickTime Player opens automatically with the file loaded and ready to play. Just click the Play button to start the video. (If you don't see a Play button, mouse over the video window to display the controls.) When you finish watching the video, click the red Close button in the upper-left corner to close the file.

Even short videos that QuickTime Player can open may not play if they use a compression/decompression format that QuickTime Player cannot process. QuickTime Player reads these formats: QuickTime Movie (.mov), MPEG-4 (.mp4 and .m4v), MPEG-1, 3GPP, 3GPP2, AVI, and DV, but you can download plug-ins for additional formats.

Recording with QuickTime Player

You have everything you need to record a video in QuickTime Player built right into your Mac. You also can connect external cameras and microphones if you want.

LET ME TRY IT

Recording a Movie

To record a movie with audio and video, follow these steps:

1. Click File in the menu bar and then click New Movie Recording. The Movie Recording window opens and you can make adjustments to sound, lighting, subject positioning, and so on.
2. When you are ready to record, click the red Record button and begin your performance.
3. When you are finished, click the black Stop Recording button. The movie appears in the QuickTime Player window and QuickTime automatically saves the movie in your Movies folder.

When QuickTime Player saves the movie file for you, it gives it a generic name (Movie Recording.mov, Movie Recording 2.mov, and so on). You might want to go immediately to the Finder and rename the movie after you shoot it.

LET ME TRY IT

Recording an Audio File

To record an audio file, follow these steps:

1. Click File in the menu bar and then click New Audio Recording. The Audio Recording window opens.

2. Click the red Record button and begin speaking.
3. When you are finished, click the black Stop Recording button. QuickTime automatically saves the audio file in your Movies folder.

The generic names QuickTime Player uses for audio files are Audio Recording.m4a, Audio Recording 2.m4a, and so on.

Recording the Screen

To record action on your computer screen, follow these steps:

1. Click File in the menu bar and then click New Screen Recording. The Screen Recording window opens.
2. Click the red Record button and QuickTime Player prompts you to click to record the entire screen or drag to record a portion of the screen.
3. Click anywhere on the screen to record the full screen or drag the mouse over a section of the screen such as a window.
4. Perform the computer operations you want to record on the screen.
5. When you are finished, click the black Stop Recording button. The movie appears in the QuickTime Player window and QuickTime automatically saves the movie in your Movies folder.

The generic names QuickTime Player uses for screen recordings are Screen Recording.mov, Screen Recording 2.mov, and so on.

Editing Movies with QuickTime Player

In the previous version of QuickTime Player, you could trim the beginning or the end of a movie and that was the extent of the editing capabilities. New Lion enhancements to QuickTime Player give you the ability to split your movies into clips, rearrange the clips, insert clips from other videos, or insert complete video files.

The steps in this section for trimming and splitting movies are the same steps you use to trim screen recordings.

SHOW ME **Media 17.1—A Video about Trimming a Movie**
Access this video file through your registered Web Edition at
my.safaribooksonline.com/9780132819091/media
or on the DVD for print books.

LET ME TRY IT

Trimming a Movie

To trim the beginning and the end of a movie, follow these steps:

1. Open the movie file in QuickTime Player.
2. Click Edit in the menu bar and click Trim.
3. If you want to trim the beginning, drag the yellow handle at the beginning of the movie to the location where you want to trim it. As you drag, the number of seconds you are going to eliminate displays above the yellow handle.
4. To trim the end of the clip, drag the yellow handle on the right to the approximate location (see Figure 17.3).

Figure 17.3 *Trimming the movie leaves only the part within the two trim handles.*

5. Click the Play button to play the entire section between the two trim handles to be sure you have what you want.
6. Adjust the handles if necessary and then click the Trim button.
7. If this is the only change you want to make to the movie, click the red Close button to save the changes.
8. Type a name for the file in Save As, select a location for Where, select a format that is suitable for your target device, and click Save.

SHOW ME **Media 17.2—A Video about Splitting a Movie into Clips**
Access this video file through your registered Web Edition at
my.safaribooksonline.com/9780132819091/media
or on the DVD for print books.

LET ME TRY IT

Splitting a Movie into Clips

Splitting a movie cuts a movie into two pieces. After you split a movie, you can select one of the pieces you split and split it. So basically, you can cut a movie into as many pieces as you want. Perhaps your question is, "Why would you cut a movie at all?" One reason is to cut out a piece in the middle of the movie that you don't want. Another reason you might cut a video is to insert a new clip where you have cut the video. To split a movie into clips, follow these steps:

1. Open the movie file in QuickTime Player.
2. Click View in the menu bar and click Show Clips.
3. Click the movie frames to select the entire clip. The movie is outlined in yellow.
4. Click the Play button and then click the Pause button when you get to the location where you want to split the movie.
5. Click Edit in the menu bar and click Split Clip. The movie is divided into two clips and both are selected, as shown in Figure 17.4.

Figure 17.4 *Now the movie is split into two clips.*

6. At this point you could do any of the following:
   - Select one of the clips and repeat the steps to split it.
   - Select a clip and delete it by pressing the Delete key.
   - Select a clip and drag it before or after the other clip to rearrange them.
   - Select one of the clips and trim it.
   - Open the Finder, drag a movie file to the QuickTime movie and drop it between the two clips.
   - Open another movie in QuickTime Player, split it into clips, and drag one of the clips from that movie to the one you are currently working on.
7. When you are finished, click the red Close button to save the edited movie. Type a name for the file in Save As, select a location for Where, select a format that is suitable for your target device, and click Save.

You also can trim an audio recording, but you cannot split it.

Sharing QuickTime Files

New in Lion on the Share menu, you can now send files to Vimeo, Flickr, Facebook, and Mail. When sending files in Mail, be aware of the fact that even a very short video (less than a minute long) can be larger than many email servers will accept as an attachment. You might want to upload the file to one of the video sites and send just the link to the video in email.

TELL ME MORE Media 17.3—A Discussion about Video Resolution and File Size

Access this audio recording through your registered Web Edition at ***my.safaribooksonline.com/9780132819091/media*** *or on the DVD for print books.*

Using iTunes

iTunes is a media player, the front door to the iTunes Music Store, a music CD burner, and currently the central location for synchronizing your Mac with your iPod or iPhone. Of course, the iCloud will probably take over the synchronizing duties when it's released in the fall of 2011.

The first time you open iTunes, you have to agree to the License Agreement, and then the iTunes video presents itself. You can watch the video to get an overview of how iTunes works.

Exploring the iTunes Window

The design of iTunes is very similar to the design of the Finder window. It has a list of sources in the pane on the left and a viewing pane on the right. It has another pane you can display on the far right, and this pane is called the Sidebar. You can hide and display the Sidebar using the buttons shown in Figure 17.5.

When you first start using iTunes, if you click any source in the Library, the viewing pane displays introductory information and links to more information or tutorials, but after you add items in the sources, the right pane displays the items (refer to Figure 17.5).

Using the View buttons in the toolbar, you can display items for certain sources in a song list, album list, a grid, or cover flow view. Figure 17.6 shows the Music library (selected in the left pane) in the song list view and in grid view.

Figure 17.5 *TV Shows is selected in the left pane and the right pane shows the TV shows I have downloaded.*

Figure 17.6 *The list view is in alphabetical order by the first word in the Artist's name and the grid view shows icons for the albums.*

Listening to a Music CD

To listen to a music CD, simply insert it in your optical drive. iTunes opens automatically due to the preference set in the CDs & DVDs pane of System Preferences. The CD doesn't start to play right away because iTunes displays a list of the tracks on the CD and the dialog box shown in Figure 17.7. Click No and then double-click the track you want to play. Use the controls at the top of the window to adjust the volume, pause and play, and go to the next or previous track. To hide everything in the iTunes window except the controls, click the green Zoom button. Alternatively, you can click View, Switch to Mini Player.

In addition to the onscreen controls, you can use the F7 through F9 keys on new keyboards to control the play of tracks.

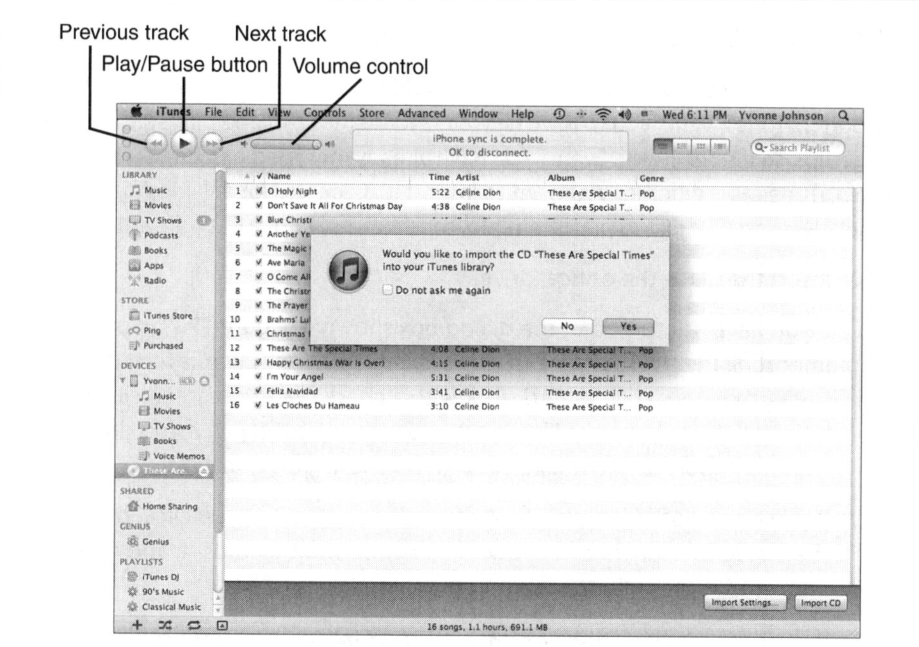

Figure 17.7 *iTunes always ask whether you want to import a CD unless you select Do Not Ask Me Again.*

Adding Music to the Library

You can add music to your library by importing tracks from a CD, by purchasing albums or single tracks from the iTunes store, by downloading the free Single of the Week from the iTunes store, or by downloading music from the Internet. When you download music from the iTunes Store or from another Internet site, iTunes adds it to its Library automatically.

SHOW ME **Media 17.4—A Video about Importing Music**
Access this video file through your registered Web Edition at ***my.safaribooksonline.com/9780132819091/media*** *or on the DVD for print books.*

LET ME TRY IT

Importing Music

Every time you insert a music CD in your disk drive, iTunes asks whether you want to import it. iTunes wants you to have all your favorite music in one place and at your fingertips, so it's persistent. Even if you have already imported a CD, if you insert it again, iTunes asks whether you want to import it. (Click Do Not Ask Me Again if you regularly insert CDs just to play them.) To import music from a CD, follow these steps:

1. Insert the CD in the optical drive.
2. If you have not turned of the dialog box shown in Figure 17.7, you can import *all* the tracks on the CD, by clicking Yes. iTunes works through the tracks, marking a completed track with a check mark in a green circle. When all the tracks have imported, you can skip to step 4. If you don't want to import all the tracks, click No for the import question.
3. If you turned off the dialog box referred to in step 2 or you clicked No in the dialog box, uncheck the tracks you don't want to import, and click the Import CD button (in the lower-right corner).
4. If the track names import as Track 01, Track 02, and so on, select them, click Advanced in the menu bar, and click Get CD Track Names.

You must be connected to the Internet to get track names because iTunes gets them from http://www.gracenote.com.

5. Click the eject button in the pane on the left beside the CD's name (Under the Devices category) to eject the CD.

If you import a track you don't want, you can select the track and press the Delete key. A confirmation dialog box opens (unless you have previously selected Do Not Ask Me Again). Click Remove and then click Move to Trash. Note that you can't delete tracks listed in the source called Recently Played, Recently Added, or Top 25 Most Played.

LET ME TRY IT

Importing Cover Art

Well, we're just so spoiled aren't we? We want iTunes to show the covers of our albums just as they appear in the store or on the Internet. And why not? It's a simple thing to ask isn't it? Yes, it is. Make sure you are connected to the Internet and then follow these steps to download the cover art for your albums:

1. Click Advanced in the menu bar and click Get Album Art. A confirmation dialog box opens because Apple wants you to confirm your choice after it advises you that information about the songs on your computer will be sent to Apple.
2. Click Get Album Artwork. The artwork is downloaded to your computer. A message displays if there are albums for which the artwork could not be found. Click OK if you get a message like this.
3. To see all the artwork, click the Grid view button.

Listening to Music in Your Library

If you are playing tracks in your Music source, iTunes plays the first track you select and continues playing the next tracks until you stop it or it gets to the end of your list. If you click the Repeat button, before you play the first track in your list, iTunes plays all the tracks in your list and then starts over. If you click the Shuffle button, iTunes plays your tracks in random order.

If you click the Repeat button while a track is playing, iTunes repeats that track.

Creating and Using Playlists

Essentially, all the tracks in your Music source make up a single playlist, but you can create smaller playlists and include only the tracks you select. You might create a playlist for a party, one for exercising, one with only country music, and so on. You can listen to your playlists on iTunes, burn them to a CD for use in a CD player, or publish them to the iTunes Store where lots of people can listen to samples of the songs in your playlist and purchase the ones they like from the iTunes Store. Additionally, people will rate your list and write reviews for it.

The iTunes DJ playlist is a live mix—that is, each time you select it, iTunes chooses songs randomly in the source you select. If you don't like the mix, click Refresh and iTunes chooses songs again.

LET ME TRY IT

Creating a Playlist

To create a playlist, follow these steps:

1. Click the Add button (+) in the lower-left corner of the window. A new playlist called *untitled playlist* appears at the bottom of the Playlists category in the left pane.
2. Type a name for the list and press Return.
3. Drag songs from the Music Library to the list.

To play a playlist, select it in the left pane and double-click the first song.

Burning a Music CD

The great thing about burning your own CDs is that you get to choose your own songs to include from different artists and albums that span all genres and all eras. Instead of Elvis's Greatest Hits, you can have My Favorite Hits.

LET ME TRY IT

Burning a Playlist to a Disc

If you want to burn a playlist to a CD, make sure the playlist is not too large to fit on the disc. When a playlist is selected, the total size of the list displays in the status bar. To burn a playlist to a disc, follow these steps:

1. Select the playlist in the left pane.
2. Make sure the check boxes for the tracks you want to include are selected.
3. Click File in the menu bar and click Burn Playlist to Disc. A dialog box opens, as shown in Figure 17.8.

Figure 17.8 *iTunes selects the format based on the type of tracks you have selected.*

4. Click the Burn button and insert a blank disc as instructed. The progress displays at the top of the window. When finished, the name of the disc, which is the same name as the playlist, displays under Devices in the left pane.

Listening to Radio

iTunes can access lots of live, streaming radio broadcasts. To listen to one, click Radio in the Library category in the left pane, click the disclosure triangle beside a stream, and double-click a radio station to connect to it. The name of the station appears in the box at the top. Additional information about the name of the song, show, or artist may appear below it. To disconnect from the station, click the Stop button in the toolbar controls.

Acquiring and Playing Podcasts

A podcast is an audio or video recording that has multiple episodes released over time. Using iTunes, you can download a single episode or subscribe to the series, in which case, iTunes automatically downloads new episodes when they become available. To select podcasts for downloading, click Podcasts in the left pane and click Podcast Directory (see Figure 17.9). (If you are a new Lion user instead of an upgrader, you'll have to open the iTunes General Preferences and select Podcasts to display in the left pane.) Browse through the podcasts and double-click one you want. Click Free (to the right of a single podcast) to download that episode or, to get all episodes automatically as they are available, click Subscribe Free. A dialog box opens; you must then click Subscribe again. To unsubscribe, click Podcasts in the left pane, click the podcast in the right pane, and click the Unsubscribe button.

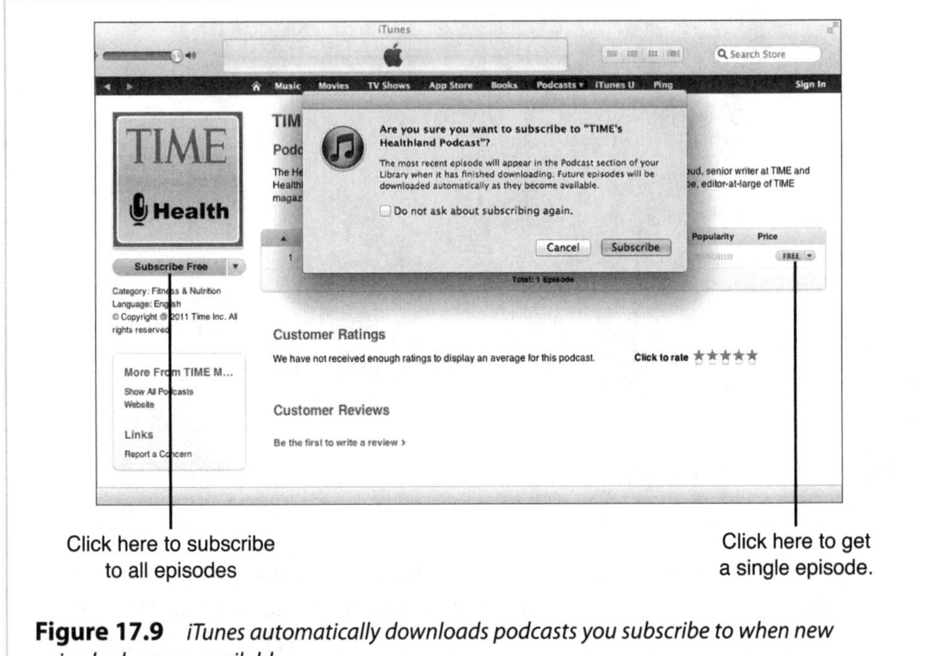

Figure 17.9 *iTunes automatically downloads podcasts you subscribe to when new episodes become available.*

To play a podcast, click Podcasts in the left pane, click the disclosure triangle for the podcast series in the right pane that you want to play, and double-click the episode you want to play.

Exploring the Genius Feature

The Genius feature can put together playlists of your existing music and find other music that you might like—music you may not even know exists—by analyzing the music you have on your computer and matching it to similar music. So before you can use the Genius, you must send information to iTunes about the music you have on your computer. You do this by clicking Store in the menu bar and then clicking Update Genius.

To use the Genius, you select a song in your list of music and click the Genius button. It's the button on the bottom right that looks like an atom. Then the Genius selects songs from your library that it views as similar or compatible and puts them together in a playlist for you. You can refresh the list if you don't like what it selected, and you also can save the list so you can play it again. The playlist is added to the left pane under the Genius category.

In the Sidebar, the Genius lists albums and songs on sale at the iTunes Store that are similar or compatible with the song you selected. If you are a regular purchaser of music from iTunes, this is a feature you would appreciate. It seems to be no different from what Netflix does in suggesting movies you might want to rent based on what you've already rented.

Using Photo Booth

Just as in the old dime-store photo booths of the 1960s, with Photo Booth, you can pose and take your own picture or take four quick pictures of yourself. (If you ever took your picture in one of those dime-store photo booths, call me, and we'll reminisce about the good ole days.) Adding a new dimension to the '60s photo booth, the Mac Photo Booth also takes videos.

The very first time you open Photo Booth (on a new installation of Lion), it opens in full-screen mode. This gives you the full effect of actually sitting in a photo booth surrounded by the red curtains as you can see in Figure 17.10. If you don't use the full-screen mode, the user interface is somewhat different as shown in Figure 17.11.

Figure 17.10 *A photo of my assistant in full-screen mode. (No wonder nothing ever gets done.)*

Figure 17.11 *The dial and Share button are replaced by a toolbar when you are not using full-screen mode.*

When working in full-screen mode, remember you can point to the top of the screen to see the menu.

Taking Pictures

Obviously, the built-in camera on a Mac is not like using a handheld camera because you really can't point it at subjects too easily, but it's great for taking pictures and videos of yourself. Now, with the new widescreen FaceTime HD camera that is built into all the new Macs, you can even take pictures and movies of a "crowd."

Older versions of the Mac have the iSight camera built in, and it still works fine with Photo Booth, but it does take lower resolution photos than the FaceTime HD camera, and it's not widescreen.

Taking a Still Picture

To take a still picture of yourself in full-screen mode, rotate the dial on the left (shown in Figure 17.10) to the middle or just click the icon in the middle. Click the red Shutter button. Three "red lights" illuminate one at a time as the camera counts down to the snap, but don't watch these buttons. Look into the camera and smile. Your portrait appears as a thumbnail in the pane that runs across the bottom of the screen.

If you are not using full-screen mode, to take a picture, click the icon for still pictures in the toolbar and wait for the countdown from three.

Taking a Four-Up Picture

To take four quick pictures in a row in full-screen mode, rotate the dial on the left all the way to the left (or just click the icon on the left). After the three lights illuminate, the camera will take four pictures in a row. You barely have time to turn your head between the pictures, so you might want to concentrate on just changing your facial expression. The four photos are grouped together as one photo and the photo is added to the other single photos and movies in the pane across the bottom.

If you are not using full-screen mode, to take four pictures, click the icon for four pictures in the toolbar and wait for the countdown from three.

Flipping Photos

In Figure 17.12 you see a photo of the book I am updating to the Lion version. As you can see, it's a mirror image of the book, and the title doesn't read correctly. To fix this problem right in Photo Booth, just select the photo, click Edit in the menu bar, and click Flip Photo.

If you are shooting a whole session of photos that will need to be flipped, you can tell Photo Booth to flip them for you automatically. Click Edit in the menu bar and click Auto Flip New Items. After the session, don't forget to disable this option by selecting it again.

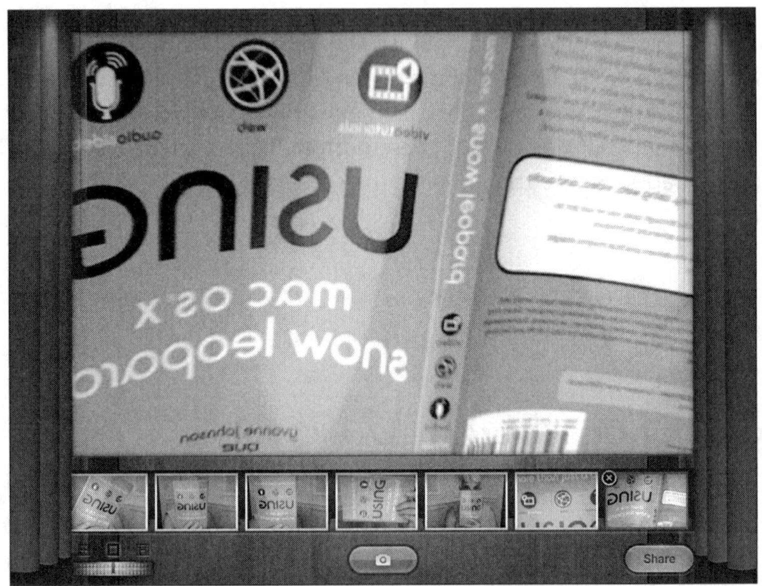

Figure 17.12 *You can flip this photo to make the text readable.*

Setting Options for Taking Photos

If you want to turn off the countdown feature so the photo is taken instantly, press the Option key when you click the Shutter button. The next time you take a photo, the countdown will return so you have to press the Option key every time you want an instant photo.

To use natural lighting when you take a photo, press the Shift key when you click the Shutter button. To turn off the flash so it is not used for any photos, click Camera in the menu bar and click Enable Screen Flash to remove the check mark beside this option.

Recording Movies

To shoot a movie in full-screen mode, drag the dial on the left all the way to the right. (You also can just click the icon on the right.) Then click the red Shutter button. Wait for the three lights to illuminate and then start performing. An elapsed time counter appears on the left to let you know how long you are filming. Click the Stop button when finished. Your movie appears as a thumbnail in the pane at the bottom, but unlike the still photos, it has a length of time on it. That's how you can distinguish a movie from a still photo in the bottom pane.

If you are not using full-screen mode, to take a movie, click the icon for video in the toolbar and wait for the countdown from three.

Trimming a Movie in Photo Booth

Recording a movie in Photo Booth without including footage of your motions to start and stop the video camera is difficult. Before the new Trim feature was added in Lion, you had to open the movie file in another program, such as iMovie, and trim these clips at the beginning and end of the movie. Now you can do it all right in Photo Booth. To trim the beginning or the end of a movie, follow these steps:

1. Select the thumbnail of the movie in the bottom pane.
2. Click Edit in the menu bar and click Trim Movie to display the controls. If the controls display automatically when you select the movie, then just click the Trim button.
3. Drag the yellow handles at the left or right to trim the beginning or the end of the clip.
4. Click the Save button (the button with the check mark).

Viewing Your Photos and Movies in Photo Booth

Use a swiping motion to scroll to the thumbnail you want to see. Alternatively, if you don't have a device that uses gestures, you can click an item and use the left or right arrow keys on the keyboard to scroll. Click the thumbnail to view it in the upper pane. If the picture is a four-up photo, you see all four pictures in the viewing area, but you can click any one of the four photos to zoom in on it.

To view a slideshow of all your photos, click View in the menu bar and click Start Slideshow. Click the play button that appears below the viewing area. The slideshow plays in a continuous loop, and it does not include videos. To stop the slide show, point to the black space under the viewing area to redisplay the controls and click the Pause button. Click the X button to exit.

To view a movie, select the thumbnail of the movie in the pane at the bottom of the screen. Move the pointer over the video to see the controls and click the Play button. To pause the movie, display the controls again if necessary, and click the Pause button.

After viewing photos or movies, you can return to picture-taking mode by clicking the Shutter button.

Deleting Items in Photo Booth

If you don't like a photo or movie you have taken, you can easily delete it. Just select it and click the *x* in the corner. To delete more than one item, Command-click the items to select them and then press the Delete key. When you select multiple items, they do not display *x*'s in the corner.

Using Effects

Selecting a special effect before you take a photo can create some very unusual results, to say the least. Some of the standard effects include black and white, sepia tone, and color pencil. The more unusual effects twirl and twist your picture into hilarious contortions. These types of effects are evidently so popular that Apple added eight new ones in Lion, including two that show birds or hearts circling overhead. The circling birds or hearts actually track with your movement. (I'm constantly amazed at the talent of Apple programmers!)

To select an effect before you take a photo, click the Effects button. There are five pages of effects you can scroll through using swiping gestures or by clicking the scrolling arrows. When you find an effect you want to use, click it to select it, and then click the Shutter button. If the special effect you select is a background, you will be asked to step out of the frame until the background is detected. After the background is detected, step back into the frame, and click the Shutter button. If the background is a movie, you can click the video icon and then click the Shutter button.

You may not be totally satisfied with the background effect feature. Everything has to be almost perfect to get a great photo. By this I mean that your hair color, skin tone color, clothes, and the color of the live background need to be in high contrast to the colors in the effect background you have chosen. If any colors are too similar you will see bleedthrough of colors from either background to the other.

Sharing Your Photos and Movies

I like to email Photo Booth photos with effects to my Mom to prove that I'm having a bad hair day or to show her how bad a head cold I really have. Additionally, my husband and I make Happy Birthday movies and Happy Anniversary movies to send when we can't be there.

To email photos or movies, select them, click the Share button (refer to Figure 17.10) and click Email (if using full-screen mode) or click the Email button in the toolbar. Mail opens with a new message and the items display full size in the body of the email. Right-click the items and click View as Icon if you prefer. Fill in the email header, type the text of your message, and click the Send button. It's that easy. (Before emailing a video, check the size of the file to make sure it's not too large to send.)

To send photos or movies to iPhoto, select the items in Photo Booth, click the Share button (in full-screen mode), and click Add to iPhoto, or if you are not using full-screen mode, click the Add to iPhoto button in the toolbar. iPhoto opens and imports the items into a single event.

To make a photo your account photo, select the photo, click the Share button, and click Set Account Picture (in full-screen mode) or click User Picture in the toolbar. When you select this option, the Users & Groups preferences window opens and your account is selected. The photo you selected in Photo Booth displays as your photo. Close the window.

To use one of your Photo Booth photos for your iChat account, select the photo, click the Share button, and click Set Buddy Picture (in full-screen mode) or click Buddy Picture in the toolbar. iChat opens, if it isn't already open, and iChat opens the Buddy Picture window for your account showing your Photo Booth picture. You can size and move the picture as you normally would and apply effects, too. Click the Set button when you have it just the way you want it. If you change your mind, just click Cancel.

Playing Games

In regards to fun and games, Mac is heavy on fun, but, unfortunately, light on games. Only one game comes with Lion and that is—no, not Solitaire—Chess. This used to be a pretty big disappointment, but the new App Store more than makes up for it. I'm surprised that the Chess game even made the cut in Lion! Really, I was expecting Angry Birds!

To launch Chess, click the Chess icon in the Launchpad. To start a new game, click Game in the menu bar and click New or press Command-N. Select the players (Human vs. Human, Human vs. Computer, Computer vs. Human, or Computer vs. Computer), select the variant, and click Start. Various menu options allow you to take back a move, see a hint for your next move, see the last move, and see a log of the game. To quit Chess, press Command-Q.

A large number of free games are available for downloading from the App Store, including Solitaire. Just type **free** in the Spotlight search box to find them.

index

A

D

E

F

J

K

L

M

N

O

P

T

U

V

W

Z